Sectarianism in Islam

Sectarian divisions within the Islamic world have long been misunderstood and misconstrued by the media and the general public. In this book, Adam R. Gaiser offers an accessible introduction to the main Muslim sects and schools, returning to the roots of the sectarian divide in the medieval period. Beginning with the death of the Prophet Muḥammad and the ensuing debate over who would succeed him, Gaiser outlines how the *umma* (Muslim community) came to be divided. He traces the history of the main Muslim sects and schools – the Sunnis, Shiʿites, Khārijites, Muʿtazila, and Murjiʾa – and shows how they emerged, developed, and diverged from one another. Exploring how medieval Muslims understood the idea of "sect," Gaiser challenges readers to consider the usefulness and scope of the concept of "sectarianism" in this historical context. Providing an overview of the main Muslim sects while problematizing the assumptions of previous scholarship, this is a valuable resource for both new and experienced readers of Islamic history.

Adam R. Gaiser is Professor of Religion at Florida State University. He has previously published two books on the early Kharijites and Ibāḍiyya: *Muslims, Scholars, Soldiers: The Origin and Elaboration of the Ibāḍī Imāmate Traditions* (2010) and Shurāt *Legends, Ibāḍī Identities: Martyrdom, Asceticism and the Making of an Early Islamic Community* (2016).

Themes in Islamic History

THEMES IN ISLAMIC HISTORY comprises a range of titles exploring different aspects of Islamic history, society, and culture by leading scholars in the field. Books are thematic in approach, offering a comprehensive and accessible overview of the subject. Generally, surveys treat Islamic history from its origins to the demise of the Ottoman Empire, although some offer a more developed analysis of a particular period, or project into the present, depending on the subject-matter. All the books are written to interpret and illuminate the past, as gateways to a deeper understanding of Islamic civilization and its peoples.

Other books in the series

1. *Islamic Historiography* by Chase F. Robinson
2. *The Formation of Islam: Religion and Society in the Near East, 600–1800* by Jonathan P. Berkey
3. *Forbidding Wrong in Islam: An Introduction* by Michael Cook
4. *Martyrdom in Islam* by David Cook
5. *Charity in Islam* by Amy Singer
6. *Prayer in Islamic Thought and Practice* by Marion Holmes Katz
7. *Paradise and Hell in Islamic Traditions* by Christian Lange
8. *Nomads in the Middle East* by Beatrice Forbes Manz

Sectarianism in Islam

The Umma *Divided*

Adam R. Gaiser
Florida State University

CAMBRIDGE
UNIVERSITY PRESS

CAMBRIDGE
UNIVERSITY PRESS

Shaftesbury Road, Cambridge CB2 8EA, United Kingdom

One Liberty Plaza, 20th Floor, New York, NY 10006, USA

477 Williamstown Road, Port Melbourne, VIC 3207, Australia

314–321, 3rd Floor, Plot 3, Splendor Forum, Jasola District Centre, New Delhi – 110025, India

103 Penang Road, #05–06/07, Visioncrest Commercial, Singapore 238467

Cambridge University Press is part of Cambridge University Press & Assessment, a department of the University of Cambridge.

We share the University's mission to contribute to society through the pursuit of education, learning and research at the highest international levels of excellence.

www.cambridge.org
Information on this title: www.cambridge.org/9781107032255
DOI: 10.1017/9781139424790

First published 2023

A catalogue record for this publication is available from the British Library.

Library of Congress Cataloging-in-Publication Data
Names: Gaiser, Adam R., 1971– author.
Title: Sectarianism in Islam : the Umma divided / Adam R Gaiser.
Description: 1. | New York : Cambridge University Press, 2022. | Series: Themes in Islamic history | Includes bibliographical references and index.
Identifiers: LCCN 2022033350 (print) | LCCN 2022033351 (ebook) | ISBN 9781107032255 (hardback) | ISBN 9781009315210 (paperback) | ISBN 9781139424790 (ebook)
Subjects: LCSH: Islamic sects.
Classification: LCC BP191 .G35 2022 (print) | LCC BP191 (ebook) | DDC 297.8–dc23/eng/20220723
LC record available at https://lccn.loc.gov/2022033350
LC ebook record available at https://lccn.loc.gov/2022033351

ISBN 978-1-107-03225-5 Hardback
ISBN 978-1-009-31521-0 Paperback

For Allison Overholt,

who left us too soon,

but now delights in God's library.

Contents

Figures and Maps

Figures

Maps

Preface

As this is a book that is interested in narratives, along with the people who enmesh themselves in narratives, perhaps the best way to thank the many who had a hand in shaping this work is by telling the story of how it came about.

Marigold Ackland first approached me about the possibility of writing an introductory work on Muslim sectarianism in 2011. As an untenured professor, being approached by Cambridge University Press was both exciting and daunting. Being subsequently asked to submit a proposal for a book that I had not conceived, within a month, to the senior editor of the Islamic studies series, Patricia Crone, was even more daunting. Yet somehow I managed to patch a proposal together. It was about six pages, double spaced, and it was mostly terrible. Professor Crone's comments on it were seven pages, single spaced. To date her first return missive stands as the single most humbling email that I have ever received in my scholarly career. I still keep it in my files for those days when my head seems to be getting too large, or when I want to imagine what being shelled in a trench feels like. After a few days of depression, I picked myself back up and revised the proposal. Professor Crone's second response was only slightly less pitiless than the first. She was right, of course, in just about everything that she said about it, so after a few more days of sulking (and the sneaky suspicion that my life was mimicking a Monty Python monologue about a castle in a swamp) I went back to the drawing board and wrote a third version of the proposal. In her next response, Patricia said something to the effect that I was being surprisingly cordial in my return emails to her. At that moment I realized that I had passed some sort of test, and that the pounding that I had received from her was her way of showing me that she believed my proposal worthy of her hammer. From then on, our collaboration was pleasant, and right up until her death she continued to guide me in expert ways. Her loss to the scholarly community is tremendous, and this book would be a pale shadow without her efforts. The emails that I initially dreaded I now miss.

With Cambridge contract in hand, I now had a book to write. However, I had to write a different book first, so the sectarianism project had to wait, giving me time to try to figure out how to write in a responsible manner about Muslim sects and schools (to use Patricia's phrasing). The nudge came from Nancy Khalek, who invited me in 2015 to a conference on sectarianism in Islam and Muslim communities. Suddenly I was forced to think about how to think about sectarianism. The result was the idea of narrative identification as a theoretical framework, and the paper from the conference became both a chapter in Danny Postel and Nader Hashemi's book *Sectarianization*, and served as the basis for the introductory chapter of this book. Najam Haider and my colleague Will Hanley both read drafts of the introduction, and helped me to see some of the faults (many of which remain) in the theory that I was proposing.

Meanwhile, a slow drip of graduate students had begun to help me put together materials for my chapters. Kim Beaver was my trailblazer, faithfully gathering, evaluating, and highlighting much of what would go into the introduction. Beena Butool, Jesse Miller, Austin Fitzgerald, James Riggan, and Darian Shump followed her with suggestions, summaries, and notes. Amanda Propst read some of the later chapters with an expert eye for my obfuscations. They and other members of my seminars, one on Shiʿism and another on Islamic sectarianism, likewise helped in the conception and formulation of the ideas in this book: Allison Haney, Gemma Sunnergren, Madeleine Prothero, and Josh Carpenter to name a few.

As my first chapters came together, I was approached by a shy undergraduate from one of my classes, Allison Overholt. Allison was enrolled in Florida State University's undergraduate research assistance program, which pairs students with professors to give them a sense of what professional research entails. I had never participated in the program because my work was mostly obscure, but now I realized that Allison was the perfect reader. She was an enormously talented religion major, well-read for her years, and she was exactly the person to evaluate the prose. And so Allison – initially shaking at the prospect of offering a professor critical comments on his work – began to evaluate my chapters. By the end of the year, we had become close collaborators and friends. She was the first reader of this book, and it is dedicated to her. In the middle of her senior year, on January 19, 2019, Allison died suddenly in her bed. I'm looking at her picture now, in my office, and thinking of how she would have enjoyed holding the finished copy in her hands. She was a rare student.

Numerous colleagues from the Islamic studies community have contributed to the conceptualization and substance of this book. I will surely forget many names here, and to them I apologize. My colleagues in the Ibāḍī studies community have been a constant source of inspiration over the years: Abd al-Rahman al-Salimi, John Wilkinson, Wilferd Madelung, Valerie Hoffman, Amal Ghazal, Ersilia Francesca, Angeliki Ziaka, Paul Love, Cyrille Aillet, Mandana Limbert, and many others. My Shiʿism chapter benefitted from the help of Vernon Schubel, Mushegh Asatryan, and Aun Hassan Ali. Additionally, Maribel Fierro, Feryal Salem, and Alan Godlas directly contributed to the last couple of chapters.

Having finally taken up archery in the wake of Allison's death (life is short, after all) the sport proved to be essential to my survival during the COVID-19 pandemic and beyond. My friends at the archery range have made my life immensely more interesting, and helped me to improve my form and skills with the bow and arrow. I could not have completed my professional work without their companionship in my personal life. Thanks to Nick, Bob, Roy, Gary, Rex, Lori, Jamie, Travis, Daniel, Mike, Richard, and others at the Tallahassee Archery Club.

And finally, this book would not have been possible without the support and love of my wife, Carolina, and my daughter, Adela.

Note on Transliteration, Dates, and Qur'anic Citations

Transliterations from Arabic follow the *International Journal of Middle Eastern Studies* system, which has all but become the standard system in the United States. In accordance with this system, I've dropped the diacritical marks on "known" words like Sunni and Shiʿite. I have retained them, however, with medieval names and groups that are not well known in English (e.g. Ibāḍī, Khārijite). Dates will be given either as a stand-alone figure followed by the designator CE, or as *hijri* year or century first, followed by a slash and then common-era year or century. For qurʾanic citations, I will use the 1923 Egyptian printed recension of Ḥafs from ʿĀṣim, which has also become the standard version. I use the adjectival form "qurʾanic" just as we use "biblical," and I prefer to refer to God as God (not as Allah).

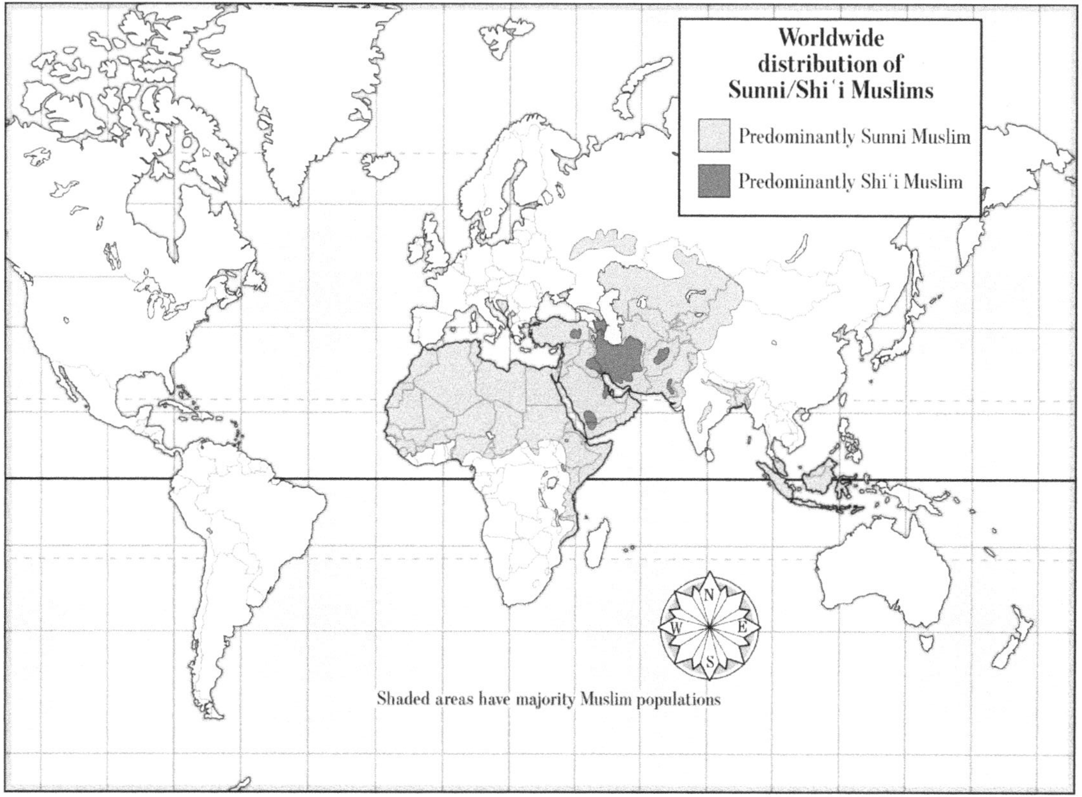

Map 1 World Sunni/Shiʿi population distribution.

1 Introduction

Approaches to Muslim Sects and Schools

Why Read a Book on Muslim Sects and Schools?

This is a book about intra-religious divisions among Muslims – what medieval Muslims might have called *firaq* (sing. *firqa*), or *niḥal* (sing. *niḥla*), and contemporary Muslims might call *ṭawāʾif* (sing. *ṭāʾifa*) or *madhāhib* (sing. *madhhab*). That is to say, it is a book about how Muslims have, over the course of their long history and in the many geographical areas where they found themselves, forged and often reforged divergent notions of what it means to be a Muslim. This process might be called "sectarianism," or even "Islamic sectarianism," though the moniker is fraught with problems, not the least of which being that several of the recognized divisions (*firaq*) among Muslims (e.g. Muʿtazilites and Murjiʾites) would not technically qualify as being "sects" according to the myriad scholarly definitions of that term. To account for this particular issue, this work focuses on Muslim sects and "schools," meaning here schools of thought, as a means of approaching what Muslim authors might have implied when they described these groups as *firaq*, *niḥal*, *madhāhib*, or *ṭawāʾif*.

At the outset, it is worth asking after the purpose of such a book. Why read it? On the face of it, it would seem that current world conditions make the answers to these questions obvious: communal unrest or outright violence in Muslim-majority countries such as Iraq, Bahrain, Lebanon, Yemen, and Pakistan (to name a few) often gets articulated in sectarian terms, not only by the actors and the victims of such violence but also by the various journalists, anchors, and writers whose task it is to report and explain these events to the rest of the world. For many popular media outlets, affiliations, such as Sunni or Shiʿa, offer convenient identity markers by bounding groups by their communal affiliation. These sectarian classifications are meant to "make sense" of conflict in the Islamic world by providing their readers a means to navigate that world, and they gain legitimacy as explanatory devices insofar as they reflect the ways that some Muslims articulate the underlying causes of their conflicts. Indeed, many

Sunnis and Shiʿa, among others, employ sectarian categories as a means to identify themselves, or as the basis for polemics (as a simple search of the Internet will show), or as a reason to engage in violence. Journalists, then, can accurately claim that their reporting reflects "local" perceptions of the situation on the ground.

Explanations that aim to be taken as more sophisticated often come seasoned with historical accounts of the first disputes among Muslims over the succession to the Prophet Muḥammad, and of the subsequent sectarian divisions that developed therefrom. In this way, contemporary conflicts between different kinds of Muslims receive a history, and sectarian conflict is presented as part and parcel of the meta-historical narrative of Muslims. Thus, the seemingly inherent nature of sectarian conflict, or – in its more sophisticated form – the *longue durée* approach to Islamic sectarianism, would be assumed to do the work of "explaining" contemporary instances of communal tension, intra-religious polemic, or violence. The simple invocation of "Sunni" or "Shiʿa" or other identifiers such as "Wahhābī," "Salafī," and "Aḥmadī" are assumed to be sufficient in and of themselves as explanatory devices. Or these conflicts are presented with reference to the origins and presumed longevity of sectarian monikers over the long course of Islamic history.

These lines of thinking remain flawed in several fundamental ways. First, the simplistic invocation of "Sunni" and "Shiʿa" (or other identifiers) as explanatory devices for contemporary polemic or conflict in the Islamic world falls apart when we encounter the equally numerous examples of Sunnis and Shiʿa, to which we could add the Ibāḍiyya, living together in relative harmony. In other words, simply being Sunni, Shiʿa, or Ibāḍī is not enough to automatically create conflict with other Muslims of a different communal affiliation. More to the point, this all-too-common move to essentialize Muslim sectarian identities obscures the very interesting questions of how Muslims acquire, maintain, and manipulate their communal affiliations, as well as the extent to which such affiliations might overlap or break down altogether. After all, Muslims are not born Sunni, Shiʿa, or Ibāḍī (nor were they born Khārijites, Murjiʾites, or Muʿtazilites in the medieval periods), but must first imbibe the meanings of such associations before they themselves go on to determine the extent to which such affiliations matter. Accordingly, the existence of historical figures who defy easy categorization as Sunni, Shiʿa, or other (such as Abū ʿAbdullāh Muḥammad b. Idrīs al-Shāfiʿī, Haji Bektāsh Veli, or Timurlane, to name a few) tends to erode confidence in the utility of sectarian markers as fixed taxonomies of identification.

Also concealed by the essentializing of sectarian identifications is the question of when, and under what conditions, sectarian differences can be mustered in the service of polemic or violence. It conceals what "activates" sectarian affiliations and makes them "gain the salience needed to elicit a shift in levels of self-definition" to the point that such groups become willing to engage in confrontation.[1] It must be noted that sectarian difference, here to be treated as a form of intra-religious identification, often stands alongside of (and sometimes in competition with) other modes of identification. For example, a person's primary outlook might also be global-humanist, interreligious, ethnic, linguistic, familial, tribal, national, or even ritual/performative (among others). In order to become a dominant mode of self-identification, sect/school identities must be imbued with significant meaning, so much so that sectarian differences begin to stand in front of other types of identification, including Qurʾan-grounded exhortations toward unity among Muslims that are embedded in the concept of the *umma* (the Islamic community writ large). Moreover, in order to effect violence sect identifications must overcome the barriers to action that seem to characterize studies of human behavior. Confrontation requires significant time and energy (as any who have engaged in formal debates know), and thus a good many, if not most, people seek to evade it by tolerating or simply ignoring other people. Moments of sectarian "activation," then, remain necessarily grounded in specifically charged, and often local, circumstances and may involve a whole host of social, political, economic, and religious issues. Simply pointing toward sectarian affiliation, therefore, obscures the ways that a given group of Muslims in a given time and place "activate" such identifications with the purpose of resisting, confronting, or possibly fighting other types of Muslims.

Equally limiting is the assumption that the *longue durée* history of sectarian difference can be marshaled to explain modern instances of violence in which sect identification is a factor. This is not to say that the long history of Islamic sects and schools is unimportant, but rather to stress that the origin and development of various Muslim groups goes only so far as a means of elucidating contemporary conflicts between, for example, Sunnis and Shiʿites.[2] History and its role in bolstering

[1] Haddad, *Sectarianism in Iraq*, 10.

[2] Many journalistic accounts of contemporary sectarian conflicts in the Islamic world do not end up providing much in the way of actual historical analysis, and thus do not really qualify as *longue durée* explanations. Many tend to provide accounts of the early succession debates, or perhaps the Battle of Ṣiffin, but then jump to the present. Implicit in such a move is the idea that Islamic sectarianism is a phenomenon with a long history (despite the fact that authors often do not provide much of that history), and that this longevity "explains" recent iterations of sectarian conflict among Muslims. In essence, such

sectarianism remains only part of this story. Historical narratives of sect identification illuminate the trajectory of ideas through time, and explain some of their inertia. However, references to events of the seventh century CE cannot explain the activities of twentieth-century actors. Thus, the recent violence between Iraqi Sunnis and Shiʿa (and the many non-Iraqis that joined in that conflict) must be elucidated, in large part, with reference to the recent history of Iraq: that is, the Iranian Revolution of 1978 that pitted a revolutionary vision of a Shiʿite-inspired Islamic government against Saddam Hussein's secular-socialist totalitarianism; the eight-year war between Iran and Iraq in which Saddam Hussein treated Shiʿites as a fifth column; the First Gulf War with its doomed Shiʿite uprising in southern Iraq; the Second Gulf War and the rise of various Sunni and Shiʿite militias; and so on (to mention but a limited number of these factors, and briefly at that).[3] So too, sectarian conflicts in Bahrain, Pakistan, Lebanon, and the Yemen must be approached by weighting the recent histories of those countries. A *longue durée* history of sectarian difference will certainly contribute to this project, but it will not ultimately explain the core issues driving these local struggles.

A third and rather insidious assumption underlying the move to explain contemporary violence and confrontation in Islamdom is the supposition that such violence is inherently religious in nature, and thus must be explained with reference to religious categories of identification. Setting aside the problems of defining "religious" violence, it is worth noting how this assumption tacitly favors a "secular" view of conflicts where religion or religious affiliations play a role. According to such a view, removing religion from the equation (presumably by introducing a "secular" element) should remove the main driver of violence. However, not only do religious identifications seem to play a contingent role in such conflicts (recalling that sectarian affiliation must be "activated" in some fashion, usually involving social, political, economic, or other motivators), but such an assumption relies on views toward religion that mark it as irrational due to its emotional appeal, instable in the public sphere, and given to provoking extreme ("fanatical," "zealous") responses in human beings. Such a simplistic view of religion is to be avoided on principle, to say nothing of how it obscures the complex of factors (including whatever we might designate as the "religious") that contribute to specific instances of tension or violence in the world.

treatments use the cover of history to essentialize Islamic sectarianism as a driver of contemporary violence between Muslims.

3 See Haddad, *Sectarianism in Iraq*, 32ff.

For all of these reasons, a book on Islamic sects and schools that provides descriptions and history of the main Muslim *firaq* will be of limited use to those who seek an understanding of the conflicts plaguing the Muslim world today. Consequently, this work is emphatically not a book that deals with today's sectarian conflicts: it ends its analysis before the twelfth/eighteenth century, and does not highlight the topic of religious violence as such. It is, on the other hand, a book about Muslims and their differences: specifically, the kind of intra-Islamic differences that are tied to religious rituals, histories, beliefs, and other kinds of things. It is a book that navigates the long development of these religious differences among Muslims, and charts the subsequent ways by which such differences were periodically made to stand between them as a marker of their specific intra-religious affiliations. And herein lies the value of an exploration of Muslim sects and schools. Religious identification turns out to be a complex process, shaped by innumerable factors, and insofar as these divergent means of articulating "Islam" allow for an appreciation of the development of different Islamic perspectives, it also illuminates the ways that human beings create identities for themselves and others. The questions raised in the preceding paragraphs about how Muslims acquire, maintain, and manipulate communal affiliations, the extent to which such affiliations might overlap or break down altogether, as well as the question of how local circumstances affect the "activation" of sect identification provide the guiding principles behind this exploration. A welcome side benefit to this approach is that it explodes the idea of a monolithic Islam, and of fixed sectarian or school identifications that can be adopted "as is" for any occasion. The rich texture of Islamic thought, herein examined through the lens of sects and schools, reflects the diversity of human thought. And if this work does nothing more than allow a glimpse into the complex, sometimes sublime, too-often tragic workings of the fellow human beings that call themselves Muslim, then it will have succeeded.

Narratives of Muslim Sects and Schools

What is a sect, and what is a "school of thought"? And why use two different English terms as the equivalent of what in Islamic literature is usually rendered by a singular term? To answer these questions, we must approach the ways that the metanarratives, what Somers also calls the "master narratives" and I have often called the "grand narratives," of sect/school division were and are articulated.[4] Medieval Muslim historians and theologians developed several concepts and taxonomies to help them

[4] Somers, "The Narrative Constitution of Identity," 619ff.

explain the existence of, and navigate their place among, the *firaq*. As we are largely dependent on the sources that they created for our own understanding of Muslim sects and schools, it behooves us to examine the ways that they conceptualized their subject. And for the same reason, we must first scrutinize the ways that we, as students and researchers in English-speaking (part of the so-called Western) academies, have inherited a discourse about sects and philosophical/theological schools of thought that guide the way that we speak and think about religious difference.

The English word "sect" derives from the Latin *secta*, meaning "manner, mode, following, school of thought," or, literally, "way" or "road." However, a common mistake, dating back even to the medieval period, was to derive the word from the Latin verb *secare* ("to cut"), thus giving the idea of a sect as something that breaks off or branches off from a main group.[5] Medieval Christians often applied the term "sect" to denote schismatics, and therefore heretics. In other words, they used it to describe those who were perceived to have deviated from true Christianity in the eyes of whatever body was making the accusation of schism. As a modern term, the popular notion of sectarianism has retained something of this polemical and pejorative sense, though academic definitions of sectarianism attempt, with varying degrees of success, to define sectarianism in a more neutral fashion. Also noteworthy is how both of the connotations of sect (as a subgroup of a religious or philosophical system, and usually as an offshoot of a larger group) inform the ways that term is understood. In fact, many academic definitions of "sect" and "sectarianism" have not deviated far from these core usages, though they have offered some important insights along the way.

Contemporary academic discussions about sectarianism begin with one of the founders of modern sociology, the German intellectual Karl Emil Maximilian ("Max") Weber (d. 1920). Weber interested himself in the study of human social behavior, its origins and development, organizations and institutions. As an aspect of these concerns, he offered the first sociological characterization of a sect, which he contrasted with the institution of the church. Weber was interested in these institutions insofar as they provided ideal types, highlighting certain contrasting features of human social organization for the purposes of comparison.[6] Specifically, Weber was interested in refuting Marx's contention that social institutions were rooted in the economic substructure of society, aiming to show that religion could operate as an independent variable in

[5] www.etymonline.com/word/sect#etymonline_v_23088.
[6] Swatos, "Weber or Troeltsch?" 131.

history.[7] For Weber, churches had certain features such as professional priesthoods, dogmas and rites, claims to universal domination; and they were compulsory organizations, meaning that the church's claims to truth went beyond individuals, compelling the church to discipline those who deviated from it.[8] This last point on the mode of membership provided for one of the main differences between churches and sects: people were born into churches, but they chose to be part of sects. This mode of membership, thereby, affected how a person acted in relation to the institution, as the church remained a "compulsory association for the administration of grace," while the sect offered a "voluntary association for religiously qualified persons."[9] Sects thus rejected the institutionalized grace of the church for the personal salvation offered by the sect. This meant that membership in the sect required specific actions, and unqualified members were removed from the group.[10] Weber also claimed that sects resisted hierarchies while churches maintained hierarchies of persons who dispensed grace, and that sects were generally apolitical, desiring to be left alone, in contrast to churches that remained tied to the world.[11]

Weber's ideas were taken up and elaborated upon by one of his colleagues, another German intellectual, Ernst Troeltsch (d. 1923). As a theologian, Troeltsch hoped to relate different kinds of religious experience to various kinds of social teachings, and to thereby discover a solution to the problems facing Christians in the modern era. He thus emphasized the social behavior of churches and sects over the particular forms of social organization that they maintained.[12] Churches, he argued, tended to accommodate the state, becoming in the process associated with the ruling classes, and thus part of the social order.[13] This willingness to compromise with the world was predicated on the church's presumed ability to remain sanctified despite individual inadequacies. Thus, the sanctity of the church superseded the individual pieties of the persons that comprised it. Sects, on the other hand, aspired toward inward perfection and personal fellowship, treating the wider society sometimes with indifference and tolerance, but often with protest or open hostility. Indeed, for Troeltsch the very values of the sect existed as a remonstration of those of the wider society. For this reason, they tended to break from the church, and to exist among the lower classes of society and those who did not get on well with the state. For sect members, attainment of salvation existed

[7] Coleman, "Church-Sect Typology and Organizational Precariousness," 55.

[8] Weber, *Economy and Society*, 1164.

[9] Weber, *From Max Weber*, 314.

[10] Weber, *Economy and Society*, 1204–5.

[11] Weber, *Economy and Society*, 1208.

[12] Swatos, "Weber or Troeltsch?" 133.

[13] Troeltsch, *The Social Teaching of the Christian Churches*, 331ff.

in tension with secular interests and institutions. Thus, for Troeltsch, the church represented an institution of grace that was enmeshed in the wider world of politics and society, while the sect presented a smaller, voluntary group that stressed individual, demonstrated ethical behavior apart from the world.

Weber and Troeltsch's typologies were heavily invested in the language and history of Christianity. They posited sects as voluntary, apolitical groups that existed in tension with their universalist parent groups, the church. Not only did their typologies draw explicitly from the history of the Catholic/Protestant splits in Europe, but both offered less a definition of church and sect, and more an attempt to establish these ideals as heuristic tools that would illuminate certain features of human social organization through comparison. Weber's aim in developing the typology was precisely to understand why capitalism and the idea of secular democracy seemed to develop only among Protestant Christians. For his part, Troeltsch hoped to find an answer to the problem of the Christian's relation to the modern world, concluding that because of its relation to society at large, the church offered the better solution.

Weber and Troeltsch's church-sect typology was itself then picked up by an American theologian, Helmut Richard Niebuhr (d. 1962), who treated churches and sects as poles on a continuum, rather than as distinct categories. Niebuhr's insight was to show how sects tended to become more church-like with time. As new generations populated the sects, and as their ways became fixed, "the original impetus to reject the norms and activities of the dominant society" gave way to acceptance.[14] Following Niebuhr, several contemporary sociologists and scholars of religion have offered elaborations of the church-sect typology, many of which developed it into full-fledged definitions of various church or sect-types, creating what has been called "quasi-evaluative" devices.[15] Thus, for example, Becker expanded the church-sect model to include denominations and ecclesia.[16] Yinger enlarged Becker's model even further, positing six types (cult, sect, established sect, class church/denomination, ecclesia, and universal church) and sub-typing sects by their accepting, avoiding, or aggressive relationship to the wider society.[17] Similarly, Johnson classified religious groups according to their state of tension with their social

[14] Swatos, "Weber or Troeltsch?" 134; Dawson, "Creating 'Cult' Typologies," 367; see also Niebuhr, *The Social Sources of Denominationalism.*

[15] Swatos, "Weber or Troeltsch?" 134–35.

[16] Becker, *Systematic Sociology*, 114–18; Becker, "Sacred and Secular Societies," 362–76; Swatos, "Weber or Troeltsch?" 135.

[17] Yinger, *Religion and the Struggle for Power*, 18–23; Yinger, *Religion, Society and the Individual*, 142–45.

environment.[18] Stark and Bainbridge defined churches as conventional religious organizations, sects as deviant religious organization with traditional beliefs and practices, and cults as deviant religious organization with novel beliefs and practices.[19] Opting for visual models, Robertson and Gustafson provided two-by-two tables, the cells of which offered elaborations on the church and sect-types using modified Troeltschian criteria,[20] while Swatos afforded a more elaborate table with five types.[21] Wilson, arguing along classic Weberian lines that religious groups should be understood according to their soteriological function, classed several types of sects according to their "deviant" responses to the world.[22] Importantly, Wilson rejected the idea that sects must be set against a church. Rather, they may be arrayed against "secular society" as a kind of protest movement.[23] Baumgarten similarly viewed sects primarily as protest groups, emphasizing the process of boundary creating by defining a sect as "a voluntary association of protest, which utilizes boundary marking mechanisms – the social means of differentiating between insiders and outsiders – to distinguish between its own members and those otherwise normally regarded as belonging to the same national or religious entity."[24] As becomes clear from a brief survey of the various sociologists and religious studies scholars who developed the Weber/Troeltsch/Niebuhr church-sect and later, cult typology, the notions of "sect" and "sectarianism" admit varying degrees of subtlety, and may be differentiated from other kinds of groups according to an array of diverse criteria. Broadly speaking, however, there is consensus among them that a sect is "a group that has separated to some degree from a parent body, and has boundary markers to indicate its separate identity."[25]

Given this broad consensus among certain "Western" academics, it is worth asking how applicable their conceptualizations of "sect" and "sectarianism" might be for the study of Muslim *firaq*. Cook has argued that Weber's notion of church-sect is, in fact, not very useful when carried over into an Islamic context. For one, Islamic sectarianism proper was first and foremost a response to religio-political developments after the death of the Prophet Muḥammad, while Weber and Troeltsch (among others) characterized sects as apolitical.[26] Secondly, membership in what might

18 Johnson, "On Church and Sect," 542; Stark and Bainbridge, *The Future of Religion*, 23.
19 Stark and Bainbridge, *A Theory of Religion*, 124.
20 Robertson, *The Sociological Interpretation of Religion*, 122–28; Gustafson, "UO-US-PS-PO," 64–68; Gustafson, "Exegesis on the Gospel according to St. Max," 12–25.
21 Swatos, "Monopolism, Pluralism, Acceptance, and Rejection," 174–85 (esp. figure 1 on 177); see also Wallis, "Scientology," 98.
22 Wilson, *Religious Sects*, 36–40. 23 Wilson, *Religious Sects*, 26–27.
24 Baumgarten, *The Flourishing of Jewish Sects in the Maccabean Era*, 7.
25 Collins, *Scriptures and Sectarianism*, 177. 26 Cook, "Weber and Islamic Sects," 276.

be considered a Muslim sect, notably the Shiʿites, but also the Ibāḍiyya, is not any less voluntary than that of other Muslim groups. And lastly, Shiʿites possess far more hierarchical characteristics than their Sunni counterparts, making them more properly the candidates for the Weberian status of "church" than the Sunnis, upon whom Weber actually bestowed the designation.[27] Given these problems, Cook concludes that "Weber is neither so obviously right, nor so interestingly wrong, as to provide a useful starting-point for our own attempts to understand the peculiar groups we know as Islamic sects."[28]

Similarly, many of the definitions of sects and sectarianism that follow Weber turn out to be fundamentally problematic when applied to the Islamic context. One of the main issues with them revolves around their notions of church, denomination, or ecclesia as somehow set against sects and cults. While a case could be made for treating Shiʿites and, perhaps more appropriately, Khārijites as sects in the Weberian-Troeltschian vein, there is no good candidate for what in the early Islamic period might qualify as the church, denomination, or ecclesia from which they separated. Something called the "Sunni" branch of Islam cannot be said to have existed before the third/ninth century (at the earliest), and the pro-ʿUthmān groups of the initial period (mainly the Umayyads) constituted no majority, nor were they as firmly established in their rule as they might have liked to have been. Certainly, the Umayyads attempted to make themselves into the undisputed, popular, religious authorities of early Islamdom, but such attempts failed, as did the later ʿAbbāsid efforts to do the same. At best, these early groups might simply qualify as other Muslim sects. None of them actually meet the requirements for "churches" or parent groups.

Even Wilson's definition of sect, which helpfully leaves aside overt notions of "church," nonetheless posits sects as protest movements (and "deviant" ones at that) to be measured against the societies in which they are located. In effect, Wilson simply substitutes "society" for "church" as the normative baseline against which sects may be classed. This is not to say that what early Muslims later dubbed *firaq* were not protest movements within the midst of their societies. Indeed, many of the *firaq* could be described as protest or revolutionary movements. Nevertheless, the yardstick for measuring protest need not be a real or imagined universal such as church/denomination/ecclesia or "society." Defining sects as "deviant" in relation to some universal, in fact, subtly replicates the historical situation of the early Christian church, revealing it to be hiding under such definitions all along.

[27] Cook, "Weber and Islamic Sects," 277. [28] Cook, "Weber and Islamic Sects," 278.

The early Islamic situation seems, rather, to be one of several groups competing for primacy, and mutually protesting, or actively rebelling against each other. There is no stable center, no "parent group," or normative society from which these groups sprung and against which they defined themselves. Moreover, while many of the *firaq* were, at some point and to a certain degree, voluntary, in the heavily tribalized societies of early Islamic period voluntarism quickly elided with tribal association such that sect and tribal affiliation can frequently be correlated. And while most of the groups that later get described as *firaq* initially arose in protest against the Umayyads, by the ʿAbbāsid era one of them (i.e. the Murjiʾites) abandoned any vestige of revolutionary protest to be eventually absorbed into the emerging Sunni consensus. In other words, the analytic church-sect-cult categories discussed above will not be much help in characterizing early Islamic sectarianism.

But what of the medieval and early modern periods? Sedgwick has argued that in the absence of an established church among Muslims, researchers might look to "general mores," the "general sociocultural environment," as well as a conventional "body of doctrine," which is "largely under the control of bodies which may be termed denominations."[29] Perhaps, following Sedgwick, it is possible to speak of Shiʿism, Sunnism, or Ibāḍism, broadly, as denominations, especially after the third/ninth century when such groups seem to have accumulated enough institutional weight in their respective locales to control bodies of doctrine, and to significantly influence their general sociocultural environments. His reminder (à la Niebuhr) that sectarian groups may become more like denominations with time remains an important one, allowing the researcher to examine the Islamic world as a patchwork of sociocultural environments, each with the potential to sustain "general mores" and normative bodies of doctrine within them (and thus, simultaneously containing the potential for more sects to arise within them).

The question, however, remains whether or not it is necessary or especially useful to employ these classificatory terms ("sect" and "denomination") to track development within the same Muslim group.[30] Given that the particularism of the categories renders them virtually useless as explanatory devices for the earliest Islamic periods, it

29 Sedgwick, "Sects in the Islamic World," 197.

30 In some cases (such as particularly technical or specialized studies), the answer might be affirmative. However, in an introductory work on Muslim sects and schools, shifting descriptors mid-chapter seems a bit like needless classificatory gymnastics. This suspicion is confirmed by noticing that Hodgson argues for the Shiʿa becoming "sectarian" precisely at the moment (i.e. third/ninth century) when Sedgwick might consider them as moving toward becoming a "denomination." See Hodgson, "How Did the Early Shiʿa Become Sectarian?" 8ff.

is hard to see how they might be introduced mid-stream as helpful descriptors for groups in the classical to late medieval eras. More to the point, the overt usage of these categories remains unnecessary insofar as the telling of a given *firqa*'s history implicitly explains how it became more accepted in such-and-such a place and time (i.e. less like a sect in tension with its social environment), and how it then established more "institutions" (thus becoming less "voluntary," and more like what Sedgwick calls a denomination). In the end, Sedgwick's categories are helpful for thinking about sects in the contemporary Islamic world (which are his core concern), but the particularism of the sect-denomination typology becomes needlessly burdensome when marshaled to tell the broader story of Muslim sects and schools.

Turning to the ways that early Muslims conceptualized the religious subgroups in their midst, it is noteworthy that they tend not to use binary, tertiary, or relational terminology ("church-sect-cult" or "sect-denomination"), but rather to abstract the main groups using a singular concept. Thus, the terms *firqa/firaq*, *niḥla/niḥal*, *madhhab/madhāhib*, and later *ṭāʾifa/ṭawāʾif* tend to evenly designate Shiʿites, Khārijites, Murjiʾites, Muʿtazilites, as well as those later known under the rubric of Sunnis.[31] This is not to say that individual Muslim authors treated these groups as equally legitimate (they most certainly did not), but merely to point out that the conceptual schema underlying the Muslim imaginary of sectarianism tended to deploy one notion to describe various kinds of groups while Christian and later "Western"/academic notions seem to replicate what is at its base a dualistic or tripartite model. Even when medieval Muslim authors designated one group as superior to the others, they tended to cite the Prophetic *ḥadīth* that mentioned the "saved *firqa*" (*al-firqa al-nājiyya*) among the other erring *firaq*. In other words, Muslims cast all of these groups as *firqa*s, be they "saved" or not.

It would seem, then, that the terminology of church-sect-cult would not be of much use in describing the Muslims' situation. And yet, we are left with few acceptable English replacements: we could avoid the language of sect altogether, describing Shiʿism, Khārijism, Sunnism, and so on, as communal groups, identifications, or affiliations.[32] Alternately, we might try to recover the term "sect" as somehow the equivalent of *firqa*, *niḥla*, and so forth. Neither option is perfect, and so, this work will attempt a little of both, approaching Muslim sectarianism as a kind of

[31] The term *milla/milal* tended to denote, following the qurʾanic usage (2:14–15; 7:86–87; 14:16; 18:19–20), divisions among discrete religious traditions, such as between Jews, Christians, Zoroastrians, and Muslims.

[32] For example, see Haider, whose introduction to *Shīʿī Islam* (1–11) avoids the language of sect and sectarianism in favor of "communal group."

affiliation, but also reappropriating the term "sect" as reflecting its accurate Latin meaning "manner, mode, following, way" or "road" to designate the primary ways, manners, and modes by which groups of Muslims differed over the religio-political succession to Muḥammad. In this sense, "sect" refers to those groups that *differed with each other* rather than with some "parent group" or normative society. Specifically, it refers to the actual Shiʿites, Khārijites, and the constellation of groups that, much later, became subsumed under the heading of the Sunnis. And as with the Islamic usage of *firaq*, and so on, this work will consistently refer to these groups as "sects" at all stages of their development, even though stricter sociological taxonomy might classify them at some point in their history as having become "denominations."

Set alongside of these groups are those which I will designate schools of thought: mainly the Murjiʾites and Muʿtazilites. This work has chosen to use a different term to describe these groups, in part, because the term "sect" does not really do them justice. Their manner of difference was not religio-political per se, but more properly philosophical-theological, and thus they turn out to be dissimilar enough from their Shiʿite, Khārijite, and Sunni counterparts to warrant, in my estimation, another descriptor. Moreover, the idea of a school of thought is familiar to students trained in the "Western"/academic tradition (e.g. the school of Athens) to approximate the extent that *firaq* such as the Murjiʾites and Muʿtazilites (among others) referred to groups set off by their commitments to primarily intellectual endeavors, as opposed to revolutionary ones. Admittedly, the resulting "Muslim sects and schools" is a bit unwieldy, and it is to be hoped that the line between "sect" and "school" would remain comfortably hazy.

Despite the serious shortcoming of church-sect typologies for the study of Muslim sects and schools, there remain some elements of these theories that might be rescued. First, Weber and later Wilson approached religion in terms of its function, highlighting how religious groups like churches and sects offered distinctive paths to salvation. They thereby distinguished sects by their soteriological responses to the world, meaning that they were interested in the ways that sectarian answers to the question "what should we do to be saved?" implied certain kinds of relations to their social environment.[33] While I do not wish to reduce religion or sectarianism to its function alone, I do hold that the idea of salvation remains a central leitmotif to what I am calling Muslim sects and schools, and that soteriology might provide an important means to distinguish between them.

[33] Dawson, "Creating 'Cult' Typologies," 366.

Second, returning in some senses to Weber's notion of the "mode of membership" in a church or sect, it is possible to see past his particular characterizations of membership toward the more general question of how human beings participate in religious groups and subgroups. More recent definitions of sectarianism view it as both a practice and a discourse,[34] calling attention to how sectarian affiliation must be "activated" if it is to move from being passive or banal to being assertive or even aggressive.[35] These definitions point to the importance of external influences, economics, shifting notions of modernity and nationalism, and to history, and myths and symbols as factors that create and sustain sectarianism in modern contexts.[36] They challenge researchers to move away from treating sectarianism as a thing-in-itself (and therefore from relying on taxonomies of church-sect-cult types) and back to sectarianism as a way of doing things, as a mode of being in the world, and as a discourse of identification.

A Narrative-Identification Approach to Muslim Sects and Schools

How, then, to best study Muslim sects and schools? If not Weberian/Troeltschian models, then what other approaches, models, and theories might assist the study of Islamic sectarianism? The answers to these questions will depend, in large part, on how the notions of sect, school, and religious difference are conceptualized. Following recent trends in the study of sectarianism, this study will treat Muslim sects and schools, in the broadest sense, as affiliations that Muslims hold. Strongly associated with these affiliations are the various institutions that perpetuate them (insofar as these institutions can be said to be accumulated products and reflections of particular kinds of Muslim sect/school identifications).[37] And because Muslim sects and schools remain indelibly tied to the Muslims who articulate and constitute them, sectarian modes of identification turn out to be remarkably unstable. After all, human modes of self-identification are often situation specific, meaning that human beings identify themselves differently depending on their situation. The fact that a person identifies as a Sunni or Shiʿite may or may not be relevant at any given moment, depending on the

[34] Makdisi, *The Culture of Sectarianism*, 6; see also Weiss, *In the Shadow of Sectarianism*, 13.
[35] Haddad, *Sectarianism in Iraq*, 25ff.
[36] Makdisi, *The Culture of Sectarianism*, 6–7; Haddad, *Sectarianism in Iraq*, 10–23.
[37] See Weiss, *In the Shadow of Sectarianism*, 13ff.; Jokiranta, *Social Identity and Sectarianism in the Qumran Movement*, 77ff.; Potter, *Sectarian Politics in the Persian Gulf*, 2–3; on the limits of the concept of "identity," see Brubaker and Cooper, "Beyond 'Identity,'" 1–47.

circumstances. For example, while having coffee with peers in a café in Baghdad, the notion that a person is a Shiʿite (or Sunni) may fade into the background, while the issue of said person's favorite soccer team, oud player, or political stance may take over. This does not mean, of course, that the person has stopped *being* a Shiʿite, but rather that the importance of such an affiliation has ceased to become a significant factor of their being in those moments, and thus, from the perspective of social science research, the person's Shiʿism has temporarily ceased to be relevant. However, when the month of Muḥarram nears, this same person's Shiʿism may come to the fore (and thus return as an object of interest to social science researchers) as she remembers al-Ḥusayn b. ʿAlī's martyrdom at Karbala in the local mosque or Ḥusayniyya. In fact, depending on the circumstances, the month of Muḥarram may cause the person's Shiʿism to become more relevant than it was previously. Thus, and as a reflection of the human beings who hold them, intra-religious differences are not fixed, immutable, or eternal, but constantly shifting, as is their salience in any given situation.

Additionally, this situation-specific nature of sect/school identification offers clues to another aspect of sectarianism and difference, namely, its connection to other elements of our personhood both as individuals and collectives. We sometimes think of our identities as something intensely personal, yet who we "are" also contains elements that are imminently communal. Thus, a person might be a Muslim, a Sunni Muslim to be more precise, and also an American of Palestinian descent, a Democrat, middle class, a veteran, an electrical engineer, a Mason, a University of Virginia graduate, a UVA Cavaliers fan, an archer, a father, husband, brother, and neighbor. Seeing sect-affiliation in relation to "commonality, connectedness and groupness"[38] renders it, following Abdul Jabbar, "a loose cultural designation" that differentiates one group affiliation from another using "religious terms."[39] It also reminds us that sect/school identification is but one aspect of a larger, and malleable, patchwork of individual and group affiliations, and that it must be approached as tangled up with these other kinds of identifications.

How, then, to study an unstable affiliation that is but one stand among many possible identifications? In this regard, the recent conversations among scholars of sociology, psychology, anthropology, philosophy, and literary criticism as to how human beings use narrative to form identities and interpret their experiences may prove useful. In particular, the work of Margaret Somers captures some of the general insights of this

[38] Brubaker and Cooper, "Beyond 'Identity,'" 19–21.
[39] Abdul Jabbar, *The Shiʿite Movement in Iraq*, 33–35.

line of inquiry. Somers builds on the idea that "it is through narrativity that we come to know, understand, and make sense of the social world, and it is through narratives and narrativity that we constitute our social identities." That is to say, human beings find themselves "emplotted" in the midst of small and large-scale narratives, relating to others as "characters" within those narratives, and navigating the roles that they choose to play with reference to the underlying "themes" and "plots" of such narratives. Such narratives feed into the individual and group identifications of human beings, allowing them to make sense of past, present, and future events through the lenses of the narratives in which they are emplotted.[40] Generally speaking, Somers argues for the idea that "all of us come to be who we are (however ephemeral, multiple, and changing) by being located or locating ourselves (usually unconsciously) in social narratives rarely of our own making."[41]

Adapting Somers' views of narrative identity to the study of Muslims sects and schools (and substituting à la Brubaker and Cooper the notion of "identity" for the more precise concept of "identification"), then, treats sect/school affiliations one particular cluster of narratives among and related to many others in which human beings find themselves emplotted.[42] Such an approach has much to commend it. First, it avoids essentializing sect and school affiliations by recognizing them as products of human beings: products that accumulate, change, and develop – even break down – over time, and in accordance with the particular situations in which people employ (or forget) them. Secondly, it allows for human agency within the social context of group affiliation,[43] viewing sect/school actors as both participating in a drama that goes beyond their individual

[40] Somers, "The Narrative Constitution of Identity," 613–14.
[41] Somers, "The Narrative Constitution of Identity," 606.
[42] See the criticism of Somers's approach in Brubaker and Cooper, "Beyond 'Identity,'" 11–12.
[43] It is mainly for this reason that I find Somers's approach to narrative identity far more useful to the study of sectarianism than the notion of the "myth-symbol complex" (see Kaufman, *Modern Hatreds*, 25; Haddad, *Sectarianism in Iraq*, 17). Though very similar to the idea of narrative identity (the myth-symbol complex is ultimately a kind of narrative), Kaufman tends to treat myth-symbol complexes as mostly static narratives that exert an almost irresistible influence over their (mostly passive) consumers. He does not adequately explain, for example, how "the existence, status and security of the groups" comes to depend on "the status of group symbols" (25). Similarly, he tends to reserve agency for "leaders" who "manipulate … symbols for dubious or selfish purposes," casting the followers of these leaders as simple dupes, or for mass movements in which the relation of group to symbol is obscure. The narrative-identification approach, on the other hand, highlights how actors participate (both actively and passively) in the narratives of sect and school. Somers's approach thus comes closer (à la Asad, "Idea of an Anthropology of Islam," 16) to treating people as participants in sectarianism as a discursive tradition.

selves, but also manipulating that drama through their participation in it.[44] Third, it recognizes sect/school identifications as part of the multiple, intersecting, and often competing identifications that constitute a person or social entity (i.e. that a person or group will be involved in several narratives of being, all of which might affect each other to varying degrees). Viewing sect/school affiliation as a kind of narrative identification thus permits the researcher of Muslim sects and schools to inquire after the narratives, themes, plots, institutions, and characters that make up – collectively – what we consider to be any given *firqa* at any given moment. In this way, it provides a potent methodology for the historical study of Muslim sects and schools. Taking a narrative-identification approach to the study of Muslim sects and schools treats the question of how Muslims create, acquire, maintain, and manipulate their communal affiliations as a question of how the master narratives of Muslim sects and schools initially develop, how subsequent Muslims began to emplot themselves or found themselves emplotted in such narratives, and what such emplotments may have meant for them at the time. It also pays attention to the ways that the narratives of sect/school identifications accumulated over time, became more refined, perpetuated themselves through institutions, frequently fragmented into subsects and schools, and sometimes disappeared altogether.

With the narrative-identification approach to Muslim sects and schools as the theoretical model guiding this book, several methodological questions remain to be addressed, starting with which sect and schools will be included in it, and which will be excluded. The answer to this question will ultimately guide us toward a more precise definition of sect and philosophical-theological school. More immediately, the answer turns out to be cautiously straightforward. At a relatively early period, medieval Muslim heresiographers established the principal divisions among Muslims, and for the most part these principal divisions remained the broad categories by which Muslims organized taxonomies of Muslim *firaq*. Although the numbers of "mother sects" range from four in the writings of al-Nawbakhtī and al-Muqaddasī to ten in al-Ashʿarī, Muslim heresiographers tended to agree that the *khawārij* (the Khārijites), *shīʿa* (Shiʿites), *muʿtazila* (Muʿtazilites), and *murjiʾa* (Murjiʾites) were four of

44 Somers recognizes several dimensions of narrativity, notably what she calls "ontological narratives" and "public narratives" ("The Narrative Constitution of Identity," 618–19). This sensitivity to the individual and collective aspects of narrativity mirrors in some ways the concerns of Brubaker and Cooper in specifying modes of identification/self-understanding and commonality, connectedness, and groupness (Brubaker and Cooper, "Beyond 'Identity,'" 14–21).

them.[45] Heresiographers that break the *firaq al-umma* into five or more usually include, using a variety of different monikers, the *ahl al-sunna* (Sunnis) – with the exception of al-Ashʿarī, who wrote before something called "Sunnism" could be said to have existed.[46] Many heresiographers who numbered the divisions of the *umma* beyond five (i.e. al-Khwārizmī, Abū al-Maʿālī, and Fakhr al-Dīn al-Rāzī) cast the *mujabbira* (Determinists), *mushabbiha* (Anthropomorphists), Karrāmiyya, and Ṣūfīs (mystics) as separate *firaq*.[47] However, it could be argued that most of those who held "determinist" or "anthropomorphic" views, along with those known as the Karrāmiyya, could all be rightly regarded in the broad sense as some variation of Sunni, however "proto" or distant. This is how al-Shahrastānī, in fact, speaks about them despite the fact that he, too, classes these groups not as Sunnis but as either *ṣifātiyya* (Attributists) or *jabriyya* (Determinists).[48] Similarly, it could be argued that Sufism is not a sect or school at all, but the mystical dimension of Islamic life, and one that often cut across sectarian boundaries. Thus, we are left with five main sects or schools, namely, the Khārijites, Shiʿites, Murjiʾites, Muʿtazilites, and Sunnis, which will form the main sect/school divisions to be investigated in this book.

Admittedly, there are problems with following medieval Muslim heresiographers in their organization of the Muslim *firaq* into five. One of the main issues, of course, is that some groups are left out of that schema, while others do not fit it exactly. For example, the abovementioned *mujabbira* (Determinists), *mushabbiha* (Anthropomorphists), and Karrāmiyya sit but awkwardly classed among the Sunnis. It is difficult to find a "place" for these groups within the fivefold *firaq* schema.

So too, the various Sufi personalities and orders (*ṭarīqāt*) that developed in the medieval Islamic world do not fit easily into the schema, and they will not be formally included in this work. However, insofar as some of these mystical orders did have a profound effect on the ways that some sectarian groups articulated their narratives, then they will be included in the discussion (as is the case with Haji Bektāsh Veli and the Bektāshiyya

[45] al-Muqaddasī, *Aḥsan al-Taqāsīm fī Maʿrifat al-Taqālīm*, 38; al-Nawbakhtī, *Kitāb Firaq al-Shīʿa*, 15.

[46] Van Ess, *Frühe Muʿtazilitische Häresiographie*, 27–28 (Pseudo-Nāshiʾ); al-Khayyāṭ, *Kitāb al-Intiṣār*, 101 (quoting Ibn al-Rawandī); al-Masʿūdī, *al-Tanbīh wa'l-Ashrāf*, 358; Sayyid, *Faḍl al-Iʿtizāl*, 164 (al-Qāḍī ʿAbd al-Jabbār); Abū Ḥayyān al-Tawḥīdī, *Kitāb al-Imtāʿ wa'l-Muʾanasa*, 2:9; Ibn Ḥazm, *al-Faṣl*, 1:368; al-Ashʿarī, *Maqālāt al-Islāmiyyīn*, 1:65.

[47] al-Khwārizmī, *Mafātīḥ al-ʿUlūm*, 24–32; Abū al-Maʿālī, *Bayān al-Adyān*, 26; al-Rāzī, *Iʿtiqādāt Firaq al-Muslimīn wa'l-Mushrikīn*, 13–20. On al-Shahrastānī and Abū Tammām, who fix the number of mother-sects at seven, see Gaiser, "Satan's Seven Specious Arguments," 191–93.

[48] al-Shahrastānī, *Kitāb al-Milal wa'l-Niḥal*, 103–4, 107.

Sufi order, or Shah Ismāʿīl and the Ṣafawiyya/Ṣafaviyya order). Nevertheless, and despite the fact that Abū al-Maʿālī and Fakhr al-Dīn al-Rāzī include the "Ṣūfiyya" in their list of *firaq al-umma*, most other medieval and modern Islamic authors do not consider the Sufi *ṭarīqāt* to be something akin to the Khārijites, Shiʿa, Murjiʾa, Muʿtazila, or Ahl al-Sunna. Of course, many Sufi groups do assert a sectarian affiliation (i.e. they identify with the "Sunni" or "Shiʿite" narrative), or, alternately, they claim access to religious insights that move human consciousness beyond what they consider to be the "surface" (*ẓāhirī*) designations of sectarianism. However interesting these subjects may be, a work of this size can offer but limited comments.

Similarly, the legal "schools" (*madhāhib*) will not be treated with any depth, as they, too, are not usually considered *firaq*. As with the Sufi orders, however, there are also some exceptions to this rule. For example, the heresiographer Abū al-Maʿālī's categorization of the Sunnis subdivides them into legal schools, as does the Ibāḍī heresiographer al-Qalhātī, who treats the separate Sunni legal *madhāhib* as discrete *firaq*.[49] Nevertheless, the legal schools are not the same kind of institutions as the five *firaq*, though they may share some profound similarities, and they sometimes acted as a sect or theological school might. One reason for the institutional difference between the legal *madhāhib* and the *firaq* can be traced to the development of Sunnism as an expansive and inclusive path that made room for a wide variety of groups. As it slowly became ascendant, Sunnism more and more became affiliated with several of the main legal schools. In this way, and like the Sufi orders, the legal schools often claimed a sectarian affiliation by identifying with specific sectarian narrative. Thus, the Mālikī, Shāfiʿī, Ḥanbalī, and Ḥanafī legal schools are usually considered "Sunni," though it is noteworthy that the eponym of the Ḥanafī legal school, Abū Ḥanīfa, was an important early Murjiʾite while the so-called Jaʿfarī legal school is identified with Ithnā-ʿAsharī Shiʿism. The Ibāḍiyya, too, boast a legal school, claiming that it predates all the others. Legal schools, then, are not here treated as sectarian per se, but reflect the influences of the sect and philosophical-theological orientations within which they developed. It must be remembered, however, that the line dividing a legal *madhhab* from a sectarian or theological *madhhab* is far from clear (especially in the developing stages of Sunnism), and that the legal *madhhab*s often behaved in ways similar to their sectarian coreligionists (e.g. the Ḥanbalīs in Baghdad).

A more glaring problem with employing the fivefold division of the *umma* as an organizing concept for the book is how this schema makes the

[49] Abū al-Maʿālī, *Bayān al-Adyān*, 26; al-Qalhātī, *al-Kashf wa'l-Bayān*, 2:373–91.

divisions among Muslims seem more solid and real than was, perhaps, the case. This is directly contrary to what a narrative-identity approach to Muslim sects and schools hopes to emphasize: namely, that sect identifications are far more contingent and fluid than is usually assumed. There are few avenues around this obstacle, however, as a book on Muslim divisions must address the main Muslim *firaq*, and it must do so in a relatively succinct fashion. Nevertheless, and to reemphasize the provisional nature of sect identifications, I will close the work with a chapter on sectarian relations and ambiguities. Chapter 7 will be devoted to the issue of sect and school affiliation and relations between communal groups, and will delve into theoretical definitional problems associated with the study of Islamic sectarianism. It is hoped that Chapter 7 might mitigate some of the potential problems caused by adhering to a rigid fivefold characterization of the *umma*'s divisions.

Having decided, following most though not all of the medieval Muslim heresiographers, to exclude Sufi orders and legal schools and focus on the so-called fivefold division of Muslim sects and schools, we have arrived at a point where we may inquire into a more precise working definition of "sect and school." If, as I have posited above, sect/school affiliation is a kind of identification, and identification is itself a process in which human beings emplot themselves in certain kinds of narratives, then our inquiry begins at the moments of divergence that created distinct kinds of narratives, or clusters of narratives, into which Muslims began to emplot themselves. It continues through how these narratives lead to the creation of discrete sects and schools, or what Muslims called *firaq* (as well as *niḥal*, *ṭawāʾif*, or *madhāhib*). A *firqa*, or sect/school, then, may be defined as participatory narrative of intra-religious difference that accretes institutionalized forms through the collective weight of the Muslims who choose to emplot themselves within it. In other words, Muslims sects and schools are here treated as accumulating stories, or grand or master narratives, in which Muslims partake, especially insofar as these narratives stake out particularized claims to religious distinctiveness.[50] Whatever unique institutional forms might arise from this participation (e.g. rituals of mourning, or theories of legitimate governance) are products of the human involvement in and elaboration of these stories.

As narratives, sect/school stories possess all of the characteristics of a narrative, which is to say that they develop their own themes, plots, characters, and so on. From a more general perspective, however, it is the

[50] This view toward Muslim sects and schools captures, I believe, what Makdisi (*The Culture of Sectarianism*, 6) meant when he claimed that sectarianism was both a practice and a discourse.

connection between the theme of salvation and the plot of truth preservation that distinguishes sect/school narratives from other kinds of identification narratives. In other words, a common theme among the various sects and schools is that they claim to offer a means to achieve perfection and/or salvation to their followers. Simultaneously, the "plot" of the sect/school story, writ large, is the preservation of this distinctive soteriology against the illegitimate forces that would seek to destroy, degrade, or forget those truths, and thus lead the community into damnation. And because the story itself is one of perfection/salvation by a particular group, participation in the sect/school story, adoption of its worldview, practicing of its rituals, and so on, can become highly significant, even to the point where people might be willing to die for it.

Recognizing the centrality of soteriological themes, combined with the plot of truth preservation, allows us to recognize when a religious tendency or inclination moves on to become sectarian. For example, holding that ʿAlī b. Abī Ṭālib, the Prophet Muḥammad's cousin, was the rightful successor to Muḥammad was a belief held by those who came to be known as the partisans or supporters (*shīʿa*) of ʿAlī. While this group and its convictions formed the nucleus of what would eventually become Shiʿism, it cannot be said that the earliest Shiʿa constituted a sect. However, when this very same conviction (i.e. that ʿAlī b. Abī Ṭālib or other members of the Prophet's family were the rightful and true successors to Muḥammad) was held to effect the fate of individual souls on the Day of Judgment, then something called Shiʿism (as a sectarian tendency among Muslims) could be said to be present.

The presence of soteriological themes also permits us to distinguish sectarian narrative identifications from other kinds of narrative identifications and to navigate our way toward understanding how sect/school narrative affiliations might bleed into other kinds of identifications. For example, economic categories (being "rich," "poor," "middle class," etc.) might not become tied to sectarian narratives unless real or perceived inequities begin to consistently impinge on a group of people who cleave to a particular narrative of sectarian salvation. If this happens, then economic disparity and class difference may become understood as persecution, threat, or harassment by hostile sectarian others. Likewise, political, national, or ethnic narratives, which we are accustomed to thinking of as separate in some senses from "religious" narratives (and thus separate from the issue of perfection/salvation), can, in fact, be linked through the theme of perfection/salvation. Thus, a political party may offer a vision of limited earthly salvation (e.g. Obama's "Change We Can Believe In" and "Hope"; Trump's "Make America Great Again"). However, by our definition of sectarianism this kind of political narrative will remain merely partisan, becoming sectarian only when a more ultimate kind of salvation is linked to membership in the truth-preserving party (as when certain American Christian groups create narratives in which Obama figures as the anti-Christ, or Trump appears as a savior figure).

The ability to view religious sect/school identifications as sometimes merging with political identifications offers a particular advantage to the study of Muslim sects and schools. In several periods of Islamic history, and especially in the early medieval Islamic period, political and religious (here meaning "ultimate" or "other worldly") perfection/salvation tended to be elided, which is to say that Muslims looked for perfection in this world as well as the next, and tended to see the two as profoundly connected. Thus, early expressions of Islamic sectarianism may be described as revolving around what we would consider to be both "religious" and "political" themes of salvation. This does not mean, though, that we cannot distinguish, however artificially, between the two. What we might think of as "political" narratives in the medieval Muslim period, narratives involving righteous or tyrannical caliphs, legitimate or unlawful violence, taxation, land practices, and so on, can be separated (however artificially) from the "other-worldly" aspects of perfection/salvation involving the proper performance of rituals, recognition of divinely guided leaders, and so forth. Thus, while this theory of Muslim sects and schools highlights claims to perfection/salvation by particular groups as the most salient element in the grand narratives of sectarianism (and school affiliation), it also allows that the theme of salvation is not the exclusive purview of "religious" narratives alone. Sect and school narratives, while distinctive, often bleed into other (notably political) kinds of narratives. In the medieval period as in the modern, "sectarianism can be political."[51]

Having determined to treat Muslim sects and schools through the lens of intra-Islamic narratives of perfection and salvation, a few more questions remain to be answered. Namely, it is time to ask whose versions of the grand sect narratives will be related, and to consider how best to tell them. The answers to these questions will be determined, in part, by which sources are available to us as historians of Muslim sects and schools, the nature of those sources, as well as by the positions we take vis-à-vis these narratives in our capacity as scholars of religion. It is a common fact that historians almost never have access to the sources for which they might wish, and must therefore learn to use those that they do possess. For example, with the exception of coins, almost nothing survives from Khārijite authors outside of poetry, a few letters, and

[51] Weiss, *In the Shadow of Sectarianism*, 11.

a creed, all of which is preserved in non-Khārijite sources. There are, however, a plethora of pro-ʿAlīd, Shiʿite, Muʿtazilite, proto-Sunni, Sunni, and Ibāḍī Muslim authors and editors that treat the subject of the Khārijites with varying degrees of sympathy or polemic. Moreover, it is often clear that these authors are using some kind of original Khārijite writings as the sources for their own accounts. The core narratives, what we might even call the central "myths," of the Khārijite sect and its subsects, then, must be reconstructed, for the most part, from hybrid, written sources that range from receptive to hostile, and the rhetorical approaches that shaped the various accounts of this core narrative must be appreciated for how they molded the interpretation of these stories.[52] This process will not give us "history" in the modern sense, but an idea of the narrative that either guided or horrified those who interacted with it. And while the problem of sources might be more acute when dealing with the Khārijites, the general problem of sources, their hybridity and their rhetorical edges, similarly plagues the study of the other *firaq* to varying degrees.

Another aspect of the issue of our sources becomes apparent in the case of groups who guard their sources as the property of an exclusive, secretive, and/or initiated elite. The Nuṣayrīs, for example, do not generally discuss their group's narratives with outsiders, preferring to keep their rituals, beliefs, cosmologies, and soteriologies a guarded secret. In many cases, then, a researcher will have to suffice with what little information is available.

When it comes to other groups, such as the Ibāḍiyya, a different situation presents itself. The Ibāḍiyya have preserved a robust literature spanning their 1,300 years or so of existence. This literature springs from two continents (Africa and Asia) and can be found in several languages, notably Arabic, Berber, and Swahili. With the Ibāḍiyya, enough primary source materials exist so as not to have to depend on hostile outside sources. However, relying exclusively on Ibāḍī narratives of their group's identity brings its own difficulties. For example, some Ibāḍī presentations of their early history differ from what academic historians of the Ibāḍiyya have discovered through critical examination of their early texts. Moreover, later narratives on Ibāḍism, such as those penned by the great Omani Ibāḍī scholar ʿAbd al-Ḥumayd al-Sālimī (d. 1914), were invested in presenting a particular version of Ibāḍism that differs in some senses from that which fell from the pens of medieval Ibāḍī scholars. Thus, just as modern historians must be selective in what they present as the "history" of any given topic, so too, Muslim writers select, edit, and simplify their materials in order to present a specific version of their group's narrative identification. This issue becomes more intractable when we recognize that sect/school

[52] See Haider, *The Rebel and the Imām*, 6–16.

authors often do not recognize their group as developing. Rather, these authors tend to view the group as preserving the unchanging and original message of Islam, and thus, not developing so much as conserving what they believe to be the pristine religion. Thus, from certain Ibāḍī perspectives, their group is believed to have existed *more or less in the same form* from the time of the Prophet until now. There are, then, both older and newer, insider and outsider, pristine and developmental narratives of Ibāḍism. And given that the narratives of sects/schools are always shifting, the question, once again, becomes: which narratives to privilege? Essentially, what is required is a means to report on a centuries-long, unfolding discourse about sect/school identification involving numerous participants, both from within and outside that tradition. Though it presents a formidable task with no easy solution, this book will attempt to present as many viewpoints as feasible within the confines of the chapters, hoping that the general development of the sect/school can be addressed alongside of what group members view as its salient features.

Lastly, there are different kinds of sources for the study of sect/school narratives, ranging from the standard fare of history, written sources, to coins, archeological sites, material culture, and art, as well as living communities. As this study revolves about the notion of sect/school as narrative identifications, it will (for the most part) privilege written sources. Written sources come with their own set of historiographical issues, many of which are well-known to students of Islamic studies, and will not be rehearsed here.[53] Moreover, in privileging written sources I do not mean to imply that archeology, material culture, art history, numismatics, and anthropology are unimportant to the study of Islamic sects and schools. On the contrary, much of the most exciting work being done on Muslim sects and schools is coming from these disciplines, and I will incorporate as much of this material as proves feasible.

The Structure of the Book, and How to Use It

Eco claims that a text, a narrative, is a "lazy machine asking the reader to do some of its work," meaning that narratives rely to a great degree on shared assumptions, cultural knowledge, and "common sense" (which is often culturally framed) to build their stories.[54] This is also the case for participants in the narratives of Muslim sects and schools. Much is assumed when the stories of particular groups become articulated and

[53] Donner, *Narratives of Islamic Origins*, 125–229; Robinson, *Islamic Historiography*, 83–158.

[54] Eco, *Six Walks in the Fictional Woods*, 3.

then set down in dusty books. Of course, for students unfamiliar with early Islamic history, or with the cultural frames of the early Islamic world, these narrative assumptions appear as blank spaces, bewildering to those without the requisite cultural knowledge. The historian, therefore, must fill them in, and it is the task of Chapter 2 to provide a background for the emergence of various sectarian and school narratives. This book, however, is neither an introduction to Islam, nor a history of Muslims, nor is it intended to be overly long. Thus, Chapter 2 focuses only on those events and processes that form the backdrop to the development of Muslim sects and schools. Those seeking a broader introduction to Islam or Muslim history should consider themselves warned, and can consult the many excellent works on these topics that have appeared in the last decades.

After laying the groundwork for the emergence of Muslim sects and schools, the following four chapters address the five main divisions among Muslims. Chapter 3 treats the Khārijites and Ibāḍiyya; Chapter 4 delves into the Shiʿa and their main subdivisions; Chapter 5 discusses the Murjiʾites and Muʿtazilites; and Chapter 6 provides an overview of the long development of Sunnism. Recognizing that these chapters might be used in isolation, I have made an attempt to repeat certain key themes from the historical overview, and to tie these chapters to grand narratives that emerge from the *longue durée* of their histories, and that seem to guide those who emplot themselves within them. These grand narratives, it should be remembered, remain malleable to a degree, as an innovative thinker can shift them in subtle ways to orient the group differently.

Chapter 7, as indicated above, attempts to provide some perspective across the narrowly focused silos of the earlier chapters. By examining areas of ambiguity in the practice, definition, and theory of Muslim sectarianism, this penultimate chapter hopes to recomplicate the too-neat chapters that preceded it, and to leave the reader with more questions than answers. The proper way, I believe, to frame a book on Muslims sects and schools is with a sober assessment of the fragility of our knowledge, and the ambiguities of our subject. This introduction and Chapter 7, then, form the theoretical bookends around the group-specific chapters of this work. If the reader is rather more familiar with Muslims sects and schools it is hoped that these chapters might provide a starting point for more abstract discussion on our topic. Chapter 8 provides a summary of the main themes of the book, reemphasizing some of the main points made in this introduction.

2 History, Sects, and Schools

Following recent insights into the place of Islam amidst the religions of late antiquity, the story of Muslim sects and schools begins not with the death of the Prophet Muḥammad, nor with the revelations that came to him over the period of his twenty-two years as a religious figure in Makka and later Madina. Rather, the narrative of Muslim sects and schools begins earlier with the religious groups that preceded Muslims in late antique North Africa, the Middle East, and Central Asia.[1] Not only did Muslims trade with, live alongside, and have intimate knowledge of the welter of sects and schools that had developed among the various Christian, Jewish, Zoroastrian, Manichean, "Pagan," and later, Buddhist and Hindu religions of late antiquity, but they also developed their own theological, heresiographical, and polemical literatures alongside the models provided by their late antique counterparts. Muslims in general, including those who later comprised the medieval Muslim sects and schools, display strong resonances with the various religious groups of late antiquity, to the extent that it becomes difficult (if not impossible) to avoid the conclusion that they all shared a significant pool of mutual assumptions and cultural knowledge.

The period of late antiquity is usually thought to cover the second to eighth centuries CE. At this time, a complex tapestry of religio-political entities, including the Western Roman Catholic Empire, the complex of Germanic tribes that later overran it, Byzantium, the Ethiopian Empire, Coptic, Donatist, Armenian, "Nestorian" (i.e. Church of the East), "Jacobite" (i.e. Syriac Orthodox Church) and so-called gnostic Christians, as well as Jews, Zoroastrians, Manicheans, stoics, pagans, Buddhists, and others were represented throughout North Africa, Central Asia, and the so-called Middle East. In the Arabian Peninsula itself, Jews and modest numbers of Christians had long lived; not only the

[1] Hoyland, "Early Islam as a Late Antique Religion," 1053ff.; Al-Azmeh, *The Emergence of Islam in Late Antiquity*, xi–xiii; Milwright, *An Introduction to Islamic Archaeology*, 29ff.; Robinson, "Prophecy and Holy Men in Early Islam," 241–62.

famous and ill-fated Christian community in Najrān, but also in Oman, Bahrain, the islands of the Gulf, and even to India.[2] These various groups populated the areas of the world with which the pre-Islamic Arabs traded, and later, after the coming of Islam and the early Islamic conquests, over which the Muslims exercised political control.

The period of late antiquity is also when several Christian empires first emerged, casting themselves as "orthodox" ("right believing") and those who differed from them as "heterodox." It was therefore, and especially among Christians, a time of overt sectarianism. Also populating the stage were the various Jewish groups that had survived the destruction of the Second Temple in 70 CE, the innumerable pagans who had persisted through the introduction of Christianity, and the Manicheans who had erupted onto the world stage in the late third century in the midst of the Sāsānian Empire. Further afield, a proliferation of Buddhist and "Hindu" religious paths flourished in Southeast, East, and Central Asia.

Closest to Muḥammad's Arabia, and therefore likely to be the most familiar, were the rival Byzantine and Sāsānian empires, who held to Christianity and Zoroastrianism respectively, as well as the Christian Kingdom of Aksum (in present-day Ethiopia and Eritrea). While many of the first Byzantine emperors followed Arianism (a form of Christianity that followed a stricter view of the Oneness of God), by the end of the fourth century CE the First Council of Constantinople (381 CE) affirmed the doctrines first put forth at Nicaea (325 CE) and set the stage for the eventual ascendancy of what is sometimes called "Chalcedonian" Christianity, or "Byzantine Orthodoxy," in the central lands of the Byzantine Empire. Allied with the Byzantines was the Aksumite Kingdom, which officially adopted Christianity with the conversion of its emperor, Ezana II, in 324 CE. Maintaining ties with the Christian church at Alexandria, the Aksumites upheld a form of monophysite (i.e. "single nature," holding that Christ possessed a single divine nature), Christianity that became known as Ethiopian Orthodoxy. Increasingly pitted against these two empires were the Sāsānians, who officially followed Zoroastrianism, a religion founded in Iran by Zarathustra in the

[2] In Oman and Bahrain, Christianity was solidly established, with a metropolitan see and Christian community at al-Mazūn. Christians could be found among the ʿAbd al-Qays of eastern Arabia, the Bakr b. Wāʾil of Yamāma and Bahrain, as well as the Ḥanīfa b. Lujaym (Yamāma). Likewise, two prominent Omani Arabs, Kaʿb b. Barsha al-Ṭāḥī and Kaʿb b. Ṣūr, were known to be Christians (the second of whom converted to Islam and eventually became the first *qāḍī* at Basra). So too, the Nestorian metropolitan at Rēv Ardhashīr (in the Bushire area) extended his responsibility for the Christian community from the Gulf all the way to Ceylon. Ṭalūn, al-Ḥaṭṭa, and Hajar were also said to have housed Nestorian bishoprics. See Finster, "Arabia in Late Antiquity," 71–72; Wilkinson, *Ibāḍism*, 70–71.

sixth century BCE. Zarathustra taught that human beings were participants in the eternal struggle between good and evil, and that their choices would affect their eternal salvation or damnation. Central to the ritual of Zoroastrianism was the sacred fire, which burned in Zoroastrian temples and houses as a symbol of purity and the illuminated mind. Framing the Arabian Peninsula, these three empires maintained their official religions, even as a number of religious minorities and sectarian groups lived within and between them.

Although religious persecution was sometimes a fact of life for those considered outsiders or heretics within these empires, ascendancy of any given official religion or "orthodoxy" was never absolute. Emperors and theologians constantly negotiated the ways, means, and extents to which "heresy" or undesirable religious minorities should be fought or tolerated. One means by which Christians bolstered the idea of "orthodoxy" came through the emerging medium of heresiography (also called heresiology). This genre of polemical writing sought to establish "orthodoxy" through the polemical classification of others as "heretics." Christian heresiological writings often presented a highly schematized taxonomy of heresies, organizing them into fixed categories and setting the "true" Christianity (those considered "orthodox" at the moment) against them. One of the most famous of early Christian heresiologies, the *Panarion* ("Medicine Chest") of Epiphanius, for example, described eighty different religious sects that were deemed "poisonous" to believers. Epiphanius offered the *Panarion* as a "stock of remedies to offset the poisons of heresy." He fixed the number of heresies at eighty based upon two verses in the Song of Songs.[3] Heresiography as a genre of writing, as well as its stylistic components, would be taken up by Muslim authors in later centuries.

Despite increasing identification as "heretics" by the empires of late antiquity, religious minorities and sects often found the means to survive and spread their doctrines. Among the Arabs, for example, the Ghassānids, vassals of the Byzantines, occupied southern Syria (i.e. present-day southern Lebanon, southern Syria, Palestine, and Jordan) and protected the borders of Byzantium against Sāsānians and Bedouin raiding parties alike. The Ghassānids adopted and promoted monophysite Christian teachings, and helped to establish what would later become known as "Jacobite" Christianity. So too, in the Western end of the Sāsānian Empire, significant Jewish, Manichean, and Christian populations existed, as had several "gnostic" Christian sects (such as the Valentinians, Messalians, Marcionites, etc.).

[3] "There are threescore queens, and fourscore concubines, and maidens without number. My dove, my undefiled, is but one" (6:8–9).

Equally familiar to the Arabs of the peninsula would have been the dynasty of the Lakhmids, who functioned as Arab vassals to the Sāsānians and made their capital at al-Ḥīra (near present-day Kufa). They adopted the dyophysite form of Christianity later known as "Nestorian" Christianity (dyophysitism taught that Christ had two natures, one divine and one human). Nestorianism was recognized as the official Christian church in Sāsānian lands, and by the late sixth century CE al-Ḥīra was said to contain several churches and monasteries, including a theological school.[4] Importantly, the pre-Islamic Arabs maintained extensive trade relations with al-Ḥīra.[5] As an Arab-Christian center, such relations would have been vital for familiarizing the Arabs of the peninsula with the basic narratives, rituals, and structures of late antique Eastern Christianity. Given that the Arabs of al-Ḥīra celebrated their liturgy in Syriac, it remains noteworthy how many of the possibly Christian loanwords that appear in the Qurʾan come via the Syriac, suggesting a strong connection to Syriac-speaking regions.[6]

Yet, al-Ḥīra was not alone in introducing sectarian forms of Christianity to the pre-Islamic Arabs. In fact, several Christian communities existed in the Arabian Peninsula before the coming of Islam. Most renowned, perhaps, was the community at Najrān, whose persecution at the hands of the Yemenī Jewish king Yūsuf Dhū al-Nuwās was made famous by early Christian writing in Greek and Syriac. The incident is also alluded to in the Qurʾan.[7] In addition to the ill-fated community at Najrān, there were several other groups of Christians living in or near the peninsula. In the Arabian Peninsula itself, Arab tribes from the north boasted Christian converts or even entire subgroups: such as the Ashʿar, and the Farāsān branch of the Taghlib that resided in Mukhā (in the Yemen). Nestorian Christians lived along the east coast and Persian Gulf, such as the Banū Asʿad b. ʿAbd al-ʿUzzā, the Kalb, Ṭayy, Tamīm and ʿIbād, Banū ʿUdhra and ʿIjl, Kinda, Taghlib and Banū Judham. Christians also could be found among the Banū Shaybān in al-Hajar (in Bahrain).[8]

The Arabian Peninsula also boasted significant Jewish communities, the most famous of which were those with whom the Prophet Muḥammad himself interacted during his time in Madina. The presence of Jews in the Arabian Peninsula may well be quite old, as the Bible in Psalm 84:6 makes possible mention of the valley of Makka ("Bakka") as

[4] Peters, *Muhammad and the Origins of Islam*, 66.
[5] Kister, "Al-Ḥīra: Some Notes on Its Relations with Arabia," 150ff.
[6] See, for example, Jeffery, *The Foreign Vocabulary of the Qurʾān*, 43ff.
[7] See Qurʾan 85:4; Cook, "The *Aṣḥāb al-Ukhdūd*," 125–48.
[8] Finster, "Arabia in Late Antiquity," 71–72; Wilkinson, *Ibāḍism*, 70–71.

a place of visitation that possessed a blessed spring. Both Jewish and Islamic traditions associate Makka with Ibrāhīm (Abraham), Hājar (Hagar), and their son Ismāʿīl (Ishmael).[9] In addition, large Jewish communities thrived in southern Arabia, and were said to have been sent there by Sulaymān (Solomon), or, alternately, by his queen, Bilqīs (i.e. the Queen of Sheba). Hard evidence for Jewish communities in south Arabia, however, is weak until after the fifth century CE, when the Ḥimyarite king Abū Karība Asʿad was said to have become the first of many southern Arabian leaders to convert to Judaism, forcing their populations to convert as well. The last of these rulers, Yūsuf Dhū al-Nuwwās, was overthrown by the invading Ethiopian Christian army around 525 CE.

Further east in the peninsula, in Oman, southern Arabian tribal groups who had migrated in several waves up the Omani coasts entered into relations with the Zoroastrian Persians, becoming in essence a subject Sāsānian population, though many of the tribes in the interior of Oman maintained their own leaders (who were recognized by the Sāsānians) and their independence.[10] The presence of farming communities of *majūs* (Zoroastrians) in Oman persisted for many centuries after the coming of Islam, and, as in other parts of the Islamic world, conversion of the local population was slow.[11] In addition, starting in the pre-Islamic period coastal Arabs had forsaken their tribal status by entering into maritime occupations (a livelihood considered “low” among other Arabs), a career that would have brought them into contact with the myriad religious communities of the Indian Ocean and down the East African coast.

Not only, then, was the Arabian Peninsula surrounded by a massive diversity of religio-political entities, but within the peninsula itself several different religious persuasions could be found. And it is this high level of awareness and contact that accounts, in part, for the Qurʾan’s sophisticated commentary on Jewish and Christian stories – narratives that the Qurʾan’s Arabic-speaking audience must have already known. Indeed, the Prophet Muḥammad saw his mission as a *restoration* of the pure monotheism that had earlier been brought to the Jews and Christians, thereby positioning the nascent Islamic community squarely within the sectarian milieu of late antiquity.

This familiarity with late antique religions clearly informs the qurʾanic exhortations to Islamic unity, which is itself profoundly tied to its commentary on the phenomenon of sectarianism. With the examples of previous late antique and monotheistic schismatics before them, Muslims were to remain unified. This was an idea enshrined in the qurʾanic concept of the *umma* as a community based on belief in and

[9] Genesis 21:17–19. [10] Wilkinson, *Ibāḍism*, 63. [11] Wilkinson, *Ibāḍism*, 318–20.

submission to God. The notion of an *umma* was to supersede the tribal milieu of first/seventh-century Arabia into which it was revealed, providing a new type of concord on the basis of worship and piety. As the Qurʾan stated: "Indeed, this your *umma* is one *umma*, and I am your Lord; so worship Me."[12] The *umma* was to be a model community, upholding justice and moderation, even to the extent that Muslims were commanded to testify against themselves, or erring family members: "O you who believe, stand firm in justice, witnesses for God, even if it is against yourselves, or parents and relatives."[13] Accompanying the lofty model of the *umma* were several qurʾanic verses that explicitly warned Muslims against breaking their community into factions or sects. For example, following the above-quoted 21:92 ("Indeed, this your *umma* is one *umma* ... "), 21:93 reads "And [yet] they divided their affair among themselves, [but] all to Us will return." 23:52–53 possess a similar structure and message: "And indeed this, your *umma*, is one *umma*, and I am your Lord, so fear Me; but the people divided the matter among them into sects (*zuburan*) – each faction (*ḥizb*) rejoicing in what it has." Likewise, other verses of the Qurʾan warn: "And do not be like the ones who became divided (*tafarraqū*) and differed (*akhtalafū*) after the clear proofs had come to them; and those will have a great punishment";[14] "Indeed, those who have divided their religion (*farraqū dīnahum*) and become partisans (*shiyaʿan*) – you, [O Muḥammad], are not [associated] with them in anything. Their affair is only [left] to God; then He will inform them about what they used to do";[15] "[And do not be] of those who have divided their religion and become partisans, every faction (*ḥizb*) rejoicing in what it has."[16] While these qurʾanic verses provide forceful admonitions against internal religious division, they also seem to point toward a fateful recognition of its inevitability. A divided *umma* was to be avoided, and yet the Qurʾan seems to acknowledge that such factionalism would surely manifest itself among human beings.

During its formative period in Makka and Madina, the Islamic *umma* turned to the Prophet Muḥammad for guidance in settling the kinds of disputes that would normally have resulted in communal factionalism. The Prophet's authority, thereby, kept the nascent Islamic community from splitting into what we might now call sects or denominations. Nevertheless, it required significant effort to keep the *umma* unified, and not all seem to have uniformly respected the Prophet's authority. Not only did the Muslims face threats from the polytheist Arabs and their allies, but the sources also provide several examples where Muḥammad

[12] Qurʾan 21:92. [13] Qurʾan 4:135. [14] Qurʾan 3:105. [15] Qurʾan 6:159.
[16] Qurʾan 30:32.

was forced to deal with divisive elements from within. The Qur'an describes some of these persons as "hypocrites" (*munāfiqūn*), who outwardly professed Islam, but inwardly worked toward its destruction.[17] It was members of this group, for example, who may have been behind the building of a mosque, known as the "mosque of dissent" (*masjid al-iḍrār*), that the Prophet Muḥammad ordered destroyed in the year 9/630.[18] And while the hypocrites cannot be considered "sectarians" proper, nor can they be seen as a "school" of Islamic thought, their existence does point toward the kind of centrifugal, intra-communal forces that would have rent the community asunder if not for the Prophet's guidance. By the end of his life, the Prophet Muḥammad had overcome his enemies (including the hypocrites), and had knit together the various Arab tribes in submission to Islam. This unity would not survive the Prophet, as his death would sorely test the fabric of the early Islamic community.

Rare are those moments in history that can claim to be as evocative and controversial as those following the Prophet's death. Indeed, nothing divided the *umma* "more profoundly or durably" than the question of succession to the Prophet Muḥammad.[19] However, the ultimate survival of Islam as a world religion speaks, in part, to the strong foundation of unity that was established under the leadership of Muḥammad. Though the *umma* is and was frequently divided, the idea of the united *umma* persists among Muslims, such that the desire for unity frequently overcomes the divisive impulses that threaten to tear it apart.

Succession to Muḥammad: The Seeds of Muslim Sectarianism

The Prophet Muḥammad died, unexpectedly as it would appear, in the year 10/632. And as with the death of many religious leaders, his passing became an important moment of choice for the community that he left behind. To survive, the *umma* needed to select a successor, but what kind of person could or should succeed God's chosen Prophet? What qualities should that person possess, and what was to be the nature of their authority? The answer to these questions – or rather, the story of the long unfolding of the answers to these questions – is, in many ways, the core concern of Muslim sectarians, even if something called Muslim sectarianism would yet take a few decades to emerge. And some Muslims

[17] Qur'an 2:8–20; 63:1–8.

[18] See Qur'an 9:107; al-Ṭabarī, *Tārīkh*, 1:1074–75; Poonawala, *The History of al-Ṭabarī*, 60–61.

[19] Madelung, *Succession to Muḥammad*, 1.

proffered answers to the questions of succession almost immediately after the Prophet's death, even as his body was being prepared for burial.

One of the groups of Muslims representing the two main constituencies in Madina, the Anṣār (the "Helpers," as the Muslims of Madina had come to be known), met at the "covered porch" (*saqīfa*) of the Sāʿida tribe to elect a leader from among themselves.[20] As they considered their political allegiance to Muḥammad as having ended on his death (as was common in the pre-Islamic tribal system in Arabia), the Anṣār sought to consolidate control over their city by selecting a leader for it. When two of Muḥammad's closest Companions, Abū Bakr and ʿUmar b. al-Khaṭṭāb, heard of this meeting they were said to have rushed to it with some of the Muhājirūn (those who had emigrated with the Prophet Muḥammad from Makka) and argued for a single leader for the Islamic community. At stake was the future of the *umma*. Without a single leader to unite them, there was a good chance that the Islamic community would have fragmented into regional/tribal constituencies. Abū Bakr and ʿUmar contended that the *umma* required such a leader, and that this person must come from the Prophet's (and their own) tribe of Quraysh because only a person from the Quraysh would command the respect of the different groups of Arabs in the peninsula. So heated was the ensuing argument that, according to some accounts, it even came to blows.[21] At some point during the meeting, ʿUmar preemptively gave his support to Abū Bakr and employed the recognized tribal handshake (*bayʿa*) that was extended to leaders by stretching out his hand in allegiance to Abū Bakr. Several, though not all, of those present followed suit, and Abū Bakr was recognized as the *khalīfa* (caliph, literally "successor") to the Prophet Muḥammad. Notably absent from the meeting was Muḥammad's family, who were busy preparing his body for burial. Their absence, and the "rushed" quality of Abū Bakr's selection, would all remain controversial among those who looked to the Prophet's family for guidance.

Those who favored the family of the Prophet Muḥammad (his family was later known as the *ahl al-bayt*, the "people of the house [of the Prophet Muḥammad]") looked especially to his cousin ʿAlī b. Abī Ṭālib. ʿAlī had much to commend him. He was an early (according to many accounts, the first male) convert to Islam, and had lived in the same house with the Prophet from a young age. He had married the Prophet's daughter Fāṭima, and had two children with her (and another by a concubine). ʿAlī possessed a vast knowledge of Islam, and was a noted

[20] Madelung, *Succession to Muḥammad*, 28ff.; Ayoub, *The Crisis of Muslim History*, 8ff.

[21] al-Ṭabarī, *Tārīkh*, 1:1823; Poonawala, *The History of al-Ṭabarī*, 194; Madelung, *Succession to Muḥammad*, 31.

warrior on behalf of it: his sword, named *dhū al-faqār*, is still famed in songs and poetry and is regarded as a visual symbol of him. Moreover, ʿAlī came from the same family as the Prophet, and the Arabs had long believed a person's character traits, their moral qualities of trustworthiness, valor, bravery, and so on, along with the physical qualities of hair, eye, skin color, head shape, and so forth, to be passed genealogically through their families. Just as in premodern Europe, pre-Islamic notions of nobility found expression in the idea of noble families, called (much as they were in Europe) the "houses" of the ʿArabs (*buyūtāt al-ʿArab*).[22] If the Prophet Muḥammad had been chosen by God above all others, and his family had been purified along with him (as could be implied in Qurʾan 33:33), then was not ʿAlī the most qualified to lead the Muslims after the Prophet's death? The Qurʾan itself seemed to imply that leadership, even prophetic leadership, passed in families: in the Qurʾan, Hārūn (Aaron) inherited prophetic leadership from his brother Mūsā (Moses), as did Sulaymān (Solomon) from his father Dāwūd (David).[23]

Some would also remember episodes during the Prophet's life when the Prophet had preferred or honored ʿAlī above other Muslims, interpreting these events as explicit designation of ʿAlī's right to succession. For example, many would look to an occasion when the community, returning from the final pilgrimage before the Prophet's death (the "Farewell Pilgrimage"), stopped at a well known as Ghadīr Khumm (near present-day al-Juhfa, in Saudi Arabia). There the Prophet addressed his followers, and in the course of his speech (of which there are many versions) was reported to have said: "By God, of whomsoever I have been master, ʿAlī is his master (*Allāhumma man kuntu mawlāhū fa-ʿAliyyun mawlāhū*)."[24] This incident, and its narration, became known as the *ḥadīth* of Ghadīr Khumm. It was interpreted by later generations of Shiʿa to be an explicit designation of ʿAlī as successor and heir to the Prophet Muḥammad.[25] So too, when the Prophet Muḥammad earlier gave his banner to ʿAlī at the Battle of Khaybar in 7/629, saying, "I give this flag to a man at whose

22 Jafri, *The Origins and Early Development of Shiʿa Islam*, 3–7.

23 Madelung, *Succession to Muḥammad*, 9–13; but see also Afsaruddin, *The First Muslims*, 22ff.

24 While there are many versions of this *ḥadīth*, with variations in wording, this particular version comes from the collection of Ibn Ḥanbal (*Musnad*, no. 950). An exhaustive compilation of Sunni and Shiʿa works on the Ghadīr Khumm tradition (running into eleven volumes) is al-Amīnī's *al-Ghadīr fī'l-Kitāb wa'l-Sunnā wa'l-Adab*.

25 Non-Shiʿa, for their part, took it as merely an acknowledgment of ʿAlī's closeness to the Prophet, but not as a political designation. And as the term *mawlā* possesses several layers of meaning (among them master, servant, client, patron, friend, partner, and ally), there is room for ambiguity surrounding the interpretation of Muḥammad's words and actions at Ghadīr Khumm (Jafri, *The Origins and Early Development of Shiʿa Islam*, 21).

hands God will grant victory; he loves God and His Messenger, and God and His Messenger love him";[26] or when the Prophet left ʿAlī in charge of Madina during the raid of Tabūk in 9/630, consoling him with the words "Do you not like to be to me like Aaron (Hārūn) was to Moses (Mūsā)?"[27] These and other events would be remembered as moments when the Prophet had unambiguously indicated his preference for ʿAlī to lead. They bolstered the convictions of some among the Muslims (including ʿAlī himself) that ʿAlī was the rightful successor to the Prophet Muḥammad. Consequently, this group viewed Abū Bakr as having usurped, in some sense, ʿAlī's rightful claim.

But ʿAlī's supporters remained a minority. Relevant to the choice of Abū Bakr over ʿAlī may have been ʿAlī's history with the prominent Makkan families who had been spared by Muḥammad after the conquest of Makka, and allowed to convert to Islam. During the warfare between the polytheist Makkans and the Muslims, ʿAlī had killed many among them, and had thus made numerous enemies. Moreover, ʿAlī was still a young man when Muḥammad died, only thirty-one years old. Thus, there are reasons to believe that even had ʿAlī been present at the porch of the Banū Sāʿida, he might not have been supported by a majority of the Muslims there. Indeed, ʿAlī did not press his claim, and after a period of several months in which he refused contact with Abū Bakr ʿAlī eventually pledged his allegiance to him out of desire to maintain solidarity in the early community.[28] Yet ʿAlī and his supporters never ceased affirming ʿAlī's right to leadership.

Those who continued to support ʿAlī became known by the general term "*shiʿa*" meaning partisan or supporter. And it is in ʿAlī's claim to political succession to the Prophet Muḥammad that the first glimmers of sectarian division among Muslims can be discerned. Yet, these are only the "roots" of the division. There is little evidence that ʿAlī or his successors linked following ʿAlī (or any other member of the Prophet's family) with perfection in this world and salvation in the next. Thus, according to the model that we have set for ourselves, we cannot as yet speak of Shiʿism as a sect, but only as a tendency to view ʿAlī as having more right to leadership than his peers.

[26] al-ʿAsqalānī, *Fatḥ al-Bārī*, 1678–79 (nos. 3701, 3702); 1849 (no. 4210).
[27] al-ʿAsqalānī, *Fatḥ al-Bārī*, 1679 (no. 3706).
[28] Bad blood may also have existed between Abū Bakr and ʿAlī, as ʿAlī had counseled the Prophet Muḥammad to divorce ʿĀʾisha, Abū Bakr's daughter, in the immediate aftermath of the "affair of the necklace." See Madelung, *Succession to Muḥammad*, 42.

Early Caliphate and Civil War

Abū Bakr governed the Islamic community as the political successor to the Prophet Muḥammad, fulfilling some of the religious duties that the Prophet had performed, such as giving the Friday oration (*khuṭba*) and leading the annual pilgrimage to Makka. However, he made no claim to any religious title or authority, and indeed, very soon after the Prophet's death, and in the wake of several "false" prophets who appeared in the Arabian Peninsula, the Prophet Muḥammad came to be seen as the last of God's chosen prophets, as the "seal of the prophets" (*khātim al-anbiyāʾ*).[29] Abū Bakr led in a style similar to that of a tribal leader. For example, he often consulted with prominent Muslims, and reached many of his decisions through compromise. His authority, like the tribal shaykhs, was based in his experience, knowledge, familiarity with the genealogies of the Arab families (and thus with their alliances), and his demonstrated ability to lead. He was also admired for his piety, and for his close companionship with the Prophet.

Abū Bakr ruled for two tumultuous years, in which the Muslim community chose to fight certain Muslim tribes who considered their agreement to pay *zakāt* annulled with Muḥammad's death, and refused to remit it to Abū Bakr.[30] The importance of this decision cannot be underestimated. In fighting the so-called *ridda* wars (often poorly translated as the wars of "apostasy"), Abū Bakr solidified the idea of a unified Islamic polity, with the caliph at its head. He tamed the divisive tribalism that would have fragmented the nascent community, preserving the Muslim "super-tribe" that the Prophet had welded together during his lifetime.[31] Unified again, by the time Abū Bakr died the Muslim community was set to turn their energies outward in conquest.

On his deathbed, Abū Bakr appointed ʿUmar b. al-Khaṭṭāb as his successor. ʿUmar ruled as caliph for ten years, and oversaw the dramatic expansion of Islamdom out of the Arabian Peninsula in the early Islamic conquests (*futuḥāt*). Under ʿUmar, the Muslims brought the Nile Valley and significant portions of the Byzantine and Sāsānian empires under their control. Yet while the conquests did enlarge the geographical area where Muslims enjoyed political dominance, they did little to spread Islam as a religion. ʿUmar, it seems, understood Islam to be a religion primarily meant for the Arabs, much as Judaism was to be for the Jews. He therefore discouraged conversion among non-Arabs, and went to considerable lengths to keep them separate. Non-Arab Christian and Jewish communities, often the very same communities that had been persecuted

[29] Qurʾan 33:40. [30] Afsaruddin, *The First Muslims*, 27. [31] Watt, *Muhammad*, 95.

by the Byzantines and Sāsānians, usually found it convenient to enter into a relationship of "protection" (*dhimma*), by which they could continue to practice their religion by paying a fixed tax known as the *jizya*. Discouraging conversion thus also protected the growing tax base of the Islamic polity.[32] When non-Arabs did choose to convert, they became associated with an Arab tribe as "clients" (*mawālī*, sing. *mawlā*), replicating in new circumstances the way that pre-Islamic Arabs had accommodated non-Arabs who traveled, lived, or did business among them in the pre-Islamic period. The status of *mawlā*, however, was considered inferior to that of a full Arab, and such prejudices spilled over into the Umayyad period. Muslims thus formed a ruling elite, and remained a minority in the lands where they held sway, which were populated by the Christian, Jewish, Zoroastrian, and even pagan populations that had long inhabited these regions.

The early Islamic conquests bequeathed another legacy to later Muslims, namely, the glorified image of the first Muslim warriors (*ghāziyūn*/*mujāhidūn*). Muslim authors depicted those who participated in the conquests as world-eschewing fighters, ever conscious and fearful of God. Unimpressed with the vast wealth around them, they were portrayed as engaging in night prayer vigils, supererogatory fasting, even celibacy. Desiring the afterlife more than this world, they were willing, some even eager, to martyr themselves "in the way of God" for the greater cause of establishing God's justice. In the words of a Christian monk sent to scout the advancing Muslim army, these ascetic-warriors were "monks by night, lions by day."[33] The caliph ʿUmar b. al-Khaṭṭāb himself was famous for precisely this type of ascetic piety.[34]

To what extent can these images be said to reflect the actual actions of the early Muslim warriors? The nature of our sources, which were written long after the conquests themselves, make answering this question difficult if not impossible. However, it is important to note that this image strongly resonated with how late antique Christian writers portrayed the militant monks and soldiers who policed the boundaries of proper Christian identity. In other words, there is a strong possibility that the well-known, late antique (and largely Christian) literary trope of the religious warrior shaped how Muslim historians themselves wrote their histories. Given the ways that Muslim militancy is popularly understood

32 Madelung, *Succession to Muḥammad*, 74; Donner, *Early Islamic Conquests*, 251–52; Afsaruddin, *The First Muslims*, 180–82.

33 al-Azdī, *Tārīkh Futūḥ al-Shām*, 115–16; Sizgorich, *Violence and Belief in Late Antiquity*, 161–64.

34 See, for example, Ibn Ḥanbal, *Kitāb al-Zuhd*, 114–15; Sizgorich, *Violence and Belief in Late Antiquity*, 162.

today, there is some irony in how the image of Muslim militancy as a kind of ascetic piety was forged alongside similar late antique portrayals of Christian militancy.

As the history of the conquests were recorded many decades or even centuries after their completion, the portraits of Muslim warriors found in the pages of conquest literature are perhaps better understood if treated as rhetoricized historical writing, and one that reflected the needs of those later Muslims who produced and consumed it.[35] Later Muslim authors introduced the notion that the conquests had been a just struggle, a *jihād*, and that God must have aided the Muslims in their expansion. How else, they likely reasoned, could such dramatic success be explained? And just as militant Christian figures such as St. George or Joan of Arc have enjoyed a long history among Christians, so too, the image of the first *ghāziyūn* and *mujāhidūn* established themselves among Muslims as models for how just warriors should fight.[36] As an early model of piety, it is also this image that made its way into later sectarian narratives.

ʿUmar ruled as caliph for ten years before he was stabbed by an angry slave in the mosque in Madina. Before he succumbed to his wounds he appointed a council of six to consult over his successor, and they selected ʿUthmān b. ʿAffān, a pious, elder Companion of the Prophet. ʿUthmān's caliphate would prove controversial. Some writings on ʿUthmān claim that he ruled justly for six years, but then he "grew soft and feeble, and came to be dominated [by his kin]."[37] Among the admired deeds of his caliphal tenure was the collection of the *sūra*s of the Qurʾan into their present form (the Prophet Muḥammad was said to have fixed the order of the verses within each *sūra*).[38] In addition, the continuing conquests opened North Africa and the remainder of the Sāsānian Empire to the Muslims. However, it was claimed that ʿUthmān was not as strict as ʿUmar, and he tended to favor his family and clan (the house of Umayya), placing them in positions of power, showering them with the largesse of the growing empire, and often refusing to punish them for their infractions. He could also be harsh to his critics. For example, when some pious early Companions criticized him, he exiled one (Abū Dharr al-Ghifārī) to

[35] Haider, *The Rebel and the Imām*, 2.
[36] On the differences between *maghāzī/sīra* and *futuḥāt* literature, see Bonner, *Jihad in Islamic History*, 64–65.
[37] ʿAbd al-Razzāq, *al-Muṣannaf*, 5:331 (no. 9838); Madelung, *Succession to Muḥammad*, 86.
[38] Notably, Muslims agree on the content of the Qurʾan (though they may differ profoundly over the interpretation of that content, and some may claim that verses specifically relating to ʿAlī were intentionally left out). This remains a good indicator that the qurʾanic verses were fixed before the advent of Islamic sects and schools, who would surely have contested it if the sects had already come into existence.

Syria, and had another (ʿAmmār b. Yāsir) beaten into unconsciousness.[39] His perceived nepotism and heavy-handedness made him unpopular among many Muslims, but especially among Egyptians, Iraqis, and Madinans.

In the last year of ʿUthmān's caliphate, a group of Iraqis and Egyptians arrived in Madina to air their grievances before him. Surrounded in his own house, and abandoned by most of the Madinans, negotiations continued for almost fifty days until sometime in the month of Dhū al-Ḥijja 35/June 656, a group broke into the house and killed him.[40] ʿUthmān was said to have been reciting the Qurʾan at the time, and the attackers also injured his wife who tried to protect him. He was buried secretly in the middle of the night.

The killing of ʿUthmān initiated what Muslims would later refer to as the first *fitna*, a word that indicated "civil war," but also meant "trial," "test," "unrest," or "strife."[41] It is with the first *fitna* that the seeds of Muslim sectarianism, planted at the death of the Prophet and rooted in the soil of late antiquity, first sprouted. In the chaotic aftermath of ʿUthmān's killing, ʿAlī b. Abī Ṭālib reluctantly agreed to accept the caliphate in Madina.[42] Older now, ʿAlī commanded the respect of a larger portion of the Islamic community. However, he was not without his detractors, and immediately faced opposition from ʿĀʾisha bt. Abī Bakr, the Prophet's youngest wife, and her supporters, specifically two Companions known as Ṭalḥa b. ʿUbaydallāh and Zubayr b. al-ʿAwwām. Muʿāwiya b. Abī Sufyān, the governor of Syria (in Damascus) and relative of ʿUthmān, also opposed ʿAlī, accusing him of harboring ʿUthmān's killers.

ʿĀʾisha gathered her forces initially at Makka, and then marched to meet ʿAlī's army in Iraq, where ʿAlī had moved to be closer to his supporters. Near the settlement of Basra the two groups met, and fought what became known as the Battle of the Camel, so called because ʿĀʾisha was present on her camel encouraging her forces.[43] Yet the battle ended in defeat for ʿĀʾisha, and both Ṭalḥa and Zubayr were killed. ʿĀʾisha retired from politics, spending the remainder of her days in Madina, where she became an important source on the life of the Prophet Muḥammad.

[39] Madelung, *Succession to Muḥammad*, 87–88; Ayoub: *The Crisis of Muslim History*, 58–62.
[40] Madelung, *Succession to Muḥammad*, 113ff.; Ayoub, *The Crisis of Muslim History*, 71–80.
[41] On the many senses of the term *fitna*, see Tayob, "An Analytical Survey of al-Ṭabarī's Exegesis of the Cultural Symbolic Construct of *Fitna*," 158–59.
[42] Madelung, *Succession to Muḥammad*, 141ff.; Ayoub, *The Crisis of Muslim History*, 81–86.
[43] Madelung, *Succession to Muḥammad*, 157–80; Ayoub, *The Crisis of Muslim History*, 86–93.

ʿAlī then prepared to meet the forces of Muʿāwiya, who had gathered the tribes of Syria to his banner by displaying the bloodied shirt of ʿUthmān.[44] Following a brief and failed attempt at diplomacy, ʿAlī marched from his base at Kufa to a place on the Euphrates known as Ṣiffīn (near present-day al-Raqqa, Syria) where their forces met. The main engagements of the two armies began on Safar 11, 37/July 26, 657, and lasted three days.[45] When it became clear that ʿAlī's forces were winning, Muʿāwiya's advisor, ʿAmr b. al-ʿĀṣ, suggested that Muʿāwiya sue for arbitration (*taḥkīm*) according to the Qurʾan. Muʿāwiya directed his armies to hoist up pages from the Qurʾan on their lances (a symbolic gesture meant to indicate that the Qurʾan was between them, and thus they should arbitrate according to it). The scheme succeeded in dividing ʿAlī's army. A significant faction insisted on arbitration, but another group held that fighting Muʿāwiya was a duty. Against his better judgment, it seems, ʿAlī accepted the arbitration offer and the two armies left the battlefield.[46]

As ʿAlī led his army back to Kufa, the faction within his army that had opposed the arbitration agreement became steadily more dissatisfied with it, and with what they saw as ʿAlī's lapse of leadership. So disillusioned were they that they broke with ʿAlī and decamped to a place outside of Kufa, elected their own leaders, and resolved to follow the qurʾanic directive to fight those who "transgress" or "rebel" among Muslims until they were beaten or returned to the fold of Islam.[47] Thus rejecting the arbitration as a sinful abandonment of a clear, qurʾanic command, and having seceded from or rebelled against (*kharajū ʿan*) ʿAlī, this group later became known as the Khārijites (*khawārij*), the first recognizable sectarian tendency within the *umma*.

The first Khārijites, known as the Muḥakkima, did not survive for very long. ʿAlī was able to coax some of their number back to his army for a time, but his insistence on the arbitration brought about a final break between them. Separating from ʿAlī's army completely, the Muḥakkima decamped north to Nahrawān, an area east of present-day Baghdad. During this time, Muʿāwiya's representative at the arbitration outmaneuvered ʿAlī's, and the arbitration was decided in favor of Muʿāwiya.[48] Also around this time, ʿAlī was said to have accepted an oath of allegiance from his supporters. This oath is sometimes taken as the beginning of Shiʿism proper. After the pledge, ʿAlī marched his army to meet the

44 On Muʿāwiya, see Ayoub, *The Crisis of Muslim History*, 92–106.

45 Madelung, *Succession to Muḥammad*, 184–238; Ayoub, *The Crisis of Muslim History*, 106–22.

46 Ayoub, *The Crisis of Muslim History*, 122–26.

47 Qurʾan 49:9.

48 Ayoub, *The Crisis of Muslim History*, 126–33.

Muḥakkima at the town of Jisr al-Nahrawān. Although some Muḥakkima left the battlefield before the Battle of Nahrawān began, the remaining were virtually annihilated on Ṣafar 9, 38/July 17, 658.

In the aftermath of the battle, three remaining Khārijites conspired to kill ʿAlī, Muʿāwiya, and ʿAmr b. al-ʿĀṣ, whom they held responsible for the deterioration of Islam's moral fabric. Only one, ʿAbd al-Raḥmān b. Muljam, succeeded in stabbing ʿAlī with a poisoned blade in the mosque of Kufa.[49] ʿAlī died some days later, and his son al-Ḥasan b. ʿAlī took over. Yet ʿAlī's army was disorganized, and so al-Ḥasan struck a deal with Muʿāwiya that insured peace for the Islamic community. According to this deal, Muʿāwiya would lead as caliph until his death, at which point leadership was to devolve on al-Ḥasan. With the first *fitna* now ended, Muʿāwiya declared himself caliph, initiating the Umayyad dynasty and ending the period that would much later become known as the era of the "rightly guided" (*rāshidūn*) caliphs.

Umayyads and ʿAbbāsids

Al-Ḥasan b. ʿAlī died in the year 50/670, before Muʿāwiya could pass the caliphate to him (it is possible that Muʿāwiya had al-Ḥasan's wife poison him). Al-Ḥasan's death opened the way for Muʿāwiya to secure allegiance to his son, Yazīd, as caliph. Thereafter, the Umayyad caliphate became hereditary, remaining within different branches of the Umayyad family until their defeat at the Battle of the Zāb River in 132/750 (and thereafter in Iberia, where the Umayyad dynasty continued until 422/1031). The Umayyads were not well regarded among many Muslims, and hatred of the Umayyads did much to solidify Islamic sectarianism in its formative period, even as the relative peace and stability established under their successors, the ʿAbbāsids, encouraged the development of Muslim philosophical and theological schools of thought.

In considering the growth of Muslim divisions, it is worth remembering that in these early centuries Islam remained largely an urban phenomenon, and thus sectarianism and the emergence of schools of Islamic thought was something that developed in the cities, though it was not uncommon for sectarian groups to "take to the hills" when threatened. The urban centers of the Umayyad and ʿAbbāsid periods, then, represent the places and times when the main Muslim sects and schools came of age, and where many of the formative elements of their stories took place.

[49] Madelung, *Succession to Muḥammad*, 308–10; Ayoub, *The Crisis of Muslim History*, 142–44.

The Umayyads ruled an as Arab dynasty, with their capital at Damascus and their power concentrated in the Syrian tribes that had backed Muʿāwiya during the first *fitna*. Over the decades of their rule, the Arabic language slowly replaced Greek and Pahlavi as the administrative language of the empire, and Arab cultural norms gradually supplanted those of Byzantium and the Sāsānians. However, this process took some time, and the Arabs subtly assimilated much from the conquered populations. As a ruling elite Arabs continued to favor other Arabs over others, and conversion among non-Arabs was, for the most part, discouraged.[50] Nevertheless, conversion of the non-Arab populations continued, but non-Arab converts, the *mawālī*, often did not receive equal treatment as their Arab counterparts. This situation would become steadily more precarious for the Umayyads as the conquests continued to bring more and more territory, and gradually more non-Arab converts, under their control. Sustained conquest over the long term likewise drained the resources of the empire, contributing to the internal weaknesses that eventually brought down their dynasty.[51]

The downfall of the Umayyads had many causes, not the least of which was sectarian unrest. In fact, so prevalent was opposition to the Umayyads that rebellion could be considered a nearly constant component of the Umayyad period, especially in the region of Iraq. Of the more serious insurrections that wracked the Umayyads in their early years was that known as the second *fitna*. On Yazīd I's ascension to the caliphate, ʿAbdullāh b. al-Zubayr (the son of ʿĀʾisha's supporter, Zubayr b. al-ʿAwwām) refused allegiance to the new caliph, and rallied resistance in the Arabian Peninsula against the Umayyads. In Kufa, supporters of ʿAlī's family invited his youngest son, al-Ḥusayn b. ʿAlī, to come to their city to claim his right as imam. Al-Ḥusayn accepted, and marched with several of his family members and followers toward the city. However, before they arrived, the newly appointed Umayyad governor ʿUbaydallāh b. Ziyād arrived and executed al-Ḥusayn's supporters, suppressing the potential rebellion before it began. When al-Ḥusayn's group was approximately two days' march from Kufa, at a place that came to be known as Karbala, they found themselves surrounded by an Umayyad army and deprived of water. On the tenth of the month of Muḥarram, the Umayyads attacked, killing most of the men, generally thought to be seventy-two in number, including al-Ḥusayn and his infant child ʿAlī al-Aṣghar, and taking the rest, including the women of al-Ḥusayn's household, prisoner. Few events in Muslim history have

50 Madelung, *Religious Trends in Early Islamic Iran*, 13.
51 Blankinship, *The End of the Jihâd State*, 223ff.

resonated so profoundly as the death of the Prophet's grandson at the hands of the reigning Muslim polity, and this event, known as the Battle of Karbala, continues to resonate among many Shiʿa as the central moment of betrayal for the family of the Prophet.

After the tragedy of Karbala, the rebel Ibn al-Zubayr himself accepted the oath of the caliphate in Makka and then consolidated his control over Madina and parts of Iraq, Iran, and Egypt, thereby creating a rival power to the Umayyads in the core geographical regions of Islamdom. Although Ibn al-Zubayr is remembered sometimes as the "anti-caliph," convincing arguments can be made that his popularity outstripped that of his Umayyad rivals. Concurrent with Ibn al-Zubayr, several Khārijite and Shiʿite revolts broke out in Arabia and Iraq, such that the Umayyads effectively lost control of these areas for more than twelve years. In part, the rebels succeeded because Yazīd's sudden death in 64/683 fueled a power struggle among the Umayyad clans, from which the Marwānid branch would claim the caliphate. Under the new Marwānid caliph, ʿAbd al-Malik b. Marwān (r. 65–86/685–705), Ibn al-Zubayr was eventually killed (probably in 73/692), Makka retaken, and the more recalcitrant Khārijite and Shiʿite rebels suppressed. However, the Umayyads had not seen the end of Khārijite and Shiʿite rebellions. Sectarian hostility to the Umayyads continued right up until their final demise. ʿAbd al-Malik's deputy and governor of Iraq, al-Ḥajjāj b. Yūsuf, did much to suppress the opposition, but his heavy-handed treatment of the Kufan general and aristocrat Ibn al-Ashʿath itself provoked another rebellion among the Kufan soldiers. Likewise, al-Ḥajjāj's poor treatment of the Muhallab family in Basra did much to solidify later opposition to the Umayyads in that city.

In the wake of the second *fitna*, ʿAbd al-Malik and the Umayyads began appealing more and more to the idea of *jamāʿa*, adhering to the community, as the mandate for their rule. The Prophet, their supporters endeavored to show, had commanded Muslims to follow the majority, which the Umayyads claimed to represent. This, along with the practice of condemning and executing "heretics" during the latter half of their rule, seems to indicate that the Umayyads envisioned their authority along the lines of the Byzantine emperors. In other words, they aspired to the kind of religious and political authority that allowed the Byzantines to determine doctrine and law, and they grounded their claims in an appeal to majoritarianism. The Umayyads, however, remained generally disliked, and they never uniformly achieved the kind of absolutist authority they desired.

The unpopularity of the Umayyads stemmed, in large part, from the perceived illegitimacy, impiety, and authoritarianism of the Umayyad administration. With a few exceptions (such as the caliph ʿUmar b. ʿAbd al-ʿAzīz), the Umayyads were widely regarded as dissolute leaders, or as outright usurpers. Their governors were often reviled, and their armies were frequently despised. Three Umayyad caliphs can be taken as examples of this dissolution. Beginning with Muʿāwiya, the first Umayyad caliph, it is relevant to recall that he was the son of Muḥammad's longtime enemy, Abū Sufyān, whom Muḥammad generously forgave and allowed to convert to Islam after the conquest of Makka. Although Muʿāwiya earned grudging respect for his political acumen, he is often blamed for transforming the highly principled early caliphate into mere kingship (*mulk*).[52] Muʿāwiya's son Yazīd (lampooned in poetry for being a drunkard) was hated for ordering the killing at Karbala of the Prophet's family, while al-Ḥusayn b. ʿAlī ascended in the memory of many Muslims as the martyr par excellence of the early Islamic period. Yazīd was also widely despised for the plunder of Madina, in which Yazīd's troops were said to have indiscriminately raped Muslim women, and the assault of Makka in which Yazīd's army assaulted the Kaʿba with flaming catapults.[53]

Nor did later Umayyad caliphs fare better in the collective memory of the Muslims. The eleventh Umayyad caliph, al-Walīd b. Yazīd (r. 125–26/743–44), for example, who was remembered primarily for his prodigious drinking, was said to have once called upon God, the angels, and all pious Muslims to bear witness "that my pleasures are listening to music, drinking wine, and biting ripe cheeks."[54] To be fair, examples of Umayyad misrule remain relatively easy to find because their history was penned under the dynasty that replaced them, the ʿAbbāsids. From such a perspective, it is easy to forget the truly spectacular artistic and cultural achievements of the Umayyads as a whole. Nevertheless, many Muslims felt something fundamental to the Islamic endeavor had been lost with the ascension of the Umayyads to power, and these disillusioned Muslims would remain a mainstay of the opposition.

Among those pious Muslims who felt that the Umayyads possessed no religious mandate to rule were many (though not all) from the nascent class of religious specialists known as the *ʿulamāʾ* (sing. *ʿālim*). The *ʿulamāʾ* remained a diverse group, several of whom found outlets for their thought in sectarian and scholastic groups. In general, they cleaved to the sources of Islamic piety, namely the Qurʾan and the *sunna* (established practices) of the Prophet Muḥammad and the early community, as

[52] Humphreys, *Muʿawiya ibn Abi Sufyan*, 115.
[53] Hawting, *The First Dynasty of Islam*, 47–48.
[54] Farrin, *Abundance from the Desert*, 130.

the source of their knowledge and authority. Thus, they held that the leader of the Muslims should be, at the minimum, pious and upright and they believed that Islamic life should not be the exclusive luxury of the Arabs alone. Grounding themselves in the early period when the Prophet had lived alongside the *umma*, they hoped to understand the implications of the Qurʾan and the way of life that the Prophet and the early Muslims had established. This endeavor to achieve some understanding (literally, *fiqh*) of God's plan for human existence through the study of the knowledge (*ʿilm*) contained within the divinely revealed sources was, in essence, an attempt to map out God's "laws," and thus the beginnings of the formal discipline of Islamic law, *fiqh*. Like their largely Christian counterparts, some of these early scholars also likely engaged in discussions and disputations over the implications of God's message, an endeavor that later became known as *kalām*.[55] Those who engaged in these processes became known as the *ʿulamāʾ* or the *fuqahāʾ* (sing. *faqīh*), while later theologians became known as *mutakallimūn*. Their accumulated discoveries and methodologies became the stuff of the *sharīʿa*, *ḥadīth* criticism, and Islamic theology (it is sometimes not helpful to separate these disciplines, as they were not often separated by the *ʿulamāʾ* who engaged in them). Like its counterparts in the Jewish tradition, Islamic law/theology covered more than the Anglophone word "law" tends to imply: it covered ethics, morality, manners, as well as traditional "legal" subjects such as divorce, marriage, inheritance, contracts, and so on. The *sharīʿa* was meant to be a comprehensive roadmap for pious living, but right from the beginning it was recognized that human situations, along with the contexts and individual cases, varied greatly, and that human beings could not finally know God's mind. For this reason, tremendous regional and personal diversity characterized the endeavor to build the *sharīʿa*. In the Umayyad period, for example, local Muslim jurists often relied on their own reasoned judgment (*raʾy*) in deciding any given case, resulting in a remarkable multiplicity of legal judgments and opinions on any legal question. In addition, the Umayyad caliphs sometimes arrogated to themselves the right to settle legal and theological questions.[56] Ultimately, however, the unpopularity of the Umayyad caliphs precluded the caliphal office from possessing any special authority in the realm of the religious sciences. If he possessed the requisite knowledge the caliph's opinion would be heard and possibly even favored, but it would remain in the long run one opinion among many.

[55] Tannous, "Between Christology and Kalām?" 707–16.
[56] Crone and Hinds, *God's Caliph*, 43–57.

By the 120s/740s the Umayyad regime found itself in serious trouble. Weakened by constant warfare against the Byzantines, Khārijite and Shiʿite revolts inside its borders, as well as the growing resentment of non-Arab Muslims (*mawālī*), the Umayyads began to falter. Massive Khārijite revolts across North Africa in the 120s/740s removed this large and lucrative geographical area from their sphere of influence. Closer to their capital at Damascus, the delicate tribal and political balance of Umayyad power in Syria was broken when rival caliphal contenders began to elicit the aid of the competing Qays (northern Arab) or Yaman/Kalb (southern Arab) groups.[57] Further afield in Khurasān (northeastern Iran), a radical Shiʿite group known as the Hāshimiyya, capitalizing on previous failed rebellions, was able to attract support among the *mawālī* with their claims to restore Islamic justice through the installation of a Prophet's family member from the ʿAbbāsid branch of the *ahl al-bayt* as caliph.[58] The Hāshimiyya boasted an able general, Abū Muslim, who in 129/747 raised the black banners of the end times and directed the revolt that would terminate the Umayyad dynasty in Damascus. By 133/751, Abū Muslim and the ʿAbbāsids had defeated the Umayyad armies, and had hunted down and killed virtually all the Umayyads that they could find. Surviving Umayyads fled to Iberia, where the Umayyad dynasty would last another 200 some years.

Once in power, the ʿAbbāsids backed away from their more radical Shiʿite supporters, and began to justify their rule in ways similar to the Umayyads (i.e. by invoking the idea of preserving and adhering to the community, the *jamāʿa*). They did, nevertheless, address some of the more pressing issues of the revolution. For example, under ʿAbbāsid rule Islam was to be universally applicable to all, without preference for the Arabs. Thus, they began to incorporate the *mawālī* into their administration, especially those who lived in the former Sāsānian regions, and removed most impediments to conversion. A universalizable Islam meant that law needed to be universally applicable, a task that the *ʿulamāʾ* of the ʿAbbāsid period set about discovering in the example of the Prophet Muḥammad. This endeavor culminated in the figure of Muḥammad b. Idrīs al-Shāfiʿī, who enshrined the principle of the Prophet's *sunna*, his example, as the reflection of the qurʾanic message, the second legitimate source (after the Qurʾan) of Islamic law. Consensus among the learned, *ijmāʿ*, and analogous reasoning, *qiyās*, would become the third and fourth sources of law for al-Shāfiʿī and his followers, whose legal methodology was coalescing into a recognizable "way" (*madhhab*) or

[57] Hawting, *The First Dynasty of Islam*, 93.
[58] Bernheimer, "The Revolt of ʿAbdullāh b. Muʿāwiya AH 127–130," 393.

school of law. At the same time, other legal scholars looked back to similar eponymous figures around which to organize their legal thinking: the Ḥanafīs to Abū Ḥanīfa, the Mālikīs to Mālik b. Anas, the Ḥanbalīs to Aḥmad b. Ḥanbal, the Ẓāhirīs to Dāwūd al-Ẓāhirī, and the Jarīrīs to Muḥammad b. Jarīr al-Ṭabarī. After al-Shāfiʿī, these legal schools shared an emphasis on Muḥammad's *sunna*, as enshrined in the *ḥadīth* literature, as the second source of Islamic law, even as they differed in how they approached this literature, and over the other sources of law.

For their part, the ʿAbbāsids incorporated more of the *ʿulamāʾ* into their bureaucracy as judges, officials, and so on, offering them, in essence, what amounted to a compromise: the ʿAbbāsids would honor and abide by the program of the pious to create an Islamic basis for living, and in return the pious would legitimate caliphal rule and not interfere with the caliph's power.[59] The caliphs came more and more to rely on the *ʿulamāʾ* for their own legitimacy, meaning that the caliphs found themselves more and more bound to honor the norms of Islamic law. The *ʿulamāʾ*, for their part, were to cease to participate in opposition or outright revolution, but were required to tolerate the absolutism and sometimes arbitrary practices of the caliphs.

The ʿAbbāsids modeled their rule along old Sāsānian lines, adopting the powers and court etiquette of the old Sāsānian kings (*shāh*s): thus, the caliph retained certain judicial powers, especially when it came to rebels and political criminals, and surrounded himself with an elaborate court replete with rituals designed to accentuate his dignity. For example, court etiquette required petitioners to kiss the ground before the caliph, and to address him as *jalālat al-khalīfa* ("his majesty the caliph"). As Jalāl was considered an epithet for God (*dhū al-jalāl wa'l-ikrām*, "He of majesty and generosity," being one of the so-called names of God mentioned in Qurʾan 55:27 and 78), applying it to the person of the caliph might border on the blasphemous. After all, the Qurʾan enjoined humility, piety, and knowledge, and the *ʿulamāʾ* continued to hold that the leader of the Muslims should possess these qualities. For the *ʿulamāʾ*, whose piety had long been a mark of their sincerity to Islam, such a situation amounted to a compromise indeed. However, many put up with or ignored caliphal excess so long as the caliph maintained order in the realm, protected Muslims, and allowed for the functioning of Islamic ritual and law.

For those who could or would not stomach the compromise, these coalesced (or, as the case may be, continued to coalesce) into various Shiʿite, Khārijite, and Ibāḍī groups, many of whom remain today, while

[59] Hodgson, *The Venture of Islam*, 1:280ff.

the rest became more and more associated with the growing consensus later dubbed Sunnism. Thus, the immediate effect of the "ʿAbbāsid compromise" on the course of Muslim sectarianism was, effectively, to separate those willing to accept rapprochement with the caliphs from those who would not, and thereby to entrench certain kinds of attitudes toward political power into recognizable sectarian tendencies.

Yet the ʿAbbāsid compromise, over the long term, appealed to enough Muslims such that the remaining sectarians increasingly found themselves a minority. Consequently, the ʿAbbāsid era by comparison saw far less sectarian violence than the Umayyad period, and appears as one of relative stability. As a result of the health of the ʿAbbāsid Empire, trade generated prosperity, which in turn drove developments in Islamic science, culture, and art. For example, in their newly established circular capital near the old city of Baghdad the ʿAbbāsid caliphs oversaw a 200-year translation movement that rendered vast corpuses of Greek, Syriac, Pahlavi, and Sanskrit works (among other languages) into Arabic.[60] The translation movement (among other things) provided material for the *mutakallimūn*, the theologically minded, especially those associated with the Muʿtazilite movement, to hone their styles of argumentation. Across the world, in Umayyad Iberia, imported irrigation techniques allowed new crops (such as rice, almonds, spinach, limes, lemons, and oranges) to be introduced as new dietary staples.[61] And in what is today Pakistan, in the fifth/eleventh century, Abū al-Rayḥān Muḥammad b. Aḥmad al-Bīrūnī calculated the circumference of the earth to within 200 miles of its actual measurement.[62] Such achievements represent but a small sampling of medieval Islamic advances in science and the arts that the ʿAbbāsid era made possible.

This relative stability also created a space for philosophical and theological schools of thought to flourish. In particular, a group known as the Murjiʾites, who had in fact begun in the Umayyad period, matured in the ʿAbbāsid era into a loosely identifiable *firqa* with a range of opinions on the notions of faith and action. So too, an Umayyad-era group known as the Qadariyya, who had debated ideas about free will, laid the ground for the emergence in the ʿAbbāsid era of one of the most important early theological schools, the Muʿtazila. Finally, the compromises of the ʿAbbāsid era allowed many of the *ʿulamāʾ* to table the question of legitimate leadership in return for the space and patronage to pursue the question of a universalizable vision of Islam. In the long run, this quest resulted in the slow emergence of a loose scholarly coalition focused on

[60] On the translation movement, see Gutas, *Greek Thought, Arabic Culture*.
[61] Fletcher, *Moorish Spain*, 62–64. [62] Scheppler, *Al-Biruni*, 89.

the Prophet's example, his *sunna*, especially as it was found in the emerging collections of *ḥadīth*, as a means of guiding Muslim life. This group would become known as the Ahl al-Sunna wa'l-Jamāʿa, the Sunnis for short, and would much later establish themselves as the majority through Seljuq patronage of their *madrasa*s (schools).

Lest the division between the caliphal and *ʿulamāʾ*'s authority be overstated, it is important to note that the early ʿAbbāsid caliphs initially laid claims to religious authority just as their Umayyad counterparts had done. This authority, however, would not endure, leaving the *ʿulamāʾ* as the primary custodians of Islam. The last and perhaps most famous exercise in caliphal authority began in 212/827 when the ʿAbbāsid caliph al-Maʾmūn instituted what became known as the *miḥna* (meaning "test," but often and poorly translated as "inquisition"). He initially proclaimed the doctrine (held by Muʿtazilites and Shiʿites at the time) that the Qurʾan was created, following up this proclamation six years later by demanding that leading scholars and officials publicly embrace the doctrine or face punishment, imprisonment, or even death. Al-Maʾmūn had argued elsewhere, in a series of letters to his governors, that caliphs were guardians of God's religion and laws, and al-Maʾmūn seemed eager to enforce this idea through the *miḥna*.

The *miḥna* continued under al-Maʾmūn's successors, the caliphs al-Muʿtaṣim, al-Wāthiq, and al-Mutawakkil (who finally abolished it). Famously, the caliph al-Muʿtaṣim had the popular Baghdadi preacher and scholar Aḥmad b. Ḥanbal imprisoned and flogged for refusing to acknowledge that the Qurʾan was created. However, the murder of the caliph al-Mutawakkil instigated an extended power struggle among the ʿAbbāsids that ultimately diminished the caliph in favor of his courtiers and Turkish slave soldiers. In the intervening power vacuum, the *ʿulamāʾ* stepped in to assume responsibility for determining questions of religion, a role that the weakened ʿAbbāsid caliphs would never again fulfill.[63] The *ʿulamāʾ* would remain the specialists in religion and law, however reliant on the caliphs and the court for their appointments and patronage they continued to be.

The diminution of caliphal authority had far-reaching consequences for Islamdom. By the fourth/tenth century, the caliphate began to lose some of its political unity and to fragment. On the surface, the caliph remained in power, and the empire remained nominally united. In reality, different clans and families had emerged in various parts of Islamdom, and had secured real control over local areas, often forcing the caliph to recognize them as governors. For example, the Būyid clan, a Shiʿite

[63] Turner, *Inquisition in Early Islam*, 137.

family from Daylām (northern Iran), conquered much of Iran and Iraq in the fourth/tenth century, forcing the ʿAbbāsid caliphs to recognize them as *amīrs* (local potentates), and effectively ruling the central lands of the caliphate for more than half a century. As Shiʿites, the Būyids did much to patronize Shiʿi scholarship and pilgrimage sites (such as Karbala), also allowing for a more public presence of ʿAlīdism within their domain, but without publicly emphasizing their sectarian identification.

The Būyids persisted until the mid-fifth/eleventh century when the invading Seljuq Turks finally ended their influence. The Seljuqs also maintained the ʿAbbāsid caliph as a kind of figurehead, adopting for their own leaders the titles Sultan and Bey. Unlike the Būyids, however, the Seljuqs aggressively adopted Sunnism and actively used it to distinguish themselves from their predecessors. Their patronage, in particular, of Sunni institutions of learning did much to establish Sunnism as the majority trend among Muslims, but it also created rivalries between them and other Shiʿite groups.

In other parts of Islamdom the ʿAbbāsids lost control completely, as they did with the Fāṭimids in North Africa and Egypt. Yet throughout this tumultuous political history, Islamic sciences and arts continued to thrive, often with local patronage, and the *ʿulamāʾ* maintained their systems of Islamic law. In other words, local communities could function with semi-independence, thereby weathering the storms that periodically raged through the upper echelons of Muslim political life. This same semi-independence allowed the various Muslim sects and schools to endure as well.

From Horsepower to Gunpowder

As important as the decentralization of political power was to the survival of Muslim sects and schools in the medieval period, so too, the nature of and limits to the projection of political power shaped the way that any given medieval Muslim polity could enforce the sovereign's will. It is therefore imperative to gain a sense of how political/military power worked in the medieval period, as well as how (and why) it changed in the late medieval era. A quote from the Muslim traveler Ibn Baṭṭūṭa, in which he praised the Ūsmānlī ruler Ūrkhān Bey whom he observed in 731/1331, nicely outlines the main features (and constraints) of the early types of power in medieval Islamdom. Describing the Bey, Ibn Baṭṭuṭa writes:

> Of fortresses he possesses nearly a hundred, and for most of his time he is continually engaged in making the round of them, staying in each fortress for

some days to put it into good order and examine its condition. It is said that he had never stayed for a whole month in any one town. He also fights with the infidels [i.e. Byzantines] continually and keeps them under siege.[64]

From Ibn Baṭṭūṭa's comments, it is immediately apparent that power centered on the person of the ruler and his army, and in the constant mobility that was required for them to maintain order. Without a doubt, the garrisons and fortresses here mentioned by Ibn Baṭṭūṭa played an important role in the defense of Ūsmānlī territory, but what is striking is that Ibn Baṭṭūṭa praises Ūrkhān Bey for *not* remaining in them for any extended period of time. Control over an area, then, lay primarily in a ruler's mobility.

Secondly, Ibn Baṭṭūṭa praises the Bey's ability to subdue enemies, and occasionally, friends. In the border region of the Anatolian Plateau where the Ūsmānlīs held territory, this meant fighting with the Byzantines, and Ibn Baṭṭūṭa commends Ūrkhān Bey accordingly. What goes unmentioned in the quote, however, is how the Ūsmānlīs often fought with their Muslim neighbors, subduing and absorbing in the course of the seventh/thirteenth and eighth/fourteenth centuries the surrounding Amīrates such that by the fall of Constantinople in 857/1453 they were set to become one of the most important empires in world history, the Ottomans.

The notion that mobility translated into politico-military power would find its most dramatic and world-altering expression in the Mongol invasions of the seventh/thirteenth century, whereby a highly mobile nomadic confederation would go on to create the largest contiguous land empire in human history, putting an end to the ʿAbbāsid Empire and disrupting the rest of Islamdom in profound ways. The Mongols were masters of mounted archery, using the composite bow and the sturdy Mongolian pony to devastating effect. They also learned different techniques (such as siege warfare) as they conquered. The Mongol invasions would be followed 200 years later by another conquering nomadic federation, that of Timurlane (also known as Timurlank, Tamurlane) (d. 807/1405). Timur likewise cobbled together a confederation of nomadic warriors and subjugated a more modest swathe of what is now Iran, Iraq, and Central Asia.

What might such configurations of power mean for sectarian minorities? In comparison with today's highly centralized surveillance bureaucracies, medieval political orders appear radically decentralized, and reliant on the ability of a capable ruler and his army to project their authority where it was needed. In such situations, it was often the ability to evade or otherwise subvert the mobility of the ruler that translated into

[64] Dunn, *The Adventures of Ibn Battuta*, 152.

long-term survival for sectarian groups. Such evasions/subversions could happen in a multitude of ways. Sectarian groups could opt for a "low profile," perhaps even officially adopting a mode of secrecy to insure their survival. With the rulers and/or their representatives (i.e. the caliph, his military officials, sultans, *amīrs*, beys, etc.) frequently on the move, secrecy allowed sectarian groups to wait out their presence in any given region or town. In a place like Baghdad, where the ʿAbbāsid caliphs increasingly found themselves delegating their responsibilities, and therefore remaining more in permanent residence in the city, sectarian minorities, such as the Shiʿites or Ibāḍīs, could practice a form of prudent secrecy (*taqiyya*) during the times when sectarian tension mounted. So too, the more local and therefore more "permanent" representatives of power, such as the governors of medieval Muslim regions, often found it convenient to ignore or come to an understanding with local sectarian groups, so long as public order was not upset too dramatically by their activities.

Another tactic, employed the world round by sectarians and other kinds of minorities, was to occupy (or flee to) geographical regions that were difficult to access, such as mountains or swamps. A glance at a topographical map reveals that Zaydī, Ismāʿīlī, Alevi, and ʿAlawī Shiʿites, along with Ibāḍīs, have survived down to the present in mountainous regions (also the Druze and Yazīdīs). Iraqi Twelver Shiʿites, the so-called Marsh Arabs, inhabited the southern marshes of Iraq. Similarly, Twelver Shiʿites in Afghanistan, the Hazāra, inhabit the mountainous areas west of Kabul. Living in geographically remote areas allowed these groups to survive mainly by obstructing the mobility of would-be sectarian oppressors, and thereby subverting the main feature of power in the medieval period.

For what might be considered the "formative period" of Muslim sectarianism, such were the configurations of political and military control, and the main Muslim sects and schools under discussion in this book interacted with those authorities accordingly. However, the destruction and disruption wrought by the Mongols changed the balances of power in many places in Islamdom, notably in the Muslim East. Scholars have noted a marked "confessional ambiguity" in the period following the Mongol conquests, such that sectarian identifications receded or collapse entirely, often to be replaced with a generalized ʿAlīd loyalism that defied easy sectarian definition.[65] Whether the result of the increased presence of mystical organizations that de-emphasized sectarian identification in

[65] Pfeiffer, "Confessional Ambiguity," 129; Hodgson, *The Venture of Islam*, 2:369–85, 445–55, 463.

favor of other (and more universal) identifications, or by other factors, Islamdom after the Mongol invasions, especially in its eastern regions, became a place where increased intra-sectarian participation and pro-ʿAlīd expressions proliferated. The extent to which this de-confessionalization manifested itself in the central and western regions of Islamdom remains to be investigated.

Another historical factor that greatly changed the way that sectarian groups and schools of thought interacted with the power centers of the time is the dispersion of gunpowder throughout the medieval world. This process began in China in the fourth/tenth century and passed to Islamdom and Europe by the seventh/thirteenth century. Gunpowder technologies gradually changed the way that warfare, and therefore political power, operated. Concurrent with changes in Islamic education, patronage structures, naval technologies (which allowed for a greater volume of trade across greater distances), and the scope and structure of the mystical orders, the emergence of gunpowder armies, and the bureaucracies required to sustain them, created a very different world for sectarian groups to navigate.

The so-called gunpowder empires of the late medieval period – the Ottomans, Safavids, Uzbecks, and Mughals – epitomize the changes happening in Islamdom, and indeed, throughout the world with the introduction of gunpowder armies.[66] The advantage of mounted archers diminished with the ability to shoot riders from their horses at long distances. However, gunpowder needed to be stored and kept dry, and cannon was weighty and difficult to move, all factors that hindered an army's mobility. Alongside mobile armies, then, depots and forts developed where standing armies could be housed closer to the centers of commerce and trade. With the slow development of the idea of the nation-state with borders, armies began to station themselves near emerging boundaries of their territory. Such far-flung (from the perspective of the medieval period) armies evolved alongside of the increasingly centralized bureaucracies that now organized, fed, housed, clothed, and directed them. Such were the gunpowder empires as they emerged with their standing armies, their centralized states, and their increasingly formalized borders. At the top of this bureaucracy sat the sultan or shah, who increasingly possessed the means to control their populations in ways nearly unthinkable to earlier medieval monarchs.

In such a situation, the ability of any given sectarian group to evade the sultan/shah and his ministers contracted as the governing forces acquired more ability to suppress dissent, and as the centralizing tendencies of the

[66] Streusand, *Islamic Gunpowder Empires*, 2–4.

gunpowder empires eroded local privilege. Nevertheless, outright suppression of sectarian groups would have remained a costly affair. Even with gunpowder technology, marching an army into the mountains, for example, required significant resources, and success was not guaranteed. Softer types of control proved more effective, such as government patronage of the *ʿulamāʾ* and their institutions combined with the suppression of the rival sectarian institutions. These types of actions increasingly defined the patterns of popular piety in late medieval Islamdom.[67] Such efforts, for example, allowed the Safavids in the early ninth/fifteenth century to convert the Iranian cities and countryside en masse to Twelver Shiʿism. These same types of efforts entrenched Sunnism as the official sectarian affiliation of the Ottomans. The advantages of geography and secrecy, then, were not completely eliminated in the period of the gunpowder empires, but they now existed alongside the imperial ability to exercise greater control, often with the aid of the *ʿulamāʾ*, in the cities and surrounding areas.

It must be remembered, however, that even with growing centralization, and an increased ability to interfere in the daily lives of their subjects, a sultan, shah, or other government official of the late medieval period nevertheless had to decide that it was worthwhile to make sectarian identification count in their empire. Put another way, if we cease assuming that sect-identification automatically mattered, and return to treating it as one type of identification among many, then we can investigate the rich tapestry of sectarian identifications and relations in the period of the gunpowder empires (or any period, for that matter) in a more responsible fashion. Much of this work remains to be completed, but a cursory glance at some of the existing scholarship reveals a complex and often shifting situation for sectarian minorities within the gunpowder empires. Winter, for example, has shown how the Ottomans integrated the ʿAlawī (i.e. Nuṣayrī) Shiʿites of the Levant into their tax regime, doing so, seemingly, without overt concern for their ʿAlawī sectarian affiliation. Moreover, he shows how Nuṣayrī rebels identified themselves along tribal (rather than sectarian/religious) lines during their initial tax revolt against the Ottoman state.[68] Thus, while it is true that sectarian friction in and between the Ottoman and Safavid empires emerged, especially after the tenth/sixteenth century, as an element in and result of imperial competition and warfare between the two groups, the case of the ʿAlawī minority initially presents that of banal sectarianism within the Ottoman Empire (whereby the sectarian affiliation appears subordinated to other

[67] Streusand, *Islamic Gunpowder Empires*, 296.
[68] Winter, *A History of the ʿAlawis*, 116–18.

concerns). However, by the twelfth/eighteenth century, the amplified presence and power of local ʿAlawī elites, along with the monies and armies that they could raise with their newfound capital, meant that they were increasingly seen as a "sect" (*ṭāʾifa*) by the Ottoman court of the time.[69] The salience of ʿAlawī sectarian identification, then, shifted over time from banal to somewhat more active, and the factors contributing to this shift had much to do with local economies, local politics, as well as the perceptions of Ottoman elites. It is hoped that further investigation might help to uncover the extent to which sect affiliation may or may not have created friction in the emerging gunpowder empires, identifying along the way the factors that pushed sectarian identification from banal to active, or vice versa.

This chapter has endeavored to focus on broad themes throughout the long history of Muslim sects and schools, namely, on those trends and events that contributed specifically to the evolution of the master narratives of Muslim sects and schools. It rooted the beginnings of these narratives in the period of late antiquity, noting how the Qurʾan and the leadership of the Prophet Muḥammad discouraged the fragmentation of the *umma*. The question of succession to the Prophet, however, sowed the seeds of sectarian division, even if these divisions only later manifested themselves in outright disputes over the identity and nature of the *umma*'s proper leader. The first *fitna*, and then the Umayyad period, witnessed the birth of Islamdom's first sectarian groups: the Khārijites and the Shiʿites initially, but later the first Murjiʾa and the Qadariyya. As the revolutionary upheavals of the Umayyad period gave way to the relative stability of the early ʿAbbāsid era, the story of Muslim sects expanded to include more philosophically and theologically minded schools of thought, with the Muʿtazilites and later Murjiʾa being the primary examples of this trend. Also during this time emerged the coalition that would articulate Sunnism, though this group cannot be considered the majority until the Seljuqs in the high medieval period established their primacy through the patronage of their institutions of learning. The chapter ended with an examination of how gunpowder changed the nature of empire in the high to late medieval period, and how those changes affected the ways that Muslim sects and schools evolved.

Ending, as this survey does, just at the outset of the twelfth/eighteenth century, Muslim sectarian affiliations and identifications stand as one strand among many that define and motivate Muslims throughout their

[69] Winter, *A History of the ʿAlawis*, 160.

long history. To say that sect and school has been unimportant to the broader story of Muslim history would be naive to the extreme. However, equally misleading would be to assume that sect/school identifications inevitably drove the engine of Muslim history. Such is simply not the case, as Muslims had, as they now have, complex motivations for acting in the ways that they did.

3 Protest and Piety

The Khārijites and the Ibāḍiyya

Arguably the earliest division to emerge among Muslims was that of the so-called Khārijites (sing. *khārijī*, pl. *khawārij*), the first of whom were said to have initially broken with ʿAlī b. Abī Ṭālib when he consented in 36/656 to arbitrate the Battle of Ṣiffin with his enemy, Muʿāwiya b. Abī Sufyān. These *khawārij* were said to have seceded from (*kharajū ʿan*) ʿAlī because they held him to have sinned through accepting arbitration, and thereby to have forfeited his status as full believer and leader of the Muslims. Insofar as later Khārijite and Ibāḍī groups looked back to these first Khārijites as their predecessors, later Khārijites were said to have held pious action to be the main criterion for accepting a person as a true Muslim, and they rejected the exclusive claims of the Quraysh (as well as the ʿAlīds) to the caliphate. As such, issues of piety and protest could be said to have framed the self-image of Khārijites and Ibāḍīs such that their narratives (insofar as they can be recovered from the sources) often tell stories of protest against tyrannical and unrighteous caliphs. These same stories also seem to narrate the repeated (and often failed) attempts of various early Khārijite groups to establish a just community under the leadership of a pious imam. Of course, the concepts of protest and piety are not exclusive to the Khārijites and Ibāḍiyya, nor are the yearnings for a righteous community led by a pious leader. Rather, it is the particular answers to the questions of just leadership and communal piety, especially that leaders and co-sectarians demonstrate their piety to some extent, that seems to distinguish those who became known as Khārijites and Ibāḍiyya from other Muslim sects and schools.

However, the "stories" of and by the Khārijites remain problematic for reasons that are related to the problem of source material for the academic study of early Islam (this is less so for the Ibāḍiyya, from whom a considerable body of sources survived). The nature of the Muslim sources on the early groups that were retroactively labeled Khārijites (*khawārij*) makes obtaining an accurate portrait of them deeply challenging, some would even say impossible. As a result of their virtual disappearance by the sixth/twelfth century almost nothing of Khārijite writings survives that hasn't been mediated through other non-Khārijite sources. And while these non-Khārijite sources do clearly use earlier Khārijite works as the basis of their narratives, later (proto-Sunni, Shiʿi, and Ibāḍī) Muslim author-editors remained hostile to the Khārijite groups about which they wrote. Additionally, both Khārijite authors and the medieval Muslim author-editors who preserved their writings were not interested in "history" in the modern sense. Rather, these authors manipulated the stuff of history to present idealized images of their subject, whether sympathetic or disparaging, and they did so by liberally employing recognized literary tropes, rhetoric, and schemata to do so. The modern historian, then, must analyze what are essentially rhetoricized images of the Khārijites that have been vilified by later Muslim author-editors. These portraits survive in non-Khārijite sources as hybrids of admiration and horror. In short, the stories of the Khārijites had many tellers, not all of whom relished the telling.

Moreover, it must be admitted that some contemporary scholars have not approached the Khārijites with the requisite caution, continuing to treat their sources as if they presented a "historical" portrait of the early Khārijite groups. This uncritical position, combined with an overreliance on heresiographical sources, has resulted in some lopsided scholarly notions about who and what the Khārijites groups did or held as true, as well as who was the most representative of them. Even the issue of whether or not to conceptualize the Khārijites as a sectarian group (as this chapter does for simplicity's sake) presents another critical scholarly issue. It is not clear that "sectarianism" is, in fact, the best theoretical framework for their study, nor that those retroactively labeled the "Khārijites" constituted a reified group. Employing the moniker "Khārijites" implies a separate and at the very least semi-coherent movement with a minimum of common features to distinguish this supposed movement from others of its kind.[1] However, groups identified as "Khārijite" diverged radically from each other, and the broad ideas that could be said to characterize them in their earliest periods were not markedly different from some basic qurʾanic notions as well as certain caricatures of early Muslims that appear in later sources. For example, before the advent of the second *fitna* (when somewhat coherent groups of identifiable and militant Khārijites do seem to emerge onto the scene), those groups described as "Khārijites" seem connected only by the vaguely outlined conviction that people demonstrated their submission to God through their actions, and that among the outward signs of submission was resisting unjust, sinful, and/or tyrannical rulers (be they caliphs or governors). The first idea is thoroughly grounded in qurʾanic

[1] Cook, "Weber and Islamic Sects," 276.

discussions of sin and disbelief (*kufr*), which strongly imply in several places that such transgressions can be intuited from actions. What, then, did the earliest Khārijites mean when they employed the term *kuffār* to describe their opponents? Did they intend, as most heresiographers and later historians would have us believe, that non-Khārijites were absolutely beyond the pale of belief? Or did the earliest Khārijites employ this term as polemic, implying that non-Khārijites had fallen short in a manner resembling (but not actually becoming) unbelievers?

Their second conviction, that piety required, among other things, resisting unfit leaders, can likewise be attested as an utterly "Islamic" ideal in the early period, meaning that it is not exclusive to the Khārijites. For example, al-Azdī's *Futūḥ al-Shām* contains a description of the early *ghāziyūn* that was given by a Christian monk who had been sent to scout the advancing Muslim army. Returning to the Roman commander, the monk described the Muslim soldiers as "a people staying up through the night praying and remaining abstinent during the day, commanding the right and forbidding the wrong, monks by night, warriors by day. Should their king steal, they cut off his hand, and if he commits adultery they stone him."[2] While this description, too, must not be confused for "history" per se, what it does reflect is a concern with portraying the first Muslim *mujāhidūn* as particularly pious, and that a marker of their piety included an eagerness to extend the qurʾanic punishments even to their leaders (their "kings" in this quote). In such a light, descriptions of the early Khārijites' willingness to label their opponents as *kuffār* or to stand up to caliphs and governors that they considered tyrannical appear as variations on this theme of early Islamic piety. In such a light, it is difficult to see how the images of the Khārijites that survive in the sources actually distinguish them from similar images that appear in other narratives about the early Muslims.

When, then, can a historian speak of a distinct Khārijite movement? At best, the first Khārijites might be considered as a loosely defined politico-religious movement, unified only by their conviction that ʿUthmān had been killed justly, and that ʿAlī had erred by agreeing to arbitrate his dispute with Muʿāwiya. Yet beyond the vague notion that leaders should be pious, and that egregiously sinning rendered a Muslim somehow less than a full Muslim, they were unable to fully agree on what the consequences of these positions should be. The idea of the Khārijites as an identifiable sectarian assemblage with their own distinct "path" is the product of later periods, though the process likely began early, possibly as early as the 60s/680s, and among nascent groups of Khārijites themselves.

[2] Sizgorich, *Violence and Belief in Late Antiquity*, 160–61.

In addition to these already weighty issues, it should be noted that the term *khawārij* itself remains awkward insofar as it was a pejorative that was applied to them by their enemies (as are most of the other terms that are often used to delineate the group). The first so-called Khārijites seem not to have employed the word at all, preferring to describe themselves simply as Muslims, or as *shurāt* (sing. *shārī*), "exchangers." The term *shurāt* likely alludes to the qurʾanic verse (9:111) promising paradise to those who "exchanged" their persons and their properties for paradise by fighting for the cause of righteousness.[3] Moreover, the only remaining representatives of this sectarian trend, the Ibāḍiyya, reject the term *khawārij* as derogatory. Despite these problems, this chapter will retain the term "Khārijite" because it has become the recognizable signifier for this particular group, and changing it would only lead to confusion. As much as possible, the Ibāḍiyya will be treated as a separate group, and this separate treatment is fully warranted given their longevity.

Given these caveats, the stories of the Khārijites, and even the terms used to describe them, must be treated with extreme caution. Nevertheless, certain recognizable themes do tend to emerge from the many descriptions of them. First and foremost, the Khārijites followed leaders that they considered pious, and they resisted (and often fought) those considered to be unjust and sinful. Those who accepted unjust imams were also considered to have sinned, possibly even to have left the realm of proper belief in some fashion. Such a stance led to a kind of separatism, whether outright (i.e. physical) or ideological (i.e. maintained through secrecy and dissimulation). It might be said that the positions taken with regard to these questions broadly define what might be said to constitute "Khārijism," as well as locating Ibāḍism in relation to them.

With these questions as their guiding stars, this chapter specifically outlines the main groups of Khārijites, as well as the Ibāḍiyya. Khārijite groups who engaged in open protest to the Umayyads and later ʿAbbāsids include the Muḥakkima, Azāriqa, Najadāt, as well as the constellation of Khārijite groups that survived in Persia. Groups who followed a quietist model of protest primarily include the Ibāḍiyya and the so-called Ṣufriyya. This last group will be scrutinized closely, as they do not seem to have constituted themselves as a separate entity as early as the sources claim. So too, the tendency to overemphasize the impact of early Khārijite groups (especially the Azāriqa and Najadāt) while ignoring the

[3] "Indeed, God has exchanged (*ashtarā*) with the believers their lives and their properties for that they will have paradise. They fight in the cause of God, so they kill and are killed. [It is] a true promise [binding] upon Him in the Torah and the Gospel and the Qurʾan. And who is truer to his covenant than God? So rejoice in your transaction which you have contracted. And it is that which is the great attainment."

importance of others (namely the Ibāḍiyya) will be noted. Moreover, this chapter treats the Ibāḍiyya as a kind of off-shoot from the earliest Khārijites, but takes care to emphasize that they developed in ways that make casual comparisons with the Khārijites problematic. The subgroups of the Ibāḍiyya will be discussed, as will developments in North Africa and the Arabian Peninsula that gave local expressions of Ibāḍism and Ṣufrism their particular colorings.

Origin and Early Development Narratives

Although recognizable groups that are later identified as Khārijites formed during the early Umayyad period, and largely in opposition to the Umayyad caliphs, traditionally Muslim and non-Muslim scholars alike traced the emergence of the so-called Khārijites to events directly preceding that period, specifically to the Battle of Ṣiffīn in 36/656 and its aftermath. The events of Ṣiffīn brought the question of an erring imam into relief, and cast the actions of the first Khārijites, known as the Muḥakkima, as paradigmatic for all subsequent Khārijite and Ibāḍī groups. Initially, those who became the Muḥakkima supported ʿAlī b. Abī Ṭālib against, first, ʿĀʾisha, Ṭalḥa, and Zubayr and then against the army of ʿUthmān's cousin and governor of Damascus, Muʿāwiya b. Abī Sufyān. Muʿāwiya, it should be recalled, had challenged ʿAlī's right to rule with the contention that ʿAlī had not done enough to punish the killers of ʿUthmān. ʿAlī and his supporters, on the other hand, regarded Muʿāwiya as a rank opportunist. Not only was he the son of the Prophet's bitter enemy, Abū Sufyān, but ʿAlī's supporters questioned the veracity of Muʿāwiya's motives. Moreover, many of them regarded ʿUthmān as having been justly killed. The two armies met outside of present-day Raqqa, in northeastern Syria, on the plain of Ṣiffīn. When the tide of battle turned against Muʿāwiya, his confidant and general ʿAmr b. al-ʿĀṣ suggested that they escape total defeat by suing for arbitration. Placing pages (*maṣāḥif*) of the Qurʾan on lances and symbolically hoisting them up between the battle lines (suggesting that the Qurʾan should judge between them), the plea for arbitration initially split ʿAlī's army. Many, including ʿAlī himself, wanted to continue fighting.[4] Others (including many who subsequently joined the Muḥakkima) pressed ʿAlī to accept arbitration, which he did. However, as the details of the arbitration emerged, discontent grew among the ranks of ʿAlī's army. A group among them, including some who had initially supported it, came to believe that there could be no agreement with Muʿāwiya. Possibly citing

[4] Madelung, *Succession to Muḥammad*, 239ff.

Qurʾan 49:9 as the proof for their line of reasoning, this group argued that God had made His intentions clear regarding the likes of Muʿāwiya: he should be fought, using the Qurʾan's terminology, until he "returned to the ordinance (*amr*) of God."[5] Arbitration (*taḥkīm*, *ḥukm al-ḥukūma*) therefore directly contradicted a clear qurʾanic command to fight rebellious and oppressive factions until they returned to obedience, and only after returning to obedience should settlement (*ṣulḥ*) be restored between them. In what became the slogan of the Khārijites (and a play on the term for arbitration, *taḥkīm* or *ḥukūma*), there was "no judgment but God's" (*lā ḥukm illā li-llāh*), and ʿAlī should resume the fight. When ʿAlī refused to restart hostilities (claiming that he would not break an agreement that he had already made), several of the dissatisfied seceded from (in Arabic, *kharajū ʿan*) ʿAlī's army, decamping initially to a place outside of Kufa called Ḥarūrāʾ where they were said to have elected provisional leaders.[6] According to many accounts, ʿAlī was able to coax some of these secessionists back to his camp by debating them, and possibly making certain promises regarding his willingness to disregard the arbitration (which ʿAlī certainly did not fully support).[7] Yet when ʿAlī did not wholly abandon the arbitration, the Khārijites again broke with him. They elected their own imam, ʿAbdullāh b. Wahb al-Rāsibī, and then escaped in small numbers to a place further up the Euphrates near a canal called Nahrawān.[8]

Along the way to Nahrawān, the Muḥakkima were reported to have killed a Companion of the Prophet named Ibn Khabāb, and possibly his family. Numerous versions of this killing exist in the sources, with very few of them actually narrating the event in the same way (notably, they do not exist in Ibāḍī narratives of the Muḥakkima).[9] Moreover, this incident was said to have compelled ʿAlī to march against the Muḥakkima at Nahrawān. It therefore behooves the student of history to regard it with extra caution. Whatever the case, ʿAlī and his army did march to Nahrawān where, after ʿAlī convinced some of the Khārijites to leave the field, the two groups engaged in battle, and ʿAlī's forces virtually annihilated the Muḥakkima remaining there.

Although decimated, some of the early Khārijites survived to propagate their ideas. Yet the main fallout from the Battle of Nahrawān occurred

[5] al-Qalhātī, *al-Kashf wa'l-Bayān*, 2:249, 234; al-Barrādī, *al-Jawhar al-Muntaqāt*, 122; Gaiser, Shurāt *Legends*, 126–27.
[6] Thus, one of the names of the Khārijites was the Ḥarūriyya.
[7] Gaiser, "North African and Omani Ibāḍī Accounts of the *Munāẓara*," 67–69.
[8] al-Qalhātī, *al-Kashf wa'l-Bayān*, 2:239; al-Barrādī, *al-Jawhar al-Muntaqāt*, 128–29; al-Ṭabarī, *Tārīkh*, 1:3363–66; al-Mubarrad, *al-Kāmil*, 3:117.
[9] Gaiser, Shurāt *Legends*, 95–96; al-Sābiʿī, *al-Khawārij wa'l-Ḥaqīqa al-Ghāʾiba*, 127–28.

after the battle when a relative of some of those killed at Nahrawān, ʿAbd al-Raḥmān b. Muljam, assassinated ʿAlī in the mosque of Kufa. ʿAlī's eldest son, al-Ḥasan b. ʿAlī, wisely decided not to challenge Muʿāwiya, instead agreeing to cede to Muʿāwiya the leadership of the Muslim community with the understanding that upon Muʿāwiya's death, the imamate would devolve upon al-Ḥasan. Muʿāwiya b. Abī Sufyān thus became in 41/661 the first Umayyad caliph, initiating the first dynasty of the early Islamic period. For those who would become the Khārijites (as well as the nascent Shiʿa), this must have seemed a terrible outcome, and "Khārijite" resistance to Muʿāwiya and the Umayyads commenced immediately.

The resistance emanated from the garrison cities of Kufa and Basra. Muʿāwiya himself faced an uprising at Nukhayla, outside of Kufa, in 41/661 from Khārijites who had deserted the battlefield of Nahrawān and sought to redeem themselves. Eliciting the help of the Kufans, the Nukhaylites were slaughtered. Other rebels and small rebellions followed in their wake. From Kufa: Shabīb b. Bajra al-Ashjaʿī, Muʿayn b. ʿAbdullāh al-Muḥāribī, Abū Maryam, Abū Layla, Ḥayyān b. Ẓabyān al-Sulamī, al-Mustawrid b. ʿUllafa, Ziyād b. Kharrāsh al-ʿIjlī, and Muʿādh al-Ṭāʾī. From Basra: Sahm b. Ghālib al-Ḥujaymī, Yazīd b. Mālik al-Bāhalī (known as al-Khaṭīm, "broken nose"), ʿAbbād b. Ḥuṣayn, Ḥāritha b. Ṣakhr al-Qaynī, Qarīb b. Murra al-Azdī, Zuḥḥāf b. Zaḥr al-Ṭāʾī, Ṭawwāf b. ʿAllāq, and Abū Bilāl Mirdās b. Udayya.[10]

What these uprisings have in common is how they are presented in the sources, which emphasize the early *shurāt*'s eagerness to perish fighting tyranny and injustice. In other words, the sources emphasize their eagerness for martyrdom (expressed as *shirāʾ*, exchange of one's life for paradise), as well as the attendant attitude of asceticism that was said to have permeated their group.[11] Several *shurāt* poems express these notions, as with the lines attributed to the *shārī* hero Abū Bilāl Mirdās b. Udayya:

> What do we care if our souls go out [of our bodies];
> What did you do with bodies and limbs [anyway]?
> We look forward to the Gardens [of paradise],
> When our skulls lie in the dust like rotten melons.[12]

This poem aptly captures the spirit of what the stoics and then later Christians called *apathea*, which was an attitude of pious disregard for the things of this life. Indeed, the *shurāt* lived in a world still teeming with Christian monks, Hellenistic philosophers, Jewish doctors, and many

[10] Ibn al-Athīr, *Tārīkh Ibn al-Athīr*, 467 (3:411); al-Balādhurī, *Ansāb al-Ashrāf*, 5:172; Ibn Khayyāṭ, *Tārīkh Khalīfa b. Khayyāṭ*, 128.

[11] Higgins, "Faces of Exchangers," 7–8. [12] ʿAbbās, *Shiʿr al-Khawārij*, 50 (no. 27).

other kinds of religious actors. Thus, the appearance of such themes in their poetry comes as little surprise. Their poetry was a literary creation of late antiquity, comprehensible to a broad spectrum of religious communities of the era.

So too, the sentiment of celibacy, nightly prayer vigils, and fighting tyranny that comes from another poem that was attributed to Abū Bilāl:

> O you who seeks good, the river of tyranny hinders
> Spending nights in vigils, if no man comes to cross.
> I do not deserve to live if I do not abstain from every beautiful woman,
> Until the flash of oppression turns to rain.[13]

This image of the pious *shārī* warrior permeates the literature on and by the early *shurāt*, and it is possible to imagine it accomplishing two things for the later Khārijites who remembered and told their stories. First, the literary image of the pious warrior aligned the early *shurāt* with the paradigmatic Muslim soldiers, the *ghāziyūn* who conquered much of the known world during the Islamic conquests. These first Muslim warriors were themselves depicted in their own literature as pious, ascetic, and filled with the eagerness to fight and to die combating injustice (that is, by insuring the political ascendancy of God's newly purified monotheists, the Muslims). Aligning the image of the first *shurāt* with that of the early *ghaziyūn* was undoubtedly a powerful recruiting tool, as well as a means by which the *shurāt* emphasized the rightness of their cause.

Secondly, the stories of the ascetics and the martyrs created a nexus for establishing communal identity, just as the narratives of the Christian martyrs and ascetics had established in the preceding centuries similar focal points of communal identity for neighboring Christians in Egypt, Syria, and Iraq. It is no accident that the stories of the Khārijite martyrs and ascetics share so much thematic and structural similarities with those of Christians. Christians (along with Jews, Zoroastrians, and others) vastly outnumbered their Muslim conquerors in Islamdom for many centuries. Muslims rubbed shoulders with non-Muslims on a regular basis, both in the cities and outside of them. And when certain groups of Muslims such as the *shurāt* began to coalesce into recognizable groups, they remembered their very special dead, their martyrs and their ascetics, in ways that resembled their Christian neighbors.

Abū Bilāl's narrative is especially illustrative of how the story of a martyr can become the focal point for community. Abū Bilāl was a hero of the early *shurāt* and of later Khārijite groups (as well as the Ibāḍiyya). He was a Ṣiffīn veteran who lived in Basra, and who counseled

[13] ʿAbbās, *Shiʿr al-Khawārij*, 49–50 (no. 26).

moderation (even condemned a few fellow *shurāt* for their excesses). As his poems above show, he was famous for his ascetic piety and his fierce commitment to justice. From Basra, Abū Bilāl was said to have rebelled with forty of his followers. Following an incredible victory at Āsik over 2,000 Umayyad troops, his group was again confronted by an Umayyad army bent on their destruction. According to one version, Abū Bilāl's band was betrayed: after agreeing to cease fighting in order to perform the Friday prayers, the Umayyad army treacherously reneged on their agreement and killed Abū Bilāl and his companions as they prayed.

As with other narratives of the early *shurāt*, Abū Bilāl's revolt became the focal point for *shārī* and later Khārijite identities. His exploits remained some of the most celebrated among *shurāt* poets, and eulogies to Abū Bilāl and his followers were quite common in their poetry. Thus, for example, the early Khārijite poet Kaʿb b. ʿAmīra sang of Abū Bilāl (here using his patronymic name Ibn Ḥudayr):

> God has bought (*sharā*) Ibn Ḥudayr's soul
> and he has embraced the paradises of Firdaws with its many blessings,
> He was made happy by a people with faces like
> The stars in the darkness when their clouds have cleared
> Forward they rode – with Indian swords and with lances
> On charging horses given to running.[14]

Remembering Abū Bilāl by turning his tragic death at the hands of the Umayyads into the victory of martyrdom with its heavenly reward was one means by which *shurāt* poets consolidated group identity and perpetuated resistance to the Umayyads. In fact, so popular was Abū Bilāl that he was claimed by several Khārijite groups, as well as the Ibāḍiyya. Even non-Khārijite groups such as Shiʿites and Muʿtazilites were said to have laid claim to his memory.[15]

Beyond what can be surmised from the poetry of early Khārijites such as Abū Bilāl, the early positions of the Khārijites prove difficult to reconstruct with any reliability. At a bare minimum, the events of Ṣiffīn and then the Umayyad period raised the problem of sinful and erring leaders into relief. In the broadest sense, the Khārijite "answer" was that leaders needed to demonstrate piety, and so long as they did so, the imam could theoretically be any Muslim. This position stood in contradistinction to what later became the standard Sunni and Shiʿi stances on the issue. Sunnis held that the imam should be from Muḥammad's tribal bloc, the Quraysh, and that his transgressions could be tolerated up to a point, while the Shiʿa looked to the family of the Prophet (the *ahl al-bayt*) as

[14] al-Balādhurī, *Ansāb al-Ashrāf*, 5:195; ʿAbbās, *Shiʿr al-Khawārij*, 61 (no. 44).
[15] al-Baghdādī, *al-Farq bayn al-Firaq*, 71–72; al-Mubarrad, *al-Kāmil*, 3:153, 200.

providing the sole legitimate leaders of the Islamic community. The Khārijite stance strongly implied that sinning imams, along with their supporters, needed to be resisted in some fashion, and they could not be regarded as full Muslims. Yet these positions left significant leeway for interpretation. Were all unjust imams to be fought, along with their supporters, at all times? Was the true Muslim community to separate themselves physically from these sinners, and to exclude themselves from their own ranks, or might it be better to practice *taqiyya* (cautionary dissimulation) until the moment was right for revolution? What did it mean to hold non-Khārijites to be less-than-full Muslims?

This last question, in particular, generated numerous interpretations in later years, and became, in part, a means by which later Muslim scholars made sense of the various subgroups of Khārijites. The Muḥakkima reportedly accused ʿAlī of all manner of transgressions, including *kufr* (unbelief). It is far from clear, however, what they may have meant by describing their opponents as "infidels" (*kuffār*). Most Muslim heresiographers (along with later historians who follow them) understand this appellation to mean that the Khārijites held non-Khārijites absolutely beyond the pale of belief.[16] Yet it is possible, following upon ways that early Christians and Jews used accusations of unbelief in their polemical writings, that the Khārijites deployed this term as polemic, implying simply that non-Khārijites had fallen short in a manner resembling (but not actually becoming) infidels.[17] The ambiguities surrounding qurʾanic discussions of sin and unfaithfulness admit these interpretations, making it difficult if not impossible to reconstruct the early interpretations of these ideas among the Khārijites.

Tafrīq, *Takfīr*, and Militancy

Beyond the apparent unity of the early *shurāt* movement, then, significant differences must have developed between various Khārijite groups. These disagreements manifested themselves in the fragmentation of the movement at the outset of the second *fitna* (that is, ca. 64/683). Later Muslim sources refer to this event as the *tafrīq* (splintering), and trace its origin to a specific incident involving Khārijite reactions to the "anti-caliph" Ibn al-Zubayr. Following al-Ṭabarī's version of this event, the death of Yazīd b. Muʿāwiya and ʿAbdullāh b. al-Zubayr's revolt in the Arabian Peninsula (i.e. events of the second *fitna*) brought a contingent of Basran Khārijites

16 al-Ashʿarī, *Maqālāt al-Islamiyyīn*, 1:167; al-Baghdādī, *al-Farq bayn al-Firaq*, 55–56; al-Iṣfarāʾinī, *al-Tabbassur fī'l-Dīn*, 38.
17 Hawting, *The Idea of Idolatry*, 49, 74.

to Ibn al-Zubayr in Makka where they considered throwing in their lot with him against the Umayyads.[18] However, they found that Ibn al-Zubayr refused to dissociate himself from ʿUthmān, and so they decided not to support him, and furthermore to declare themselves dissociated from him. Those present were said to have differed amongst themselves regarding the "status" of sinners (meaning, in this case, Ibn al-Zubayr). Nāfiʿ b. al-Azraq (eponym of Azāriqa/Azraqites) took the most extreme stance when he held the sinner to be unfaithful in the same fashion as a polytheist. This position implied that sinners and non-Khārijites had to be fought in the same fashion as those in the Prophet Muḥammad's era. ʿAbdullāh b. Ibāḍ (eponym of the Ibāḍiyya) condemned Ibn al-Azraq for taking this stance, considering it too extreme, while ʿAbdullāh b. Ṣaffār (the name differs depending on the version) condemned them both, meaning that he criticized Ibn al-Azraq for going too far and Ibn Ibāḍ for not going far enough. In this way, according to the *tafrīq* narrative, the Azraqites, Ibāḍiyya, and Ṣufriyya were established.

The *tafrīq* narrative remains a popular anecdote, even today. However, it is not likely to be based in historical fact. First, the distinctions between the groups are a bit too neatly drawn, and they do not match other narratives of these groups' founding (especially what can be surmised about the founding of the Ibāḍiyya). Second, a strong color symbolism undergirds the story whereby the most extreme stance is associated with blue (al-Azraq), the most moderate with white (al-Abyaḍ), and the moderate position with yellow (al-Aṣfar).[19] Such color symbolism could be imagined to function in a number of ways. For example, it could be a conceptual tool that simplified the differences between the three main "Khārijite" subsects. However, it likely does not reflect history as it unfolded, but rather the craft of good storytelling.

Yet the *tafrīq* anecdote offers insight of another kind. More often than not it seems that more militant sectarian groups achieve a kind of definition and a sense of group mission, and thus coherence as a sub-*firqa*, before those who adopt moderate/quietist stances. In other words, militants, because they are militant, tend to organize themselves into recognizable groups and get noticed before the moderates (who tend to hide themselves better). And it is true that the militant Khārijite subsects, namely, the Azāriqa, Najadāt, and their many offshoots, do seem to

[18] al-Ṭabarī, *Tārīkh*, 2:516–20.
[19] On the other hand, there are references to the Ṣufriyya having "yellowed faces" (see al-Ṭabarī, *Tārīkh*, 2:881; Ibn ʿAbd Rabbih, *al-ʿIqd al-Farīd*, 1:285, 2:369). Fierro argues that these references to the yellow faces of the Ṣufriyya may also have some connection to the south Arabian practice of physically dyeing the face yellow. See Fierro, "Al-Aṣfar Again," 204ff.

have commenced their activities around the time of the second *fitna* (i.e. ca. 63–79/683–98), and to have achieved a sense of self-definition around that time. By contrast, those moderate Khārijites (who survived for far longer and about whom there is much to say) do not appear to have achieved doctrinal or practical coherence until decades later. Yet equally true is how militants, also because of their militancy, tend to attract the *wrong kind* of attention: their violence often loses them the support of the local population and causes governments to send their armies against them. Militant movements, therefore, tend to be relatively short-lived in comparison to the relatively longer lasting quietist/moderate movements. This was also true of the Khārijites.

As the first militants to emerge from the Basran Khārijite milieu, the Azāriqa remain, perhaps, the most notorious. Following Nāfiʿ b. al-Azraq, the Azraqite answer to the question of who was the rightful leader remained the same as the other Khārijites, namely, that the leader could be any pious Muslim. However, their answer to what they should do in the face of illegitimate leaders and what was to be their stance vis. those who do not join them was radically different. To the Azraqites, theirs was a narrative of a righteous remnant, the last band of true Muslims surrounded by the unfaithful. In such a situation, their solution was to fight the unfaithful wherever and whenever they encountered them, and when not fighting to separate from the rest of Islamic (meaning to them, non-Islamic) society. They were to dissociate themselves from (*barāʾū min*) those who did not fight (i.e. the "sit-outers" [*al-qaʿada*] who refrained from battle), or who practiced *taqiyya* in either word or deed.[20] Although nothing aside from poetry and coins survives from the Azraqites themselves, reports about them in the histories and heresiographies paint a more or less consistent picture of them. For example, the second/eighth-century Ibāḍī heresiographer Sālim b. Dhakwān censors them for classifying their *qawm* (i.e. non-Khārijī Muslims) as idolaters (*ʿabadat al-awthān*), and for subsequently severing inheritance relations and refusing to intermarry with them or to grant them protection. He reports that they deemed it permissible to enslave their *qawm*, take their women and property as spoils, kill their children, and indiscriminately slaughter them (*istiʿrāḍuhum*).[21] Ibn Dhakwān also mentions a "test" (*miḥna* – but not to be confused with the historical event also known as the *miḥna*) administered to non-Azraqīs who wished to join their camp, and that they anathematized those who did

[20] al-Mubarrad, *al-Kāmil*, 3:200; Ibn Ḥazm, *al-Fiṣal*, 3:125.

[21] Accusations of *istiʿrāḍ* bear a strong whiff of polemic, but it is also true that this practice dovetails with the belief that those not with a group remain against them.

not fight (*al-qaʿada*), declaring their lives and property licit, and refusing to associate or even to pray for forgiveness for them.[22]

Much of what Ibn Dhakwān says about the Azāriqa finds its counterpart in the writings of the Islamic heresiographer al-Ashʿarī, who states that the Azraqites anathematized as unfaithful (*kuffār*) all Muslims who did not emigrate (make the *hijra*) to their camp. He claims that they administered an examination (*miḥna*) of those who came to them. When fighting, they allowed the killing of the women and children of their enemies (i.e. of those they considered polytheists, *mushrikūn*), believing that these were also in hell.[23] The Azāriqa thus appear in the pages of Muslim history as a stringent group, holding that once a person had sinned (as ʿUthmān, ʿAlī, or Ibn al-Zubayr had done) or refused to join the true Muslims, they stopped being Muslim altogether and became a legitimate target of violence. *Kufr*, for the Azraqites, equated to absolute nonbelief, the equivalent even of idolatry (*shirk*). Important to remember is that these Azraqite stances were considered excessive by other Khārijites, and also by the Ibāḍiyya.[24] Thus, the eponymous founder of another early militant Khārijite group, Najda b. ʿĀmir, was said to have written to Nāfiʿ b. al-Azraq in a letter: "You strayed away from the right path, and declared those whom God excused in His Book for staying at home to be unfaithful on account of their weakness."[25]

Thus, central to the disagreements among these groups was the distinctive Khārijite and Ibāḍī doctrines concerning faithfulness and its absence. One of the more (perhaps the most) unique Khārijite and Ibāḍī principle is that someone who does not profess Khārijism or Ibāḍism cannot be considered a full Muslim. They remained a less-than-full Muslim as a kind of unfaithful person. To use the actual terminology of the era, they were *kuffār* (sing. *kāfir*), the Latin *infidelis* (infidel) meaning literally someone who is not faithful, but closer in linguistic meaning to the Latin *ingratus* (ingrate), someone who is not grateful for God's blessings. The act of designating a person a *kāfir* is known as *takfīr*, a term and later doctrine that more and more came to be synonymous with the Khārijites (despite the fact that many non-Khārijites also practiced *takfīr*).[26] As with much of what the Azraqites were said to profess, the Azraqite position on *kufr* (that is, that the *kāfir* clearly and definitively stopped being a Muslim altogether) along with the kind of militancy

[22] Crone and Zimmerman, *The Epistle of Sālim Ibn Dhakwān*, 100–05.
[23] al-Ashʿarī, *Maqālāt al-Islāmiyyīn*, 1:168–74.
[24] Ibn ʿAbd Rabbih, *al-ʿIqd al-Farīd*, 2:373; see also Crone and Zimmerman, *Epistle of Sālim Ibn Dhakwān*, 100–03.
[25] al-Mubarrad, *al-Kāmil*, 3:201.
[26] As, for example, the early Zaydiyya: see Haider, *Origins of the Shīʿa*, 18.

toward non-Azraqites that this stance implied represented the most extreme position on the matter. It was rejected as such by many if not most other Khārijite groups, along with the Ibāḍīs. It is unfortunate that many scholars, along with many Muslims, assume that the Azraqite interpretation of *takfīr* is typical of the Khārijites as a whole.[27]

As might be expected, these extreme positions resulted in limited popular support among the wider Muslim community, as well as the massive counter-responses from the Umayyads that resulted in the virtual extinction of these militants within a relatively short period of time. Thus, the Azāriqa did not last that long: about fourteen or fifteen years. Their eponym Nāfiʿ b. al-Azraq was killed in the Azraqites' first battle at Dūlāb, in 65/685, and he was followed by several other leaders. One of these, Qaṭarī b. al-Fujāʾa, an orator and poet, led the group into mountains east of Basra. There the group minted coins (see e.g. Figure 3.1), itself an indicator that the Azraqites were perhaps not as militantly separatist as we are led to believe. In the end, the Umayyad general (and later hero of the Ibāḍiyya) al-Muhallab b. Abī Ṣufra relentlessly hunted them down,

Figure 3.1 Arab-Sāsānian-style coin of the Azraqite Khārijite Qaṭarī b. al-Fujāʾa.
Photograph by Daniel Kariko.

[27] The most egregious scholarly example is Dabashi, who dubs the Azraqites "the representation of the original Kharijite position" (*Authority in Islam*, 125).

sowed dissention in their ranks by splitting the Arabs from the non-Arabs, and finally eliminated them.

A related group, known as the Najadāt or Najdiyya after their founder, Najda b. ʿĀmir (d. 73/692, with many variations of his name), was founded when Najda and his followers broke with Nāfiʿ b. al-Azraq and the Azraqites over the status of those who do not fight (*qaʿad/quʿūd*) and other questions. For example, the Najdites reportedly allowed the practice of *taqiyya* and tolerated those who refused combat, though Najda was said to have preferred those who fought.[28] They also reportedly considered it lawful to marry and eat the meat of non-Khārijites, even though they considered them akin to idol worshippers (*ʿabadat al-awthān*).[29] On the question of sinners, Najda was said to have held that those who persist in minor sins became unbelievers qua polytheists (*mushrikūn*), but that a Muslim (meaning Khārijite Muslim) who commits a major sin, but then repents, remains a Muslim. Those who did not join the Najdite camp were considered "hypocrites" (*munāfiqūn*), a usage which suggests that they were not absolutely anathematized.[30] Indeed, Ibn Dhakwān claims that the Najdites made those among them who refused to fight admit to hypocrisy, which granted them safety, but that they would declare an infidel those who would not admit to it.[31] Moreover, Najda was said to have excused sins committed in ignorance, though this was not universally held by all Najdites and led to some friction in the group. Thus, while the Najdites count among the militant Khārijites due to their belief that those who do not join them from the greater Muslim community became unbelievers (with a status equivalent to the polytheists), Najda did apparently moderate some of the more stringent stances of the Azāriqa.

It is possible that his moderated stances led to the limited successes of the Najdites in the Arabian Peninsula during the second *fitna*: as Najda was a member of the Ḥanīfa tribe, he led his band into the Arabian Peninsula, where he rallied the Banū Ḥanīfa to his cause and enjoyed somewhat widespread success during the course of the second *fitna*. In essence, the Najdites came to control the Arabian countryside while Ibn al-Zubayr controlled the cities (esp. Makka and Madina). Toward the end of the second *fitna*, however, fatal divisions developed within the group. Two prominent Najdites, ʿAṭiyya b. al-Aswad (d. 78–79/698–99) and Abū Fudayk (d. 73/693) broke from Najda, and Abū Fudayk later killed him. Abū Fudayk's group was said to have stayed in the Arabian Peninsula, while those who followed ʿAṭiyya went east into the Iranian

[28] al-Shahrastānī, *al-Milal wa'l-Niḥal*, 123–24; al-Baghdādī, *al-Farq bayn al-Firaq*, 67–70.

[29] Crone and Zimmerman, *The Epistle of Sālim Ibn Dhakwān*, 104–11.

[30] al-Ashʿarī, *Maqālāt al-Islāmiyyīn*, 1:174–75; Ibn Ḥazm, *al-Faṣl*, 3:125; Van Ess, *Theology and Society*, 2:228.

[31] Crone and Zimmerman, *The Epistle of Sālim Ibn Dhakwān*, 110–11.

highlands where they broke into several small subgroups, notably the ʿAṭawiyya, from whom split the ʿAjārida with its many purported subsects.[32] According to al-Ashʿarī these were the Maymūniyya, Khalafiyya, Ḥamziyya, Shuʿaybiyya, Ṣaltiyya, Khāzimiyya, and Thaʿāliba;[33] the hereiographer al-Shahrastānī adds the Aṭrāfiyya.[34] What distinguishes many of these subgroups is their stance toward the status of children. The ʿAjārida reportedly excluded them from Islam until they reached maturity and could formally accept it,[35] while the subsects of the ʿAjārida tended to accord them a more neutral stance until puberty.[36] Note that there is great confusion regarding these subsects as well as their purported offshoots, most of whom were defeated in the same series of campaigns that rid Fārs and Kirmān of the Azāriqa.[37] Some clearly survived, however, as the Ḥamziyya Khārijites led a revolt in southern Khurāsān against the ʿAbbāsids from 179/795 until 195/810.[38] So too, remnants of the original Najdites in the peninsula were said to have persisted up to the fifth/eleventh century (reportedly in Bahrain), and to have come to the position that the imamate was optional due to the fact that every person had equal capacity to reach the relevant conclusions in religious matters (that is, to practice *ijtihād*).[39] Beyond the sixth/twelfth century, nothing is recorded of the militant Khārijites, none of whom survived.

"Militant" or "activist" Khārijites, then, advocated fighting unrighteous rulers and their supports (even passive supporters) as the only means to establish the kind of just social order advocated by God in the Qurʾan and through His Prophet. This very same militancy, however, resulted in limited popular support for their movements, as well as the counter-responses from the Umayyads that resulted in their virtual extinction within a relatively short period of time.

"Quietist/Moderate" Khārijites and the Emergence of the Ibāḍiyya

Less militant Khārijites fared better in the long term, but they do not appear to have achieved doctrinal or practical coherence until decades after their militant counterparts. Like the militants, the moderates also

32 Van Ess, *Theology and Society*, 2:574–76.
33 al-Ashʿarī, *Maqālāt al-Islāmiyyīn*, 1:177–83.
34 al-Shahrastānī, *al-Milal wa'l-Niḥal*, 130–31.
35 al-Ashʿarī, *Maqālāt al-Islāmiyyīn*, 1:128; Ibn Ḥazm, *al-Faṣl*, 3:126–27; Van Ess, *Theology and Society*, 1:132.
36 al-Ashʿarī, *Maqālāt al-Islāmiyyīn*, 1:129ff; Van Ess, *Theology and Society*, 2:576ff.
37 Madelung, *Religious Trends in Early Islamic Iran*, 58–59.
38 Van Ess, *Theology and Society*, 2:584–88.
39 Crone, "A Statement by the Najdiyya Khārijites," 67.

disapproved of tyrannical and sinful imams and looked to any competent, pious coreligionist as theoretically qualified to replace them. However, whereas the militants advocated separatism and warfare as the primary (if not the only) means to resist sinning imams and their followers, rejecting in the process all nonmilitant Khārijites as non-Muslims, the moderates proved more practical on these counts. In general, the moderates seem to have accepted (even advocated) secrecy over physical separatism, and to have rejected (on the whole, but with some notable exceptions) the reckless pursuit of martyrdom in favor of inconspicuously building the institutions and support necessary for successful resistance (which, in turn, allowed the moderates to mount more traditional military campaigns). Furthermore, although they treated non-Khārijites as less-than-full Muslims, they did not count them as outright polytheists (*mushrikūn*). This last point meant that moderates were more willing to interact with non-Khārijites than their militant counterparts, a fact that undoubtedly contributed (especially in the case of the Ibāḍiyya) to their long-term survival as Khārijite subgroups.

The terms "quietist" or "moderate," however, can be misleading, and it is important before proceeding further to understand the potential misunderstandings of them. First, it is better to think of "moderate/quietist" and "militant" Khārijism not as two ends of a spectrum, but as a kind of mass, out of which militant offshoots emerge first, leaving the rest to coalesce into the various forms of quietist Khārijism that developed after the second *fitna*. Many if not most of the recorded Khārijite groups (insofar as we can reconstruct their stances) would actually display traits of both militancy and moderation. As an example, the Najdite propensity to consider their enemies as polytheists would make them a "militant" offshoot, but their qualified acceptance of *taqiyya* would push them further toward the "quietist" center. Another early Khārijite subsect, the Bayhasiyya, are harder to locate. Reports on the Bayhasiyya indicate that although they held non-Khārijī Muslims to be unbelievers (that is, *kuffār*) and also encouraged separation from them, they also were said to have nevertheless considered it permissible to live amongst them and to intermarry with and inherit from them.[40] Where, then, to place the Bayhasiyya? They seem to occupy many places.

Second, the terms "quietist" or "moderate" might be taken to imply that groups so labeled gave up on the notion of fighting altogether. However, these terms should not imply the practice of pacifism, which neither the Khārijites nor the later Ibāḍiyya accepted. Rather, the "quietists" and "moderates" allowed for *taqiyya*, waiting amidst the wider non-Khārijite population until the circumstances were right for armed action (thus their

[40] al-Shahrastānī, *Kitāb al-Milal wa'l-Niḥal*, 126–27; Crone and Zimmerman, *The Epistle of Sālim Ibn Dhakwān*, 214; Van Ess, *Theology and Society*, 2:594–600.

acceptance of those "sitting out" the fight). Relatedly, these groups could be defined by their rejection of obligatory emigration (*hijra*) to a separate "camp." Theirs was often a separation within the midst of society, a stance that the Ibāḍiyya would refine with great precision. Given these caveats, it is possible to stake out certain traits that make up the "quietist" or "moderate" wing of the Khārijites, and to locate the Ibāḍiyya (and Ṣufriyya) in relation to them. Quietists/moderates, then, tended not to consider non-Khārijites/non-Ibāḍīs as polytheists (*mushrikūn*) proper, but rather as less-than-full Muslims (*kuffār* or *munāfiqūn*) of some kind. In practice, this meant that moderates eschewed physical separation, preferring secrecy, and they remained more willing to treat non-Khārijites as they would fellow Muslims (i.e. to allow intermarriage, inheritance, eating the meat that they prepared, etc.).

For the Ibāḍiyya, it is possible to paint a more precise picture of their thought. As with other groups considered to fall under the Khārijite branch of Islam, the particularly Ibāḍī answers to the questions of what should be done in the face of illegitimate leaders, as well as the status of those who did not join the movement, distinguished the Ibāḍiyya as a unique group. While eschewing association with the Khārijites, Ibāḍīs nevertheless accepted the central premise shared by other Khārijite groups that the leader of the Muslim community could be any pious Muslim. In fact, the Ibāḍiyya have had several imams throughout the centuries of their existence, the most recent being the Omani imam Ghālib b. ʿAlī (imam until 1959, d. 2009). In general, the Ibāḍiyya held that fighting should only be pursued if there was a reasonable chance of success (they did, however, make limited provisions for the practice of revolt, known as *shirāʾ*, by a select group). Otherwise, the Ibāḍiyya had recourse to the practices of *taqiyya* and secrecy (*kitmān*).

Regarding non-Ibāḍī Muslims, the Ibāḍiyya held them to be unfaithful (*kuffār*), but distinguished their particular type of unfaithfulness from that of polytheism. There were, in other words, different degrees of unfaithfulness. First, there was polytheism proper (*kufr shirk*), which applied only to those who worshipped a multitude of gods. Next, there was the *kufr* of other monotheistic communities (Zoroastrians, Jews, Christians), which was an unfaithfulness that involved rejecting the prophecy of Muḥammad. Finally, there was the *kufr* of ungratefulness or hypocrisy (*kufr al-niʿma/kufr nifāq*), which is how various Ibāḍīs of different ages described the unfaithfulness of non-Ibāḍī Muslims.[41] As the category

[41] Although I have used the term "non-Ibāḍī Muslims" as a way to avoid confusion, this is not how Ibāḍīs theology treats non-Ibāḍīs: Ibāḍīs consider non-Ibāḍīs to be, technically, non-Muslims or, as I prefer, less-than-full Muslims.

closest to the Ibāḍiyya themselves, those guilty of *kufr al-niʿma/kufr nifāq* enjoyed virtually all the legal protections and permissions granted to Ibāḍīs. Ibāḍīs could intermarry with them, inherit from them, eat the meat that they slaughtered, and honor contracts with them. During times of peace non-Ibāḍī Muslims enjoyed the protection of the Ibāḍīs, while during a time of war they should be first summoned to accept the truth before they could be fought. At no time could their property be taken, nor could their wives and offspring be killed or treated as spoils, nor could non-Ibāḍīs be assassinated or killed in secret.[42] The specifics of these positions required in some cases several decades to articulate, and only in the case of the Ibāḍiyya do scholars possess a more or less reliable record of that process. Nevertheless, these non-Ibāḍī Muslims were not considered full Muslims, and Ibāḍīs were to formally maintain an attitude of dissociation (*barāʾa*) with them, just as they were to hold other Ibāḍīs in formal association, called *walāya*, and to abstain from adopting a position (that is, to practice *wuqūf*) if the status of a person was unknown.

Of the other distinguishing features of Ibāḍism one of the most distinctive remains their acceptance of imams that are neither from the tribe of Quraysh nor from the family of the Prophet Muḥammad. In addition, Ibāḍīs recognize different kinds of imams for different kinds of situations that their community might face. Thus, the *imām al-ẓuhūr* (manifest imam) is an ideal type of leader who rules when Ibāḍīs can openly practice their particular form of Islam.[43] If, however, the conditions for the imamate were not optimal, the imamate may go into abeyance (as is the case in North Africa since the early fourth/tenth century), or Ibāḍīs may choose to elect one of several types of provisional imams. They may, for example, establish a temporary imam for the purposes of defense, known as the *mudāfiʿī/difāʿī* imam (sometimes given as *al-imām ʿalā al-difāʿ*). Omani Ibāḍī literature also speaks of "weak" (*ḍaʿīf*) imams who rule in conjunction with the religious scholars. Alternately, Ibāḍīs may establish an imam, known as the *imām al-shārī* (the imam of "exchange"), whose purpose was to lead volunteer soldiers (known as *shurāt*, "exchangers") in instituting an Ibāḍī polity. This imam and his soldiers were to be willing to "exchange" their lives (that is, martyr themselves) to establish Ibāḍism. During conditions of concealment (*kitmān*) when the imamate ceased to exist, Omani literature allowed for a provisory (*muḥtasib*) imam, who was actually a religious scholar who advised the community until a proper imam could be established. North African imamate theories postulate the

[42] Crone and Zimmerman, *The Epistle of Sālim Ibn Dhakwān*, 132–41; on the term *kufr al-niʿma* (*kufr* of ingratitude), see 200.
[43] Gaiser, *Muslims, Scholars, Soldiers*, 212ff.

idea of an *imām al-kitmān* (imam [during the condition] of concealment) but this feature of the imamate tradition seems theoretical, with its main purpose being to rationalize a continuous imamate tradition from the Prophet Muḥammad to the first North African dynasty of Ibāḍīs, the Rustumids. In the state of *kitmān*, Ibāḍīs held that most *ḥudūd* punishments go into abeyance (because there is no imam to properly administer them), and that Friday prayers should be held only in cities in which justice prevails (other opinions on the status of Friday prayers exist). Additionally, they hold that the duties of *walāya* and *barāʾa* become suspended during *kitmān*. Modern iterations of Ibāḍī imamate theory harmonize the various types of imams that could be found in medieval North African and Omani literature into four imam-types: the *imām al-ẓuhūr*, *imām al-kitmān*, *imām al-difāʿī*, and the *imām al-shārī*.[44]

Several theological and legal tenets also distinguish the Ibāḍiyya from their Muslim counterparts. Their conviction that non-Ibāḍīs are not full Muslims (they are technically a kind of *kuffār*, and thus *zakāt* should not be given to them), but are nevertheless treated as nearly Muslims, distinguished the Ibāḍiyya from other more militant Khārijite groups. Ibāḍīs also hold, for example, that reward and punishment are eternal in the afterlife and that there will be no intercession. On the question of free will vs. determination, some Ibāḍīs held an initial interest in limited free will (*qadar*), but now Ibāḍīs follow the more common Sunni, specifically Ashʿarite, position of determinism. Unlike Ashʿarites, however, Ibāḍīs offer no anthropomorphic descriptions of God, use reason as a supplement to revelation (and they formally state that they are doing this), and hold to the unity of God's essence and attributes. They also hold the Qurʾan to be the created speech of God (though this was also a contested position in early Oman).

In the realm of Islamic law, there are several positions (too many to list) that distinguish the Ibāḍiyya. As the preparation for and performance of the ritual prayers (*ṣalāt*) has long been a means by which Muslims actually recognize differences between themselves, some specifically Ibāḍī rulings on prayer are here offered as examples: along with many Shiʿa the Ibāḍiyya reject the notion of "wiping over the sandals/shoes" as part of the ablutions before prayers; uniquely, at noon and afternoon prayers only the opening chapter of the Qurʾan (*fātiḥa*) is recited; Ibāḍīs pray with their arms at their sides (like many Shiʿa and some Mālikī Sunnis); they offer no "amen" (*āmīn*) after the *fātiḥa*; nor do they curse the enemies of Islam (called *qunūt*) in the predawn prayer; and a shortened type of prayer is required during journeys.

[44] Ennami, *Studies in Ibadhism*, 229–38.

When attempting to describe how this history and indeed, the history of the quietists in general, came about, several difficulties arise. For example, the origins of quietist groups like the Ibāḍiyya and Ṣufriyya are much harder to determine than their militant counterparts. Several kinds of origins narratives can be found amidst the various sources available to the researcher. To take the example of the so-called Ṣufriyya Khārijites, al-Ṭabarī's *tafrīq* narrative ascribes their origin to ʿAbdullāh b. Ṣaffār whose stance vis-à-vis Ibn al-Zubayr positioned him in relation to Nāfiʿ's Azraqites and Ibn Ibāḍ's Ibāḍiyya. However, one early version of the *tafrīq* leaves out altogether both the Ṣufriyya and the Ibāḍiyya from its account of the event, substituting in their places the Bayhasiyya.[45] This would seem to complicate the orderly narrative that is presented elsewhere in the sources. Moreover, al-Shahrastānī's account of the Ṣufriyya gives Ziyād b. al-Aṣfar as the name of their founder (five more versions of his name appear in different sources), but provides only a list of doctrines ascribed to him without providing an origin narrative.[46] The early Ibāḍī heresiographer Ibn Dhakwān does not mention the Ṣufriyya at all. In terms of origins narratives, then, the case of the Ṣufriyya Khārijites is muddled, to say the least.

Lewinstein proposes a solution to the confusion reigning in accounts of the Ṣufriyya. He argues that they were a group projected back in time, imagined after the Ibāḍiyya had come into existence for the purpose of accommodating the quietist figures, doctrines, and rebellions that could not be readily classified as Ibāḍī or as some other form of early quietist Khārijism.[47] In other words, as the different pockets of undefined quietists developed into distinct groups the "leftovers" who had not found a classification were back-projected into the category "Ṣufriyya." This is the reason for the lack of a coherent founding narrative (there wasn't one), as well as the instability of the group's eponym (he was imagined to some degree). This does not mean that there were no groups of quietist Khārijites who could later be identified as Ṣufrī. The Midrārid dynasty of Sijilmāsa (in present-day Morocco) is one example of a distinct Ṣufrī Khārijite group in North Africa, and an aspect of what made them distinct involved association with certain tribal groups in North Africa. Likewise, several later Khārijite rebellions in northern Iraq and Armenia seem to be "Ṣufrī" insofar as they were not Ibāḍī and involved groups of Arabs not associated with the Ibāḍīs. Lewinstein's point is that these groups, and other figures identified as "Ṣufrī" (such as the Iraqi rebels Ṣāliḥ b. al-Muṣṣariḥ, Shabīb

[45] Ibn Khayyāṭ, *Tārīkh Khalīfa b. Khayyāṭ*, 157.
[46] al-Shahrastānī, *Kitāb al-Milal wa'l-Niḥal*, 138; on the various names of the Ṣufrī founder, see Lewinstein, "Making and Unmaking a Sect," 79.
[47] Lewinstein, "Making and Unmaking a Sect," 93–96.

b. Yazīd, and Daḥḥāk b. Qays), can only be identified as such retrospectively, and in relation to other quietists (mainly the Ibāḍiyya) who were simultaneously achieving a more reified kind of self-definition. For this reason, there is significant overlap in the early periods between those later identified as "Ṣufrī" and Ibāḍī. Both, for example, are associated with Abū Bilāl and the poet ʿImrān b. Ḥaṭṭān, and some Ibāḍīs were said to have supported Ṣāliḥ b. Muṣarriḥ's rebellion in Iraq. The real difference between the two groups, in fact, may have been their emerging tribal affiliations. In Iraq the Ibāḍīs more and more recruited from the southern Arabian tribes of Kinda and Azd while those labeled Ṣufrī are associated with the north Arabian tribes of Rabīʿa (such as the Banū Shaybān b. Bakr).

In Iraq, so-called Ṣufrī Khārijite uprisings included that of the ascetic preacher Ṣāliḥ b. Muṣarriḥ al-Tamīmī in northern Mesopotamia in 76/695, which was taken up after Ṣāliḥ's death by Shabīb b. Yazīd al-Shaybānī. Shabīb's rebellion (more an extended tear through Iraq) included taking Kufa for a brief period. It was eventually put down by the Umayyads. Ṣufrī Khārijism, with its ties to the north Arabian tribes in northern Iraq and Azerbayjān, continued: Shawdhab (Bisṭām) al-Yashkūrī rose in 100–01/718–20 and was killed; Buhlūl b. Bishr (near Mawṣil) and Shabīb b. Yazīd's son al-Ṣaḥārī (near Jabbul) rose in 119/737 and were killed. A larger Ṣufrī rebellion erupted in 126/744 following the murder of the Umayyad caliph al-Walīd II. Initially led by Saʿīd b. Bahdal al-Shaybānī and then after Ibn Bahdal's death by al-Ḍaḥḥāk b. Qays al-Shaybānī (whose followers were sometimes counted a separate sect called al-Ḍaḥḥākiyya) and swelled by large groups of Ṣufriyya who had previously operated in Armenia and Azerbayjān, al-Ḍaḥḥāk's army seized Kufa and Wāsiṭ (causing the Umayyad governor to surrender and pledge allegiance to al-Ḍaḥḥāk). Al-Ḍaḥḥāk was killed fighting Marwān II in 128/746. The remaining Ṣufriyya were chased out of Mawṣil, briefly backed the ʿAlīd rebel ʿAbdullāh b. Muʿāwiya, and met their end in Oman fighting the Ibāḍī-backed army of al-Julandā b. Masʿūd in 134/751–52. Ṣufrī rebellions in northern Iraq continued into the early fourth/tenth century. Most were short-lived affairs that ended with the death/martyrdom of the rebels. A few larger rebellions gave the ʿAbbāsids cause for concern, such as that of al- Walīd b. Ṭarīf al-Taghlībī (in 178–79/794–96) who alarmed the caliph Hārūn al-Rashīd. Likewise, Musāwir b. ʿAbd al-Ḥamīd al- Bajalī (252–63/866–77) and Hārūn b. ʿAbdullāh al-Bajalī (267–83/880–96) both seized control of large swaths of territory in northern Mesopotamia.

In North Africa, uprisings labeled "Ṣufrī" and later "Ibāḍī" wrested much of western North Africa away from the Umayyads in the 120s/740s (these revolts even spilled over into the Iberian Peninsula). By 122/739–40 the emerging Ṣufriyya under Mayrasa al-Maghṭarī had taken Tangiers. Maysara, however, was killed by his own followers, and replaced by Khālid b. Ḥamīd al-Zanatī who led the fracturing coalition to two victories against the Umayyads in 123/740. However, by 124/742, the Umayyads had pushed these groups away from Qayrawān, inflicting defeats on them in two other decisive battles. Ṣufrī uprisings (or, uprisings later identified as Ṣufrī in the sources) again harassed the Umayyads in the west of Tūnis in 130/748, but after the Ibāḍī imam Abū al-Khaṭṭāb seized Ifrīqiya in 141/758–59, to be followed by ʿAbbāsid consolidation of their strength in Ifrīqiya, the Ṣufriyya under the leadership of Abū Qurra established themselves at Tilimsān (Tlemcen). Unable to defeat the ʿAbbāsids at Ṭubna in 148/765, the Ṣufrīs found themselves more and more squeezed out of the Tilimsān region by the expanding Idrīsid state, as well as by the ʿAbbāsids. They migrated again to the region of Tāfilalt, where in 140/757 the Ṣufrī scholar Abū al-Qāsim Samghū b. Wāsūl had earlier founded the city of Sijilmāsa. Although the Ṣufrīs had recognized a black man named ʿĪsā b. Mazyad as their leader, in the 150s/770s this ʿĪsā was deposed (and reportedly tortured and killed for some sort of transgression) and Samghū assumed control of the city. From his line came the Ṣufrī Midrārid leaders, who governed the city of Sijilmāsa into the mid-fourth/tenth century.[48] By the end of the Midrārid dynasty, Ṣufrī Khārijism seems to have waned, to disappear finally with the rise of the Fāṭimids.

The only enduring remnant from the constellation of groups that emerged out of the Muḥakkima and *shurāt* movements is the Ibāḍiyya. Their survival to the present day in North and East Africa, as well as in Oman, has resulted in the preservation of a truly impressive corpus of Ibāḍī materials. Consequently, several works discuss their origins and development and provide the researcher with a cornucopia of material. It is therefore possible to investigate the origins and history of the Ibāḍiyya in a way that is not possible with other quietist Khārijites, such as the Ṣufriyya. However, as with other groups, there is some divergence between how the group itself narrates its origins and development, and what some scholars have proposed. Modern Ibāḍī articulations of their earliest history trace their origins to the figure of Jābir b. Zayd, a famous legal scholar, Successor to the first generation of Muslims, and *ḥadīth* transmitter (he is considered a *ḥadith* transmitter by Sunnis also).[49] Ibāḍī sources claim that he hailed from Firq, near Nizwa, Oman,

48 On the Midrārids, see the outstanding article by Love, "The Sufris of Sijilmasa," 173–88.
49 al-Dhahabī, *Kitāb Tadhkirat al-Ḥuffāẓ*, 1:72.

moved with his family to Basra, and eventually returned to Firq, where he died.[50] He was said to have studied under the early scholar ʿAbdullāh b. ʿAbbās (d. 67/687), and to have heard *ḥadīth* from the Prophet's youngest wife, ʿĀʾisha bt. Abī Bakr (d. 58/678). In Basra in the late first/sixth and early second/seventh centuries, Jābir was said to have organized the quietists and trained disciples, including Abū ʿUbayda Muslim b. Abī Karīma, whom Ibāḍīs consider an important early leader and imam, as well as their eponymous founder, ʿAbdullāh b. Ibāḍ, who is considered a kind of lieutenant to Jābir b. Zayd.[51] Ibāḍīs attribute some of the more important institutions of their early period to Jābir's pupil Abū ʿUbayda and his leadership. For example, to Abū ʿUbayda they attribute the treasury, *bayt al-māl*, which was organized during this time, as well as the training of missionaries (called *ḥamalāt al-ʿilm*, carriers of knowledge).[52] These *ḥamalāt al-ʿilm* were said to have spread Ibāḍī teachings to every corner of the Islamic world, and achieved the success in North Africa and Arabian Peninsula that would later result in the establishment of Ibāḍī imamates in these locations. After Abū ʿUbayda, the Ibāḍiyya looked to succeeding imams in Basra, notably al-Rabīʿ b. Ḥabīb al-Farāhīdī (d. ca. 175/791). To him is credited the main collection of Ibāḍī *ḥadīth*, known as *al-Jāmiʿ al-ṣaḥīḥ* (*The Sound Collection*). Such is the story of Ibāḍī origins as modern Ibāḍīs might tell it.

Scholarly reevaluations of this origin narrative have pointed out some difficulties with it. Jābir b. Zayd seems not to have been an Ibāḍī per se, but probably an early sympathizer with (and possibly an important authority for) the early quietist community of Basra. Of ʿAbdullāh b. Ibāḍ there is wildly contradictory information, to the point that scholars can claim to know almost nothing of the eponym of the group (even as late as the fifth/eleventh century the Iberian scholar Ibn Ḥazm writes that even the Ibāḍīs of al-Andalus did not know of Ibn Ibāḍ, their alleged founder). Lastly, Abū ʿUbayda seems not to have been an imam proper, but an important early scholar, enjoying the company of several other important scholars (such as Ḥājib al-Ṭāʾī) without being the leader of them. Moreover, while Ibāḍīs undoubtedly began training and sending out missionaries possibly as early as the 100s/720s, there is no evidence

[50] al-Shammākhī, *Kitāb al-Siyar*, 1:182ff; al-Darjīnī, *Kitāb Ṭabaqāt al-Mashāyikh bi'l-Maghrib*, 2:205ff.

[51] al-Shammākhī, *Kitāb al-Siyar*, 1:189; al-Darjīnī, *Kitāb Ṭabaqāt al-Mashāyikh bi'l-Maghrib*, 2:214; Ennami, *Studies in Ibadhism*, 24–29.

[52] al-Shammākhī, *Kitāb al-Siyar*, 1:196ff.; al-Darjīnī, *Kitāb Ṭabaqāt al-Mashāyikh bi'l-Maghrib*, 2:238ff.; Ennami, *Studies in Ibadhism*, 82ff.

that the term *ḥamalāt al-ʿilm* was used to describe them as such. Scholarly reevaluations of the Ibāḍī origin narrative, then, view the Ibāḍiyya as having emerged out of the quietist Khārijite scholarly circles of Basra, but from far murkier origins than assumed by later Ibāḍiyya. In fact, it seems that the first real imam of the Basran Ibāḍī community was al-Rabīʿ b. Ḥabīb, who enjoyed wide support among the Ibāḍīs of North African and Arabia. This revisionist view of the origins of the Ibāḍiyya accords with the equally problematic and murky origins of the other main quietist group, the Ṣufriyya, both of whom seem to have emerged from the relatively undefined groups of early quietist/moderate Khārijites.

As noted above, understanding the emergence of coherent quietist subgroups requires an appreciation of the tribal element of their sectarian identities. For the Ibāḍiyya, it is vital to understand how Umayyad maltreatment in the 80s/700s of a famous early general, Ibn al-Ashʿath, from the Kinda tribe, as well as the persecution of the popular al-Muhallab family of the Azd tribe, helped to push these tribal blocs toward local anti-Umayyad movements, one of which was the nascent Ibāḍiyya. In Basra, quietists began to successfully proselytize among the (southern Arab tribes of) Kinda and Azd (whereas earlier Khārijite movements were dominated by different and northern Arab tribes of Tamīm, Bakr, Shaybān, and Yashkur). These connections to southern Arab tribal groupings paid off in several ways for the later Ibāḍiyya. Although Basra remained the center for early Ibāḍism well into early 180s/800s, by the late third/ninth century Basran Ibāḍism had died off there and the prominent Basran Ibāḍīs moved to Oman (the home of the Azd tribal grouping). Moreover, tribal affiliations with Kinda and Azd led to two important uprisings in late Umayyad/early ʿAbbāsid revolutionary periods in the ancestral homes of these groups. In Yemen (home of the Kinda tribal grouping), the Ibāḍī-inspired uprising of ʿAbdullāh b. Yaḥyā al-Kindī (aka Ṭālib al-Ḥaqq) controlled the holy cities of Makka and Madina for a time before falling to the invading ʿAbbāsid army. In Oman, the Ibāḍī-inspired uprising of al-Julanda b. Masʿūd aligned the old ruling elites of Oman, the Julanda, toward Ibāḍism. Although both rebellions ultimately failed, Ibāḍism became firmly implanted in these areas. It is also in this period, the mid-second/seventh century, when we can confidently begin to speak of something called Ibāḍism (as opposed to "emergent" or "nascent" or "proto-" Ibāḍism).

In Oman, the failed uprising of al-Julanda b. Masʿūd paved the way for Ibāḍīs to continue to agitate there, and in 177/793 to establish an imamate that would survive for roughly a hundred years. With its capital at Nizwa, this period, sometimes called the second Ibāḍī imamate in Oman, witnessed the consolidation of Ibāḍism, especially in the interior regions.

On the coast, Ibāḍī maritime law enabled Suḥar to become a main port on the Indian Ocean and East African trade routes (the Ibāḍī imam Ghassān b. ʿAbdullāh was said to have rid the coast of pirates). However, the second imamate ended in controversy (at heart, a tribal quarrel) with the deposition of Imam al-Ṣalt b. Mālik al-Kharūṣī in 272/886. This act brought civil war and, by 280/893, an invading ʿAbbāsid army.

However, Ibāḍism survived as a vibrant force in Oman, and indeed continues to survive up to the present day. Ibāḍīs in Oman have periodically reestablished the imamate, as they did in 407/1016 with al-Khalīl b. Shathān al-Kharūṣī (r. 407–20/1016–29). During their third imamate, tribal rivalries were often present, and frequently translated into religious rivalries. To an extent, such tribal rivalries underlay the main medieval division of Omani Ibāḍīs over the deposition of al-Ṣalt b. Mālik into the Rustaq and Nizwa "schools." The Nizwa party argued that there was no means to evaluate al-Ṣalt b. Mālik's deposition, and that later Ibāḍīs should therefore suspend judgment on the matter. Against the Nizwa party, the Rustaq school, represented by the scholars Ibn Baraka and al-Bisyānī, brooked no abstention (*wuqūf*) in the process of declaring dissociation (*barāʾa*) from those who had participated in the wrongful deposition of the imam (so forceful was this stance that the modern Ibāḍī scholar Nūr al-Dīn al-Sālimī writes of them: "the people of truth renounce their treatises and reject their extremism").[53] This position, upheld by the Rustaqī imam Rāshid b. Saʿīd al-Yaḥmadī (r. ca. 420–45/1029–53), led the Arabian Hadramawti Ibāḍīs to break from their Omani brethren and form their own imamate under Abū Isḥāq Ibrāhīm b. Qays. The short-lived Yemeni imamate collapsed, and Ibāḍism thereafter all but disappeared from the Yemen. Tribal and religious divisions in Oman led the Omani imamate to collapse at end of the sixth/twelfth century. In the period of Sunni rule that followed, Ibāḍī scholarship moved closer to Sunni norms (a phenomenon that can be seen among North African Ibāḍīs as well), a process that has been called by a leading scholar of Ibāḍism "madhhabization."

In the eleventh/seventeenth century, Ibāḍī rule emerged again in Oman under the Yaʿrubid dynasty, whose first imam was Nāṣir b. Murshid al-Yaʿrubī (r. ca. 1624–49), in the course of their struggle against the Portuguese. Ibāḍism enjoyed something of a renaissance in this period, with several of the seminal works of Ibāḍī law and theology being penned at this time. This dynasty was replaced in 1749 by Imam Aḥmad b. Saʿīd Āl Bū Saʿīdī (r. 1749–83), founder of the present ruling family of Oman, the Āl Bū Saʿīdīs. Succeeding Āl Bū Saʿīdī rulers eschewed the title of

[53] al-Sālimī, *Tuḥfat al-Aʿyān*, 1:210.

imam, preferring to rule as sayyids (an honorific title) and later sultans. The late ruler of Oman Sultan Qābūs b. Taymūr hailed from the Āl Bū Sa'īdī dynast, as does the current sultan, Ḥaytham b. Ṭāriq. The Āl Bū Sa'īdīs also (re-)extended the influence of Ibāḍism down the East African coast (there is evidence of Ibāḍism in East Africa as early as the sixth/twelfth century). Several sultans ruled Zanzibar from 1832 until 1964 (see e.g. Figure 3.2), when it became part of Tanzania.

Ibāḍism also spread to North Africa, beginning with the undefined quietist Khārijite missionaries who arrived in the 100s/720s. At this early period there did not seem to be much difference between Ṣufrīs and Ibāḍīs (and sources on/from this period reflect this difficulty). But with time, the Ibāḍiyya would become more and more associated with the Berber tribal groupings of the Hawwāra, Nafūsa, and some elements of the Zanāta. Ṣufrī Khārijites of North Africa aligned themselves with the Miknāsa primarily, but also the Barghawāṭa, Maṭghara, Maghīla, and

Figure 3.2 1896 stamp of Zanzibar depicting the Ibāḍī imam Ḥamad b. Thuwaynī.

Ifrān. During the North African Khārijite uprisings of the 120s/740s (i.e. the "Berber Revolt"), the emerging coalitions of Ibāḍīs established footholds in Tunis (in the Djerid and the Fezzān) and in Libya (in the Jabal Nafūsa region). They even took Qayrawān for a time, but were beaten back by the ʿAbbāsid armies. In 161/778, one of the *ḥamalāt al-ʿilm*, ʿAbd al-Raḥmān b. Rustum (the son of a Persian *mawlā*), moved part of the Ibāḍī community to Tāhart (in Algeria) and established the Rustumid dynasty, one that would last until the Fāṭimids destroyed it in 296/909. The Rustumids consolidated the gold and slave trades in West Africa, and they enjoyed excellent relations with both the Iberian Umayyads, Ṣufrī Midrarids, and even at times the Muhallabid governors of Qayrawān. Sectarian differences seemed to fade in the late second/eighth century as these groups all became fantastically wealthy from the slave/gold trade.

After the death of ʿAbd al-Raḥmān b. Rustum, the imamate passed to his son, ʿAbd al-Wahhāb, giving rise to a hereditary dynasty. Given that a fundamental principle of Ibāḍism was that leadership should devolve of the most qualified and pious (and not necessarily on families), it is no surprise that several Ibāḍīs objected to the idea of hereditary leadership. Two of these groups, who became known as the Nukkār and the Khalafiyya, split from the Ibāḍīs at Tāhart and formed their own sub-groups, with their own leaders. The Nukkār spread amongst other Ibāḍī groups of North Africa, and survived to the eighteenth century in Jerba, Tunisia, and down to the 1970s in Libya.

After the Fāṭimids destroyed the Rustumid dynasty in 296/909, the Ibāḍiyya of North Africa made no further attempts to reestablish the imamate, with the exception of the spectacular revolt of Abū Yazīd Makhlad al-Kaydād al-Nukkārī (nicknamed *ṣāhib al-ḥimār*, "he of the donkey") and his son against the Fāṭimids in the mid-fourth/tenth century. Instead, North African Ibāḍīs governed themselves through local councils of scholars (*ḥalāʾiq*/*ʿazzāba*), an institution that survives to the present among them. Ibāḍī communities can now be found in Algeria, Tunis, and Libya. These groups became quite active during the Ibāḍī "renaissance" of the tenth/sixteenth century, growing steadily closer to their Omani counterparts. Indeed, the printing press and the jet engine have reconnected communities that were once separated.

The Khārijites and later, the Ibāḍiyya, formed in the crucible of opposition to Muʿāwiya, ʿAlī, and, perhaps most profoundly, the hated Umayyads. Given the conviction that the Umayyads had betrayed the central mission of the Prophet to establish a just and ethical social order on earth, it is no surprise that notions of justice and piety became central to the Khārijites and Ibāḍiyya. Indeed, so central were these ideas that they became the anchor point for the two defining ideas of Khārijism and Ibāḍism: first, that the leader of the Islamic community must be pious, so much so that piety outweighed the concern that the imam be from the Prophet's tribe or family. Second, that this commitment to piety distinguished the members of the true Islamic community to the point that non-Khārijites and non-Ibāḍīs could not be considered as full Muslims. The details of these positions, especially the extent to which non-Khārijites or non-Ibāḍīs should be actually treated as non-Muslims, staked out to a certain extent the subsequent differences between militant and quietist Khārijites, and distinguished the Ibāḍiyya as the most moderate among them.

The virtual extinction of the Khārijites, as well as the small numbers (and low profile) of Ibāḍīs in the present day, have rendered these sectarian groupings difficult to comprehend. On the one hand, the Khārijites and their image has been so tarnished and so abused over the centuries that an accurate portrait of their activities and doctrines is supremely problematic (some would say impossible) to achieve. On the other hand, the Ibāḍiyya survive to the present, preserving much of their medieval writings and making an accurate portrait of them easier to attain. Despite their differences, modern Ibāḍīs, perhaps wisely, have chosen to emphasize their similarities with other Muslims.

4 Devotion to the Family of the Prophet

The Shiʿa

Shiʿism, in general, stresses "personal allegiance and devotion to the Prophet and his family as the most crucial element and sign of one's submission to the will of God."[1] This allegiance has important consequences that distinguish it (and thus, Shiʿism) from the collective devotion that all Muslims felt and feel toward their Prophet and his descendants. Allegiance to the family of the Prophet (known as the *ahl al-bayt*, the "people of the house [of the Prophet Muḥammad]") elevates the issue of leadership to one of paramount importance, such that adherence to the *sharīʿa* and understanding of the fundamentals of Islamic doctrine flow from the love and obedience that is shown to the imams. Thus, the stories of the family of the Prophet receive heightened attention, as not only did the imams serve as sources of guidance and inspiration for the community, but the stories of their betrayal often elicited intensely emotional responses. Underlying many of these narratives, and formally articulated initially by Imāmī Shiʿa and then Ithnā-ʿAsharī (i.e. "Twelver") Shiʿa after the disappearance of their twelfth imam, as well as Ismāʿīlī Shiʿa of various stripes, was the conviction that God was so merciful that (out of His grace, *luṭf*, and His justice, *ʿadl*) He would not cut off access to divine guidance, even after the death of the last Prophet. He would always remain accessible to human beings through the family of the Prophet Muḥammad. This meant that the central mission of the prophets to establish a just and ethical social order on earth continued under the guidance of their family. Human beings were to hope for and work toward justice on earth, commanding good and forbidding evil, and they were to oppose tyrants. This was to be accomplished with the leadership of the imams. Later, when rationalist (Muʿtazilite) ideas were more and more imbibed by Shiʿite theologians, it was understood that God was just in a manner that was understandable to human beings, and that they were endowed with the capacity to recognize what was good and what was evil and were thus able to grasp the importance of the

[1] Schubel, *Religious Performance in Contemporary Islam*, 17.

imams to humankind.[2] Moreover, it was later held that they were free to choose the good or evil because God did not constrain their choices through predestination. Thus they were free to accept or reject the imams.

In this manner, Shiʿism is the story of the imams and of human beings' responses to them. It is the answers to questions about what kind of persons they were. It asked, who was the proper imam and how did a believer recognize the imam? In all cases, obedience to God's chosen leader was expected, though it was not always uniformly given. As with the Khārijites, the answers to these questions delineated different kinds of Shiʿa, some of which survive into the present day as the main Shiʿite representatives, while others disappeared into the historical record. In particular, questions over the role of the imam – was he primarily a revolutionary or a source of knowledge? – delineated the activist Shiʿa from what might be called the quietist and provide the blueprint upon which the history of Shiʿism unfolded.

Origin and Development Narratives

Although there are many branches of Shiʿism which diverge on important points of doctrine and practice, the narrative of the Shiʿite path begins with the figure of ʿAlī b. Abī Ṭālib, cousin to the Prophet Muḥammad and an early convert to Islam. The issue of succession to the Prophet Muḥammad has already been mentioned: how certain Muslims looked to the family of the Prophet Muḥammad, and especially to ʿAlī, as more entitled to lead the community after the death of the Prophet. In later years, different Shiʿa elaborated this expectation into a number of complex "proofs" for ʿAlī's candidacy. The proofs revolved around a few points. First, and perhaps most universally, it focused on the idea that ʿAlī had been explicitly singled out by the Prophet as his successor at the pool of Ghadīr Khumm. The event and the *ḥadīth* associated with it are something that nearly all Shiʿa groups acknowledge, even to the extent that it has become a yearly celebration in some areas of Islamdom (the Islamic Republic of Iran, for example, issues postage stamps for it; see Figure 4.1). Other formal articulations of proofs for ʿAlī's candidacy point to his designation at the *yawm al-dār* (the "day of the house"). This event was said to have happened early in ʿAlī's lifetime, when the Prophet Muḥammad was directed to make his mission public and ʿAlī was held to have been appointed as his successor. Shiʿa also looked to ʿAlī's role as Muḥammad's double during the attempted assassination of the Prophet at the time of the *hijra* and to ʿAlī

[2] Haider, *Shīʿī Islam*, 21.

Figure 4.1 1991 stamp of the Islamic Republic of Iran commemorating "the Day of Ghadīr."

being appointed as the "brother" to Muḥammad when the Prophet established networks of support for his newly emigrated community in Madina. They looked to ʿAlī's marriage to Muḥammad's daughter Fāṭima, as well as to ʿAlī's exploits on the battlefield.[3] Many of these early discussions emphasized the merits (*faḍāʾil*) of ʿAlī in relation to other candidates, notably Abū Bakr, the underlying assumption being that as the most meritorious, ʿAlī remained the clear choice as leader.

Various arguments for ʿAlī's leadership also pointed to Prophetic traditions that singled out ʿAlī as special. For example, the Prophet was recorded as saying, "I am leaving you with two safeguards, the Book of

[3] Haider, *Shīʿī Islam*, 57–58.

God and the members of my household. As long as you cling to these two you will not go astray"; "the likeness of my family is Nūḥ's [Noah's] ark; whoever takes refuge therein is saved and whoever opposes it is drowned"; "just as the stars are a means of securing the people of the earth against drowning, my family is a means of securing my people from division"; "I am the city of knowledge and ʿAlī is its gate"; (and speaking to ʿAlī) "your rank in relation to me is that of Hārūn (Aaron) in relation to Mūsā (Moses)."[4] Although many of these traditions were only later mustered to defend the position of ʿAlī and his Shiʿa, these narrations of the Prophet have become some of the most important "proofs" for ʿAlī's candidacy.

In the early period, there were other reasons why it would make sense for some Muslims to expect a member of the Prophet's household to succeed him. There is evidence that the idea of "noble" Arab families, called the *buyūtāt al-ʿArab*, existed before the coming of Islam.[5] Noble traits, such as honor, bravery, generosity, and so on, that were valued by the Arabs were thought to have been passed down in families, much in the same way that physical traits (eye color, facial shape, etc.) were passed down through families. This notion gave rise among the pre-Islamic Arabs to the existence of certain lineages ("houses," *buyūt*) within particular tribal groups that were known for their strong and noble ancestry. And if God had chosen Muḥammad to be His Messenger and had purified him (as is mentioned in Qurʾan 33:32–33), then Muḥammad's family would be assumed to also partake of some of these noble traits as well. Such assumptions may have predisposed certain persons to look toward the family of the Prophet for guidance after his death.

Similarly, the Qurʾan in general places great importance on familial relations and narrates several instances when family members of prophets inherit their material and spiritual status after the death of the prophet. Thus, in the Qurʾan Ibrāhīm's (Abraham's) two sons Isḥāq (Isaac) and Yaʿqūb (Jacob) became his heirs (38:45–47); Mūsā (Moses) asked God to make his brother Hārūn (Aaron) his helper (7:142); Sulaymān (Solomon) inherited the role of leadership from Dāwūd (David) (27:16); as did Yaḥyā (John) from Zakariyya (Zacharias) (19:5–6). Additionally, the line of prophecy sketched in the Qurʾan (from Adam to Noah to Abraham to Muḥammad) follows one family. In this way, individual instances of succession in the Qurʾan remain within families of the prophets, while the overarching narrative of prophecy in the Qurʾan is that of a single prophetic

[4] Haider, *Shīʿī Islam*, 58–59.
[5] Jafri, *The Origins and Early Development of Shiʿa Islam*, 1–10.

family.[6] Such qur'anic proofs have offered powerful reasons for Shiʿa over the centuries to believe that after the death of the Prophet Muḥammad, leadership was meant to devolve onto his cousin and family member ʿAlī, and then through ʿAlī to other members of the Prophet's household.

Nevertheless, and to the disappointment of himself and his supporters, much of the community passed ʿAlī over and entrusted leadership to Abū Bakr. There might have been several reasons for why a majority of early Muslims accepted Abū Bakr over ʿAlī, including ʿAlī's young age, and the fact that he had killed relatives of several prominent Makkans who after their subsequent conversion to Islam became powerful figures in the Muslim community. Yet for many if not all later Shiʿa, this abandonment of the person who came to be understood as God's intended ruler amounted to a betrayal by the early Companions. Although ʿAlī himself eventually made peace with Abū Bakr, reportedly out of a concern for the unity of the community, he was again shunted aside at Abū Bakr's death, and then again when the council appointed by ʿUmar to decide the succession opted for ʿUthmān. It was only after ʿUthmān's violent killing that ʿAlī assumed the helm of the Islamic community, and his tenure as caliph was fraught with civil war and dissention.

To ʿAlī's partisans (literally, his *shīʿa*) his status as the rightful successor to Muḥammad merited their unflinching loyalty and devotion. One of the first public displays of this loyalty, an event that is sometimes taken to indicate the birth of Shiʿism itself, came after the Battle of Ṣiffīn and following the Khārijites' secession from ʿAlī's army at Kufa (but before the Battle of Nahrawān). At this time, ʿAlī's followers were said to have taken a pledge to "be the associates of those with whom you [ʿAlī] associate and the enemies of those whom you make your enemy."[7] This display of charismatic loyalty, known as *walāya*, was the mark of those who accepted God's divinely chosen leader of humanity, and it later became one of the fundamental acts (*farʿ*) of Shiʿism.[8]

ʿAlī's death at the hands of the Khārijite Ibn Muljam tragically ended the life of the man that his partisans believed was Muḥammad's divinely appointed successor. On ʿAlī's death, his eldest son, al-Ḥasan b. ʿAlī, briefly assumed leadership of the community, but soon came to an agreement with Muʿāwiya, who was stronger militarily. Muʿāwiya agreed to pass the caliphate to al-Ḥasan on his death, in return for al-Ḥasan's acquiescence to Muʿāwiya assuming the caliphate in the interim. However, al-Ḥasan died before he could succeed Muʿāwiya. Many

6 Madelung, *Succession to Muḥammad*, 10–12. 7 al-Ṭabarī, *Tārīkh*, 1:3350.
8 Dakake, *The Charismatic Community*, 60.

Shiʿa maintained that al-Ḥasan b. ʿAlī was poisoned, which was a distinct possibility given how Muʿāwiya often dealt with his rivals. Leadership then passed to Muʿāwiya's unpopular son Yazīd, who was widely regarded as ill-suited to the job of ruling. For those who remained convinced that the Umayyads possessed no mandate for the caliphate, the ascension of Yazīd presented them with both further proof of this fact as well as an opportunity to exploit.

Such was the feeling among ʿAlī's supporters in Kufa, who wrote to ʿAlī's younger son, al-Ḥusayn b. ʿAlī, in 61/680 asking him to come to Kufa and assume his rightful title as imam. In what is regarded as one of the most tragic episodes in Muslim history, al-Ḥusayn accepted the invitation and began marching with several of his followers toward the city.[9] In the meantime, the newly arrived Umayyad governor of Kufa, ʿUbaydallāh b. Ziyād, executed al-Ḥusayn's main supporters and turned the tide against revolt. When al-Ḥusayn's contingent was approximately two days' march from Kufa, at a place that came to be known as Karbala, they found themselves facing an Umayyad army. The army surrounded al-Ḥusayn and his supporters and deprived them of water. On the tenth of the lunar month of Muḥarram, they attacked. Reports place the Umayyad army at anywhere between 4,000 and 30,000 troops, while al-Ḥusayn's group numbered between 100 and 150. Badly outnumbered, most of the men, generally thought to be 72 of them, including al-Ḥusayn's infant child ʿAlī al-Aṣghar, were killed and the rest, including the women of al-Ḥusayn's household, taken prisoner.

For many Muslims, the death of the Prophet's grandson at the hands of a caliphal army confirmed their worst suspicions about the Umayyads and drove many into the ranks of the opposition. For many Shiʿa, the Battle of Karbala, as it came to be known, assumed a central place in their communal memory and thus in their identification as Shiʿa. The battle story itself admits many interpretations: al-Ḥusayn and his companions' martyrdom became a rallying cry and model for resistance, a symbol of justice delayed but not forgotten, and a tragedy to be mourned by any who would consider themselves faithful. It would become a central motif in much Shiʿa literature, and it is commemorated by many Shiʿa annually during the first ten days of Muḥarram with mourning, public processions, remembrance sessions (*majālis*), and other forms of devotion (which can include striking the chest and in some cases self-flagellation). For other Shiʿa, Karbala became a tragedy that needed to be righted. It was not enough to passively mourn the injustice done to Muḥammad's family.

[9] For a helpful discussion on the sources for the early history of the Karbala episode, see Borrut, "Remembering Karbalā'," 249–82.

For this group, devotion meant active resistance to the Umayyads. This resistance marked some of the first actions of groups that could be recognized as Shiʿite.

Activist Shiʿism: The *Ghulāt* and Zaydiyya

In the early period of Islamic history, many different kinds of Muslims looked to different branches of the Prophet's immediate family and clan for leadership. A large portion of this support came from those with scholarly inclinations, or those for whom active resistance to the Umayyads was not appealing or practicable. These Shiʿa might be called, after their Khārijite counterparts, the "moderates" or "quietists," and they looked to their imams as sources of religious guidance and knowledge. Initially, however, the story of the quietist Shiʿa is difficult to find, if indeed it can be found at all. More commonly narrated in the sources for early Islamic history were those Shiʿa groups who adopted a more activist or militant approach. These looked toward the family of the Prophet to provide military leadership and a focal point for revolutionary yearnings. They were the first to catch the attention of the wider Muslim community and thus to end up chronicled in the many historical sources on and by scholars. It is for this reason that the story of Shiʿism after the death of al-Ḥusayn continued with groups that were later labeled *ghulāt* ("exaggerators/those who go to extremes"), most of whom appeared in ʿAlī's former capital, Kufa. More than any other place in the early Islamic world, Kufa became the center of the emerging Shiʿa.[10]

The first *ghālī*, and indeed the first Muslim to be considered almost universally as a religious deviant, is usually the mysterious figure of ʿAbdullāh b. Sabāʾ, who was said to have established an early Shiʿite group known as the Sabāʾiyya.[11] A Yemeni convert from Judaism, some later Sunni sources remember Ibn Sabāʾ as the originator of Shiʿism itself, which in their estimation was enough to condemn him. Other sources attribute to Ibn Sabāʾ the belief in ʿAlī's divinity as well as the idea that ʿAlī had not died but had gone into hiding and would return at some point in the future (this was known later as the doctrine of return, *al-rajʿa*). Both beliefs were later associated with *ghulāt* Shiʿism, and in some versions of the Ibn Sabāʾ narrative they angered ʿAlī so much so that he either exiled Ibn Sabāʾ or burned him alive. Yet in other versions of the story, Ibn Sabāʾ expressed these views after the death of ʿAlī. Given the many, and often contradictory, versions of the Ibn Sabāʾ narrative, it is unsurprising

10 al-Qāḍī, "The Development of the Term *Ghulāt* in Muslim Literature," 295ff.
11 Anthony, *The Caliph and the Heretic*, 2–3.

that scholarly opinion is uncertain about him, to the point that several scholars even doubt his existence.[12] Although the layers of polemic that surround him renders an accurate historical portrait of Ibn Sabāʾ unlikely, it seems fair to regard him as something of a mascot for those among the early Shiʿa who held to the apocalyptic notion that ʿAlī would return in victory, even despite ʿAlī's apparent death.[13] Such a view renders the notion of the "Sabāʾiyya" as a coherent subsect problematic, though such subgroups of Shiʿites appeared not long thereafter.

Almost immediately following the disaster at Karbala, a certain Sulaymān b. Surād began calling in 65/684 on those who supported ʿAlī's family to repent for their failure to aid al-Ḥusayn b. ʿAlī and to avenge his slaughter. His followers became known as the Tawwābūn ("Penitents"), and they marched to Karbala where they pledged themselves to resist the Umayyads. Moving up the Euphrates toward upper Iraq, and joined by the remnants of a Zubayrid army that had earlier that year been defeated at Marj Rāhit, the Tawwābūn met an Umayyad army at a place called ʿAyn al-Warda. It took three days for the Umayyad army to defeat them, and the remnants of the Tawwābūn trickled back to Kufa where they joined another militant Shiʿa uprising in the making, that of al-Mukhtār b. Abī ʿUbaydallāh al-Thaqafī, in 66/685.

Al-Mukhtār raised his revolt by calling for revenge for the massacres at Karbala. He claimed to have the support (and to be working on behalf) of ʿAlī's son, Muḥammad b. al-Ḥanafiyya (named al-Ḥanafiyya because his mother was a Ḥanafī concubine). For his part, Ibn al-Ḥanafiyya neither affirmed nor denied any connection to the rebels.[14] Nevertheless, al-Mukhtār attracted a large number of non-Arab Muslims (*mawālī*) and took control of the city, where they executed several Umayyads who had participated at Karbala. Despite initial successes in and around Kufa, al-Mukhtār was killed and his followers were defeated in 67/687 by Ibn al-Zubayr's governor of Basra (and brother), Muṣʿab b. al-Zubayr.[15]

Those who followed al-Mukhtār, initially called the Mukhtāriyya, became known as the Kaysāniyya.[16] Several distinctive teachings were attributed to al-Mukhtār and the Kaysāniyya, especially the belief in the imamate of Ibn al-Ḥanafiyya and the notion that he was a messianic figure around which the oppressed and exploited could rally. The idea of

[12] Anthony, *The Caliph and the Heretic*, 4–5.
[13] Anthony, *The Caliph and the Heretic*, 313–14. [14] al-Ṭabarī, *Tārīkh*, 2:607.
[15] Tucker, *Mahdis and Millenarians*, 21–23.
[16] The name's origin is disputed: it could have been that al-Mukhtār was given the nickname Kaysān, or that a *mawlā* of ʿAlī who was named Kaysān gave al-Mukhtār the inspiration for his ideas, or that it came from the leader of al-Mukhtār's personal guard at Kufa, Abū ʿAmra Kaysān.

a messianic figure, later identified as the Mahdī, was and is something generally held among different kinds of Muslims (thus, medieval and modern Sunnis have ideas about who and what the Mahdī is and does). However, the Kaysāniyya seem to be among the first early Shiʿite group in which expectations of the imam's return were clustered around a specific person, namely Ibn al-Ḥanafiyya, and tethered to the idea that Ibn al-Ḥanafiyya would reestablish justice and right religion. Thus, when Ibn al-Ḥanafiyya died, a portion of the Kaysāniyya were said to have awaited his return (*al-rajʿa*), while another group held that the imamate passed to his son ʿAlī b. Muḥammad b. al-Ḥanafiyya.

Other distinctive ideas are often attributed to the Kaysāniyya. They (or more likely a group among them) were supposedly known as the Khashabiyya ("club bearers") because they elected to fight only with clubs, eschewing iron weapons until such time as the Mahdī returned. Alternately, it could have been that they regarded Kufa as a holy site because of al-Ḥusayn's death, and therefore iron weapons should not be used in it. Another report tells of how al-Mukhtār claimed to have the chair of ʿAlī, which might give some indication that the Kaysāniyya regarded the material objects of the *ahl al-bayt* in much the same way as early Christians regarded the relics of their saints.[17] There is no way to verify such reports, and as colorful as they remain, it should never be forgotten that the authors who recorded these stories were far removed in time from the Kaysāniyya and often hostile to them.

The Kaysāniyya are important to the history of early Shiʿism insofar as they represent the first of many small groups said to have revolted out of Kufa against the Umayyads. Groups whose names appear in the various heresiographers of later centuries, such as the Bayāniyya, Mughīriyya, Manṣūriyya, Jahāniyya, and others, reportedly made the province of Iraq, and the city of Kufa in particular, a difficult province for the Umayyads to govern. One group, the Hāshimiyya, deserves mention for the role that they played in the ʿAbbāsid revolution. This group held that a descendant of Ibn al-Ḥanafiyya (Abū Hāshim ʿAbdullāh b. Muḥammad b. al-Ḥanafiyya) had transferred the imamate to the clan of ʿAbbās (their cousins) via the father (Muḥammad b. ʿAlī) of the first two ʿAbbāsid caliphs (i.e. al-Ṣaffāḥ and al-Manṣūr). Claiming revenge for the killing of the Prophet's family, and adopting the symbols of the expected Mahdī (black banners and robes), the Hāshimiyya allied themselves with the dispossessed merchant class of eastern Central Asia, equipped themselves with an able general (Abū Muslim) and an army of non-Arab (*mawālī*) supporters, and proceeded to cut a bloody swathe through the ailing

[17] Tucker, *Mahdis and Millenarians*, 25–28.

Umayyad dynasty. Once installed in power, however, the ʿAbbāsids realized that their association with a fringe Shiʿa movement would not result in the kind of consensus that they needed to rule the empire, and so they cut their ties (and in some cases, several throats) and began promoting themselves as the guardians of communal unity (*jamāʿa*).

As with the Khārijites, the sources available for the study of these early activist Shiʿa render an accurate portrait of them difficult if not impossible to obtain, and the historicity of these reports can and should be questioned. For example, numismatic evidence shows that the group that preceded the Hāshimiyya, known as the Jahāniyya, controlled a larger area than textual evidence suggests, and that the Hāshimiyya (especially their general, Abū Muslim) appropriated both the members and the message of that movement into his own. In this sense, the revolt of the Jahāniyya could be considered a "dress rehearsal" for the later ʿAbbāsid revolution. This is a perspective that remains submerged in the textual sources.[18]

Equally problematic is the term *ghulāt*, one whose meaning is difficult to pin down in part because its referent tended to shift over time. Initially, the label *ghulāt* seems to be used in reference to a group within the Mukhtāriyya who held that ʿAlī had not died and would not die until he had driven the people with his stick. This group might have constituted the remnants of the early admirers of Ibn Sabāʾ, and the term was applied to them because of their "exaggeration" (*ghuluw*) of ʿAlī's role in the end times scenario. However, after the establishment of the ʿAbbāsids, Shiʿites began defining *ghuluw* differently, using it for people who treated the imams as prophets, or who believed that God could incarnate in human form (called incarnationism, *ḥulūl*) and/or held to the transmigration of souls into new bodies (*tanāsukh*), or who rejected various aspects of the *sharīʿa*. Among non-Shiʿa, the concept of *ghuluw* came to designate "exaggeration" or "going beyond bounds" generally in religious matters.[19] In this fashion, the latitude of the term *ghulāt*, combined with the questionable character of the sources on those labeled *ghulāt*, makes it very difficult to obtain an accurate portrait of the groups so labeled.

From a historical perspective, many *ghulāt* groups (or, groups labeled as such) constituted the activist Shiʿa of the early period. Other *ghulāt* Shiʿa seem to have been organically integrated into the larger Shiʿa community in Kufa and did not emerge as separate until the disappearance of the twelfth imam of the Ithnā-ʿAsharī branch of Shiʿites (to be discussed presently). Several of the early *ghulāt* authorities, such as

[18] Bernheimer, "The Revolt of ʿAbdullāh b. Muʿāwiya AH 127–130," 393.
[19] al-Qāḍī, "The Development of the Term *Ghulāt* in Muslim Literature," 295ff.

Mufaḍḍal al-Juʿfī, were associates of the sixth imam, Jaʿfar al-Ṣādiq. And although they sometimes incurred the rebuke of the imams, they remained important to the early Shiʿa community of Kufa in their roles as moneychangers.[20] As such, the quietist *ghulāt* community of Kufa seems to have constituted an elite who were interested in esoteric ideas that they did not share with the wider Shiʿa community for fear that it would be misinterpreted. As the result of being a small and insular elite, their writings display a certain consistency, and a number of themes do seem to emerge across the spectrum of surviving *ghulāt* writings. For example, in the *ghulāt* tellings of the creation, God was said to have first created either Muḥammad or the imams from shadows (*aẓilla*) and/or apparitions (*ashbāh*) and to have delegated (*fawwaḍa*) the remainder of the creative act to them. Likewise, these writings exhibit a tendency to attribute supernatural powers or knowledge to the Prophet/the imams (and in some cases, their representatives), treating these as reflections of the Divine. *Ghulāt* versions of the creation story also tell of how God created believers and unbelievers according to how they responded to His manifestation of Himself. They tell also of the creation of seven heavens, seven Adams, and the establishment of seven covenants (*amthāq*) with each of them. These *ghulāt* held that human beings could ascend or descend the chain of being, being reborn in human, animal, or even vegetable form according to their exertion and the acquisition of proper knowledge. Higher forms of knowledge, such as the knowledge that the religious duties were, in fact, persons, erased the necessity to perform the religious duties. To the accusation that they had gone to extremes in religion, the *ghulāt* responded that their detractors did not fully appreciate the extent of the imams' knowledge and abilities nor their role in the cosmos. Accordingly, they called their opponents "shortcomers" (*muqaṣṣirūn*) because they sold the imams short.[21] Many of these persons, only later identified as *ghulāt* by historians hostile to them, remained integrated into the Shiʿa community of Kufa, keeping their ideas secret and preserving them long after the revolutionary *ghulāt* disappeared.

However, not all *ghulāt* kept a low profile, and the revolutionary activities of the early activist *ghulāt* seem to have led to their downfall, inciting the Umayyads to quash their uprisings, imprison and kill their leaders, and ultimately extinguish their movements. ʿAbbāsid-era revolutions of the so-called *ghulat*, such as that of Abū al-Khaṭṭāb (who divinized the sixth imam) in Kufa in 138/755, were likewise squashed. Yet like the

[20] Asatryan, "Bankers and Politics," 9ff.
[21] Asatryan, *Controversies in Formative Shiʿi Islam*, 137ff.

Khārijites, a secretive elite survived amidst the general Shiʿa population of Kufa.

Later, as the Shiʿa of Kufa grappled with the disappearance of the twelfth imam and worked to find some rapprochement with the reigning ʿAbbāsids, many of the surviving *ghulāt* decided to move themselves to Syria, far away from the centers of both ʿAbbāsid and Imāmī Shiʿite power. There these *ghulāt* eventually became the Nuṣayrīs, a private and quietist group who held their founder, Muḥammad b. Nuṣayr (d. after 254/868), to be the gateway (*bāb*) to the salvific knowledge of the imams. Ibn Nuṣayr claimed to be a representative of the twelfth imam and laid the foundation for the movement that took his name. After further elaboration by Abū ʿAbdullāh al-Ḥusayn b. Ḥamdān al-Khaṣībī (d. 969), the group became solidly established in Jabal Anṣāriyya (near Latakiyya in northern Syria) in the fourth/tenth century. This area remains their heartland. They are sometimes known as the ʿAlawī Shiʿites (ʿAlawiyyūn), though "ʿAlawī" simply means "follower of ʿAlī."

The Nuṣayrīs remain a secretive group, consisting mostly of Arabic speakers who, in the high medieval period, found themselves squashed between the Ottoman, Mamluk, Ilkhānid, and later Safavid empires. Although they were frequently reviled and sometimes persecuted (the medieval Sunni scholar Ibn Taymiyya, for example, considered them worse than idolaters, Christians, and Jews and claimed that fighting them was pleasing to God), they managed to exist in the midst of the Ottoman state. Unsurprisingly, *taqiyya* has been an important aspect of their survival, with the Nuṣayrīs often publicly adopting Twelver Shiʿite rituals. This makes the Nuṣayrīs extremely difficult to study, as they do not usually divulge their secrets to the uninitiated.

Nevertheless, a basic outline of Nuṣayrī ideas can be sketched from what is known about them: like the Ismāʿīlīs (to be discussed presently), the group posits secret knowledge of the universe as the key to salvation and communicates the knowledge through a narrative about the nature of the cosmos (in the field of religious studies, this is sometimes called a "cosmology"). To truly understand the full ramifications of this cosmic drama, a person must be initiated into the group. Nuṣayrīsm is thus initiatic and "gnostic" insofar as it posits its secret knowledge as the key to salvation.

Nuṣayrī cosmology posits a cosmic significance to the figure of ʿAlī b. Abī Ṭālib, who plays a central (and seemingly divine) role in the Nuṣayrī drama whereby, in pre-eternity before time, the Nuṣayrīs were held to be heavenly bodies made of light.[22] They did not eat, drink, or

[22] Olsson, "The Gnosis of Mountaineers and Townspeople," 177–79.

pass excrement, but simply beheld God, who had the form of ʿAlī b. Abī Ṭālib. But then, the narrative tells, they became prideful and boasted of their own excellence, so God/ʿAlī created a veil between Himself and them, and, when they continued to show disobedience, eventually cast them down into material form and set the Devil to tempt them. Moreover, they were condemned to reincarnate in this world until they found the means to escape it.

However, the story continues, God/ʿAlī, out of His mercy, appeared to humankind in order to lead them back to their original state of perfection. God/ʿAlī was said to have appeared seven times on earth as various Persons, and always accompanied by two others to form a triad. Thus, God Himself was said to have appeared as the inner truth made flesh, who is known as the *maʿnā* (the "meaning"). The *maʿnā* was accompanied by one who spoke for Him, called His "*ism*" (literally, "name" but indicating a kind of spokesperson), as well as one who controlled a kind of access to Him (known as His "gate" – *bāb*). God was thus held to have appeared with the other two as *maʿnā*, *ism*, and *bāb* (the idea is similar to, but not to be confused with, the Christian notion of a trinity) seven times. In His seventh appearance, God was said to have appeared as ʿAlī b. Abī Ṭālib, with Muḥammad the Prophet as His *ism*, and the early Companion of the Prophet, Salmān al-Fārisī, as His *bāb*. The *bāb* (Salmān al-Fārisī) was held to have created five beings known as the *aytām* (the "incomparables") who then created the local Nuṣayrī religious authorities. In other words, the narrative cosmology of the Nuṣayrīs implies that there is a hierarchy of beings in the universe who control access to the proper knowledge of how the universe works. Salvation thus comes through initiation into the hierarchies of knowledge whereby the soul ascends back to its original state as eternal being of light, which is a process accompanied by a rigorous spiritual discipline and is only open to males who have two Nuṣayrī parents. Nuṣayrī women who lead a virtuous life are held to be reborn as men, but those who sin can be reborn as animals. Nuṣayrī men undertake the spiritual path under a religious authority, known as the imam.

Nuṣayrīs celebrate a series of festivals throughout the year (too many to mention), but the ʿĪd al-Ghadīr, the celebration of ʿAlī's designation at Ghadīr Khumm, holds pride of place in the Nuṣayrī religious calendar. So too, a religious gathering known as *quddās* (the Nuṣayrī "mass") involves the recitation of lengthy prayers praising ʿAlī's divine attributes and the trinity of ʿAlī, Muḥammad, and Salmān al-Fārisī. It also involves consecration and consumption of bread and wine (symbolizing the intoxication in and love of God as well as the reunion of God and human beings). Given that these actions would be considered highly controversial to most Muslims, the ritual of *quddās* is most often performed in private homes or other sequestered places. It is also quite clearly similar to the Christian practice of communion, such that Nuṣayrīsm has been called "syncretic" (meaning that it amalgamates different religions and practices into itself).

Although the Nuṣayrīs hail from the traditions that have been labeled *ghulāt* by other Muslims, they cannot be classed along the same line of the more "activist" *ghulāt* of Kufa. Rather, they have adopted secrecy (notably the practice of *taqiyya*) and, in general, political quietism. This (in addition to their relocation to a mountainous region) has helped them to survive to the present in the midst of a general Muslim population who often find their ideas strange, if not highly controversial.

Less controversial by far of the activist Shiʿa proper were the Zaydī Shiʿa, who maintained the expectation that their imams would lead revolutions (and thus, they qualify as activist Shiʿa), but who held less provocative stances (especially in their early iterations) vis-à-vis the wider Islamic and Shiʿite communities. The beginnings of what is now known as Zaydī Shiʿism can be traced to a failed revolt in Kufa in 122/740 by Zayd b. ʿAlī. Zayd's uprising was quickly defeated, as was that of his son Yaḥyā b. Zayd in 125/743.[23] Other revolts followed that were later considered "Zaydī," such as that of Muḥammad b. ʿAbdullāh (al-Nafs al-Zakiyya, "The Pure Soul") against ʿAbbāsid caliph al-Manṣūr, which ended in al-Nafs al-Zakiyya's killing in 145/762. Some of his followers expected his return, but still others turned to Muḥammad b. Qāsim (a descendant of al-Ḥusayn b. ʿAlī), who was arrested by the ʿAbbāsid caliph al-Muʿtaṣim in 219/834 and died in prison. Some of his followers in northern Iran expected his return, and in 250/864, a relative, al-Ḥasan b. Zayd, founded a Zaydī polity there in Ṭabaristān. Later in 301/913, Zaydīs established imamates in Daylān and Gilān (also in northern Iran) and also enjoyed for a time the patronage of the Būyid Shiʿite family. In North Africa, Zaydī missionaries began their activities in 171/788, eventually establishing the Idrīsid dynasty in what is present-day Morocco. In al-Andalus, offshoots of the Idrīsids founded the short-lived Ḥamūdid dynasty in the fifth/eleventh century. Moreover, Zaydīsm became established as a permanent aspect of the Yemeni political landscape with a Zaydī polity that began in 288/901, and in third–fourth/ninth–tenth centuries, Zaydīs enjoyed periods of political ascendance in parts of what in now Saudi Arabia.

Such proliferation of Zaydī polities and revolts across different geographies and eras has meant that, as a whole, Zaydīsm lacked a coherent

[23] Haider, *Shīʿī Islam*, 85.

center. Accordingly, Zaydī Shiʿism has a strongly regional character, with the Zaydīs of northern Iran, Yemen, and North Africa preserving their own traditions and interpretations of what it means to be a Zaydī Shiʿite. Moreover, and as a result of the *longue durée* of Zaydīsm, what could be said to characterize Zaydī doctrines and practices have shifted over time. Nevertheless, some broad notions have tended to remain stable across geographies and through the various eras: particularly the idea that the imamate was the common property of any descendant of ʿAlī's sons (through al-Ḥasan and al-Ḥusayn), that any qualified descendant could claim the imamate by calling others to his cause and rising up in rebellion against the oppressive rulers of the day. If an imam rose in rebellion, then Muslims were required to respond to this call and to aid the rightful imam.

Beyond these notions, however, what falls under the rubric of "Zaydīsm" has witnessed some important changes. For example, the earliest Zaydīs (called "Batrī" Zaydīs) appear to have accepted the caliphates of Abū Bakr, ʿUmar, and ʿUthmān (during his first six years) as "less worthy" (*al-mafḍūl*), yet still legitimate. And this belief in "less-worthy" leaders continues to be how some Zaydīs view the "lesser" imams of the Imāmī Shiʿites. Early Zaydīs also held that the knowledge that the imam possessed was not inherent, but learned, and thus the imam could study with the prominent scholars of his generation. The imam had to demonstrate his knowledge of Islamic law and its ritual obligations and would employ independent reasoning (*ijtihād*) and learned opinion (*raʾy*) to do so. These early Zaydīs, however, seem to have become absorbed into the emerging Sunni consensus when it came into being (and thus, early Zaydī Shiʿism often seems closest to what would become Sunni positions).[24]

Later Zaydīs, however, modified or abandoned some of the tenets to which their predecessors held. What became known as Jarūdī Zaydīsm, for example, held that the first three caliphs were *kuffār* (unbelievers) and usurpers of the rights of the *ahl al-bayt*. Moreover, the Jarūdīs believed that the imam's knowledge was inherent, and that every descendant of Fāṭima possessed exactly the same kind and same amount of special knowledge (even if he were a child). For this reason, there was no need for *ijtihād* or *raʾy* as the imam could simply issue an authoritative statement and it was expected to be followed (a move that effectively restricted law to the decisions of the descendants of Fāṭima).[25] Against other Shiʿites, later Zaydīs rejected the idea of the hidden imam as well as return of the Mahdī. To them the imam should be a living person, who demonstrates their ability. Likewise, their imams were not considered

[24] Haider, *Shīʿī Islam*, 87–90, 105–7. [25] Haider, *Shīʿī Islam*, 107–8.

infallible nor capable of performing miracles. In other areas where Zaydīs flourished, in the Yemen for example, sustained interactions with Sunnis brought about a process of Sunnification whereby certain Zaydī scholars imbibed the norms of Sunni law and tradition, creating a reformed Zaydīsm that clashed with more classically minded Zaydīsm.[26]

What knits activist Shiʿism together in both its *ghulāt* and Zaydī expressions is the conviction that the imam was primarily a champion for justice. In these cases, devotion to the family of the Prophet translated into actively joining and supporting revolution led by (or in the name of) the imam. In the Umayyad period, such activism mingled with dissatisfaction with the caliphs and found a somewhat more fertile atmosphere to proliferate. However, as the revolutionary fervor of the Umayyad era gave way to the ʿAbbāsid revolution and the subsequent stability of the ʿAbbāsid period, the insurrectionist tendencies of these early groups either failed to mobilize sufficient support (as in the case of the *ghulāt*), succeeded in remote or far-flung areas (as was the case with the Zaydīs), or transformed itself into something altogether different (as with the Hāshimiyya). For this reason, the most numerous remaining early activist Shiʿa group, the Zaydīs, survived in the mountainous regions of Yemen and northern Iran, as well as in the far Maghrib, while the Nuṣayrīs survived in the mountains of southern Turkey/northern Syria.

Imāmī Shiʿism and Its Offshoots

For those Shiʿa who eschewed revolution, for whom the imam was primarily a source of guidance, the scope of their initial presence is difficult to evaluate in the sources. Despite the later Shiʿa traditions' propensity to look back toward a numerous and highly structured beginnings, it seems that the early quietist Shiʿa were loosely organized at best. Later tradition looks back to al-Ḥusayn's son, ʿAlī b. al-Ḥusayn, known as Zayn al-ʿĀbidīn (d. ca. 95/712), as the successor to the imamate of al-Ḥusayn (for a chart of the imams, see Figure 4.2). However, evidence for a significant following is problematic to decipher. More certain is that a moderate Shiʿite community began to form around Zayn al-ʿĀbidīn's son and grandson, the imams al-Bāqir and al-Ṣādiq, respectively.

Muḥammad b. ʿAlī (d. 114/733), known as al-Bāqir (the shortened form of *bāqir al-ʿulūm*, the "revealer of knowledge"), advocated a quietist approach against his more revolutionary brother, Zayd, and against the many *ghulāt* groups of Kufa. Al-Bāqir was said to have advocated *taqiyya* (cautionary dissimulation) and to have discouraged his followers and

[26] Haider, *Shīʿī Islam*, 115–21.

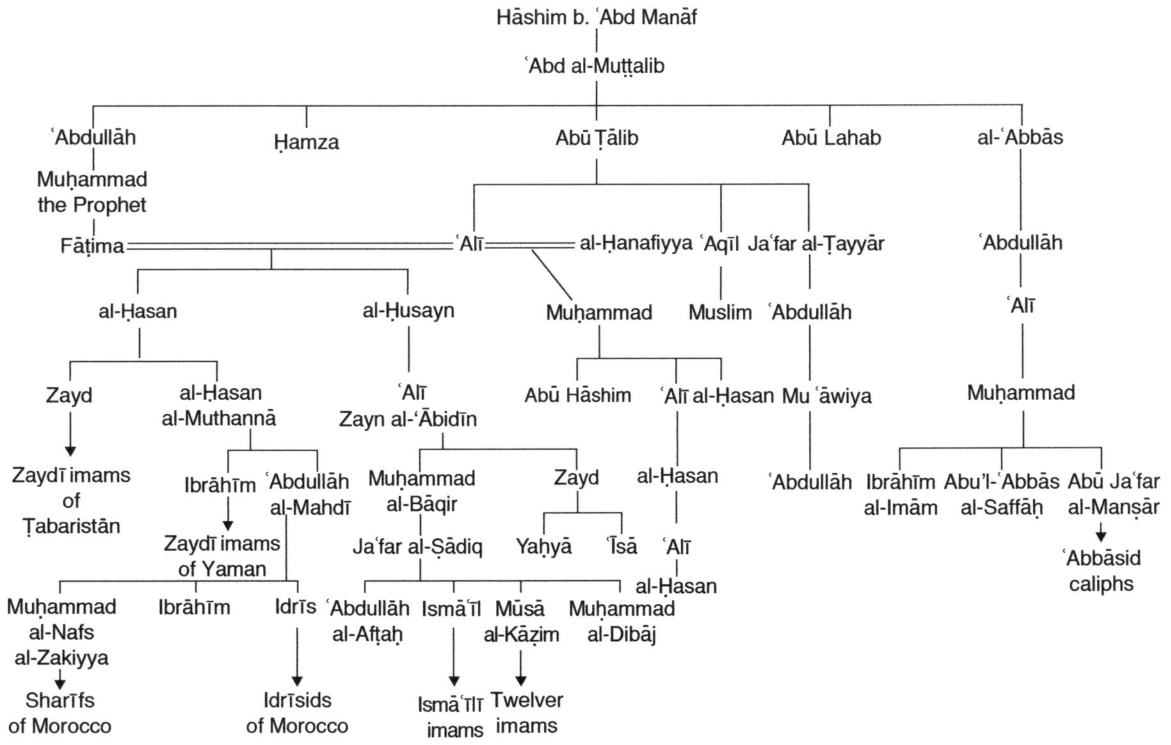

Figure 4.2 The Hāshimids and early Shiʿi imams.

admirers from engaging in rebellious activities.[27] His knowledge was widely respected in the Islamic community, especially among those who held the elevated place of the *ahl al-bayt*. His legal opinions began to set the emerging quietist Shiʿite community, later known as the Imāmiyya, apart from other types of Shiʿa, especially in Kufa. Some of these opinions are worth examining in some detail as they allow for an important insight into the nature of Islamic sectarianism in the early period. Thus, for example, against the opinion of other Muslim jurists al-Bāqir required the washing of the feet during ablution, subsequently forbidding the wiping over the socks/shoes (what is known as *maṣh ʿalā al-khuffayn*).[28] He required saying the *basmala* aloud during prayer and required the voicing of "curses and invocations" (what is known as *qunūt*) in all obligatory prayers.[29] Against Abū Ḥanīfa and his followers, who allowed the limited consumption of an alcoholic date brew known as *nabīdh*, al-Bāqir forbade drinking any kind of alcoholic beverage.[30]

What is noticeable about these rulings is how they speak, whether directly or indirectly, to the issue of ritual prayer (*ṣalāt*) among Muslims. This focus on ritual detail reveals, to an extent, how Muslims conceptualized sectarian identity in early periods.[31] Ritual often functioned as a marker of sectarian identity in the early second/eighth century. Differences in the performance of rituals (such as prayer) were visible to others, whereas beliefs and doctrinal stances were not. Thus, delineating the specific ways that a community, in this case the nascent Imāmī Shiʿi community, performed their public rituals created a means by which communal loyalties could be demonstrated. Prayer became a means for signifying and determining affiliation, such that prayer became shorthand for determining the reliability of the person performing it. For this reason, *ḥadīth* scholars would examine the prayer of a person before relating traditions from that person.[32] For the nascent Shiʿa, the importance of ritual to sectarian identity was reinforced by the gradual sect-affiliation of mosques in Kufa, where mosques progressively shifted from being tribally organized to being sect-organized and also by the performance of public pilgrimages to sacred places.[33] Indeed, Imāmī literature emphasizes the importance of pilgrimage to sacred sites such as Karbala and ʿAlī's tomb.

[27] Lalani, *Early Shiʿi Thought*, 88–91. [28] Lalani, *Early Shiʿi Thought*, 121.
[29] Lalani, *Early Shiʿi Thought*, 122–23; Haider, *Origins of the Shiʿa*, 71–74, 109–114.
[30] Lalani, *Early Shiʿi Thought*, 122; Haider, *Origins of the Shiʿa*, 156–59.
[31] The Qurʾan addresses the issue of coming to prayers drunk in 4:43. The verse appears to limit (though not absolutely forbid) the consumption of alcohol among Muḥammad's early followers.
[32] Haider, *Origins of the Shiʿa*, 219. [33] Haider, *Origins of the Shiʿa*, 231ff.

Ritual, mosque attendance and organization and pilgrimage all present "non-theological" markers of sect identity, and they seem to be the most important methods of sectarian self-identification in the early Islamic periods. Alternately, there remains a significant amount of doctrinal ambiguity among certain important thinkers in the early Islamic period. Thus, it is not hard to find examples of prominent personalities who, although later accepted as "Sunnis," seem to have been involved in "Shiʿite" activities. Thus, the legal scholar Abū Ḥanīfa, who lent his name to one of the four accepted Sunni legal schools, is reported to have monetarily supported Zayd b. ʿAlī's uprising, while al-Shāfiʿī, eponym of the Shāfiʿī legal school, was himself involved in a Shiʿite uprising in the Yemen.[34] These examples point toward two important sectarian realities in the early Islamic period. First, the importance of ritual over doctrine in defining the boundaries of sectarianism, and second, the range of ambiguities in identifying those supporting the family of the Prophet.

Al-Bāqir's son, Jaʿfar b. Muḥammad (d. 148/765), known as al-Ṣādiq (the "truthful one"), and also as al-Fāḍil ("most excellent") and al-Ṭāhir ("purified"), inherited the mantle of his father and led the emergent Imāmī Shiʿite community through the late Umayyad period, the ʿAbbāsid revolution, and into early ʿAbbāsid era. In this early period, the imams lived in Madina, but many of their followers hailed from Kufa. Among the many important scholarly milestones attributed to al-Ṣādiq and his followers was that they articulated the quietist Shiʿite doctrine of the imamate. Central to the imamate doctrine was the question of legitimate succession among the *ahl al-bayt*: what is the nature of succession and what characterizes the true imam? The fully articulated Imāmī theory of the imamate (which, in fact, matured over two centuries) postulated that God was just (*ʿādil*) in a manner that was understandable to His creatures, and in a fashion that made compelling the important conclusion that God would not leave humanity without access to divinely guided leadership in the form of the imams.[35] The issue of succession and leadership was simply too important for God to leave up to human beings. Jaʿfar al-Ṣādiq and his followers thus came to hold that imams explicitly designated (*naṣṣ*) their successors, and that they possessed a special knowledge (*ʿilm*) of religious matters that was passed from imam to imam. Thus, Imāmī Shiʿa held that God had chosen Muḥammad, purified and guided him, and given him exclusive knowledge of the Qurʾan and the strictures of religion. Muḥammad had designated ʿAlī (at Ghadīr

[34] Van Ess, *Theology and Society*, 1:214–15; Khadduri, *Al-Shāfiʿī's Risāla*, 8–16.
[35] Haider, *Shīʿī Islam*, 18ff.

Khumm) and on his death passed this knowledge to ʿAlī, who had then passed it to al-Ḥasan, who passed it to al-Ḥusayn. Al-Ḥusayn designated his son Zayn al-ʿĀbidīn before his martyrdom at Karbala, who then passed the imamate to al-Bāqir, who passed it to al-Ṣādiq. As it was ultimately God Himself who, out of His mercy and just nature, had purified and guided the family of the Prophet and endowed them with exclusive knowledge of religion, it was up to human beings to recognize the imams as God's chosen leaders for humanity, and to follow them. The imam was God's proof (*ḥujja*) to humankind, proof of God's mercy and justice to them, and proof that God had not abandoned them after prophecy ended with Muḥammad. Later Shiʿa also held that God protected the imams from making errors in conduct and judgment, holding them to be *maʿṣūm*(a term sometimes interpreted to mean "infallible").[36]

Equally important to the Imāmī theory of the imamate is what is not included in it, namely, any requirement that the imam need enjoy actual political power or participate in obtaining it. In sharp contrast with activist *ghulāt* or Zaydī understandings of the imamate, Imāmī Shiʿites essentially fashioned an apolitical imamate doctrine, separating as much as possible the religious function of the imam from the political authority that leaders were usually assumed to wield. There were good historical reasons in the failed *ghulāt* movements as well as in the failed revolts of Zayd b. ʿAlī and his sons (such as al-Nafs al-Zakiyya) for consciously following a politically quietist role for the imam. Subtler still was the process by which the ʿAbbāsid revolution and its aftermath convinced many who sympathized with the *ahl al-bayt* that the ʿAbbāsids, as rival claimants from the Prophet's family (albeit ones who less and less relied on these claims to bolster their rule) had, in fact, established a more or less workable system of government and addressed the most pressing concerns of the Umayyad-era revolutionaries. As many of these supporters threw in their lot with the ʿAbbāsids and became more and more aligned with the emerging Sunni consensus, Jaʿfar al-Ṣādiq's theory of the imamate preserved a space for those whose devotion to the *ahl al-bayt*, now narrowly defined as descendants through ʿAlī's son al-Ḥasan and al-Ḥusayn, remained the primary lens through which they understood what submission to God (*islām*) entailed and meant. Put another way: al-Bāqir and al-Ṣādiq articulated a narrative of Shiʿism by which God had made the imams His authoritative leaders on earth through their knowledge rather than through their ability to seize and hold power. This turned out to be an astute move, given the religio-political climate of

[36] Haider, *Shīʿī Islam*, 42–43.

the ʿAbbāsid era, and it allowed quietist Shiʿism to survive into the coming centuries in various guises.

Imāmī Shiʿism was the baseline from which the main contemporary Shiʿa groups, namely the Ithnā-ʿAsharī and Ismāʿīlī Shiʿites, sprung, and it was the issue of succession to al-Ṣādiq that created the main divisions among them. Al-Ṣādiq's succession became a source of division even before his death in 148/765, although it was his death that brought such divisions to the fore. Jaʿfar al-Ṣādiq had three sons, the eldest of whom, ʿAbdullāh (known as al-Aftaḥ – the "broad shouldered"), claimed the imamate after his father's death. However, ʿAbdullāh died not seventy days after his father, and apparently without a son, causing some of his followers (who became known as the Fatḥiyya) to regard him as the returning savior. Others claimed that ʿAbdullāh secretly had a son called Muḥammad and followed this hidden son as the next imam. This (secret) son, however, also apparently died without children, leading some of his followers to also make messianic claims about him. Nothing came of the Fatḥiyya and their offshoots. They largely disappeared from the scene or began to follow other imams, leaving only a passing testimony to their existence.[37]

Other of al-Ṣādiq's followers had been dissatisfied with ʿAbdullāh, claiming that he was not knowledgeable enough in religious matters to be the imam. Some of these followers looked to al-Ṣādiq's second son, Ismāʿīl, as the legitimate successor. Ismāʿīl, however, died even before his father. For those who became known as the Ismāʿīlīs, the line of legitimate imams went through Ismāʿīl to his son (Jaʿfar al-Ṣādiq's grandson), Muḥammad b. Ismāʿīl.

A third contingent held that Jaʿfar al-Ṣādiq had passed the imamate to his youngest son, Mūsā (known as al-Kāẓim), after the death of Ismāʿīl. Those who followed this line of imams became known, much later, as the Ithnā-ʿAshariyya. During his lifetime, Mūsā remained true to his father's legacy and maintained an apolitical stance. He was nevertheless imprisoned in 179/795 by the ʿAbbāsid caliph Hārūn al-Rashīd largely because of his following among the Shiʿa. Mūsā al-Kāẓim was said to be the first to organize collection of funds (both *zakāt* and *khums*, the "fifth" of the spoils given to the Prophet and paid by the Shiʿa to his family after his death) using deputies (*wakīl/wukalāʾ*). Despite his refusal to get involved in the politics of his day, al-Kāẓim nevertheless managed to create a system for amassing monies as well as a network of deputies who could serve as mouthpieces for imprisoned imams. Al-Kāẓim was poisoned four years after his arrest (i.e. in 183/799), and his body was

[37] Haider, *Shīʿī Islam*, 91–92.

interred in the Kāẓimiyya mosque in Iraq.[38] In what was becoming a predictable pattern, a group of Shiʿa refused to believe that he was dead, and held him to be the returning savior.

The rest of the Imāmī community looked toward Mūsā al-Kāẓim's son, ʿAlī al-Riḍā (d. 203/819), as his successor. In the succession struggle to the ʿAbbāsid caliph Hārūn al-Rashīd, the caliph al-Maʾmūn courted favor with Shiʿa by naming al-Riḍā his successor and even ordered coins to be minted proclaiming al-Riḍā as the next caliph. However, al-Maʾmūn had al-Riḍā poisoned in 203/819 while the imam was traveling with the caliph in Khurasān. For this reason, al-Riḍā is buried in present-day Mashhad (northeastern Iran).[39] He was succeeded by his son, Muḥammad al-Taqī al-Jawwād (d. 220/835), who enjoyed one of the shortest imamates of all of the imams (lasting sixteen years). By the era of al-Jawwād, the ʿAbbāsid caliphs knew that the Shiʿa looked to their imams for guidance, and so they often ordered them to be isolated in their houses. Al-Jawwād was poisoned in Baghdad and buried with his grandfather (Mūsā al-Kāẓim) in the Kāẓimiyya mosque.[40]

Al-Jawwād was succeeded by ʿAlī al-Hādī al-Naqī (d. 254/868), who assumed the imamate at the young age of seven or eight. Although his youth initially presented questions as to the nature of the imam's knowledge (i.e. whether such a youth would possess the knowledge sufficient to function as the imam), ʿAlī al-Hādī is remembered as a great scholar and teacher. He was also suspected by the caliph al-Mutawakkil as harboring plans for a revolution (the collection of *khums* had by this time become something that the caliphs suspected) and was "invited" to the new capital Samarra to join the caliph. There he was poisoned by a later ʿAbbāsid caliph (it is unclear which one).[41]

ʿAlī al-Hādī was succeeded by his son, al-Ḥasan al-ʿAskarī (d. 260/874), who spent his entire imamate under house arrest in Samarra. Like his father, al-Ḥasan al-ʿAskarī was remembered as a great teacher (a qurʾanic commentary, *tafsīr*, is attributed to him), though his succession to the imamate was not universally recognized among the Shiʿa.[42] After he was poisoned, like many imams before him, a group held him to be a messianic figure. He was buried with his father in the "ʿAskarī" mosque in Samarra.[43]

[38] Momen, *An Introduction to Shi'i Islam*, 39–41.
[39] Momen, *An Introduction to Shi'i Islam*, 41–42.
[40] Momen, *An Introduction to Shi'i Islam*, 42–43.
[41] Momen, *An Introduction to Shi'i Islam*, 43–44.
[42] Modarressi, *Crisis and Consolidation*, 65.
[43] This mosque gained notoriety in the second Iraq War by being twice bombed by al-Qaida, first in 2006 and then again in 2007.

Al-Ḥasan al-ʿAskarī's son, Muḥammad b. al-Ḥasan, the twelfth imam of the Imāmī Shiʿite line, was said to have assumed imamate at the age of five. He thus lived the entirety of his imamate under house arrest, isolated from his followers, from an early age. In fact, few Shiʿa ever saw this imam, who was said to have communicated with his followers through four deputies (*nāʾib*/*nawāʾib*) during the period between 260/874 and 329/941. This period later became known as the period of the "lesser" occultation (*al-ghayba al-ṣughrā*). When the last of Muḥammad b. al-Ḥasan's deputies died, a group of Shiʿa held the imam to have entered a "greater occultation" (*al-ghayba al-kubrā*) whereby God hid him from sight until such time as God would make him return at the end of time as the awaited messianic savior. With the growing articulation of this idea, the twelfth imam became associated with titles such as *qāʾim* (one who rises) and *mahdī* (rightly guided), and he was expected to "fill the earth with justice as it is now filled with injustice."[44] Some sources indicate that Muḥammad b. al-Ḥasan sent a letter to his followers explaining the occultation and his messianic role to them. In this way, the messianic expectations of many Shiʿa found a durable focal point (recall that several of the imams had been the objects of messianic expectation after their deaths) in Muḥammad b. al-Ḥasan al-ʿAskarī, and Ithnā-ʿAsharī ("Twelver") Shiʿism was born.

The idea of the twelfth imam as the awaited Mahdī is, obviously, quite an important and defining belief for the Ithnā-ʿAshariyya. Some of the titles used for the twelfth imam provide a sense of his role and function. He is regarded as al-Muntaẓir (the awaited one), al-Mahdī (the rightly guided one), Ṣāḥib al-Zamān (master of the age), al-Qāʾim (the one who rises [with the sword]), and al-Ḥujja (the proof [of God]).[45] Messianic expectation among Twelver Shiʿa has, for the most part, been interpreted as patiently awaiting the return of the Mahdī. However, every now and then it assumes a more "activist" form when certain Shiʿa have decided to pave the way for the Mahdī's return.

The notion of the awaited Mahdī has also exerted a powerful effect on how Ithnā-ʿAsharī Shiʿa have regarded government. Since the only truly legitimate government is that of the twelfth imam, and no one finally knows when the imam will return, Shiʿa scholars have traditionally eschewed politics in favor of political quietism and religious scholarship. As the "heirs to the prophets," to use the phrasing of the oft-quoted *ḥadīth* from the Prophet Muḥammad, the Twelver Shiʿa *ʿulamāʾ* have devoted themselves to answering the religious questions of their followers,

[44] Modarressi, *Crisis and Consolidation*, 89–90.
[45] Sachedina, *Islamic Messianism*, 58–70.

directing piety toward the remembrance of the imams, and offered a model of patient expectation for the Mahdī's return. Thus, there is little by way of Ithnā-ʿAsharī polities in the classical Islamic period. It wasn't until the fourth/tenth century (at the earliest) that Twelver Shiʿism became fully articulated, and it remained largely an urban phenomenon guided by religious scholars.[46]

Certain early political groupings did possess a kind of general sympathy for the *ahl al-bayt*, but it was the Būyid family (i.e. the Buwayhids) who initially adopted and then patronized Ithnā-ʿAsharī Shiʿism. As one of the many powerful local families who assumed real power during the waning of the ʿAbbāsid caliphs, the Būyids controlled the central regions of the ʿAbbāsid Empire. At their height they controlled a territory stretching from Syria to Afghanistan in the fourth/tenth and fifth/eleventh centuries. Although they officially recognized the ʿAbbāsid caliph, the Būyids effectively ruled the central regions until the coming of the Seljuq Turks. Having first adopted Zaydīsm, once secure in their power the Būyids turned to the more politically quietist Twelver form of Shiʿism as more favorable to their continued reign. They built up the pilgrim complex at Karbala and Najaf, and the first Būyid ruler, Aḥmad b. Būya (who adopted the title Muʿizz al-Dawla), officiated in the first public commemoration of ʿĀshūrāʾ (in Baghdad, in 333/945).[47]

It is telling that the Būyids chose ʿĀshūrāʾ, the commemoration of the martyrdom of al-Ḥusayn, as a centerpiece of their public embrace of Ithnā-ʿAsharī Shiʿism. ʿĀshūrāʾ (Ashura) remains one of the oldest and most important ritual events among mainly Twelver (as well as ʿAlawī) Shiʿites, dating from just a few years after the event of Karbala itself (61/680). The Umayyad caliphs frequently attempted to stop the commemoration, while the ʿAbbāsids alternately supported or suppressed the pilgrimage (*ziyāra*) to Karbala (the caliph al-Mutawakkil, for example, had the site razed to the ground).[48] ʿĀshūrāʾ thus early on became a symbol for those who held the *ahl al-bayt* in high regard, and a means by which their devotion could be publicly and ritually enacted. By publicly promoting the commemorations at Karbala, the Būyids were thus loudly and clearly announcing their affiliation as Shiʿa, but doing so in a way that large majorities of Muslims (with their general affection for the Prophet and his family) could also find meaning. In this way, it is difficult to interpret their actions as purely "sectarian."

Moreover, the late antique (and largely Christian) context for the first commemorations of ʿĀshūrāʾ remain rather straightforward. In late

[46] Modarressi, *Crisis and Consolidation*, 96ff. [47] Busse, "Iran under the Būyids," 250ff.
[48] Aghaie, *The Martyrs of Karbala*, 10; Haider, *Shīʿī Islam*, 74–75.

antiquity it was common to visit the tombs of martyrs, use their bones, clothes, and other objects that they had touched as relics and to consider the places where they were killed/buried as having been sanctified by their deaths. Public commemorations of martyrs that celebrated their "birthday" (meaning the day that they were born anew in heaven) took place at martyriums all across the late antique world. That Muslims early on commemorated the death of al-Ḥusayn at Karbala on its anniversary, the tenth day of the lunar month of Muḥarram, known as ʿĀshūrāʾ, and then forty days later (on Arbaʿīn), is therefore hardly surprising.

Even as the influence of the Būyids waned, Twelver Shiʿism continued, mainly in the cities, surviving the staunch Sunnism of the Seljuqs and the destruction of the Mongols. Later, beginning in the tenth/sixteenth century, the Safavid era ushered in several important changes to the public performance of Shiʿism. The Safavids emerged from groups of nomadic Turkic peoples who fled westward from the Mongols invasions toward Anatolia. This conglomeration, sometimes known after their conical red hats as the *qizilbāsh* (literally, "red heads"), populated the highlands between Anatolia and Iran. Many melded their antinomian ("*ghulāt*") Shiʿism with Sufism, especially with that associated with Haji Bektāsh Veli (in Arabic, Ḥājj Baktāsh Walī [d. 1271]), a Persian saint, born in Nīshāpūr, and a descendant of the seventh imam, Mūsā al-Kāẓim (see Figure 4.3). Haji Betāsh Veli had himself fled to Anatolia in the wake of the Mongol conquests and began teaching a version of the mystical path strongly focused on ʿAlī and the twelve imams. He eventually settled in a town that now bears his name and hosts his tomb, Hacibektash, in Anatolia. Some of his followers established the Sufi order after his death.

As groups of *qizilbāsh* settled, they associated with the emerging Ottoman Empire. Some became followers of various dervish groups, including the nascent Bektāshī Sufi Order, an order with a strong sense of ʿAlīd loyalism, but not one that would count as Shiʿism proper. A strong Bektāshī element eventually aligned itself with the Janissaries (the elite military forces of the Ottoman Empire), who, with the strengthening of the Ottoman Empire, increasingly saw themselves as defenders of Sunnism.[49] Among Turkic groups that remained nomadic, however, their Shiʿism blended with Bektāshī Sufism in other ways, eventually forming what is now known as "Alevi" (not to be confused with ʿAlawī/Nuṣayrī) Shiʿism.

The Alevis of Anatolia looked to the teachings of Haji Bektāsh Veli as the basis of their particular understanding of religion. This combined the practice of a mystical path with the realization of love for and unity of all

[49] Karamustafa, *God's Unruly Friends*, 84.

Figure 4.3 1970 Turkish stamp depicting Haji Bektāsh Veli.

beings. For them, reality has both an inner and outer aspect. Outwardly it is plural and diverse, but inwardly it is unified. The persons of the Prophet Muḥammad and ʿAlī were thus reflections of God, creating a triad of Ultimate Truth (*ḥaqq*), Muḥammad, and ʿAlī. Likewise, the twelve imams of the Ithnā-ʿAsharī system were reflections of ʿAlī, and the divinely appointed leaders for humankind. The purpose of a good life was to learn to love God, through His prophets and imams, and to perfect one's being, becoming at the last stages of this path of mystical perfection a perfected human being (*al-insān al-kāmil*). Alevis held that Muḥammad, ʿAlī, the imams, and Haji Bektāsh Veli were all perfected human beings and that the potential to become such also exists within each person.

Alevis ground their thinking in a collection of scriptures known as the Buyruks, which consists of qurʾanic verses, sayings of ʿAlī and the imams, the life of Haji Bektāsh Veli, and also poems from important figures, such as Yunis Emre, Pīr Sulṭān, and even the founder of the Safavid dynasty, Ismāʿīl I. Their mystical path (known as the *yol*, which simply means "path" in Turkish) follows four stages: the first stage involves following the religious precepts and laws common to all Muslims. All Muslims are thus imagined to be on the path to perfection in some way, yet the Alevi tradition posits that to progress further or faster, they must be initiated into the second stage, which involves following a living spiritual guide. These are known to the Alevis as *dede*s (literally "uncle" in Turkish), *pīr*s, or *murshid*s. The *dede*s are the spiritual and social leaders of the Alevi community. The third stage of the path involves accumulating knowledge (*maʿrifat*) of the true nature of reality, and the last stage comprises the realization of that reality and the perfection of one's being. It is held that most Alevis live their lives in practice of the second stage. The third and fourth are thought to be reserved for the spiritual elites. Alevism, like Nuṣayrīsm, is initiatic and secretive and involves the pursuit of a rigorous mystical discipline under the guidance of a spiritual master.

Alevi communal worship is held on Thursdays and is known as the cem or jem. It is held in an edifice known as the Cemevi. A *dede* leads the service and is assisted by twelve other persons (representing the twelve imams). A cem consists of music, singing, dancing, and discussion. The prototype of this service is Muḥammad's ascension into heaven (*miʿrāj*), whereby the Prophet witnessed a vision of heaven, forty saints, and their leader, ʿAlī.[50] The music, song, and dance have particular messages for their hearers. The music is played on the Saz, or Balgama, even the physical parts of which are held to have mystical significance. So too, the *samaḥ*, ritual dancing, done by men and women together, signifies various aspects of the Alevi mystical path. Another aspect of the cem service is drinking of fruit juice (sometimes wine), called *dem* ("blood"), which represents the intoxication of the lover in the beloved (and the extinguishing of the human consciousness of diversity in the unicity of God). The service ends with a discussion of meaning, called the *sohbet*. As with the Nuṣayrīs, the Alevis exhibit strong parallelism with some aspects of Christianity and have been described as strongly syncretistic. It is

[50] Schubel, "When the Prophet Went on the *Miraç*," 330–31.

important to remember, however, that religious traditions whose core truths involve the realization of the unity of all things in God do not necessarily see themselves as amalgamating different things: to them all is One, after all, when the true nature of reality is grasped.

Like their Nuṣayrī cousins, Alevi communities have survived in the mountainous regions of Anatolia and have often practiced secrecy or simply kept a low profile. They do celebrate certain communal festivals. The spring equinox, known as Nawrūz, is important, as are the festivals commemorating the mysterious prophet al-Khiḍr (who is sometimes conflated with St. George) and the various saints' days (such as those of Pīr Sulṭān or Haji Bektāsh Veli). The pilgrimage to Makka is generally not observed, with Alevis visiting the saints' tombs instead. Like other religious minorities, maintaining a generally inconspicuous public presence has helped them to survive the long term.

Even further east in Iraq and Persia, another Shiʿa qua Sufi order emerged from among the *qizilbāsh*: this was the Safaviyya, founded by Shaykh Ṣāfī al-Dīn Ardabīlī (d. 734/1334). A later leader of this group, Shaykh Junayd (d. 864/1460), turned the order toward *ghulāt* Shiʿism (it was said, for example, that some of his followers divinized him). He also militarized them and sent them raiding into Armenia and Georgia. Shaykh Ḥaydar (d. 893/1488) continued conquests into Circassia and Dagestan, and it was his troops (mostly Azerī Turks) who became known as "*qizilbāsh*," and who regarded their leaders as semi-divine beings. The grandson of Shaykh Ḥaydar, Ismāʿīl, began conquering Iran, Iraq, and into Turkey and Central Asia in the early 900s/1500s. He claimed that he was *murshid-i-kāmil* (the perfect master) and the Mahdī, and he established an empire that would last 200 years, the Safavids. Most importantly for the story of Muslim sectarianism, Shah Ismāʿīl forced the conversion of this area to Twelver Shiʿism (he probably realized that his own form of antimonian Shiʿism would not be accepted by the majority). To do so, he took Ithnā-ʿAsharī scholars from Najaf and relocated them in Iran in the shrine city of Qom. In 920/1514, the Ottomans inflicted a serious defeat, from which the Safavids recovered, but which damaged Ismāʿīl psychologically. He died shortly thereafter.

The Safavid Empire survived and thrived under Ismāʿīl's successors, especially Shah ʿAbbās (r. 995–1038/1587–1629), the most eminent of Safavid rulers. Shah ʿAbbās established the lavish Safavid capital at Isfahan. Moreover, he created a standing army (undermining the power of *qizilbāsh*) and claimed absolute authority as the *murshid-i-kāmil*. The empire declined after death of Shah ʿAbbās as European sea trade diverted commerce away from the Silk Road to sea routes and as taxes for the army overwhelmed the population. In 1134/1722, Afghan tribes invaded the Safavid Empire and ended the dynasty, after which a period of anarchy followed with many different groups vying for power. In this situation, the Shiʿite *ʿulamāʾ* often became de facto governors of towns. By the 1200s/1800s, a *qizilbāsh* tribe known as the Qajars gained control of the former Safavid Empire and shifted the capital to Tehran.

Beginning in the Safavid era, ʿĀshūrāʾ commemorations assumed new forms and meanings when deployed by the emerging Safavid nation-state. This process could be said to begin with Kamāl al-Dīn Ḥossain Vāʾiz Kāshefī's *Rowzat al-Shuhadāʾ* (*The Meadow of the Martyrs*). Based on earlier works, such as Saʿīd al-Dīn's *Rawḍat al-Islām* (*The Meadow of Islam*) and al-Khawarizmī's *Maqtal Nūr al-Aʾimma* (*Murder of the Light of the Imams*), Kāshefī's objective was to produce a distinctly Persian account to replace existing Arabic-language narratives.[51] His work became canonical within the Persian tradition in part because the Safavid political elite monopolized the *Rowzat al-Shuhadāʾ*, as well as the public sermons, known as *rowzeh khānī*, that were based upon it. Their patronage established a set of distinctly Shiʿi rituals that legitimated their rule as it demarcated the state from the Sunni Uzbeks to the east and the Ottomans to the west.[52]

In the Qajar period, the Karbala narrative became a site of contestation insofar as its public and dramatic recreation, known as *taʿziya*, was patronized by both state and social elites. Lacking the religious legitimacy of the Safavids, the Qajars patronized *taʿziya* performances to legitimate their rule.[53] However, the Iranian Shiʿite *ʿulamāʾ* also patronized these rituals, thereby contesting the authority of the Qajar elites to use the Karbala narrative as an effective method for social and political legitimation.[54] In this way, Qajar-era deployments of the Karbala narrative continued to play an important role in the creation, maintenance, and re-creation of the Persian/Shiʿa sociopolitical order.

The prestige attached to the scholarly centers of Najaf and Qom as well as the trade networks connecting these centers to Shiʿa throughout the Islamic world, meant that the largely Safavid-to-Qajar-era forms of Karbala commemoration have profoundly molded the trajectory of how Shiʿa observe ʿĀshūrāʾ.[55] Thus, in addition to wearing mourning attire during the ten days leading up to and including ʿĀshūrāʾ, many Shiʿa attend sermons, poetry, and retellings of the event of Karbala (in Iran, India, and Bahrain, for example, these can include lavish *taʿziya*, which

51 Amanat, "*Meadow of the Martyrs*," 258.
52 Aghaie, *The Martyrs of Karbala*, 11–12; Lambton, "A Reconsideration of the Position of the *Marjaʿ al-Taqlīd*," 115–16.
53 Aghaie, *The Martyrs of Karbala*, 13–16.
54 Aghaie, *The Martyrs of Karbala*, 17.
55 Cole, *Sacred Space and Holy War*, 78–94.

are reenactments of the martyrdom of al-Ḥusayn, known especially in Iran). Over the years, a number of public traditions have sprung up around ʿĀshūrāʾ: there are often public processions, which might include a ritualized form of striking the chest or possibly even shedding blood (called *matham/laṭmiyya* or *maṭam*) in commemoration of the sufferings of al-Ḥusayn. The bloodier displays of Shiʿite commemoration during ʿĀshūrāʾ are often the ones most commonly, consistently, and recently condemned by Shiʿite leaders.

Different Shiʿa throughout the centuries have found a range of narrative meanings in the story of Karbala.[56] For Ithnā-ʿAsharī (and ʿAlawī) Shiʿa, the martyrdom of the Prophet's grandson is a story of resistance to injustice, oppression, and tyranny. It is the story of an abandoned imam who marched to his death at the hands of iniquitous rulers. On the one hand, the response to such a story has been mourning and remembrance, and assurances that the awaited Mahdī will at some point arrive to bring the justice that has been delayed. On the other hand (and, on the whole, more rarely), the story of Karbala can invoke a more activist response by encouraging its hearers to resist injustices in the present or to emulate al-Ḥusayn by actively fighting against tyranny. In all cases, the Karbala narrative offers a potent locus of memory through which the Shiʿa express their devotion to the Prophet's family.

Ismāʿīlī Shiʿism

For quietist Shiʿa, allegiance to the imam is vital for salvation because God chooses the imam, invests him with religious knowledge and authority, and thereby establishes him as the sole legitimate source of guidance for humankind. Only by following the divinely chosen leader can a person correctly perform their *islām* (submission), and for this reason Shiʿite subgroups were initially defined by the imams that they chose to follow, with doctrinal, ritual, and legal differences generally flowing from those decisions. For those quietist Imāmī Shiʿa who looked to Jaʿfar al-Ṣādiq's son Ismāʿīl as the designated imam, his death before his father did not invalidate his earthly imamate, and they looked to Ismāʿīl's son, Muḥammad b. Ismāʿīl, as the imam after his father. Yet Muḥammad b. Ismāʿīl was said to have gone into hiding in southwest Persia, initiating what later Fāṭimid Ismāʿīlīs would call a period of "concealment" (*satr*). This absence was said to have caused a split among his followers. Some, known later as the "pure" Ismāʿīliyya, held that Muḥammad b. Ismāʿīl was the Mahdī and the Qāʾim ("one who rises") who would return at the

[56] Haider, *Shīʿī Islam*, 71–73.

end of time to establish justice. Others, known as the Mubārakiyya (after a title of Ismāʿīl, *mubārak*, "the blessed one"), held to the continuity of imamate through his progeny. This group likely consisted of his supporters during his lifetime, and they seem to have largely disappeared after his death, leaving the "pure" Ismāʿīliyya to await the return of Muḥammad b. Ismāʿīl as the Mahdī.[57]

These early (pre-Fāṭimid) Ismāʿīlīs moved their activities to Salamiyya (in present-day Syria) and established an extensive religious outreach and missionary movement (*daʿwa*) into southern Iraq. The *daʿwa* was initially successful in rural areas, especially among disaffected Imāmī Shiʿites trying to make sense of the apparent disappearance of the twelfth imam. From Salamiyya, the early Ismāʿīlī movement evolved into a secretive, hierarchical group that used initiation and the gradual disclosure of religious truths to establish their followers as a spiritual elite within the early Islamic world. That is to say, early Ismāʿīlīs believed that outer realities veiled hidden truths (*ḥaqāʾiq*), and that only the imam's exercise of esoteric interpretation (*taʾwīl*) uncovered these truths. This truth, however, would only be shared with those initiated into the Ismāʿīliyya, meaning that an elite (*khawāṣṣ*) consisting of the imam and his loyal followers had access to this esoteric knowledge while the rest (the "masses," *ʿawāmm*) would simply be left with the outer meanings of religion.

The structure of a secretive, initiatic group that introduced its initiates gradually to hidden truths matches that of several other kinds of religious groups in the late antique period, the most obvious being the various so-called gnostic Christians, but also Neoplatonic-inspired groups of all stripes. The philosophies of Neoplatonism likewise seem to have left a strong mark on what can be reconstructed of early Ismāʿīlī doctrines. Neoplatonism can be traced to the third-century philosopher Plotinus (d. 270 CE). This current of thought enjoyed widely popularity in the late antique world and survived into the medieval period in Europe, North Africa, and the Middle East. Consequently, Neoplatonism's specific articulations became many and varied. Nevertheless, certain general concepts, many of them found in the writings of Plotinus, can be found across the Neoplatonic spectrum. Especially, Neoplatonic groups share an idea of the One, the ineffable, unknowable first principle of reality, from whom emanated the creation and to whom all beings hoped to return.[58] For many Neoplatonists, the world was conceived as

[57] Daftary, *The Ismāʿīlīs*, 102–4.
[58] Fakhry, *A History of Islamic Philosophy*, 22–26; see also Dillon and Gerson, *Neoplatonic Philosophy*, xiii–xxii.

a material prison from which the spirit sought to escape. Such notions, familiar as they were among the communities of late antiquity, provided scaffolding upon which various religious communities would elaborate a cosmology of salvation through ascetic praxis.

This Neoplatonic nexus of ideas can be seen reflected in several early Ismāʿīlī ideas. For example, early Ismāʿīlīs taught that time progressed through a series of seven successive prophetic eras. Each new era was initiated by an "enunciator" or "speaker" (*nāṭiq*) of a divinely revealed message (for early Ismāʿīlīs the first six were Adam, Noah, Abraham, Moses, Jesus, and Muḥammad), the outer form of which imposed a religious law (*sharīʿa*). The inner and hidden meaning of the divine message of each era was passed to a legatee (*wāṣī*) (also called the "silent one" (*ṣāmit*), and the "foundation" (*asās*)), who propagated the secret among select elites of their age (the legatees of the first six ages were Seth, Shem, Ishmael, Aaron, Simon Peter, and ʿAlī b. Abī Ṭālib). These *wāṣīs* themselves had seven successors, the imams, who protected and taught the knowledge, the last of which became the *nāṭiq* of the next age (who abrogated the previous laws and promulgated a new law). Thus, history cycled through different ages with different types of religious authorities, until the seventh and final era. In the seventh era, Muḥammad b. Ismāʿīl (the last of the imams after ʿAlī b. Abī Ṭālib and thus *nāṭiq* of the last era) would combine the roles of *nāṭiq*, *wāṣī*,and imam and would usher in a golden age of justice at the end of time by making the secret available to all people.[59] For this reason (among others), the early Ismāʿīlīs considered him a unique figure.[60]

Early Ismāʿīlī cosmology likewise displays a strong Neoplatonic coloring, as Ismāʿīlīs paired the cyclical nature of history with a "gnostic"-inspired cosmology. Like Plotinus and other Neoplatonists, Ismāʿīlīs conceived of the creation as a series of emanations from God. Thus, God first said "be" and a primal being (called "Kūnī" or "Be" in the feminine) was formed.[61] This emanation of the principle of being was immediately followed by another, this one a primal being of

[59] The Nizārī Ismāʿīlīs do not consider al-Ḥasan b. ʿAlī to have been a full imam, considering him a type of nonhereditary imam known as a "trustee" (*mustawdaʿ*) imam and thus making Muḥammad b. Ismāʿīl the seventh in their reckoning. Likewise, the later Mustaʿlī Ismāʿīlīs considered ʿAlī the foundation (*asās*) of the imams and not counted as the first per se, similarly leaving Muḥammad b. Ismāʿīl as the seventh imam. By contrast, the Ithnā-ʿAsharī Shiʿites counted the imamate as having passed from al-Ḥasan to al-Ḥusayn, thus making Jaʿfar al-Ṣādiq's son Mūsā al-Kāẓim the seventh imam by their reckoning.

[60] Daftary, *The Ismāʿīlīs*, 104–5, 139–40.

[61] Note that in many earlier "gnostic" systems, the first being was often considered feminine, as it was here among the early Ismāʿīlīs. See, for example, Layton, *Nag Hammadi Codex II*, 2–7, 158–59, 252–53.

determination called Qadar. Qadar was the active principle that animated Kūnī and allowed it to act because existence without an animating principle is static. From the primal dyad of Kūnī-Qadar, the seven letters (of their names) formed the stuff from which the rest of the alphabet flowed, from which the "names" of all things and knowledge of their true nature emanated, on down into their reality in material form, such as angels, humans, the earth, and so on.[62] Early Ismāʿīlīs thus held to a sonic emanation of the universe, and one in which the macrocosmic structure corresponded to the microcosmic structure in such a way as to make the universe a series of reflections of itself. Thus, the dyad Kūnī-Qadar was respectively connected to the "pen" and "tablet" mentioned in the Qurʾan as existing with God; the seven letters of their names (the sonic building blocks of the universe) were associated with the seven *nāṭiq*s of each age. In such a universe, association with the true reality (God), and thus the appropriate form of submission (*islām*) to that Being, came through proper knowledge of the hidden structure of the universe. Only the prophets and imams possessed such knowledge, becoming thereby the gatekeepers of salvation.

Such was early Ismāʿīlism, sustained by a missionary movement out of the Levant, until the so-called split of 286/899. In that year, ʿAbdullāh (var. ʿUbaydallāh) b. al-Ḥusayn (who would become the first Fāṭimid imam), a descendant of Muḥammad b. Ismāʿīl, claimed the imamate in Salamiyya by arguing that his ancestors had always been imams, but had hidden this fact out of fear. Up to that point, Ibn Ismāʿīl's progeny had only ever publicly adopted the title of *ḥujja* (proof), maintaining that they were in contact with the imam/Mahdī Muḥammad b. Ismāʿīl. Thus, contrary to the teachings of the early Ismāʿīlīs of that time, ʿAbdullāh b. al-Ḥusayn contended that the line of imams had not ended with Muḥammad b. Ismāʿīl, and that the notion of Ibn Ismāʿīl's Mahdī-ship had been misunderstood. In fact, he asserted, the title of Mahdī had been collectively bestowed on the entire line of Muḥammad b. Ismāʿīl's descendants. According to this reinterpretation, there was more than one heptad in the age of Islam. This effectively postponed the seventh and final era to a later messianic time.[63]

ʿAbdullāh b. al-Ḥusayn's announcement split the movement into those who held to the original line of interpretation about Muḥammad b. Ismāʿīl as the Mahdī, the seventh imam of the seventh age whose return would usher in a reign of justice at the end of time, and those who cleaved to the new interpretation offered by ʿAbdullāh b. al-Ḥusayn. The old school followed Ḥamdān Qarmaṭ, who opposed ʿAbdullāh b. al-Ḥusayn,

[62] Daftary, *The Ismāʿīlīs*, 142–43. [63] Daftary, *The Ismāʿīlīs*, 125–29.

and collectively became known as Qarmaṭī Ismāʿīlīs (pl. Qarāmiṭa). The followers of ʿAbdullāh b. al-Ḥusayn became known with time as the Fāṭimiyyūn, the Fāṭimids.[64]

Early Qarmaṭīs continued to expect the return of Muḥammad b. Ismāʿīl as the Mahdī. Based on astrological speculations, several expected him as early as 317/928.[65] These Ismāʿīlīs were successful for a time in the eastern regions of former *daʿwa,* mainly Iraq, before falling into a kind of obscurity. The Qarmaṭīs of Baḥrayn and Khurasān established themselves for a rather longer period. These groups are remembered by and large for sacking Makka in 319/931, stealing the black stone, and taking it back to Baḥrayn (it was ransomed to the ʿAbbāsids in 339/950). But the Qarāmiṭa were gradually overshadowed and missionized by the Fāṭimids, and they eventually disappeared and/or were absorbed into the Fāṭimid movement.[66]

The Ismāʿīlīs who looked to ʿAbdullāh b. al-Ḥusayn (and referred to him as al-Mahdī) encouraged him to revolt in Salamiyya. He refused and fled for North Africa in 289/902 pursued by ʿAbbāsid agents. Finding his way across North Africa to Sijilmāsa (in present-day Morocco), he was jailed there by the Midrārid rulers of the city. However, the imam had dispatched his deputies and missionaries throughout North Africa. One of these, the able Abū ʿAbdullāh al-Shīʿī, worked with the Kutāma Berbers in Algeria and converted them to Ismāʿīlism. By 297/909 (and despite the imam being imprisoned), Abū ʿAbdullāh al-Shīʿī had conquered in the name of the imam the Ibāḍī Rustumids of Tāhart, the Zaydī Shiʿite Idrīsids of Fez, and Aghlabid (ʿAbbāsid governors) of Ifrīqiya, and had marched on Sijilmāsa and freed the imam, who was promptly proclaimed caliph and ruled as such until 322/934. He assumed the titles *al-mahdī bi'llāh* (God's Mahdī) and *amīr al-muʾminīn* (Commander of the Faithful).[67] Successive Fāṭimid imam-caliphs also adopted titles, by which they were and are often known.

ʿAbdullāh b. al-Ḥusayn al-Mahdī established in 308/921 a new capital at al-Mahdiyya (in modern-day Tunis) and expanded their conquests to Sicily and across Libya. Like many newly established polities, he faced a number of internal and external threats. His decision to secretly execute Abū ʿAbdullāh al-Shīʿī and his brother, for example, enraged his Kutāma Berber supporters, some of whom promptly revolted.[68]

Despite their overall successes, revolt would plague the early Fāṭimids in North Africa. Al-Mahdī's successor, al-Qāʾim Bi'llāh (Muḥammad

64 Daftary, *The Ismāʿīlīs*, 129–30. 65 Daftary, *The Ismāʿīlīs*, 130.
66 Daftary, *The Ismāʿīlīs*, 131. 67 Daftary, *The Ismāʿīlīs*, 134–36.
68 Daftary, *The Ismāʿīlīs*, 153.

b. ʿUbaydallāh al-Mahdī), never left Mahdiyya after assuming the caliphate, in part because of the popular and widespread uprising of Abū Yazīd Makhlad b. Kaydād, an Ibāḍī rebel who besieged him there for a year before being defeated. On al-Qāʾim's death, al-Manṣūr (Ismāʿīl b. al-Qāʾim) moved the capital to a new location, al-Manṣūriyya (near Qayrawān in present-day Tunisia). Under his successor, al-Muʿizz (Maʿad b. al-Manṣūr), the Fāṭimids conquered Egypt in 358/969 and established their new capital near the old city of Fusṭāṭ. They named it al-Qāhira (the "Victorious," Cairo) after a name for Mars, the star in the sky at the time of the victory. Cairo remained the seat of the Fāṭimid dynasty until it fell in 564/1169 to the Ayyūbids.[69]

At their height, the Fāṭimids extended across North Africa and into the Hijaz and Levant. They traded all throughout the Mediterranean, including with the Venetians and Genoese. They even sent emissaries to the Pope on several occasions (mainly during the Crusades). Egypt itself was not strongly Shiʿite, and so the Fāṭimids found themselves a minority in their own capital. With the wisdom of ecumenicalism and tolerance, the Fāṭimids often employed Sunnis, Christians, and Jews in high positions in the Fāṭimid administration.[70] Kutāma Berbers initially formed the backbone of the army, but later Turkish and Armenians, and still later black slave soldiers, joined the ranks of the Fāṭimid army. As a secretive, initiatic sect, Fāṭimid Shiʿism could exist as a religion of the specialized few while the empire incorporated many different kinds of ethnicities and sect/school persuasions.

In his capacity as living guide for humanity and leader of the Ismāʿīlī movement (a role restricted to the elite followers who accepted him as such), the imam-caliph presided over "sessions" of learning (*majlis/majālis*) in which he taught the elect. He was often aided in this capacity by the person of the chief judge (*qāḍī*) who also functioned as the head missionary, *dāʿī* (an institution established by al-Muʿizz).[71] The head *dāʿī* was often an original thinker in his own right. Such was the case, for example, with al-Qāḍī al-Nuʿmān, who served four successive Fāṭimid caliphs in Cairo until his death in 363/974. Jurist, historian, and exegete, al-Qāḍī al-Nuʿmān provided a popular (i.e. exoteric, *ẓāhirī*) justification for the Fāṭimid imamate that drew upon Ithnā-ʿAsharī and Zaydī sources. His work *Daʿāʾim al-Islām* (*The Pillars of Islam*) established the basis for Fāṭimid jurisprudence, while *Iftitāḥ al-Daʿwa wa Ibtidāʾ al-Dawla* (*The Beginning of the Mission and the Founding of the State*) provided a history of the beginnings of the Fāṭimid polity, and the *Kitāb al-Majālis*

69 Daftary, *The Ismāʿīlīs*, 154–76.
70 Daftary, *The Ismāʿīlīs*, 185.
71 Daftary, *The Ismāʿīlīs*, 225.

wa'l-Musāyarāt (*The Book of Sessions and Excursions*) chronicled the caliphal sessions of learning. Given this interest in scholarship, it is small wonder that the Fāṭimids established al-Azhar University, the oldest continually functioning university in the world.[72]

The chief *dāʿī* also oversaw the missionary movement outside of the Fāṭimid heartlands. Working from the main training center, Dār al-ʿIlm (House of Knowledge), in Cairo, the Fāṭimid missionaries divided the Islamic world up into twelve "islands" (*jazā'ir*), each of which had a head missionary (*dāʿī*) who was in charge of their area. These missionaries won converts to Ismāʿīlism and initiated them into the sect. It is an intriguing testimony to their missionary movement that Ismāʿīlism was far more successful in the Levant, Persia, Central Asia, and northern India than it was in the heartland of North Africa.[73]

As Fāṭimid missionaries in the eastern regions of Islamdom slowly won converts to Ismāʿīlism, they also came back into contact with non-Fāṭimid Ismāʿīlīs, many of whom eventually aligned themselves with the Fāṭimids. Such alignments brought several older Ismāʿīlī currents of thought back into the Ismāʿīlī fold. For example, the non-Fāṭimid Iranian Ismāʿīlism of Najm al-Dīn ʿUmar al-Nasafī and his followers (Abū Ḥātim al-Rāzī, Abū Yaʿqūb al-Sijistānī) was initially aligned with Qarmaṭī Ismāʿīlism. These thinkers propagated a more thoroughly Neoplatonic (and less "gnostic") vision of the cosmos and salvation that was endorsed by later Fāṭimid imams.[74]

Another great systematizer of Ismāʿīlī philosophical systems was Ḥamīd al-Dīn Aḥmad b. ʿAbdullāh al-Kirmānī, an Iranian *dāʿī* and quite possibly their most famous philosopher. Al-Kirmānī posited God as the absolutely Unknowable, a Being completely removed from the world. The active element of God in the world was known as the "first intellect," who emanated the creation in a series of nine intellects from this first (for a total of ten realms/intellects). Physical matter and form came into being with the third intellect, with the subsequent intellects likewise maintaining a relationship to the corporeal world. Salvation from the prison of matter came through attaining proper knowledge and thereby re-ascending the steps of creation back to its source. And it was the *dāʿīs* and ultimately the imam who provided this knowledge and thus remained the keys to salvation.[75] Such thoroughly Neoplatonic cosmologies and soteriological systems hint at the extent to which Ismāʿīlism remained a secretive sect. Such philosophical systems would not only be

[72] Daftary, *The Ismāʿīlīs*, 228–33. [73] Daftary, *The Ismāʿīlīs*, 228–29.
[74] Daftary, *The Ismāʿīlīs*, 234–44. [75] Daftary, *The Ismāʿīlīs*, 245–46.

deeply offensive to the average Muslim, but their intellectual sophistication would remain rather baffling for most.

Later medieval Fāṭimid history is dominated by several schisms, the first of which was the Nizārī-Mustaʿlī schism. When the caliph al-Mustansir died (in 487/1094) he appointed his son Nizār as imam. However, one of al-Mustansir's generals, an Armenian named Mālik al-Afḍal, arranged for another son, al-Mustaʿlī, to step into the role of imam. Securing allegiances for al-Mustaʿlī, al-Afḍal also made the imam, in effect, dependent on him for this position. In opposition, Nizār and his followers rose in rebellion in Alexandria, but they were defeated and Nizār imprisoned, where he later died.[76] The succession dispute split the community into those who followed Nizār, the Nizārīs, and those who followed al-Mustaʿlī, the Mustaʿlī Ismāʿīlīs.

The caliph al-Mustaʿlī witnessed the first Crusades as well as the further weakening of Fāṭimid power. At the assassination of al-Mustaʿlī's son and successor, al-Amīr, the community further split into Ḥāfiẓī and al-Ṭayyibī factions (al-Ḥāfiẓ was al-Amīr's cousin, but some looked to al-Amīr's two-year-old son al-Ṭayyib Abū al-Qāsim as the rightful imam). The Ḥāfiẓī Ismāʿīlīs survived for a time in Syria and Egypt, but largely disappeared with the downfall of the Fāṭimids. Many Ḥāfiẓīs merged with the Ṭayyibīs, who held out in Yemen and India, especially in the Indian province of Gujarat. There they became known as the Bohras (from a word meaning "trade"). The Ṭayyibīs held that the imamate existed in a state of *satr* (concealment) after the last imam, al-Ṭayyib Abū al-Qāsim, went into occultation in 524/1130. In the Ṭayyibī community, authority was (and still is) exercised by the *dāʿīs*, the head of which is known as the *dāʿī al-muṭlaq* or "absolute" *dāʿī*. Several succession splits followed, such that the Bohra community fragmented into Dāwūdī, Sulaymanī, and Alevi Bohras.

Medieval Nizārī Ismāʿīlism also survived into the medieval and modern eras. During the Crusades, they acquired a questionable reputation as the so-called assassins of medieval European imagination. This legend told of how al-Ḥasan b. Ṣabbāḥ, the "old man of the mountain," fed his followers hashish, served them food and wine, and surrounded them with young women, claiming that this was the promised paradise that they would have if they went out into the world and assassinated the enemies of the Nizārīs. There was little to no truth in these stories, but the myth of the assassins that has persisted nevertheless.[77]

[76] Daftary, *The Ismāʿīlīs*, 261–63.
[77] Daftary, *The Ismāʿīlīs*, 17–22; Daftary, *The Assassin Legends*, 1–7.

The Nizārī Ismāʿīlīs found fertile ground for their missionary work in the eastern regions of Syria, Iraq, and Iran. The late fifth/eleventh century witnessed the emergence of the Turkic and nomadic Seljuqs into the central regions of the ʿAbbāsid caliphate. These Turks were largely disliked by non-Turkic-speaking Muslims, an opportunity that the Ismāʿīlī *dāʿī*s exploited. The aforementioned *dāʿī*, al-Ḥasan b. Ṣabbāḥ (in Persian, Ḥasan-i-Ṣabbāḥ) had been born in Qom to a Twelver Shiʿite family, but had converted to Ismāʿīlism. After a period in Cairo, Ḥasan-i-Ṣabbāḥ left (by some accounts he was banished) to become active on behalf of the *daʿwa* in Iran. In 483/1090 he seized the mountain stronghold of Alamut, and from this castle began to exert his influence over the surrounding territories after death of the Seljuq leader Mālik Shah in 486/1093.[78] Ḥasan-i-Ṣabbāḥ found favor with the local populations by more equitably distributing wealth and by using the Persian language (the Seljuq Turks were a hated ruling class, and so also was their language). He used other means of persuasion as well, including the use of targeted assassinations by devoted followers known as the *fidāʾiyyūn* (sacrificers).[79] After Nizār's rebellion and death, Ḥasan was recognized as agent (literally a "proof," *ḥujja*) of the Nizārī imams who were concealed or not known at the time.[80] A line of *ḥujja*s followed, ruling from Alamut, and as Nizārī-Seljuq relations became something of a stalemate in the early sixth/twelfth century, the Nizārīs slowly acquired a series of mountain castles stretching from Central Syria (such as that in Maysaf) to the highlands of Iran.

In the fastness of their mountain strongholds, the Nizārī *ḥujja*s consolidated the doctrines of Nizārī Ismāʿīlism and shored up the support for their conglomerate of city-states. In particular, they taught that each imam possessed his own unique doctrines that were exclusive to him and his time. This was known as the doctrine of *taʿlīm*, the autonomous teaching authority of each imam in his time. This doctrine stressed absolute authority of the imams as well as obedience to their representatives, the *ḥujja*s.[81]

In 559/1164, the Nizārī imam Ḥasan II, whom the Nizārīs called *ʿAlā dhikrihi al-salām* ("On whose name be peace"), emerged from concealment and claimed his title as imam of Alamut. Accompanying this claim to the imamate was the controversial announcement that the *qiyāma*, usually taken to mean the Day of Resurrection, had arrived with his debut, and that the esoteric truths were now available and that therefore, the outer law (*sharīʿa*) had been abrogated. While this event is only hazily described by the sources (all of which are hostile of the Ismāʿīlīs), it does

[78] Daftary, *The Ismāʿīlīs*, 339.
[79] Daftary, *The Ismāʿīlīs*, 358.
[80] Daftary, *The Ismāʿīlīs*, 350.
[81] Daftary, *The Ismāʿīlīs*, 369–70.

seem as if Ḥasan II attempted to effect some changes in how the traditional religious rituals of Islam were observed. He was murdered a year and a half after the declaration.[82]

His son and successor, Nūr al-Dīn Muḥammad, modified the doctrine of *qiyāma*, claiming that his father was in fact an imam in the line of Nizār, but that the *qiyāma* was meant to emphasize commitment to the imam. His successor, Jalāl al-Dīn Ḥasan, attempting a further rapprochement with the Seljuq-backed Sunni caliph, reemphasized the traditional understanding of the *sharīʿa* and invited Shāfiʿī jurists to instruct his people.[83] However, the Nizārī conglomerate was not to survive the Mongol invasion. The Great Khān Möngke's brother, Hülagü, entered Persia in 654/1256 and began besieging and destroying the fortresses of the Ismāʿīlīs. The last leader, Rukn al-Dīn Khurshāh, surrendered Alamut as part of a bargain with Hülagü. The Mongols, however, killed its inhabitants and destroyed the castle along with its libraries. Moreover, the ruling Mongols made it punishable by death to be an Ismāʿīlī and frustrated the limited attempts to regain control of their fortresses.[84]

According to Nizārī tradition, the Mongol destruction forced the imams and their followers to wander about as iterant Sufis, concealing their identity out of fear for their lives. Unsurprisingly, this period saw the profound influence of Sufism on Nizārī Ismāʿīlism. In the eighth/fourteenth century, the imamate reemerged in the Iranian village of Anjudān (near Qom). From Andujān, the Nizārī Ismāʿīlīs reignited their missionary movement, sending *dāʿī*s back into Iran, Central Asia, and India. This brief period of political stability lasted until a new wave of Central Asian conquerors, this time under the leadership of Timurlane, sacked the city and dispersed its inhabitants.

Nevertheless, the Nizārī community survived in Iran, India, and parts of Central Asia. After Shah Ismāʿīl and the Safavids converted most of the population of what is now Iran to Ithnā-ʿAsharī Shiʿism, the Ismāʿīlī communities there sometimes found themselves the object of scorn or persecution. This situation lasted into the Qajar period, as was the case in 1232/1817 when the forty-fifth Nizārī imam Shah Khalīl Allāh was killed by an Ithnā-ʿAsharī mob. Seeking official protection, his wife took their son, the new imam Ḥasan ʿAlī Shāh, to the Qajar emperor, Fāth ʿAlī Shāh, in Tehran. Fāth ʿAlī Shāh wed his daughter Sarv-i-Jahān to the new imam, and awarded him the title Aga Khan (Lord Chief).[85] The imams of the Ismāʿīlīs have been known by this title ever since.

[82] Daftary, *The Ismāʿīlīs*, 387–91.
[83] Daftary, *The Ismāʿīlīs*, 392–95.
[84] Daftary, *The Ismāʿīlīs*, 427–28.
[85] Daftary, *The Ismāʿīlīs*, 504–5.

Whether as a revolutionary leader or as an unfailing source of religious knowledge, Shiʿa have expressed their submission to God by committing themselves to those they hold to be God's appointed leaders for humankind, the imams. This is because (according to its later, formal quietist theological iteration) God is just and merciful, and through His grace (*luṭf*) He does not leave the world without access to divine guidance after the Last Prophet, Muḥammad. For the activist Shiʿite this meant (and means) a warrior, who fought with his sword against injustice. For the quietists, devotion entailed recognizing the imam through whom inspired wisdom and secret knowledge of religious matters flowed. For most Ismāʿīlīs, this man walks the earth today in the form of the Aga Khan, while for the Ithnā-ʿAshariyya ("Twelver") Shiʿa he is alive, but hidden, waiting for the end of days to return as the Mahdī and establish justice in an unjust world. The story of Shiʿism is thus one focused on its main characters, the imams, around whom the expectations, allegiances, and devotions of the community revolve, and through whom God's guiding hand still leads them to salvation.

5 Muslim Schools of Thought

The Murjiʾa and the Muʿtazila

The story of the Murjiʾa (Murjiʾites) and the Muʿtazila (Muʿtazilites) is one with many twists and turns as well as a sometimes baffling host of characters. While both of these groups in one way or another find their origins in the Umayyad period, their later manifestations, the ones generally taken by heresiographers and historians to reflect their most emblematic or "mature" articulations, come into being in the ʿAbbāsid period. Both also disappeared from the landscape of Islamdom, albeit for different reasons: the Murjiʾa essentially merged with the nascent Ahl al-Sunna wa'l-Jamāʿa, lending some of their particular ideas to what would become Sunnism. The Muʿtazila faded by the sixth/twelfth century, their demise a combination of intellectual besting by their opponents and the Mongol invasions. Important elements of Muʿtazilite thought, however, survived insofar as aspects of it were taken up by the Ithnā-ʿAsharī, Ismāʿīlī, Zaydī, and other Shiʿa groups (their thought also finds its reflection in some elements of Ibāḍī theology).

Equally important to the story of the Murjiʾa and the Muʿtazila is how the ʿAbbāsid period pushed these groups to evolve into very different types of *firaq* than their Khārijite or Shiʿite counterparts. In part, this process was propelled by the conditions of the ʿAbbāsid age. After the ʿAbbāsid revolution, Muslims largely accepted the de facto rule of the ʿAbbāsid caliphs, even if they were not always entirely satisfied by the caliph's behavior. This was true for the Imāmiyya Shiʿa, who crafted an essentially apolitical imamate ideal and then bequeathed that ideal to their Ithnā-ʿAsharī and Ismāʿīlī offspring (of course, later Ismāʿīlī Fāṭimid rulers would challenge the ʿAbbāsid caliphs for legitimacy). It was true in a different way for the quietist Khārijites and Ibāḍiyya. In North Africa the Midrārid and Rustumid dynasties quickly established economic ties with the Umayyad *amīrs* of Iberia. These relations allowed them to become wealthy from trading slaves with the Aghlabid governors of Ifrīqiya (who were vassals to the ʿAbbāsids). In Oman, the mountain fastness of the imamate capital of Nizwa, as well as the relative isolation of Oman, allowed the Omani Ibāḍī imamate to thrive, disappear, and then reemerge with relatively little attention from the ʿAbbāsid caliphs.

While the issue of legitimate leadership waned as a compelling concern in the lives of most Muslims, the relative political stability of the early ʿAbbāsid era encouraged economic activity, bringing the benefits that came from a rejuvenated economy. These benefits included the exchange of technologies, literatures, arts, foodstuffs, and sciences, the overall result of which collectively benefitted the varied peoples who lived in Islamdom.[1] In essence, the relative stability brought by the ʿAbbāsid caliphs allowed the issue of legitimate leadership to be diminished or even tabled in favor of other topics for discussion. For the most part, those topics tended toward the scholastic and theological, a fact which nicely reflects the material and historical conditions of the ʿAbbāsid period. The grand narratives of the Muʿtazilites, and to a lesser degree the Murjiʾites, is one of intellectual activity enabled by the relative stability of the ʿAbbāsid period.

The Early Murjiʾa

The term "*murjiʾa*" remains a bit confusing because it enjoyed such a wide usage in the early sources. It can refer to a range of people, from those who cleaved to some vague notion of *irjāʾ* ("postponement"), to late Umayyad revolutionaries, to early ʿAbbāsid theologians, to those for whom the terms seems to be a general putdown. In other words, Muslim historians and heresiographers accused and labeled lots of different kinds of Muslims as Murjiʾites, and this variety presents far more persons than could actually be Murjiʾa in a realistic sense. Another difficulty arises when it is recognized that Murjiʾism, so-called, originated as something of an attitude or popular trend and only later took on the characteristics of a more organized *firqa* in the highly contradictory writings of the heresiographers.[2] At best, Murjiʾism as a movement finds its articulation among the followers of Abū Ḥanīfa in Central Asia. Yet even here there does not seem to be much to distinguish "Murjiʾite" doctrines beyond certain conceptualizations of faith, and these were the same notions that made their way into an emerging Sunni consensus. How, then, can Murjiʾism be distinguished as a coherent and separate group from Sunnism if one of its central tenets ends up being part and parcel of

[1] It is also for these reasons that the early ʿAbbāsid period is often, and somewhat speciously, imagined as the "golden age" of Islamdom. It is important to note, however, the reasons for rejecting the "golden age" characterization: the early ʿAbbāsid period, was, in fact, a period of tremendous economic, intellectual, and cultural activity. Imagining this period as the "golden age," however, implies that what followed was a steady "decline," or that there were no more periods of florescence for Muslims – a position that cannot be sustained by the evidence.

[2] Agha, "A Viewpoint of the Murjiʾa in the Umayyad Period," 2.

Sunnism? Yet some order must be imposed on this chaos, and so it is helpful to think of Murjiʾism as a story, albeit a messy one, that unfolds in several stages.

The earliest phase of Murjiʾism can be characterized as a noncommittal attitude toward the question of whether ʿUthmān or ʿAlī had sinned egregiously enough to warrant their denigration and/or outright rejection as a Muslim.[3] This stance, combined with unqualified approval of the first two caliphs, Abū Bakr and ʿUmar, offered an appeal to Muslim unity. Remembering that the Khārijites regarded both ʿUthmān and ʿAlī as sinners (for many Khārijite groups, this rendered them outside of the realm of belief proper) and that ʿAlī's supporters regarded ʿUthmān as having transgressed, while the reigning Umayyads and their staunch supporters had ʿAlī cursed weekly for his sins from the pulpits (called *minbars*) in the mosques, it is unsurprising that some Muslims (perhaps a great many of them) found all of these options untenable. Had not ʿUthmān and ʿAlī both been beloved friends of the Prophet Muḥammad? Must such an unappealing either/or choice be made between them? Adopting a position of "postponement," then, allowed the issue of ʿUthmān and ʿAlī to be evaded altogether. It also placed the one who professed such a notion outside of these emerging sectarian and political affiliations and offered a way back to the unity that Muslims had remembered during the time of the first two caliphs.

This stance took on extra importance in the wake of the second *fitna*, especially for those, such as the Zubayrids, who found themselves defeated. It is noteworthy how the first formal articulation of *irjāʾ* came from the son of Muḥammad b. al-Ḥanafiyya, the disinclined candidate of the Kufan activist Shiʿa during the second *fitna*. Al-Ḥasan b. Muḥammad b. al-Ḥanafiyya is credited with the first formal articulation of the concept of *irjāʾ* in a letter to his followers, citing 9:106 as the qurʾanic precedent for "postponing," suspending, or deferring judgment on ʿUthmān and ʿAlī in absentia.[4] It is not difficult to imagine why al-Ḥasan b. Muḥammad might want to promote such a position: It minimized the consequences to the Shiʿa after their failed revolts, and it allowed al-Ḥasan b. Muḥammad to reach an understanding with the ruling Marwānid branch of the Umayyads without him having to cast aspersion on his grandfather, ʿAlī b. Abī Ṭālib. Cleaving to *irjāʾ* in this instance offered a neutral strategy for holding the community of believers together by refusing to commit to the question of ʿUthmān and ʿAlī while

[3] Agha, "A Viewpoint of the Murjiʾa in the Umayyad Period," 3.
[4] The verse reads: "And [there are] others deferred until the command of God – whether He will punish them or whether He will forgive them. And God is Knowing and Wise."

tenuously promoting the newly reestablished Umayyad order. However, it was not yet the basis for a vibrant movement, although it did offer some theological groundwork upon which to build such a movement: The early Murji'a called for the current rulers to adhere to the principles of justice, and they generally maintained, like virtually every Muslim of the time, a theory of predestination. Sinning Muslims could be considered misguided believers (*mu'minūn ḍullāl*) rather than anathematized as unbelievers (which was the Khārijite stance), and this was the case, in part, because they came to believe that faith (*īmān*) was not categorically linked to conduct (*'amal*).[5] Yet on the whole what could be thought of as early Murji'ism was a case for withdrawing from politics and sectarian argument, pled by a war-weary would-be revolutionary at the end of his days, and it became popular in places like Kufa where Muslims found themselves equally exhausted by war and sectarian division.

However, continued Umayyad heavy-handedness brought about a second wave of Murji'ite thought, and this time it was married to revolutionary fervor. The Umayyad governor al-Ḥajjāj's vindictive policies in the early 100s/700s against figures like Ibn al-Ash'ath and the al-Muhallab family turned many Muslims in Iraq against the Umayyads and toward sectarian groups such as the Khārijites, Ibāḍiyya, and Shi'a. It also turned some toward the early Murji'ites, who participated in the revolts of Ibn al-Ash'ath and the Muhallabids against al-Ḥajjāj and the Umayyads. And though their core ideas counseled suspending judgment on cases where a person was not alive to witness them, it simultaneously upheld the need for living Muslim rulers (who could be judged because people were alive to witness their actions) to uphold the standards of Islamic justice. When such living rulers fell short, they could be resisted.

In addition, the general Umayyad policy of treating non-Arab Muslims (*mawālī*) as second-class Muslims had increasingly begun to chafe those who belonged to this category. Murji'ism, however, offered the idea that the mere confession of belief sufficed to make one a full believer. For those craving full acceptance into the Islamic fold, such a belief in combination with dissatisfaction with the Umayyads began to animate revolutionary tendencies among the *mawālī*. In 116/734 the most prominent of these Murji'ite-*mawālī*-inspired revolts broke out in Transoxania and spread to Khurasān.[6] It was led by al-Ḥārith b. Surayj and his mysterious secretary, Jahm b. Ṣafwān. Ibn Surayj and Ibn Ṣafwān, in fact, managed to unite the dissatisfaction of the local Arab populace in Central Asia with those of the *mawālī*, channeling their anger through appeals to justice, and

[5] Watt, *Formative Period of Islamic Thought*, 126–27.
[6] Blankinship, "The Early Creed," 44.

a demand to return to the Qurʾan and *sunna*. From what little can be reconstructed of the thought of Jahm b. Ṣafwān, he seems to have emphasized an "extreme" Murjiʾite stance whereby faith was conceptualized as "internalized knowledge in the heart" requiring no actions whatsoever.[7] He may well have been among the first Muslims to speak of the principle of reason (*ʿaql*) and how it could be used to derive opinions from propositions.[8] By 119/737 the Umayyad armies had worn down the rebellion to the point where Ibn Surayj entered into an alliance with a non-Muslim Turkish prince. Jahm was captured and executed in 128/746, and although pardoned in 127/745, al-Ḥārith b. Surayj was killed and the rebellion finally scattered later in the same year.

Later heresiographical writings would attribute several ideas of a different sort to Jahm and would accuse him of being associated with another *firqa*, the Muʿtazilites. Some even posited the existence of a group called the Jahmiyya. Ḥanbalī legal scholars in particular applied these terms to anyone whom they suspected of harboring Muʿtazilite tendencies, and Aḥmad b. Ḥanbal was said to have written a refutation of their thought.[9] However, the proto-Muʿtazilite ideas attributed to Jahm may not have actually been held by him. It is difficult, for example, to imagine how Jahm upheld the notion of the created Qurʾan long before such an issue became important (simultaneously, it is easy to see how later authors might interpolate this issue into the discussion as a way for them to "refute" it). As for the so-called Jahmiyya, it is noteworthy that those accused of being a member of the sect were often associated with other sectarian groups (notably the Muʿtazilites), such that the Jahmiyya appears to be a wholly made-up and polemical category. It seems that considerable confusion set in early over who was a Murjiʾite and what that term meant.

An actual proponent of early Murjiʾism, such as it was in the Umayyad period and into the early ʿAbbāsid period, was the Kufan legal scholar Abū Ḥanīfa, eponym of the Ḥanafī legal school and the person who arranged for the pardon of Ibn Surayj from the Umayyad caliph. In what is the earliest surviving Muslim creed, the *Fiqh al-Akbar I*, Abū Ḥanīfa upheld what might be considered many of the basic principles of Murjiʾism. In it, he spoke of a deferral of judgment on ʿUthmān and ʿAlī (combined with an embrace of the Companions generally), a belief in predestination, and a statement on God being in the heavens.[10] Less typical of "Murjiʾism" are some of the other statements in the *Fiqh al-Akbar I*, such as that guaranteeing damnation to any "Jahmite" who

[7] Watt, *Formative Period of Islamic Thought*, 143–44. [8] Schöck, "Jahm b. Ṣafwān," 56.
[9] Watt, *Formative Period of Islamic Thought*, 144. [10] Wensinck, *Muslim Creed*, 103–4.

denies the torment in the grave. That many of these ideas would later become standard aspects of Sunnism shows just how close Murjiʾism was to what became later Sunnism (indeed, most Sunni Muslims consider Abū Ḥanīfa a model Sunni). Yet Sunni he was not: Abū Ḥanīfa's followers made Balkh their center, which was known as "Murjiʾabād" (Murjiʾa-town) for a time.

It is difficult to think of Murjiʾism as a coherent sect or philosophy in its early stages. Rather, an apolitical tendency seems to have gathered supporters, often for different reasons, throughout the Umayyad period such that by the end of the Umayyad period a set of semi-intangible doctrines appear to animate the rebellion of Ibn Surayj and gain a certain amount of articulation in the creed of Abū Ḥanīfa. Yet Murjiʾism as such cannot still be considered a *firqa* in the same manner as the Khārijites and early Shiʿa. It is, rather, an attitude toward faith and a school of thought in formation, and with the ʿAbbāsid period this nascent theological trend gained somewhat more definition.

Later Murjiʾa

Later Murjiʾism formed alongside a growing ʿAbbāsid-era interest in *kalām* (*ʿilm al-kalām*) (theology, theological discourse/debate). Islamic theology was broadly focused on questions about the nature of God (oftentimes by deducing God's nature from His creation, the natural world) so that human beings could thereby determine how they should act in relation to God. The theological speculations of the ʿAbbāsid era shaped the direction and focus of Islamic sectarian groups of the time in profound ways. Most weighty in consequence was how the ʿAbbāsid revolution and the "compromise" established between the ʿAbbāsid caliphs and the religious scholars addressed many of the most pressing issues of the late Umayyad period. Gone was the Arab chauvinism of the Umayyads, replaced by a universalist vision of Islam that demanded a universal (i.e. "catholic") legal system grounded in an emergent interest in *ḥadīth*. And for those who more or less accepted the "compromise," the issue of God's justice, with its potential for revolutionary appeal, was lessened in the face of ʿAbbāsid caliphal order. The relative stability of the ʿAbbāsid period further reinforced anti-revolutionary tendencies among the *ʿulamāʾ*. Only scattered Khārijites and militant Shiʿa, mostly Zaydīs, maintained an interest in violent revolt, while their quietist brethren among the Ibāḍiyya and Imāmiyya remained staunchly pragmatic and/or apolitical.

In the face of such conditions, the pointed questions of the Umayyad era over the question of ʿUthmān and ʿAlī gave way to more general questions on the nature of faith. Muslims began to ask, what is faith? What makes a person faithful? Alternately, what is sin? What is the nature of sin? How is it punished? These questions sat alongside other theological questions, such as how the idea of predestination accorded with the notion of human responsibility, or the nature of God's actions (such as His speech). Several figures later identified with the Murjiʾa offered what we now identify as more or less distinct "Murjiʾite" answers to these questions. As a school of thought, however, it should be remembered that Murjiʾism (as an "ism") was much the product of heresiographical imagination, its coherence as a *firqa* exaggerated for the purposes of contrasting it with whatever "orthodoxy" the heresiographical author wished to peddle.

For these reasons, some of the ʿAbbāsid-era figures associated with the Murjiʾa in fact held a variety of views. One such figure was Bishr al-Mārisī (d. 218–19/833–34), an advisor to the ʿAbbāsid caliph al-Maʾmūn. Bishr held that faith consisted of belief plus its verbal expression, and thus unbelief had to be verbally expressed for it to count as actual unbelief (*kufr*). As an example, Bishr proffered that bowing to the sun was not unbelief proper, but only an indication of unbelief. This permissibility in the realm of defining belief, more than any other quality, identified Bishr as a Murjiʾite (like most, he held to a position of predestination). His other theological views anticipated some of the later theological discussions of the ʿAbbāsid era. Like his near contemporary Ḍirār b. ʿAmr he denied the notion of torment in the grave, but he also held (in anticipation of the later Sunni view) that sinners would not be eternally tormented in hell. He believed that the Qurʾan was created, and he also made simple distinctions between God's essential attributes (which for him were His knowledge, will, power, and creativity) and all the other attributes, which he considered figurative. This view anticipated later discussions over the essential and active attributes of God.[11]

Bishr's student, al-Ḥusayn al-Najjār (d. 218–21/833–36), differed from his teacher in some important ways. Al-Najjār held that faith consisted of belief and the profession of belief, but he appended "acts of obedience" to this (also anticipating the later Sunni stance on the issue). On the question of whether faith could increase or decrease, he held that it would not decrease. He also taught that Muḥammad could intercede (this doctrine was called *shafāʿa*) for believers who found themselves in hell, and that Muslims would not therefore suffer in hell forever. Expressing a more formal view of predestination, al-Najjār taught that God created the power to act in human beings, and that this power

[11] Blankinship, "The Early Creed," 46.

subsisted along with the act itself, but that such power to act needed to be created again with each new act. On the issue of seeing God on the Day of Judgment, al-Najjār showed his originality: He held that people would see God, but only with a special eye or unique knowledge that God gave them on that day.[12]

Perhaps more important than the Iraqis who were identified as Murjiʾa were the Murjiʾa of Transoxania, where this theological tendency found a center around the emerging Ḥanafī legal school. As the heartland of Ibn al-Surayj's rebellion, it is perhaps not surprising that Murjiʾism took root there. The scholars of Balkh reportedly traveled to Kufa to study with Abū Ḥanīfa himself, and during Abū Ḥanīfa's lifetime, a student of his, ʿUmar b. Maymūn al-Rammāḥ (d. 171/787–88), became *qāḍī* of Balkh, a position he would hold for two decades. Later Central Asian jurists would codify both Ḥanafī legal positions and Murjiʾite theological positions. Abū Muṭīʿ al-Balkhī (al-Hakam b. ʿAbdullāh) (d. 197/812–13) penned the so-called *al-Fiqh al-Absaṭ* in which he collected Abū Ḥanīfa's theological positions, including the affirmation that a Muslim convert in the territory of polytheism who confessed Islam without any knowledge of the Qurʾan or any of the religious obligations of Islam was a true believer (*muʾmin*).[13] The same Abū Muṭīʿ also transmitted the *Kitāb al-ʿĀlim wa'l-Mutaʿālim* (*The Book of the Scholar and Learner*), an exposition of Abū Muqātil al-Samarqandī's doctrine of *irjāʾ*, which Abū Muqātil attributed to his teacher Abū Ḥanīfa. These two works formed the basis of all later Murjiʾite theology of eastern Ḥanafism, a theology that itself became part and parcel of an emerging Sunnism.[14]

With the gradual emergence of Sunnism in the third/ninth to fourth/tenth centuries, many of the central tenets of "Murjiʾism," including the all-important belief that faith was somewhat separated from works, predestination, and the idea of intercession, made their way into the Sunni consensus (despite initial pushback from luminaries like al-Ashʿarī and the Ḥanbalīs). Abū Ḥanīfa and his legal school became one of the four accepted legal schools among Sunnis and the founder himself was gradually shorn of any connections to a movement increasingly deemed unacceptable. Yet heresiographers such as al-Shahrastānī continued to write about the Murjiʾa as if they were a recognized *firqa*, meaning that their continued salience offered some sort of rhetorical value to them.[15] But why continue to write about a *firqa* that probably never existed as such

[12] Blankinship, "The Early Creed," 47. [13] Madelung, "The Early Murjiʾa," 37.
[14] Madelung, "The Early Murjiʾa," 38–39.
[15] al-Shahrastānī, *al-Milal wa'l-Niḥal*, 139ff.

in the first place, and with whom the main proponents (Abū Ḥanīfa and his followers) could no longer be directly associated?

In part, this compulsion to reify the Murjiʾa can be explained by the heresiographical need to create seventy-two sects. Heresiographers continued to use a distinctive *firqa* called the "Murjiʾa" with its various subsects to round out their taxonomies. After all, earlier luminaries such as al-Ashʿarī and Aḥmad b. Ḥanbal had written of Murjiʾites as if they were a coherent group, and so they may well have been. It was left to the heresiographers, then, to muster enough individuals to satisfy the requirement for a group called the Murjiʾites. That heresiographers and others went about imagining the Murjiʾites in different and even contradictory ways is evident from the lists of persons who supposedly made up the sect. The early Shiʿi heresiographer al-Nawbakhtī, for example, claims that the Murjiʾa consisted of four groups: the Jahmiyya, who followed Jahm b. Ṣafwān; the Ghaylāniyya, who followed Ghaylān b. Marwān al-Dimashqī; the Māṣiriyya, who followed ʿAmr b. Qays al-Māṣir (a group which included Abū Ḥanīfa and his followers); and the Batriyya or the Ahl al-Ḥadīth, including Sufyān al-Thawrī, Shārik b. ʿAbdullāh, Ibn Abī Layla, al-Shāfiʿī, Mālik b. Anas, and many others.[16] Analyzing al-Nawbakhtī's list, it becomes apparent that "real" Murjiʾa are hard to find. Jahm b. Ṣafwān was associated with al-Ḥārith b. Surayj, an early Murjiʾite of sorts, and Ghaylān al-Dimashqī was said to have held to *irjāʾ*, but also to have believed in *qadar* (and therefore associated with a different group known as the Qadariyya).[17] ʿAmr b. Qays is obscure, and it is into this group that al-Nawbakhtī slips Abū Ḥanīfa and his followers. The Batriyya were a Zaydī Shiʿa group that eventually merged with Sunnism in Kufa, while the rest of those included in al-Nawbakhtī's list of Murjiʾites comprise prominent early proponents of *ḥadīth* as well as the eponymous founders of three of the four Sunni legal schools (Abū Ḥanīfa, al-Shāfiʿī, Mālik). What comes through is that the Murjiʾites are either obscure religious figures, persons with dubious Murjiʾite credentials, or persons who later became strongly associated with Sunnism.

Comparing this list with that given in al-Shahrastānī (also a Shiʿi heresiographer, but an Ismāʿīlī who extensively used Ashʿarī sources) is instructive in how the playing field of Murjiʾism can shift depending on the needs of the heresiographer in question. Al-Shahrastānī's list of Murjiʾites also breaks the group into four: the Khārijite-Murjiʾa, for whom he provides no examples; the Qadarī-Murjiʾa, who include the

[16] al-Nawbakhtī, *Kitāb Firaq al-Shīʿa*, 6–7.
[17] Watt, *Formative Period of Islamic Thought*, 86.

followers of Ghaylān al-Dimashqī and Muḥammad b. Shabīb al-Ṣāliḥī; the Jabriyya-Murji'a (elsewhere al-Shahrastānī has a chapter on the Jabriyya proper, which includes the Jahmiyya, and two other groups known as the Najjāriyya and the Dirāriyya); and the "pure" Murji'a, whom al-Shahrastānī proposes to discuss in his chapter, and who include the various followers of Yūsuf b. 'Awn al-Numayrī, 'Ubayd b. Mukta'ib, Ghassān al-Kūfī, Abū Thawbān, and Ṣāliḥ b. 'Umar al-Ṣāliḥī.[18] Of Abū Ḥanīfa, al-Shahrastānī says that "it is true that Abū Ḥanīfa and his followers were called Sunni-Murji'a, and many writers on this *firqa* have regarded Abū Ḥanīfa as a Murji'ite."[19] However, for al-Shahrastānī, Abū Ḥanīfa could not have been a Murji'ite, despite his insistence on faith as a belief in the heart that neither increases nor decreases because Abū Ḥanīfa simultaneously favored action as requisite to being considered a Muslim. Al-Shahrastānī also notes that anyone who opposed the Qadarites and Mu'tazilites was often labeled by them a Murji'ite. Thus, and declaring that "God knows best," al-Shahrastānī remains skeptical over whether Abū Ḥanīfa was, in fact, a Murji'ite.

Comparing al-Nawbakhtī's early list with that of the sixth/twelfth-century al-Shahrastānī, it is easy to conclude along with Watt that heresiographers more and more populated their chapters on the Murji'a with ambiguous figures, such as Ghaylān al-Dimashqī (who also held to *qadar*, and is sometimes described as a Qadarite), with persons whom no Muslim theologian would be eager to defend, such as 'Amr b. Qays al-Māṣir, or with those who were already considered unacceptable, such as Jahm b. Ṣafwān.[20] Those who could be considered actual Murji'ites, such as Abū Ḥanīfa, virtually disappear from the record as Murji'ism blended with what became Sunnism. Nowhere is this process clearer than in the progression from the pre-Sunni-era heresiographer al-Nawbakhtī, in which the Abū Ḥanīfa-Ahl al-Ḥadīth connection is quite clear, to the post-Sunni heresiographer al-Shahrastānī, in which Abū Ḥanīfa's connection to Murji'ite thought is treated with extreme skepticism.

Thus, Murji'ism is a sectarian story seemingly without a founding narrative, and whose main characters gradually leave the stage to be replaced by minor figures. Those who did seem to associate themselves with something called the Murji'a did so for reasons that varied widely, and they appear to tell a story of Murji'ism only briefly. Their stories are quickly taken over by heresiographers who blend these tales of Murji'ism into a grander whole, a whole far bigger than the individual strands of

18 al-Shahrastānī, *al-Milal wa'l-Niḥal*, 139–46.
19 al-Shahrastānī, *al-Milal wa'l-Niḥal*, 141.
20 Watt, *Formative Period of Islamic Thought*, 142.

Murjiʾism seem to merit. Moreover, these heresiographers appear to need such a tale of Murjiʾism for their own taxonomical reasons.

The Qadariyya

As with the Murjiʾa, the origins of the Muʿtazila, one of the great intellectual movements of medieval Islamdom, remain difficult to discern with any certainty. From the perspective of intellectual history, Muʿtazilite notions of free will appear to have their antecedents in an Umayyad-era group known as the Qadariyya. The Qadariyya derived their name from their promotion of the concept of *qadar*, which is usually rendered as "free will," but can also take the sense of "measure" insofar as God is held to have measured out a modicum of latitude for human beings to choose good or evil. This belief in human free will ran counter to the predominant notion of predestination, but its aim in the early period seemed to emphasize that human beings were responsible for their sins. That is to say, human beings could be considered accountable for their actions only if they were free to choose their actions. It is difficult to argue that human beings should be rewarded or punished if the source of their actions is, in fact, God Himself.

Considering the widespread perception of the Umayyads as suspect or corrupt, preaching human free will and the consequent doctrine of human responsibility for action could be taken as a political act. Al-Ḥasan al-Baṣrī, a popular Basran preacher and pietist, for example, was said to have caught the attention of the Umayyad caliph ʿAbd al-Malik, for preaching something akin to *qadar*, and thereby suggesting that human beings (including caliphs and governors) were to be held accountable for their actions. A letter attributed to him, allegedly in response to the caliph's request for clarification, emphasizes that evil acts come from human beings, who have a modicum of free will. Later Muʿtazilites considered al-Ḥasan al-Baṣrī a Qadarite, though some contemporary scholars have been skeptical about the extent of his purported Qadarism as well as the authenticity of his letter.[21] Given the popularity of al-Ḥasan al-Baṣrī, his stance certainly represented a political act, albeit one that did not involve rebellion, unlike some other Qadarite movements.

The alleged "founder" of the Qadarī movement was Maʿbad b. ʿAbdullāh al-Juhanī, a Basran *ḥadīth* scholar (*muḥaddith*) and a respected member of the Umayyad elite. He was executed in 80/699, either by the caliph ʿAbd al-Malik or his deputy, al-Ḥajjāj b. Yūsuf. While many sources claim that it was

[21] Judd, "Ghaylan al-Dimashqi," 180n4.

his Qadarī beliefs that led to his execution, a report suggests that he participated in the failed revolt of Ibn al-Ashʿath.[22] One of the bitter enemies of the Qadariyya, ʿAbd al-Raḥmān al-Awzāʿī, claimed that al-Juhanī learned Qadarism from the Christians, a polemical move that likely served to isolate al-Juhanī from the mainstream, as well as de-emphasizing the importance of al-Ḥasan al-Baṣrī by making al-Juhanī the "first" Qadarite.[23] Such claims can thus be treated with some skepticism.

Al-Juhanī's most important associate, and possibly his pupil, Ghaylān al-Dimashqī, was another who became associated with the Qadariyya. However, he is also identified in heresiographical sources as a Murjiʾite. Among the beliefs attributed to him in these sources are his deferring the judgment of sinners to God, and holding that faith was a secondary knowledge of God (both beliefs associated with the Murjiʾa), as well as the idea that sin came from human action, while good deeds came from God (notions associated with Qadarism). Ghaylān was, like his teacher, an Umayyad bureaucrat, one who reportedly gained the confidence of the Umayyad caliph ʿUmar b. ʿAbd al-ʿAzīz for a time (Ghaylān was one of his secretaries and also ran the Damascus mint) before the caliph reportedly dissociated himself from him (ʿUmar b. ʿAbd al-ʿAzīz reportedly penned a long treatise attacking the notion of *qadar*). Ghaylān also served in the Umayyad army, but reportedly ran afoul of his superiors. Ghaylān was later executed in Damascus, purportedly for his Qadarite beliefs.[24]

Another early pietist, Abū ʿAbdullāh Makhūl b. Abī Muslim, reflected the extent to which frontier soldiers shaped the expectations of the early Qadariyya. Makhūl was an Iranian captive who had been stationed on the frontier, and whose religious zeal and knowledge made him into a respected legal expert among his fellow soldiers. This frontier zeal, combined with grievances from the southern Arab soldiers at their treatment in Syria, fueled the Syrian Qadariyya and may have led them into supporting a putsch that brought the Umayyad caliph Yazīd b. al-Walīd (Yazīd III) to power.

After the execution of Ghaylān, many of the Qadariyya became openly political, finding a champion in the caliph Yazīd b. al-Walīd (d. 126/744).[25] Yazīd b. al-Walīd used Qadarism as a means to challenge his cousin, the caliph al-Walīd b. Yazīd (Walīd II, d. 126/744), who advocated an intense belief in of predestination. Both Murjiʾites and Qadarites were said to have supported Yazīd b. al-Walīd, to have constituted his inner circle, and to have used the doctrine of *qadar* as a means to justify

22 Judd, "Muslim Persecution of Heretics," 5.
23 Judd, "Muslim Persecution of Heretics," 5.
24 Judd, "Ghaylan al-Dimashqi," 163; Judd, "Muslim Persecution of Heretics," 10.
25 Judd, "The Early Qadariyya," 51.

political violence against al-Walīd, who used predestination to argue for a divine mandate. Several Qadarites seem to be present at the court of Yazīd III. However, some months into his caliphate, Yazīd reneged on his Qadarī agenda, and died shortly thereafter of a brain tumor. His successor, Ibrāhīm, showed little interest in the Qadariyya, and the movement lost whatever patronage it might have garnered. Qadarī groups certainly survived, but they were to be eclipsed (and possibly absorbed) by the rise of the Muʿtazilites.

The Muʿtazila

Like many of the *firaq* examined in this book, the origins of the religious movement known as the Muʿtazila, which would go on to become one of the most important medieval theological schools in Islamdom, remain obscure, and the sources available for the study of early Muʿtazilism present serious problems. Consequently, there is considerable variety in how to approach the beginnings of this group. Of the later development of Muʿtazilism there is more material, and thus, more consensus on the fundaments of what animated them as well as what caused them to decline among Sunnis (while remaining a prominent feature of certain Shiʿite theological inquiry). Muʿtazilism could be said to have three phases: an origin, early, and scholastic phase. Of these three, the origin period is the most difficult to reconstruct.

Muslim sources often tell a story of how the Muʿtazila began in Basra with Wāṣil b. ʿAṭāʾ and ʿAmr b. ʿUbayd, both pupils of al-Ḥasan al-Baṣrī.[26] One of the more popular stories concerning their origins speaks of Wāṣil's "withdrawal" (*iʿtizāl*) from the study circle of his teacher over the question of the sinner. Wāṣil was said to have interrupted al-Ḥasan when he was speaking about the state of the sinner, declaring that there was an "intermediate position" between considering the sinner either a believer or nonbeliever. Having made this declaration, Wāṣil was said to have "withdrawn" to a different corner of the mosque, signaling his formal break with his teacher.

Whatever the entertainment value of this story, it is unlikely to be a strict historical account of the origins of the Muʿtazila. The narrative is a bit too neat and seems tailor-made to account for the name of the group. Modern scholars, however, offer little consensus on the possible historical origins of the group. Some of the first scholars of the Muʿtazila offered semantic analysis of the term, arguing that it indicated how the

26 Bennett, "The Muʿtazilite Movement (II)," 144; El-Omari, "The Muʿtazilite Movement (I)," 134–35.

early Muʿtazila were pious ascetics, who withdrew from the wider society, or from the political wrangling of the early period, or, alternately, from specific persons such as ʿAlī.[27] More recent scholarship has tended to focus less on the semantic roots of the word and more on the persons said to be associated with the group. It examines, for example, how Wāṣil b. ʿAṭāʾ appeared to have connections to Muḥammad b. al-Ḥanafiyya and along with him adopted a generally pro-ʿAlīd stance.[28] He reportedly held that the imamates of Abū Bakr, ʿUmar, and ʿUthmān were valid though they were not the most excellent (*afḍal*) candidates. Rather, ʿAlī was the most excellent candidate in his estimation. Overall, these stances indicated a position of political neutrality, yet still one that favored the ʿAlīds. Moreover, Wāṣil was said to have given sermons to the Umayyad governor and to have sent his followers out from Basra as missionaries (much like the Ibāḍīs of Basra were doing), spreading his views through *kalām*, surviving through commercial activity, and providing a pious example of asceticism. His embrace of the concept of free will (*qadar*) probably earned him, as an outsider (who reportedly could not pronounce the letter "r"), a place in the city that teemed with Qadarites. On his death, many of Wāsil's students were said to have gone to North Africa.[29]

Equally important to the early Muʿtazila was the figure of ʿAmr b. ʿUbayd (d. 144/761), a traditionalist who was strongly associated with the concept of free will.[30] Also a student of al-Ḥasan al-Baṣrī, his asceticism even earned him the grudging admiration of his opponents. Contrary to Wāsil, Ibn ʿUbayd upheld the leadership of "most worthy" and was reportedly sympathetic to ʿUthmān. He was not interested in *kalām*, and he seems more known for his piety and asceticism as well as his consequent mistrust of the political elites of his age. His stature surely helped the Muʿtazila spread in Basra. After the ʿAbbāsid revolution, ʿAmr spoke often and fearlessly at the court of the ʿAbbāsid caliph al-Manṣūr, who respected him and praised him in a eulogy after his death.[31] It is possible that his appearance in al-Manṣūr's court was aimed at securing the same kind of political neutrality that ʿAmr had encouraged during the ʿAbbāsid revolution. Some of his students, however, apparently participated in the revolt of the Zaydī rebel al-Nafs al-Zakiyya after ʿAmr's death, eschewing the political neutrality of their teacher.

[27] El-Omari, "The Muʿtazilite Movement (I)," 132–33.
[28] El-Omari, "The Muʿtazilite Movement (I)," 135.
[29] El-Omari, "The Muʿtazilite Movement (I)," 135–36.
[30] El-Omari, "The Muʿtazilite Movement (I)," 135.
[31] El-Omari, "The Muʿtazilite Movement (I)," 136–37.

The doctrinal stances of the first Muʿtazila are difficult to discern. Wāṣil b. ʿAṭāʾ probably developed the notion of the "intermediate rank" of the sinner (later formalized as *al-manzila bayn al-manzilatayn*), whereby a gravely sinning Muslim was neither a full believer nor full unbeliever, but occupied a middle rank between these two categories. Like others, Wāṣil likely used the term *fāsiq* (grave sinner) to describe this person, and held that they would be punished in hell forever. The designation of *fāsiq*, however, did not imply temporal judgment, nor excommunication from the community of Muslims (both stances associated with the Khārijites), nor that these sinners could be considered akin to the qurʾanic hypocrites (*munāfiqūn*). To Wāṣil, it seems that sinful behavior could coexist with the knowledge of God, thus forging a conceptual middle ground between the two perceived extremes of Khārijite rejection and Murjiʾite acceptance.

The political ramifications of Wāṣil and Ibn ʿUbayd's stances are likewise difficult to determine. Van Ess argues that the doctrine of political neutrality shared by both offered a unique identity to the emergent Muʿtazilite movement as well as a sense of unity.[32] El-Omari, however, has argued that Wāṣil and Ibn ʿUbayd appear less as neutral toward the politics of their day and more as tolerant of political choices.[33] This stance might offer a way to understand how several of Ibn ʿUbayd's students participated in the revolt of al-Nafs al-Zakiyya. Ibn ʿUbayd tolerated the political stances of his day, favoring himself a generally apolitical stance. Some of his followers, however, did not remain neutral, but joined the fight against the newly established ʿAbbāsid state, while a great many continued to remain neutral.[34]

Yet the revolt of al-Nafs al-Zakiyya seems to bookend a first generation of Muʿtazilites, whose concerns were stoked in the fires that burned away the Umayyad dynasty. The ʿAbbāsids proved more successful at selling themselves as the preservers of *jamāʿa*, and thus the revolutionary concerns that drove the first generations of Muslim sectarians gradually gave way to a new set of concerns. In the relative stability of the ʿAbbāsid caliphate, in which most scholars had made their peace with the ʿAbbāsids (however difficult that peace may have actually been for them to make), new questions, along with new answers to old questions, arose, along with new persons to ask and answer them.

The second generation of Muʿtazilites, as it were, engaged with a series of philosophical and theological questions, only some of which could be

[32] El-Omari, "The Muʿtazilite Movement (I)," 136; Van Ess, *Theology and Society*, 2:348.
[33] El-Omari, "The Muʿtazilite Movement (I)," 137.
[34] El-Omari, "The Muʿtazilite Movement (I)," 137.

said to be completely novel. Theirs was a movement of rationalist inquiry, and although it cannot be said to be fully systematized during the first two centuries of the 'Abbāsid period, the figures of this generation cemented the Mu'tazilite reputation for serious scholarly examination. Ḍirār b. 'Amr (d. ca. 200/815), a student of Wāṣil b. 'Aṭā' and Ibn 'Ubayd, operated in Baghdad after 170/786; al-Aṣamm (d. ca. 200/816) succeeded him as a leader of the Basran "school" of Mu'tazilism. Another, Abū al-Hudhayl (227/841), though considered the formative figure among the early Mu'tazilites, was not as well regarded as his compatriots. Mu'ammar b. 'Abbād (215/830) taught in Basra; his student Bishr b. Mu'tamir (d. 210/830) went on to lead the local Mu'tazila of Baghdad. So too, Abū Isḥāq Ibrāhīm al-Naẓẓām (230/845), a nephew of Abū al-Hudhayl, friend of the poet Abū Nuwās and teacher to al-Jāḥiẓ, distinguished himself among the early Mu'tazilites.[35]

Whereas the first Mu'tazila distinguished themselves through asceticism, the second generation of Mu'tazilites embraced the courtly and literary circles of Baghdad and Basra. The salons of the Barmakids, an influential family close to the 'Abbāsid caliphs, hosted their philosophical speculations, as did some later 'Abbāsid caliphs themselves, such as Hārūn al-Rashīd and al-Ma'mūn. Famously, al-Ma'mūn and his successors adopted the quasi-Mu'tazilite doctrine of the createdness of the Qur'an during the *miḥna*. The *miḥna* episode, however, seems less a story about the influence of Mu'tazilism, however much that might have operated, and more a story about 'Abbāsid attempts to establish caliphal religious authority in the face of rising juridical-scholarly authority in religious matters.[36]

Several theological questions occupied the second generation of Mu'tazilites and to Abū al-Hudhayl al-'Allāf (d. ca. 841) is attributed a rather too neat five-point program that purports to characterize five of the main concerns. Although the "five principles," as they are known, might not actually distinguish the Mu'tazilites overly from their doctrinal opponents, the principles are worth discussing insofar as they became, in both Muslim and Western scholarship, strongly associated with that which typified 'Abbāsid-era Mu'tazilite positions. As one scholar notes, these are more areas of discussion rather than settled doctrines, and they represent significant areas of disputation when one scans the breadth of Mu'tazilite thought.[37] Nevertheless, they illustrate some of the basic underlying principles of Mu'tazilism, namely, that human reason stood

[35] Bennett, "The Mu'tazilite Movement (II)," 144–45.
[36] Turner, *Inquisition in Early Islam*, 150.
[37] Bennett, "The Mu'tazilite Movement (II)," 146.

capable of grasping the essentials of faith and propelling human society forward into justice, just as the human conscience could guide a person to salvation through the exercise of free will.

A fundamental tenet of Muʿtazilī thought came to be the assertion that God was just in a manner that human beings could understand.[38] God would not do evil, and He chose to hold Himself to the promises that He made in the Qurʾan. And because He was just, God therefore provided the means for human beings to do right and to reform. In particular, God gave human beings *ʿaql* or the ability to reason. Their reasoning capacity allowed human beings to know and recognize good and evil, and thereby to have responsibility for their actions in some way. Human beings were therefore expected to "command good and forbid evil" (to employ the qurʾanic idiom). They were responsible for reforming society as a consequence of the demands for justice. This trait was, perhaps, a holdover from the late Umayyad period insofar as opponents of the Umayyads often used appeals to justice. Nevertheless, it does point to a concern for combatting moral and social indifference.

The insistence on God's justice also, perhaps, accounts for how the Muʿtazilites imagined a middle position for the sinner (*al-manzila bayn al-manzilatayn*). A sinner could be reformed because God provides opportunities to humankind to reform their action. Put another way, God was bound by His justice to allow a sinner to repent. But by the same token, God was also bound to carry out His threats, and so another "principle" came to be the Promise and the Threat (*al-waʿd wa'l-waʿīd*) whereby God must punish evil and reward good. If God did not do this, some Muʿtazilites argued, He was neither just nor God (in fact He would be a liar).[39]

Finally, the Muʿtazilites held a particular view toward the unicity of God (*tawḥīd*), such that they were sometimes called the "people of unicity and justice" (*ahl al-tawḥīd wa'l-ʿadl*). They imagined God as a pure essence (*dhāt*) without attributes (*ṣifāt*). God thus knew, according to Abū al-Hudhayl, "with a knowledge which is He Himself."[40] The point of such scholastic discussions can be difficult to appreciate, but they did have a "real-world" consequence. The Muʿtazilite stance on God's essence and attributes played into how they viewed the speech of God, namely, the Qurʾan. If the Qurʾan was the speech of God (as Muslims held), then how exactly did God speak, and what was the nature of this speech when it entered the temporal world? Many if not most held that God's speech was eternal and that the Qurʾan, in a manner that

[38] Haider, *Shīʿī Islam*, 18. [39] Blankinship, "The Early Creed," 50.
[40] Bennett, "The Muʿtazilite Movement (II)," 153; Blankinship, "The Early Creed," 48.

participated in the way that God Himself was uncreated, was likewise uncreated. The implications of this stance, that the Qurʾan was uncreated, implied that God's commands must simply be followed without question, and that the seeming anthropomorphisms of certain qurʾanic verses – for example, verses that spoke of God's "throne" or of the "face of God" – referred to an actual Throne and Face.

The Muʿtazilites, on the other hand, held that God's speech, once uttered, came into the world and participated in the existence of the world. It existed in time and space, and thus the speech of the Qurʾan was created, just as the things of the world were also created things. The Qurʾan, then, could be apprehended by human beings through their reason, even though this understanding would itself be time bound and flawed. What seems to lie behind this concern with the Qurʾan as created speech was a desire to keep the questions of religion relevant to their time. If human beings could apprehend the Qurʾan through their reason, then it offered an endless source of contemplation, inspiration, and guidance. Seeming anthropomorphisms in the Qurʾan were not to be taken literally, but as metaphors: God's throne and face were indicators of His majestic station.

In these questions of the nature of qurʾanic speech, it is hard to miss the reflections of the Christological debates of early centuries. The status of Christ (as the "word" of God made flesh) as fully human or fully divine, or both, was something that exercised the early Christian community, forcing it to articulate stances that created orthodoxies and heresies. Islamic theology owes a debt to Christian theology, and this is one of the legacies of the translation movement.

Beyond the "five principles," other questions occupied the early Muʿtazilites. They were atomists, meaning that they conceived of the world as being made up of discrete particles, atoms (*ajzāʾ*, though sometimes *jawāhir*), as well as the force which inhered and animated these particles, known as the "accident" (*ʿaraḍ*). A great variety of Muʿtazilite positions on atomism existed, but overall these positions pointed to a concern with the physical makeup of the universe, with causality, and with the work of God in creating and commanding the elements.[41] This concern allowed the Muʿtazilites to show how human beings became responsible for their actions. Human action created chains of causes such that they caused, for example, the pain that they chose to inflict in others, not God (who, according to some, merely created the "capacity" to cause pain in others). Here the freewill legacy of the early Qadariyya found a new home.

[41] Bennett, "The Muʿtazilite Movement (II)," 147–50.

The turn of the fourth/tenth century initiated the final and "scholastic phase" of the Muʿtazilite movement, one in which the individualistic and scattered concerns of the early period gave way to coherent doctrinal systems articulated by two distinct Muʿtazilite schools. The first, the Basran school, was led by Abū ʿAlī al-Jubbāʾī (d. 303/915–16), while the second, the school of Baghdad, was headed by Abū al-Qāsim al-Balkhī (d. 313/931).[42] Abū ʿAlī al-Jubbāʾī took up the work of Abū al-Hudhayl, refining and sometimes refuting elements of it to create a comprehensive philosophical system. His son, Abū Hāshim al-Jubbāʾī, claimed leadership of the Basran Muʿtazila after his father's death, though several opponents of Abū Hāshim's leadership emerged and later coalesced as the Ikhshīdiyya. Abū Hāshim's group became known as the Bashamiyya. Until recently, texts from the Basran Muʿtazilites existed only in quotations from later works.[43]

Abū al-Qāsim al-Kaʿbī al-Balkhī, the leader of the Baghdad school of Muʿtazilism in the early to mid-300s/900s, heavily influenced not only later Muʿtazilites, but also Sunnism, specifically Ḥanafism in Central Asia, and especially al-Māturīdī, who considered al-Kaʿbī his foil. He also influenced Shiʿite thinkers such as al-Mufīd. The thought of al-Kaʿbī must be reconstructed, largely from the work of his student (and later pupil of ʿAbd al-Jabbār), Abū Rashīd al-Nīsābūrī.

The succeeding luminary of the Baghdadi Muʿtazila, ʿAbd al-Jabbār al-Hamdānī, became their leader in 369/980. He had joined the Bashamiyya movement as a young man, having been a pupil of Abū ʿAbdullāh al-Baṣrī. Under the Būyids, ʿAbd al-Jabbār was appointed chief judge (he was Shāfiʿī in his legal orientation) of their territories and their capital, Rayy. His position enabled him to attract several students, including Zaydī and Imāmī Shiʿites. These turned Rayy into an intellectual center of the Muʿtazilite movement.[44] Of ʿAbd al-Jabbār's numerous works, *al-Mughnī fī Abwāb al-Tawḥīd wa'l-ʿAdl* (*The Enricher of the Gates of God's Oneness and Justice*) remains one of the most important sources for later Muʿtazilite doctrine. ʿAbd al-Jabbār's students and successors, Abū Rashīd al-Nīsābūrī, Abū Muḥammad al-Muttawayh, and Abū Jaʿfar Muḥammad b. ʿAlī b. Mazdak, were likewise important figures. Another significant representative of Bashamī Muʿtazilism was Abū Saʿd al-Muḥassin b. Muḥammad b. Karrāma al-Bayhaqī, a Ḥanafī judge who followed Muʿtazilite theology and wrote an important

42 Schmidtke, "The Muʿtazilite Movement (III)," 159.
43 Schmidtke, "The Muʿtazilite Movement (III)," 162. For newly published Basran Muʿtazilite works, see Adang et al., *Basran Muʿtazilite Theology*.
44 Schmidtke, "The Muʿtazilite Movement (III)," 166.

encyclopedia, the *Sharḥ 'Uyūn al-Masā'il (Elucidation of the Sources of the Questions)*. Later in life he became a Zaydī Shi'ite.[45]

Abū al-Ḥusayn al-Baṣrī (d. 436/1044) led a rival school of Baghdadi Mu'tazilism after he challenged his teacher, 'Abd al-Jabbār, on certain points of Bashāmī doctrine. Raised a Ḥanafī and a Mu'tazilite, Abū al-Ḥusayn also pursued both medicine and Aristotelian philosophy in Baghdad. He challenged several standard Mu'tazilite views, such as that on the nature of God's existence, earning him condemnation, and even some accusations of unbelief (*kufr*), from some of his fellow Mu'tazilites.[46] One of his important works was the *Kitāb Taṣaffuḥ al-Adilla (Examining the Evidence)*. His most popular work was *al-Mu'tamad fī Uṣūl al-Fiqh (The Convention on the Sources of Jurisprudence)*, a work on legal theory. Despite his disagreements with the main group of Bashamiyya, his thought had a great impact on his contemporaries and successors. He taught a large circle of students and had several successors, such as Ibn al-Walīd, Abū al-'Āṣim al-Wāḥid b. 'Alī b. Barhan al-'Ukhbar al-Asadī, and al-Qāḍī 'Abdullāh al-Saymarī, who led the prayers over Abū al-Ḥusayn on his death. His thought also left an impression on later Ash'arite thinkers, such that the Ash'arī scholar al-Juwaynī relied on Abū al-Ḥusayn's notion of contingency when he formulated his proof for the existence of God. He was even quoted by the staunch Sunni Ibn Taymiyya.[47]

Abū al-Ḥusayn's group of Mu'tazilites, however, represented the last effective generation of Mu'tazilite theologians, who increasingly found their theology challenged and eclipsed by that offered by Abū al-Ḥasan al-Ash'arī and his followers. Mu'tazilite modes of thinking and reasoning, as well as many of its core doctrines, would live on among Zaydī and other Shi'ite thinkers, but by the sixth/twelfth century it was waning in the heartlands of Islamdom. The Mongol invasions wiped away the last traces of it, with the exception of those Shi'ites who had adopted Mu'tazilī ideas of rationalism and justice and applied them to their own theological speculations.

The narratives of Murji'ism and the Mu'tazilites shift the focal point of Islamic sectarianism away from the revolutionary fervor of the Umayyad era to the relative stability of the 'Abbāsid period. In that era of relative prosperity, these two 'Abbāsid-era schools of thought matured into highly specialized intellectual schools, developing philosophies/theologies that

[45] Schmidtke, "The Mu'tazilite Movement (III)," 167–69.
[46] Schmidtke, "The Mu'tazilite Movement (III)," 170.
[47] Schmidtke, "The Mu'tazilite Movement (III)," 174.

would indelibly mark Muslim scholasticism across its spectrum. Although both groups disappeared, the Murjiʾa would lend their thought to an emerging Sunni consensus, while the Muʿtazila shaped the way that Shiʿa (and it could be argued, Ibāḍī) groups continue to reason even today.

6 Emulating the Prophet and Cleaving to the Community

The Sunni Consensus

The narrative of Sunnism is one that emphasizes the importance of adhering to the community and emulating the Prophet Muḥammad above other concerns, and it is therefore a narrative predicated on reconciliation.[1] This emphasis on compromise and community has shaped Sunnism in profound ways, from its earliest beginnings among a diversity of smaller and often competing groups, to the late medieval period (and indeed, up to the present day) where the appellation "Sunni" is applied across a great variety of Muslims. It is reflected in the full name of the Sunnis, the *ahl al-sunna wa'l-jamāʿa*, the "people of the *sunna* and the community," whereby adherence to the *sunna* of the Prophet promised a universal standard for Islamic life, just as the idea of *jamāʿa*, cleaving to the community, presented an ideal through which the differences between those who adhered to this standard could be downplayed. Sunni Islam thus evolved expansively, such that this narrative embodies, in some senses, many common denominators among Muslims. In other words, to be a Sunni involves emplotment in narratives that other non-Sunni groups share, to an extent. This is not to say that Sunni Islam fails to be unique among the other Muslim *firaq*. Indeed, there is a distinctive legal-theological apparatus that defines Sunnism against the Shiʿa, Khārijites, Murjiʾites, and Muʿtazila. Rather, it is to point out that the spirit of community and reconciliation allowed the nascent Sunnis to absorb from rivals (notably, the Murjiʿa) that which suited their project. Their story, then, is one of pragmatic expansiveness tethered to the irresistible belief in the rightness of their community, grounded in the conviction that they follow the example of the Prophet.

This same pragmatic expansiveness of Sunnism makes its history difficult to pin down and its features problematic to define. The Sunni Muslim path formed after the other four classical Muslim *firaq* (that is, after the Khārijites, Shiʿa, Murjiʾa, and Muʿtazila) and their history

[1] Hallaq, "On the Authoritativeness of Sunni Consensus," 428; Barzegar, "'Adhering to the Community,'" 142.

reflects the complicated path of their emergence. So too, the tenets of Sunnism echo their broad concerns of universalism and community. At best, Sunnism might be described as a rubric with a few broad elements, namely: grounding in the *sunna*, which meant in practice a focus on *ḥadīth*; the recognition of the first four caliphs as legitimate; the refusal to grant any special political or religious role to the descendants of ʿAlī; adherence to one of the four recognized legal schools; and adherence to broadly distinctive positions on legal theory and theology. Much else could be said to be an aspect of "Sunnism," so imagined, but this functions as a minimal definition.

Adhering to the *Jamāʿa*

Because Sunnism resulted from a combination of many different groups, its origins and formation are different from the other groups that this work describes. In particular, the many groups that could be said to have contributed, in some way, to the trajectory of what would become Sunnism were often at odds with one another. A case in point are the Umayyads and their supporters. The notion of *jamāʿa*, adhering to the community, which remains a (if not the) crucial element of the later Sunni story, gained wider traction among Muslims during the reign of the Umayyad caliph ʿAbd al-Malik b. Marwān.[2] In the wake of the second *fitna*, ʿAbd al-Malik and his supporters emphasized their role as restorers of the fractured *umma*, and this appeal found fertile ground among those Muslims exhausted by years of civil war. This trend continued among subsequent Umayyad caliphs and their supporters. For example, a letter from the Umayyad caliph Walīd II speaks of the need to adhere to the community.[3] And yet, the Umayyads continued to curse ʿAlī from their pulpits, and to garner the skepticism, if not outright ire, of a great many Muslims by their misdeeds. Their pretensions to caliphal power failed resoundingly in creating a kind of centralized neo-Byzantine caliphate, resulting in a highly localized legal system that likewise could not function as an institution of universalism. Thus, while a crucial element of later Sunnism, the concept of adhering to the community, can be said to have originated with the Umayyads, they themselves remained uninterested in the kind of reconciliation that characterized later Sunnism. Their policies of Arabism excluded large numbers of non-Arab Muslims, just as their general unpopularity alienated many Arab Muslims.

[2] Barzegar, "'Adhering to the Community,'" 144.
[3] Crone and Hinds, *God's Caliphs*, 120; Barzegar, "'Adhering to the Community,'" 144–45.

It was thus, and somewhat ironically, that the Shiʿite-inspired ʿAbbāsid revolution set the stage for the emergence of Sunnism insofar as the compromise that emerged as the heart of the ʿAbbāsid endeavor paved the way for reconciliation and universalism. The ʿAbbāsids themselves quickly realized that their brand of Shiʿism, later classed among the *ghulāt*, would not be acceptable to most Muslims, and they turned away from it. Their able general, Abū Muslim, was murdered so as not to pose a threat to the new regime, and their more zealous Shiʿite followers pushed to the edges of the court. In the place of staunch ʿAlīdism, the ʿAbbāsids appealed to the notion of *jamāʿa* as that which legitimated their authority. Unlike the Umayyads, however, ʿAbbāsid appeals to the unity of the community ultimately succeeded, in part because the ʿAbbāsids and the *ʿulamāʾ* found a workable compromise. It was a universalizable Islam in return for the *ʿulamāʾ*'s and thereby the masses' support and legitimation of the ʿAbbāsid caliphs.

This compromise took some time to discover, and it was not without its difficulties. It seems clear, for example, that the Umayyads conceptualized the need to adhere to the community (*luzūm al-jamāʿa*) as adherence to their own rule and their authority. Similarly, the ʿAbbāsids seem to have attempted a bid to power in the *miḥna* not unlike similar bids that the Umayyad caliphs had attempted before them, and they were equally unsuccessful (albeit for different reasons). The chaos succeeding the murder of the caliph al-Mutawakkil not only effectively ended the *miḥna*, but it also opened a space for the emerging legal schools to solidify their place as religious authorities among Muslims.[4] Thus, the failure of caliphal religious authority and its flight to the nascent legal-theological schools forced decentralization on the early ʿAbbāsid state. The caliphal "role," then, in bolstering Sunnism, lay in how history forced them backward from their pretensions to religious authority, a process that in turn ceded some measure of authority to the *ʿulamāʾ*. The ʿAbbāsid caliphs never fully backed away from their vision of a quasi-Byzantine caliph-emperor (patronage is, after all, a means of control, and the ʿAbbāsids patronized the scholars). Yet after the murder of al-Mutawakkil the caliphs operated in the shadow of their slave-soldiers and viziers (from the Arabic term *wazīr*), ceding religious authority to the *ʿulamāʾ*, who cleaved to a vision of Islamic universalism.

The decentralization of religious authority and the institutionalization of Islamic universalism among the emerging legal schools remains one of the most important achievements of the early Islamic period, and one that remains vital to the emergence of the Sunni consensus. Already the

[4] Turner, *Inquisition in Early Islam*, 150.

ʿAbbāsid revolution had forced an important question to the forefront of Muslims. If Islam was to be equally applicable and meaningful to all who accepted the faith across the vast space of Islamdom, then a mutually acceptable basis for such an endeavor needed to be found. Universalizable legal-ethical institutions were necessary, along with a universalizable narrative of salvation history and a coherent theology. Many scholars also imagined portraits of good governance. These elements would take a long time to develop themselves into what became Sunnism, and each group that contributed to the process imagined itself to have the optimal solutions. In the end, Sunnism would become a blending of many solutions, but what fused and then held them all together was the vision, itself a carefully constructed memory, of a unified Muslim community and the promise of the *jamāʿa*. This ideal, as powerful and alluring as any around which human beings have imagined communities, sat at the center of what became Sunnism.

The need for a unifying vision was made more pressing by the material conditions of the ʿAbbāsid caliphate. Numerically, Muslims were still a minority in the regions that they administered. It is likely that conversion rates were as less than 10 percent in the Umayyad period, going up to 40 percent in the ʿAbbāsid period.[5] Those newly minted Muslims counted among themselves groups ranging from Central Asia to North Africa, all of which housed revolutionary groups who had opposed the Umayyads. For their part, the ʿAbbāsid caliphs and their courtiers likely realized what their Byzantine forerunners had suspected before them, namely, that a degree of social unity afforded them a greater share of control over their far-flung empire. As the ʿAbbāsids rejected the Arabism of the Umayyads, a kind of Islamic catholicism was all the more necessary in their diverse and expanding polity. Not forgotten by the ʿAbbāsids was the role of the non-Arabs, the *mawālī*, in bringing down the Umayyads. Yet this degree of social unity would be a delicate balance, and the ʿAbbāsid ideal of *jamāʿa* required institutions that would inculcate it more universally, and more carefully, than was done under the Umayyads.

To begin with, an appeal to *jamāʿa* required some means to placate and possibly reintegrate the different politico-religious groups that had emerged during the Umayyad period around issues of the *fitna*. The ʿAbbāsid solution, one that also suited their propaganda against the Umayyads, was to regard all four of the first leaders as legitimate and pious caliphs. Citing the *ḥadīth* that referenced the "rightly guided caliphs" after the Prophet, the ʿAbbāsids promoted the notion of the

[5] Bulliet, *Conversion to Islam*, 22–23.

rāshidūn, the "rightly guided" caliphate of the early period, and aligned themselves with its restoration.[6] This rehabilitated ʿAlī and the *ahl al-bayt* in the wake of Umayyad-era slander against them, but it also placed Abū Bakr, ʿUmar, and ʿUthmān on an equal footing with ʿAlī. The ʿAbbāsids could thus appeal to the widespread and general feeling of loyalty toward the *ahl al-bayt* without subsequently ceding political authority to them, a move which undercut the claims of the militant Shiʿa, who held that political and religious authority should be unified in the person of the imam. It also forced a question on the quietist ʿAlīds, insofar as it obliged those who looked to the *ahl al-bayt* as especially qualified religious authorities to decide whether their devotion to the Prophet's house would, in fact, be the centerpiece of their submission to God or just a feature of it.

The limits of ʿAbbāsid ʿAlīdism were thus clarified in relation to the nascent Imāmī Shiʿism of Jaʿfar al-Ṣādiq as well as the revolutionary fervor of al-Nafs al-Zakiyya and the Zaydiyya. For the ʿAbbāsids, the Prophet's family were to be respected and honored, but their luminaries were neither especially knowledgeable nor were the insurgents from the Prophet's house to be given special consideration. Naturally, the ambiguity between nascent ʿAbbāsid-era expressions of Islam and what we now recognize as quietist (Imāmī) Shiʿism, Zaydism, and so on, led to a robust debate within and between these groups as they emerged. In this fashion, Sunnism developed as a kind of anti-Shiʿism. This antagonism, however, must not be overstated. It was often at the level of caliphs, imams, notables, and scholars that acrimonious polemic and apologetics operated (as a survey of the existing polemical literature shows). On the ground, as it were, it is not clear the extent to which Muslims were overly interested in such debates, or even if they placed much stock in these emerging sectarian identities.

The extent of ʿAbbāsid-era anti-Shiʿism can be explored in what became the Sunni theories of political authority. In what became one of the first formal iterations of the theory of the caliphate, the scholar al-Māwardī posited that the caliph should be from the Prophet's tribal group, the Quraysh, but he need not be necessarily from the *ahl al-bayt*.[7] He should be pious, capable, and knowledgeable, but in practice, the state could and often did function when the caliph was none of these things. Nascent Sunni political theory, therefore, rejected both the religious and revolutionary authority attributed to the imams by their various supporters, favoring instead a practical approach to political power.

[6] On this *ḥadīth*, see Melchert, "The Rightly-Guided Caliphs," 63–79.
[7] al-Māwardī, *Aḥkām al-Sulṭāniyya*, 6–7.

Focusing too much on the anti-Shiʿism of nascent Sunni political theory, however, risks underappreciating the more profound realizations of ʿAbbāsid-era statecraft. These were that the caliph's central role was to maintain order, and that in reality the caliph might be nothing more than a figurehead. After the *miḥna*, "maintaining order" more and more meant protecting the borders of Islamdom and keeping the peace within it, while ceding religious authority to the religious scholars. As the power of the caliphs diminished, it also meant that the duty to maintain order often fell to whoever actually administered the territories of Islamdom on which they sat, be they powerful families (even powerful Shiʿite families such as the Būyids), slave-soldiers, or Turkic tribesmen.

Al-Māwardī and his successors' writings on the caliphate thus reflect both the cold pragmatism and anti-Shiʿism of the ʿAbbāsid era. This pragmatism, the willingness to cede actual political power to those who could take and wield it, has often been taken cynically as a betrayal of qurʾanic principles of morality as well as the Prophet's model of good governance. However, it is helpful to recall that successful governments must offer both pragmatic solutions to their populace, while at the same time maintaining their own legitimacy. Those who would become the Sunnis found pragmatic solutions to their actual circumstances, and the empire thrived for several centuries. If maintaining order meant sacrificing some legitimacy, or even countenancing outright tyrants (or allowing Shiʿite families de facto control over the territories), then this was deemed a price worth paying. The community could not be kept together when chaos reigned or enemies threatened. So long as *fitna* was avoided and Islamdom protected, most Muslims contented themselves to tolerate the excesses of the caliphs and the local potentates.

Islamic Universalism, *Sunna*, and the Law

A related aspect of imagining the Sunni community lay in the promise of a universally applicable basis for Islam. At the end of the Umayyad period, the Islamic *umma* was far from unified. Pro-ʿAlīd *mawālī* had helped push through the revolution, as had an array of Qadarites, Murjiʾites, Shiʿites, and Khārijites, yet these were far from united in their aims and aspirations under the new ʿAbbāsid order. In addition, Islamic law in the Umayyad period had developed in local contexts, resulting in a fragmented and provincial legal tradition that relied heavily on the personality of individual jurists. Although the Umayyads made attempts to position themselves as the sole arbiters of God's will, resistance to their rule had created several competing centers for what was shaping into the formal discipline of Islamic law.

Most jurists operated according to their own methods, giving legal advice and opinions based upon their own reasoned understanding (*ra'y*) of God's intentions. The result was a patchwork of different approaches and solutions to what it meant to be a Muslim.

The promise of a unified Islamic community, however, required a universalizable basis for Islamic law and morality. The Sunni solution, which took several decades to formally articulate and even longer to become widely accepted, lay in the abiding interest in the person of the Prophet Muḥammad. Pious persons had long been interested in the figure of the Prophet and the early community. Along with professional storytellers who regaled audiences with stories of the Prophet's life, scholars and pious persons had, right from the beginning, circulated and collected sayings from and about him and his Companions. This endeavor ultimately led in divergent directions among the Sunnis to the genres of Prophetic biography, biographical dictionaries, and to the science of *ḥadīth*. Yet the impetus at its heart was to discover the truths embedded in the example of the man whom God had chosen as His messenger, along with those who first responded to the message. It was an endeavor to discover the Prophet's "manner of proceeding" (*sīra*) with regard to certain affairs as well as authoritative precedents (*sunna*) that the Prophet and others had established for the community. Those who preceded and eventually became the Sunnis built from these elements, albeit piecemeal, a universalizable Islam.

One of the first to articulate a broad (meaning nonlocal) theory of Islamic law – one that was based, at some distance by modern standards, in the example of the Prophet – was the Madinan jurist Mālik b. Anas (d. 179/795). His means of achieving this ideal relied on the notion that proper *sunna* and therefore practice was best preserved and reflected in the community in which the Prophet had actually lived. And that was Mālik's community at Madina.[8] Mālik reasoned that the Madinan praxis, their way of doing and being Muslim, should be the basis for Islamic legal and moral decisions because of their temporal and geographical proximity to the Prophet. In his view, this closeness insured that the *sunna* of the Madinan Muslims was closest to the *sunna* of the Prophet and early community. In other words, a specific community, that of Madina, collectively preserved the *sunna* of the Prophet, and thus it should serve as a model for Islamic living. Mālik's notion proved popular, insofar as it pointed Muslims toward the Prophet and early community as a universalizable model for Islam. Yet Mālik's theories were simultaneously local, favoring his community above others.

[8] Hodgson, *Venture of Islam, Vol. 1*, 318–22.

A student of Mālik, Abū ʿAbdullāh Muḥammad b. Idrīs al-Shāfiʿī (d. 204/820), took his teacher's ideas to a kind of logical conclusion: if God had chosen Muḥammad, purified him, and made him His prophet, then the life of the Prophet was a reflection of the truths that God had revealed through the Qurʾan. Authoritative example for how to live an Islamic life, therefore, could be found in the figure of the Prophet Muḥammad and thus in his, not any specific community's, *sunna*. Even more to the point, specific examples could be found in the narrations that the entire community had preserved about what the Prophet had said, did, or silently confirmed, which were gathered in the *ḥadīth*s that circulated among the community. Al-Shāfiʿī's ideas proved far more persuasive than Mālik's insofar as they (theoretically) removed regional specificity from Islamic law, relying instead on the remembered examples that could be gleaned from *ḥadīth*.

Moreover, al-Shāfiʿī (or more likely, his students) prioritized the sources of Islamic law in such a way as to make room also for the growing importance of scholarly consensus, while at the same time acknowledging a role for juristic reasoning. The Shāfiʿites preferred the Qurʾan and *ḥadīth* as the main sources of law for a jurist. However, al-Shāfiʿī also recognized that not every possibility could be examined using these authoritative sources alone. Reflecting the rising prominence of the *jamāʿa* in Muslim social and political discourse, al-Shāfiʿī and his students recognized that the consensus of the legal scholars (*ijmāʿ*) on a given point could constitute a basis for decisions in law. Likewise, the informed opinion of a jurist if tied by analogy to a *ḥadīth* in what was called *qiyās* could serve as an authoritative source of legal decisions. Al-Shāfiʿī and his students thus prioritized what became known as the "sources of jurisprudence" (*uṣūl al-fiqh*) beginning with the Qurʾan and Prophetic *sunna* (as found in the *ḥadīth* literature), followed by scholarly consensus (*ijmāʿ*), and then analogical reasoning (*qiyās*). And with this methodology, which was to become broadly accepted with some variations across the Sunni legal spectrum, al-Shāfiʿī and his followers provided a universalizable vision of Islamic law that was not tied to any given geographical location or individual jurist.

While not diminishing the contributions of al-Shāfiʿī and his students to the project of Islamic universalism, it is worth noting that their ideas were very much a product of their times. Already al-Shāfiʿī's teacher, Mālik, had gathered *ḥadīth* from Madina into a collection known as the *Muwaṭṭaʾ*, as had al-Shāfiʿī's Yemeni contemporary, ʿAbd al-Razzāq al-Ṣanʿānī (d. 210/826), in his *Muṣannaf*. So too, Aḥmad b. Ḥanbal advocated the expansive use of *ḥadīth* as a ground for a proper Muslim life, amassing an enormous collection in his *Musnad*. A generation later, and utilizing the growing field of *ḥadīth* sciences (*ʿilm al-ḥadīth*) that determined the reliability of *ḥadīth* by analyzing those who transmitted them, al-Bukhārī (d. 256/870) and Muslim (d. 261/875) would sift through the vast *ḥadīth* material available to them, choosing only the most "sound" (*ṣaḥīḥ*) for their collections. These would much later become known as the "Two *Ṣaḥīḥ*s" (*al-Ṣaḥīḥayn*), and they formed an essential component of Sunnism's legal-moral apparatus, along with several other *ḥadīth* works that followed. Viewed from this perspective, it becomes clear that al-Shāfiʿī and his students were part of a larger ʿAbbāsid trend among certain scholars of *ḥadīth* that looked to it as the proper source for Prophetic *sunna*, and that did so in the name of Islamic universalism. Those who concerned themselves with finding the *sunna* of the Prophet in the *ḥadīth* were later known as the *ahl al-sunna*, and it is in them that the earliest articulation of something called Sunnism can be seen taking shape.

There were, of course, ranges of reactions to the growing popularity of *ḥadīth*. Underlying these reactions was the dynamic tension between those who viewed reason as an essential component of understanding revelation, and those who tended to focus more exclusively on revelation. In part, the genius of the nascent Sunni consensus was to accommodate a larger range of those reactions in the field of Islamic law. Thus, the followers of Abū Ḥanīfa countenanced a larger role for reasoned juridical opinion in law, though increasingly (following the insights of al-Shāfiʿī) they grounded that opinion in analogy with the *ḥadīth*. Along with the followers of al-Shāfiʿī, these groups found themselves in the core regions of the Middle East and also in Central Asia. The followers of Mālik likewise found a balance between the reasoned opinions of a jurist and the revelatory reflections of the *ḥadīth*. Geographically, the Mālikī school predominated in North Africa and Spain with the patronage of the remaining Umayyads of al-Andalus. The followers of Ibn Ḥanbal, long concentrated in Baghdad, eventually moved out into the main urban centers of Islamdom. Their legal methodology placed a stronger emphasis on *ḥadīth* than the other three schools, but in the areas of the law where the *ḥadīth* were silent, they allowed considerable leeway for juridical reasoning and effort (*ijtihād*).

Once the legal schools had formalized themselves into recognized "schools" or "ways" (*madhāhib*) of doing law – a process that involved not only a legal methodology that could be shown to rely on the sources but also a body of legal specialists who were loyal to that methodology[9] – adherence to one of those schools and its jurists more and more came to

[9] Hallaq, *Authority, Continuity and Change*, 236.

be expected as part and parcel of what it meant to be a practicing Sunni Muslim. This process was far from easy, as competition between the emerging legal/theological positions caused significant controversy in the first few centuries of the emergence of Sunnism. This absorption of the legal schools under the banner of Sunnism is also, in part, a reason that the four Sunni *madhāhib* did not develop into separate *firaq*, but remained classed as Sunnis.[10]

Not all emerging legal schools made it into the Sunni consensus or survived long enough to be considered part of that consensus. For example, the Ẓāhirī *madhhab*, pioneered by Dāwūd b. ʿAlī b. Khalaf al-Ẓāhirī (d. 270/884) of Kufa, held that the apparent (*ẓāhir*) meanings of the Qurʾan and *sunna* were sufficient as legal sources. Consequently, the Ẓāhirīs rejected *qiyās*. The Ẓāhirī school enjoyed modest support in the Islamic East and official patronage in Iberia in the sixth/twelfth century under the al-Muwaḥḥidūn (Almohads). However, and especially after the demise of the Almohads, it declined such that Ibn Khaldūn considered the school defunct by the eighth/fourteenth century. So too, the short-lived Jarīrī school, traced to the famous scholar Muḥammad b. Jarīr al-Ṭabarī (d. 310/923), lasted a mere two centuries after his death before falling into obscurity.

Sunni Theologies and Creed

Just as the Sunni consensus required an expansive view toward communal inclusion and legal norms, so too Sunnism developed a moderately flexible attitude toward its theologies and creeds. This is not to imply that what we understand to be Sunnism has no fixed notions of what constitutes proper beliefs about God, but rather to point out that these notions are broadly distinctive, rather than exclusive. It is also worth noting that Sunni theology, so-called, developed over a long period of time, just as did other aspects of Sunnism, resulting in a complex tapestry of theological positions that coalesced slowly.

Some of the components of Sunni creed find their roots in the Murjiʾite movement associated with Abū Ḥanīfa. Among them was the notion that the verbal declaration of faith (*shahāda*) was sufficient for a person to be considered and treated as a full Muslim. This position solved several problems for the nascent Sunnis. First, it offered (as it had for the first Murjiʾites) a politically neutral solution to the question of the *fitna*,

[10] Once this distinction between legal school and sect affiliation became common among the Sunnis, Shiʿites and Ibāḍīs asserted the existence of their own legal "schools." Ibāḍīs, in fact, claim to have the oldest *madhhab*, dating back to Jābir b. Zayd.

insofar as adopting this stance allowed for both ʿAlī and ʿUthmān to be considered full Muslims. Such a stance harmonized well with the concept of the *rāshidūn* caliphs as all equally meritorious. Likewise, the abstract concept of "postponement" allowed for the question of sinning Muslims to be tabled in favor of a more inclusive stance on the community. Grave sinners could be punished according to Islamic legal standards, but they were not considered unbelievers. So too, Muslims who were ignorant of or neglected their ritual duties were still Muslims, which was a position favorable to the newer converts from non-Arab descent (many of whom, it should be recalled, had brought the ʿAbbāsids to power), or to those who (for whatever reason) neglected their religious duties. Several of these positions can be found in two early creedal statements (*ʿaqāʾid*), known as the *Fiqh al-Akbar I* and *II*.[11] Later Sunnis attributed both of these texts to Abū Ḥanīfa, whom, after his canonization as the founder of the Ḥanafī *madhhab*, they disassociated from the Murjiʾite movement.

In addition to its distinctively Murjiʾite qua Sunni stances of sin and belief, the *Fiqh al-Akbar I* also articulates a (familiar) position on predestination and offers an eloquent statement on communal inclusion: "difference of opinion in the community is a token of divine mercy."[12] Indeed, few statements capture so succinctly the pragmatic inclusiveness that lays at the heart of developing Sunni views toward law and theology. This idea that a variety of views constitutes a blessing and a source of strength for the community allowed for a variety of groups to find common cause under the banner of Sunnism and created the kind of broadly based community that the ʿAbbāsids were interested in establishing.

Not all of the groups who fed into the Sunni consensus, however, acted from a position of pragmatic inclusiveness. Their contributions to what would become Sunnism are no less profound, even if they are more limited in scope. One such group, the Ahl al-Ḥadīth, also featured the founder of a legal *madhhab*, Aḥmad b. Ḥanbal, as one of its more outspoken proponents. The Ahl al-Ḥadīth were a movement of popular piety centered in Baghdad.[13] As their name implies, they championed revealed sources, notably *ḥadīth*, as a more proper basis for discovering Islamic creed and praxis. They tended to mistrust, if not outright reject, theologians or those who relied too heavily on human reason, which they considered limited in its ability to grasp God's plan and intentions for human beings. As such, the Traditionalists (as they are also called) opposed much of what the Muʿtazilites articulated as their theology (many of these positions were held outside of strictly Muʿtazilite circles).

[11] See Wensinck, *Muslim Creed*, 102ff., 188ff. [12] Wensinck, *Muslim Creed*, 104.
[13] On the nature of this piety, see Melchert, "The Piety of the Hadith Folk," 427–34.

Thus, for example, Aḥmad b. Ḥanbal was said to have held the Qurʾan to be uncreated and coeternal with God, as was its recitation (this last part was considered excessive by later Traditionalists, such as al-Bukhārī).[14] Similarly, the Ahl al-Ḥadīth opposed the notion that God gave a modicum of free will to human beings, focusing instead on God's overwhelming majesty and power. Such a Being was surely in control of all things.

In general, the Ahl al-Ḥadīth stance tended toward anthropomorphic descriptions of God. This stance harmonized well with the overall popular understanding of a merciful God who interacted at an intimate level with human beings, even if the Qurʾan itself offered but sparse opportunities for anthropomorphistic interpretations. In comparison with the Muʿtazilites, whose vision of God was far abstracted from popular understandings, the Ahl al-Ḥadīth approached the anthropomorphic descriptions of God's throne, face, and hands with a pragmatic scripturalism. Mistrusting theologians, they recommended not overthinking the qurʾanic descriptions of God, but accepting them, in words attributed to Ibn Ḥanbal himself, "without asking how nor about their meaning" (*bi lā kayfa wa lā maʿnā*). In other words, qurʾanic descriptions of God could be accepted without subsequently having to enter into overly theological debates about the literal meanings of the verses in question. The Ahl al-Ḥadīth thus offered a pragmatic religiosity, largely shorn of theological complications. Nevertheless this stance was positioned strongly within the field of those making arguments about the nature of God and His relation to His creatures.

Ahl al-Ḥadīth piety, however, was not enough to formally articulate a theological stance that would be acceptable to the more *kalām* minded. This came from a Muʿtazilite convert, Abū al-Ḥasan ʿAlī b. Ismāʿīl al-Ashʿarī (d. 324/936), who along with Abū Manṣūr Muḥammad b. Muḥammad b. Maḥmūd al-Samarqandī (d. 332/944), known as al-Māturīdī after his neighborhood, would put their stamp on formal Sunni theological speculation. Al-Ashʿarī was born in Basra, where he studied Muʿtazilite thought under the famous scholar al-Jubbāʾī (d. 302/915). At the age of forty, the Prophet was said to have visited him in a dream during Ramadan, commanding him to support the *ḥadīth*. Sometime after this experience (which is surely apocryphal), al-Ashʿarī broke with the Muʿtazilites and began using their method of reasoning against them, and in support of his own theories. He also moved to Baghdad, where he died. Some 400 works of theology and polemic were attributed to him.

[14] Blankinship, "The Early Creed," 51.

Against the Muʿtazilites, al-Ashʿarī argued that a strong focus on God's justice limited God's power in an unacceptable fashion. Divine justice could not be defined in human terms because human reason was limited and therefore flawed. It could not fully grasp God's designs. Faith, to al-Ashʿarī, was not something that could be rationalized. Moreover, he argued, the Muʿtazilite insistence on reason came dangerously close to placing reason on the same level with revelation, and this too was unacceptable. For al-Ashʿarī, God was powerful over all things, and He could do as He liked. This position had several important consequences for how al-Ashʿarī viewed the world and the human being's place within it.

First, al-Ashʿarī maintained that all actions take place because of the will and good pleasure of God. Not only did this engender a strong sense of determinism (*al-qaḍāʾ*) among al-Ashʿarī and his followers, but it led him to conceptualize the workings of the cosmos in a strongly determinist fashion. For Ashʿarites, God created the ability (*qudra*) to act in a person, the will to act, and the actual act itself. How, then, did al-Ashʿarī reconcile God's absolute power over human action with the qurʾanic notion of human responsibility and punishment? To this, the age-old problem of determinism, al-Ashʿarī adopted an earlier concept of "acquisition" (*kasb*).[15] According to this idea, God created the actions of human beings, who then "acquired" them because they attached themselves to a person's will.

Al-Ashʿarī also adopted a view toward the world that meshed with his strongly determinist stance. For al-Ashʿarī, God willed and created each moment as it came into existence, a doctrine elsewhere known as occasionalism. And because God willed each separate moment into existence, there was in reality no cause and effect. Objects fell toward earth because God willed them to do so, not because of some abstract law of gravity. If God chose to will things differently, then He could do so (the moments when God chose to will things differently from how He was accustomed to doing so in the past were perceived by human beings as miracles). In the face of such awesome and overwhelming power, human beings could merely accept God's will, along with the revelations that God chose to send with His prophets, "without asking how" (*bi lā kayfa*).

Although al-Ashʿarī's conceptualization of an all-powerful God might seem alienating, in fact, it appealed to many Muslims. The Muʿtazilites had removed God from the human realm by insisting on His absolute essence, portraying God as distant from human affairs. Al-Ashʿarī, by contrast, spoke of God as intimately involved in human affairs, down to

[15] Thiele, "Between Cordoba and Nīsābūr," 232.

the passing of each moment. More abstractly, al-Ashʿarī spoke of God's attributes (*ṣifāt*), such as speaking, knowing, as separate from His essence. Thus, and in accordance with how many Muslims already understood the revelation, the Qurʾan was uncreated and timeless, and it partook some of the power of God.

Al-Ashʿarī defended his positions in numerous tracts, but he also offered "apologetic theology" that challenged the groups that he considered illegitimate. His heresiography, the *Maqālāt al-Islāmiyyīn* (*The Positions of Those Who Profess Islam*), is one of the earliest and most read of the genre. With the defense of his doctrines, and the passing of time, Ashʿarism became popular in central Islamic lands and also in the Maghrib. It was accepted, in particular, by the Ḥanafī legal scholars of Baghdad, who spread it beyond the city. Although the Ahl al-Ḥadīth initially rejected it, as they rejected most theological speculation, it eventually permeated their thinking as well.

Al-Ashʿarī, however, was not the only medieval theologian to become a cornerstone of Sunni theology. Further east, Abū Manṣūr al-Māturīdī gained popularity among those who would eventually count themselves as Sunnis, also and initially among the eastern Ḥanafīs. Al-Māturīdī was himself a follower of Abū Ḥanīfa, and the importance of Murjiʾism to Abū Ḥanīfa, notably concerning the doctrine of faith and the topic of human action, has already been noted. Al-Māturīdī followed Abū Ḥanīfa in some of these doctrines. He regarded faith as assent and confession, to the exclusion of works. Against the Ashʿarites' strong stance on predestination, al-Māturīdī and his followers found a certain amount of choice (*ikhtiyār*) in the actions of human beings. Moreover, they held that good and evil could be rationally known: by contrast, al-Ashʿarī held that good and evil were known only because God revealed what is good and what is evil. Last, Māturīdīs held that the attributes of action subsisted in God's essence, but that other attributes were separate from it.

Māturīdism became associated with the Seljuq Turks, who favored the Ḥanafī legal school and who spread Māturīdism along with Ḥanafism when they assumed control of eastern Islamdom in the sixth/twelfth century. The Mongols, after converting to Islam, also tended to favor Māturīdism, such that by the ninth/fifteenth century, it was generally accepted on a par with Ashʿarism as a strand in the broad fabric of Sunni theology. As with other aspects of Sunnism, what characterizes its theological positions is the expansiveness with which Sunnis have embraced a range of acceptable views.

Further broadening Sunnism's embrace of multiple religious paths remains the towering figure of Abū Ḥāmid al-Ghazālī (d. 505/1111), who has been called "the greatest Muslim after Muhammad."[16] Al-Ghazālī was a reformer, who ultimately made the mystical path, known as Sufism (*al-taṣawwuf*), more acceptable among Sunnis, while at the same time insisting on adherence to the legal aspects of Sunnism among the practitioners of Sufism. Al-Ghazālī displayed a penchant for learning at an early age, accepting under Mālik Shah, the Seljuq ruler of his time, a position in the newly established collegiate system of the Niẓāmiyya, where he would dictate to his students his works. There, for example, he wrote *Taḥāfut al-Falāsifa* (*The Incoherence of the Philosophers*), a critical examination of Muslim philosophy that was so popular that it was translated into Latin and used by St. Aquinas to attack the philosophers of Europe. However, at some point in his life, al-Ghazālī experienced doubts and left his position at the Niẓāmiyya for a ten-year journey in search of certainty. This he found among the Sufis, who, al-Ghazālī explained, experienced (in his words, "tasted") religion through their exertions and piety. Eventually, al-Ghazālī returned to the Niẓāmiyya and resumed his teaching and writing. Among his numerous publications from that time are an account of his journey in search of certainty, *al-Munqidh min al-Ḍalāl* (*The Deliverer from Error*), and his famous multivolume explication of the inner meanings of Muslim practices, the *Iḥyāʾ ʿUlūm al-Dīn* (*Revival of the Religious Sciences*). For his attempts to re-enliven religion in his time, many Sunnis regard al-Ghazālī as the *mujaddid* (renewer) of his age, a figure whom God sends to renew religion. From the wider perspective, al-Ghazālī can be seen as a more visible example of Sunni Muslims who were increasingly incorporating the mystical dimensions of Islam into the practice of Sunnism. With al-Ghazālī, Sunnism's pragmatic expansiveness incorporated the insights and practices of the mystical paths.

A final question needs to be posed when discussing the development of Sunnism: When and how did it become the majority position of most of the world's Muslims? This question can be deceptive, as there is a great difference between when Sunnism can be said to have been fully articulated and when it gained widespread popularity. As noted above, the first recognizably Sunni figures were *ḥadīth* scholars from the late second/eighth century, many of whom espoused a *ḥadīth*-centered notion of *sunna* in Baghdad and other cities central to Islamdom. As early as the third/ninth century, and most certainly by the fourth/tenth century, something recognizable as Sunnism had emerged from the intellectual milieu of the early ʿAbbāsid period. This "sect" (following others I have called it a "consensus") drew from many sources: popular piety movements, the emergence of legal schools, theological speculation and

[16] Watt, *Al-Ghazali*, 180.

debate, and mystical tendencies. Animating it was a desire to preserve the unity of the community by grounding Muslim practice in the Qurʾan and authoritative example of the Prophet Muḥammad, which in practice meant focusing on the *ḥadīth* literature as a, if not the, main source of *sunna*.

However, as compelling an idea Sunnism might have been in the fourth/tenth century, it does not appear to have been widespread. Politically, Shiʿite dynasties, such as the Fāṭimids, or ruling families, such as the Būyids, dominated the era, such that the century has been called "the Shiʿite Century."[17] Intellectually, legal and theological schools (who would later be subsumed in the Sunni consensus) competed fiercely with one another for political patronage and popular influence. In these conditions, it is unclear how those *ʿulamāʾ* who had embraced the Sunni path might have spread their ideas in any meaningful way.

It was, rather, in the centuries succeeding the fourth/tenth century that Sunnism became popularized. This came about when Sunnism gained the political backing of the invading Seljuq Turks, who adopted Sunnism as a means of establishing their legitimacy against the largely Shiʿite groups whom they had largely displaced and with whom they sometimes clashed. It was also the Seljuqs who established the *madrasa* (school) system, initially via the Niẓāmiyya. The *madrasa*s taught a standard curriculum that incorporated the four Sunni legal schools, as well as Sunni theologies, creeds, and mysticism, all of which were based in the study of the Qurʾan and *ḥadīth*. The importance of the *madrasa* to the popularization of Sunnism can hardly be understated. It is with this institution that Sunnism gradually became the majority position and this by the sixth/twelfth or possibly the eighth/fourteenth century.

The Limits of Reconciliation: The Karrāmiyya

Sunnism, so imagined, thus took several centuries to develop and before the fifth/eleventh or sixth/twelfth century (and indeed, after it) fierce rivalry (even to the point of violence) existed between groups that would later be recognized as equally "Sunni." For example, Ḥanafīs and Shāfiʿīs competed for resources in medieval Nīshāpūr, as did Ḥanbalīs and Shāfiʿīs in Baghdad. Such are some of the conflicts that have been documented by scholars. There was surely more of the same throughout Islamdom. With Seljuq patronage, however, a broadly inclusive Sunni consensus finally emerged that claimed the majority loyalties of

[17] Hodgson, *Venture of Islam, Vol. 2*, 36; see also Baker, *Medieval Islamic Sectarianism*, 77–90.

the Muslim *umma*. This consensus, of course, excluded the Khārijites, Ibāḍiyya, Shiʿites, and Muʿtazila, and it absorbed most if not all of the Murjiʾa, such that actual Murjiʾism disappeared.

Less well known to the grand narrative of Sunnism are the groups that, had circumstances been different, might have ultimately become part of that consensus. Muslim history is littered with failed legal *madhhab*s, and they are relatively well-known.[18] However, more obscure are the nearly-Sunni *firaq* that, for one reason or another, did not become accepted as Sunnis. One such group was the Karrāmiyya. Their eponym, Abū ʿAbdullāh Muḥammad b. Karrām (d. 255/869), a man of deep mystical inclinations, was an Arab who had grown up in a Persian environment. He was jailed twice in Nīshāpūr and died in exile in Jerusalem, but his following grew to considerable numbers in Islamdom's East.[19]

Doctrinally, the Karrāmiyya appear quite similar to their fellow Easterners, the Ḥanafīs, even to the point that one heresiographer wrote of them as a branch of Ḥanafism.[20] Following Abū Ḥanīfa's lead, they espoused what was essentially a Murjiʾite, and thus also Ḥanafite, doctrine of faith, whereby faith (*īmān*) was legally defined as affirmation (*iqrār*) by the two testimonies of faith (*shahādatayn*), without having to be found in the heart. They also adopted several moderately anti-Muʿtazilite stances that appear similar to their Ḥanafī coreligionists. They held, for example, that human beings can know a modicum of good and evil without the aid of revelation, but that this good and evil occurred in accordance with the will of God, and that God alone created the acts of human beings. Like the Traditionalists, such as the Ahl al-Ḥadīth, they defended the anthropomorphic imagery found in the Qurʾan against metaphorical interpretations, such as those proffered by the Muʿtazilites and other schools.[21]

Although similar in doctrinal outlook to the Ḥanafīs and other traditionalist anti-*kalām* schools, the Karrāmiyya were not mainly a theological school nor were they a legal *madhhab*. Primarily, they presented themselves, and history remembered them as, pious ascetics, akin to the Sufi mystics who had begun to populate medieval Muslim cities. Their founder, Ibn Karrām, was famous for prohibiting economic gain (*taḥrīm al-makāsib*) and for his exclusive reliance on God (*tawakkul*). Ibn Karrām and his followers argued that having a livelihood distracted one from the worship of God, which was a position that was highly debated in this period. Their answer to it earned them condemnation in

[18] For example, see Hodgson, *Venture of Islam, Vol. 2*, 31.
[19] Madelung, *Religious Trends in Early Islamic Iran*, 39.
[20] Madelung, *Religious Trends in Early Islamic Iran*, 40; Zysow, "Karrāmiyya," 15.
[21] Madelung, *Religious Trends in Early Islamic Iran*, 41; Zysow, "Karrāmiyya," 257.

an official creed of the ruling Sāmānids. So thorough were their ascetic practices that they earned the nickname *al-mutaqashshifa*, "the self-mortifiers." It was thus as an ascetic movement that stressed personal piety and reliance on God that the Karrāmiyya made their name in medieval Islamdom.

With their main center of operations in Nīshāpūr, the Karrāmiyya spread through Iran and Central Asia, but also established circles in Jerusalem, Egypt, and Lebanon after Ibn Karrām's exile to the Levant. To them has been credited the institution of the *khānaqā*, a center akin to a retreat or a convent, where active members of the Karrāmiyya could live in community and dedicate themselves to asceticism and worship. They also functioned as centers for meeting and missionary work. The Karrāmiyya maintained an extensive network of *khawāniq*, such that the medieval historian al-Maqdisī associates the institution exclusively with them.[22] They also maintained at least three *madrasa*s in Nīshāpūr as well as one in Herat.[23]

Why, then, did the Karrāmiyya fail to gain acceptance within the Sunni consensus? By all metrics, they should have: At their height they commanded considerable numbers, even outside of the city of Nīshāpūr. In addition, they maintained institutions such as the *khānaqā* and the *madrasa* to propagate their doctrine support their community. Finally, their teachings and doctrinal stances did not differ substantially from other groups that became "Sunni." Why, then, did they attract such hostility from their rivals?

The answer is elusive, but accounting for the failure of the Karrāmiyya, it seems, it has something to do with their emphasis on asceticism and trust in God to the exclusion of economic gain. This question was, in fact, widely debated in medieval Islamdom, with some Muʿtazilite groups rejecting commerce in a fashion similar to the Karrāmiyya. However, in the busy trading hub of Nīshāpūr, commerce was the lifeblood of the city, and the Karrāmiyya's rivals, the Ḥanafīs, Shāfiʿīs, Shiʿites, and Sufis had, more or less, accepted the notion that commerce and religion were compatible. The intensity of the Karrāmiyya's rejection of worldly profit intensified the rivalries between them and these other groups.

This enmity was further inflamed during the short period when the Ghaznavids appointed a Karrāmī, Abū Bakr b. Isḥāq b. Maḥmūdshadh, to the headship (*riyāsa*) of Nīshāpūr. Abū Bakr used his position to actively and aggressively promote Karrāmism, and he persecuted his rival Ḥanafīs, Shāfiʿīs, Sufis, and Shiʿa. These actions, unsurprisingly,

[22] Madelung, *Religious Trends in Early Islamic Iran*, 45.
[23] Malamud, "Politics of Heresy," 42.

alienated a large portion of the city's notables and forced the reigning Ghaznavids to withdraw their support of Abū Bakr. A coordinated backlash followed, which effectively broke Karrāmī power in the city. Their disenfranchisement continued with the advent of Seljuqs, who favored Ḥanafīs and Shāfiʿīs, and throughout the course of the fifth/eleventh century Karrāmī influence waned while Ḥanafī and Shāfiʿī power grew. During this time, Sufism in Khurasān gradually merged with Shāfiʿism, and the Sufis established their own *khānaqās* that displaced those of the Karrāmiyya. By the end of the fifth/eleventh century, the Karrāmiyya had virtually disappeared, and they entered the heresiographical literature as deviants and heretics.[24]

Thus, the Karrāmiyya probably would have been part of the Sunni consensus if not for one unscrupulous city official and an extreme insistence on asceticism. This fact communicates something important about sectarianism: It remains as inconsistent and unpredictable as the people who articulate and embody the sectarian and scholastic groups that litter the historical landscape of Islamdom. The example of the Karrāmiyya also points to a shortcoming of this book. This and the previous three chapters have artificially isolated the grand narratives of the Khārijites, Shiʿites, Murjiʾa, Muʿtazila, and Sunnis for the purposes of introducing them in a semi-coherent fashion. Doing so, however, has foregrounded these stories, at the expense of others, and made them appear much clearer and cleaner than was, perhaps, the case. The case of the Karrāmiyya, however, reminds us that the process of sectarianism is far from clear or consistent. Such is an excellent transition back into the actual and messy history of sectarianism, which will occupy us in Chapter 7.

[24] Malamud, "Politics of Heresy," 44–51.

7 Sectarian Ambiguities, Relations, and Definitions

The remainder of this book will be devoted to undercutting or problematizing claims that this book has made in the Introduction about the nature of sectarianism as well as those which are implied in the structure of the work. This is done not to second-guess the narrative-identity approach to Islamic sectarianism, but precisely because that approach demands an appreciation of complexity. Put another way: the narrative-identity approach remains a helpful heuristic device to accomplish certain tasks. One of those tasks is to recognize that sectarian identifications are not clean, exclusive, or permanent (as the neat division of the chapters of this work seems to imply). In addition, the definition of "sect," "school," or *firqa* remains neither stable nor fixed. Therefore, this chapter asks a few key questions that are meant to probe these issues further. It asks, for example, what it means for the study of Muslim sects and schools when sect identification is not primary or obvious. It delves into the nature of relations between sectarian and communal groups in the early period, looking at what this can tell us about the idea of "sectarianism." It explores further some times and places where the definition of sectarianism itself breaks down and becomes unhelpful. As an aspect of human identity-making, the questions and ambiguities surrounding sectarian identifications need to remain, in some senses, under-answered, meaning that we as scholars need to remind ourselves that sectarian identifications are as complex as the human beings who manipulate them. It is the goal of this chapter to offer brief thoughts on these topics, recognizing that each one could become full-length studies in their own right.

Sectarianism without Sectarianism

In an article entitled "Religion without Religion," Hughes emphasizes the porous nature of religious identities in late antiquity as a means of examining anew the origins of Islam.[1] In a similar fashion, much of the new

[1] Hughes, "Religion without Religion," 869.

research on medieval Muslim groups, the *firaq*, suggests that discrete sectarian communities appear later than has generally been assumed. By appreciating anew the murky beginnings of many of these groups, we can more responsibly move to think about their further development as well as how such groups-in-formation interacted with one another.

Haider, for example, draws attention to the ambiguities surrounding the narratives of Zaydī origins in Kufa. While something resembling Imāmī Shiʿism does seem to coalesce around the figures of Muḥammad al-Bāqir and Jaʿfar al-Ṣādiq, what later heresiographers identified as Zaydī Shiʿism changes dramatically from its Batrī to Jarūdī forms, and this in response to changing social and political circumstances. Early Batrī Zaydī legal stances, for example, did little to distinguish the early Zaydīs from their proto-Sunni counterparts. And as Batrī Zaydism gave way to a more staunchly pro-ʿAlīd Zaydī Shiʿism of the Jarūdīs, the remaining Batrīs seem to have merged with the nascent Sunnis.[2] Where, then, is early Kufan "Zaydism"? What heresiographers of later centuries seem to have collapsed into a coherent group seems, in fact, to be far more ambiguous in the earlier periods of its existence.

In this regard, it is also helpful to remember that both Abū Ḥanīfa and Muḥammad b. Idrīs al-Shāfiʿī, among others, supported "Zaydī" uprisings at points during their respective lifetimes. Abū Ḥanīfa gave financial support to the uprising of Zayd b. ʿAlī (and was briefly jailed for it), comparing the rebellion to the Prophet's fight against the unbelievers. Moreover, he advocated for the Zaydī rebels Ibrāhīm b. ʿAbdullāh and his brother, Muḥammad al-Nafs al-Zakiyya, in 145/762, a move that was said to have gotten him imprisoned.[3] Similarly, the caliph Hārūn al-Rashīd nearly sentenced al-Shāfiʿī to death for aiding an ʿAlīd uprising in the Yemen. While neither of these actions renders Abū Ḥanīfa nor al-Shāfiʿī a Zaydī Shiʿite per se, it is worth asking what their actions say about the nature of sectarian identity in the early period. Is it more helpful to think of their support for "Zaydī" causes as robust manifestations of pro-ʿAlīdism? Or is it better to unthink the strong boundaries separating what we now imagine as reified *firaq* in the early Islamic period, imagining instead permeable identities that allow for multiple and less-defined allegiances? Categorizing Abū Ḥanīfa continued to give later Muslim intellectuals difficulty. The heresiographer al-Shahrastānī, for example, hedged on whether or not Abū Ḥanīfa should be counted among the Murjiʾa, asking rhetorically how a legal scholar who was interested in deeds could disregard action in favor of faith alone.[4] And yet, it is well

[2] Haider, *Origins of the Shiʿa*, 192. [3] al-Khaṭīb al-Baghdādī, *Tārīkh Baghdād*, 13:329.
[4] al-Shahrastānī, *al-Milal wa'l-Niḥal*, 141, 146.

established among contemporary historians that Abū Ḥanīfa and his followers were important sources for early Murjiʾism.[5]

The medieval revolt of the Zanj in early Islamic Iraq offers another example of ambiguous (or at least downplayed) sectarian identities. Talhami argues, for example, that while the leader of the revolt, ʿAlī b. Muḥammad, adopted an ʿAlīd genealogy, he did not espouse openly Shiʿi doctrines and opted for the "Khārijite" (I would say Ibāḍī) egalitarian ethos that the most qualified person should rule. Moreover, descriptions of the banners and the existing coinage from the Zanj revolt included qurʾanic verses (e.g. 9:111) often associated with Ibāḍī and Khārijite discourse. This, combined with indications that some Qarmaṭī Ismāʿīlīs fought alongside of the Zanj (indeed, Hamdān Qarmaṭ was said to have met with ʿAlī b. Muḥammad) indicates a mixed sectarian space where such identifications remained subordinated to other concerns, even if they presented themselves on banners, coins, and through claims of ʿAlīd genealogy. ʿAlī b. Muḥammad appears to have been consciously manipulating sectarian identifiers to increase his appeal as a leader. Other examples of numerous and different communal groups participating in revolts could surely be found, as in the case of revolt of the Khārijī al-Ḍaḥḥāk b. Qays in Kufa in the late 120s/740s, as many pro-ʿAlīd supporters, were said to have joined his movement. Clearly, sect identification is not always a primary motivator where revolt is concerned, and it is not clear the extent to which it was operative or not as an organizing factor in this uprising. In the case of the Zanj and al-Ḍaḥḥāk, dissatisfaction with the ruling elites, be they Umayyads or ʿAbbāsids, seems to have overshadowed whatever sect identification the rebels claimed.

Ambiguity might also exist within any given sect or school. For example, recent research has questioned the degree of separation between what we could classify as quietist Shiʿa and the so-called *ghulāt*. Asatryan, for example, has shown that Jaʿfar al-Ṣādiq maintained a (more or less) good relationship with at least one of the many Kufan moneychangers, Mufaḍḍal b. ʿUmar al-Juʿfī, despite accusations that al-Juʿfī was associated with the Khaṭṭābiyya, a Shiʿa group much later classed among the *ghulāt*. Similarly, several of al-Juʿfī's associates, who would also be condemned as *ghulāt* in later texts, appear to have operated comfortably within the context of the Shiʿi community in Kufa. Asatryan concludes that "in the early period, the Ghulat mixed freely with other Shiʿis and, despite episodes of mutual enmity, they were an integral part of the communal fabric of Iraq."[6] Later in the ʿAbbāsid period this situation

[5] Madelung, *Religious Schools and Sects in Medieval Islam*, 36.
[6] Asatryan, *Controversies in Formative Shiʿi Islam*, 79.

began to change, as the moderate Shiʿites of Qom began more and more to condemn the *ghulāt* as outside the pale of acceptable Shiʿi belief. At this point, Shiʿite historians wrote the *ghulāt* out of the early history of the quietist Shiʿite community in Kufa. Early interactions, however, appear to be far more complex.

If the relationship between the quietist and activist Shiʿa is not always clear in the early period, so too the line between Shiʿism proper and devotion to the family of the Prophet – what Hodgson called ʿAlīd loyalism – was (and often still is) equally fuzzy. Hodgson, in a now classic article, noted that Sunnism "can be called at least half Shi'ite" because of the Sunni reverence for the family of the Prophet.[7] For Hodgson, the ʿAbbāsid revolution forced the Shiʿa to either acclimate to the disappointments of the ʿAbbāsids and the emerging Sunni consensus or to cleave to the notion of an apolitical imamate that was being articulated by Jaʿfar al-Ṣādiq and his associates. In this fashion, the quietist Shiʿa "became" sectarian.

This book, however, has adopted Schubel's distinction between ʿAlīdism and Shiʿism, treating devotion to the family of the Prophet as the most crucial aspect of submission to God. This behavior would classify a person as Shiʿite, whereas devotion that does not place itself in such a fashion would be ʿAlīdism, and thus, nonsectarian. While Schubel's definition is, in my opinion, a very good one, it is worth noting a potential difficulty involved in adopting it, namely, that this definition of Shiʿism might also apply to certain Sufi Muslims. Hoffman, for example, has drawn attention to how modern Egyptian Sufis consider their devotion to the Prophet and the *ahl al-bayt* as central to their understanding of Islam and as vital for their salvation.[8] These Sufis, according to Schubel's definition, would qualify as Shiʿites, even though they do not identify themselves as such. Hoffman also notices that devotion among these Sufis is not restricted to the *ahl al-bayt*, but might also include masters not associated with the family by blood but rather through initiate lines (*silāsil*). Conversely, for Shiʿa, the efficacy of the master is not necessarily the key to salvation. These features might offer some means to distinguish Sufism from Shiʿism, but in all cases it is worth remembering the significant overlap and fluidity while attempting definitions of these groups.

Further ambiguity between Shiʿites and Sufis emerges when a scholar considers the early development of Sufism, which incorporated into itself several luminaries of early Shiʿism. ʿAlī b. Abī Ṭālib, for example, figures as the first link of nearly every Sufi order's chain of transmission (*silsila*),

[7] Hodgson, "How Did the Early Shiʿa Become Sectarian?" 4.
[8] Hoffman-Ladd, "Devotion to the Prophet and His Family," 626.

meaning that ʿAlī is considered the main link from the Prophet for the mystical knowledge transmitted down to the order. Similarly, to the figure of the sixth imam, Jaʿfar al-Ṣādiq, is attributed an important early mystical commentary (*tafsīr*) on the Qurʾan, in which several important mystical concepts are discussed.[9] More generally, the notion that secret knowledge was passed down among a spiritual elect is an idea that both Sufis and Shiʿites share, as was the notion that this knowledge could not be given to just anyone. Visitation to Karbala and the tombs of the Shiʿite imams, and hoping for their blessings and favors, finds its counterpart in the Sufi practice of visiting the tombs of the saints (*awliyāʾ*). So too, the Shiʿite notion of divinely sanctioned leadership (*al-imāma*) mirrors in many ways the Sufi notion of God's "elect" (*abdāl* or *awliyāʾ*).[10] Ambiguity between Shiʿism and Sufism, then, is not simply a matter of definition, but also extends into practices and notions central to both groups.

Many more examples could be offered to make the point that the origins of sectarian groups often entail a significant amount of ambiguity and overlap with "other" sectarian (or even nonsectarian) groups, such that the very idea of discreet sectarian confessions at the periods of their alleged origin needs to be questioned. Labeling a group Khārijite, Shiʿite, Sunni, Muʿtazilī, or Murjiʾī can be a convenient shorthand, but the limited utility of this shorthand needs to be recognized and frequently undercut if analysis of a group is to become more profound and meaningful.

Durable Sectarian Categories?

Equally problematic is the assumption that sects and schools, once "formed," continue to operate as meaningful and distinct entities, and that they do so all the time. This does not seem to be the case. Rather, there are moments in the long histories of sect/school movements when the importance and particularity of sect/school identifications are difficult to determine for various reasons: Either because it has become neither the primary motivator of action nor the main factor in identification among sectarian groups or that sect/school identity becomes something that is downplayed or rejected altogether. Makdisi, for example, draws attention to how relations between Christians and Druze in the mountainous region of Jabal Druze in Lebanon underwent a significant process of reformulation in relation to both colonial and Ottoman policies. Initially, groups in these regions identified socially as either peasants or

[9] Sells, *Early Islamic Mysticism*, 76–77. [10] Karamustafa, *Sufism*, 127–28.

nobles, with their Christian or Druze identifications subordinated to the social stations that they occupied.[11] However, by the 1850s, the increased presence of Christian missionaries, the propensity of colonial administrators to view Middle Eastern societies in terms of religious affiliation, and the Ottoman turn toward *tanzīmāt*-era reforms (that reified religious identifications) all contributed to a shift in sectarian affiliation to a more primary mode of social identification. While this example does not utilize Muslim sectarian identifications, it does illustrate the notion that sect identification is not always primary and must be made primary by a host of factors. It is an excellent example of "sectarianism without sectarianism" before such identifications became more salient.

In other instances, sectarian identification might be active, but not the dominant mode of social identification. Winter, for example, shows how the Nuṣayrīs (ʿAlawites) in what is now northwestern Syria were "not the deviant, marginal phenomenon it has retrospectively been made out to be but, on the contrary, constituted, and was treated by the contemporary authorities as, a normal mode of rural religiosity in Syria."[12] The Nuṣayrīs seem to have been well integrated into the Ottoman state apparatus, which was aware of their sectarian affiliation and taxed them in a different fashion from other groups. However, the Ottoman state chose to take little interest in their profession of ʿAlawism, such that by the eleventh/seventeenth-century Nuṣayrī families appear in state registers as local dignitaries and servants of the Ottoman state.[13] In this example, Nuṣayrī sectarian identification was active, but not the primary driver of identification vis-à-vis the Ottoman authorities.

In yet other instances, sectarian affiliation of a group or institution might shift over time. For example, the medieval confraternities known as *futuwwa* seem to have been largely Sunni in outlook before the ninth/fifteenth century, though they held ʿAlī in high esteem as the purported founder of the *futuwwa* groups. After the ninth/fifteenth century, however, these groups seem to have moved closer to Twelver Shiʿite norms, exhibiting more classically Shiʿite forms of devotion such as displays of love for the family of the Prophet and the imams as well as remembrances of al-Ḥusayn's martyrdom at Karbala.[14]

Moreover, there are cases where sectarian identification might be actively downplayed as unimportant, or even as a hindrance to salvation. The seventh/thirteenth-century Andalūsī mystic Ibn al-ʿArabī adopted an extremely tolerant view of other religious paths, including non-Muslim

[11] Makdisi, *Culture of Sectarianism*, 35. [12] Winter, *A History of the ʿAlawis*, 11.
[13] Winter, *A History of the ʿAlawis*, 158.
[14] Yildirim, "Shīʿitisation of the *Futuwwa* Tradition," 62–63.

ones. His pluralist outlook was informed by a kind of perennialism, whereby the mystics recognized the esoteric kernel at the core of the various religious systems that God had created. A similar perennialism informed the pluralist attitudes of the fourth/tenth-century Ismāʿīlī group the Ikhwān al-Ṣafaʿ, who likewise held that all religious paths contained some element of validity.[15]

Another example of a figure who actively downplayed sect affiliation was the seventh/thirteenth-century Sufi Jalāl al-Dīn Rūmī. He wrote several couplets in his famous *Masnavī* that indicate how Rūmī viewed sectarianism (playing on the Prophetic *ḥadīth* of seventy-two sects) as an unhelpful deterrent to the pure love of God:

> Love is a stranger to both worlds,
> To love, seventy-two [sects] is insanity.[16]
>
> Love's religion is not among the seventy-two sects,
> To love, the thrones of kings are [nothing but] splints.[17]
>
> Because of such imagination [coming from desire and fear],
> [which is] a highway robber on the road of certainty,
> The folk of religion became seventy-two sects.[18]

Whether a form of insanity, a false kind of religion, or an imaginary consciousness stemming from desire and fear, Rūmī places the love of God as a superior narrative of self-identification far above that of sectarian or school affiliation. Nor is Rūmī alone among the Sufis in considering sectarianism among Muslims as a false and misleading type of piety. The eighth/fourteenth-century Persian Sufi poet Ḥāfeẓ wrote:

> Forgive all wars between the seventy-two sects;
> Since they did not see the truth, they followed the way of myth.[19]

What all of these figures have in common is their conviction that sect and school identifications are unimportant in relation to other – they would say "truer" – forms of religious identification and consciousness.

Equally interesting are instances of ambiguous sectarian identity among some later Muslim figures. This chapter has pointed out how in the early period, sectarian identification can be complicated, a fact that points to the murky origins of sectarianism and the difficulty in determining when such identifications actually take shape. So too, there are instances of ambiguous sectarian identification from the high medieval

[15] Ebstein, "'Religions, Opinions and Beliefs,'" 514.
[16] Rūmī, *Mathnawī*, book 3, line 4719. I'm grateful to Alan Godlas for both these references and these translations.
[17] Rūmī, *Mathnawī*, book 3, line 4721. [18] Rūmī, *Mathnawī*, book 5, line 2656.
[19] Quoted in Mottahedeh, "Pluralism and Islamic Traditions," 158 (thanks again to Alan Godlas for the better translation).

periods. Indeed, several scholars have argued that in the wake of the Mongol conquests Muslim identifications underwent a process of de-confessionalization, where the importance of sectarian or even broader confessional boundaries blurred or collapsed altogether into a generalized form of ʿAlīd loyalism.[20] One example of an ambiguous figure from this era is the eighth/fourteenth-century Central Asian leader Timur (Tamerlane, Timurlane, Timur the Lame). Given their official patronage of the Ḥanafī law school, Timur and his followers were generally considered Sunnis. At the same time, they displayed a strong devotion to ʿAlī and went on pilgrimage to Shiʿi sites so frequently that one historian commented that "an 'officially' Shi'i dynasty could hardly have been more obsequious."[21] In his history, Ibn Khaldūn notes how Timur had a reputation for favoring the descendants of the Prophet, and after Timur's death, his successors more explicitly amplified this devotion.[22] In the words of Moin, Timur's sectarian ambiguities reflect the larger picture of the eighth/fourteenth century, "in which Sufi and Shi'i elements came together in the light of a 'reachieved Islamic unity.' This was a time when allegedly Sunni and Sufi figures were producing texts that would later become canonical Shi'i works; when popular stories and oral legends were being integrated with formal doctrine to shape new devotional narratives centered on the memory of Ali."[23] In other words, Timur existed at a time when de-confessionalization rendered the distinctions between Sunni, Shiʿi, and Sufi practices less meaningful, and thus there is no "contradiction" in his devotions, which can no longer be considered exclusively "Shiʿi" or "Sunni" in the context of his time.

Of course, the historical record of individuals, groups, and dynasties presents its own difficulties to the researcher insofar as later generations, with their own concerns and agendas, usually write their histories. The example of the medieval saint Haji Bektāsh Veli can be helpful in considering how the memories and images of religious figures were often constructed by later generations for their own purposes. Haji Bektāsh Veli became an important figure for the Bektāshī Sufi order, an order that was associated with the military and bureaucratic cadres of the Ottoman Empire.[24] When the Bektāshī Order was said to have taken shape, during the reign of Süleyman I (r. 926–73/1520–66), it was depicted as having incorporated "many loosely affiliated groups known for heteropraxy like the Abdâls, Kalenders, and Hurûfis, deepening its adherence to Twelver

[20] Hodgson, *Venture of Islam, Vol. 2*, 445–55.
[21] Moin, *Millennial Sovereign*, 40, quoting Amoretti, "Religion in the Timurid and Safavid Periods," 616.
[22] Moin, *Millennial Sovereign*, 37–39. [23] Moin, *Millennial Sovereign*, 40.
[24] Karamustafa, *God's Unruly Friends*, 84.

Shi'i themes, and institutionalizing under its 'second pir' Balim Sultan."[25] However, by the thirteenth/nineteenth century, a time when the Ottomans were emphasizing Sunni identifications, Ahmed Rifat in his *Mir'ātü'l-Mekāsid (Mirror of Objectives)* portrays "as unquestionably orthoprax and essentially Sunni not only Haji Bektash, but also the order founded in his name."[26] Sectarian affiliation, in other words, is sometimes the product of later generations of historians who require it for their argumentation. This is a different kind of sectarian ambiguity, but it is no less important to remember given that our historical sources are always written by interested parties. To what extent, then, are sectarian identifications emphasized, de-emphasized, or even created by later historians?[27]

These examples underscore a point made in the Introduction, namely, that sect/school identifications are dependent on the ways that people make them, or choose not to make them. Such an important insight into how human beings employ sect/school identifications might get lost in the clean divisions of this book's chapters. It is therefore worth revisiting (with some concrete examples) how sects and school identifications lose or gain importance and shift according to the needs of the human beings who live them or later frame narratives around them.

Sectarian Relations

Another method of getting at the kind of ambiguities that interpenetrate and complicate the study of Muslim sectarianism is through analysis of relations between sect and school groups. To the extent that the historical record allows for these types of relations to be studied, this can be achieved in any number of ways. For our purposes it will be helpful to begin with the investigation of the legal, political, and social aspects of interaction between (for the most part) Sunnis, Shiʿa, and Ibāḍīs. Kakar once described the association between Hindus and Muslims in India as being that of "more than strangers, not often enemies, but less than friends."[28] This quote, though focused on Hindus and Muslims in modern India, nicely captures the difficulties in pinning down relationships that span centuries and encompass many different peoples. There are simply too many variables to accurately generalize how different confessional Muslim groups interacted with one another over the *longue durée*. Defaulting to a position of either happy tolerance or ancient hatred may

[25] Soileau, "Conforming Haji Bektash," 435.
[26] Soileau, "Conforming Haji Bektash," 444.
[27] On this point, see Baker, *Medieval Islamic Sectarianism*, 77–88.
[28] Haddad, *Sectarianism in Iraq*, 55.

offer a convenient (albeit intellectually lazy) way for some journalists and politicians to simplify complex issues, but this course veers to extremes in how sectarian relations seem to happen over the long term.

To conceptualize Muslim communal groups as "more than strangers" is to remind ourselves that sect and school identifications must be made to matter. There are, however, several other ways that Muslims have imagined and classified themselves: for example, medieval Muslims often wrote of elites (*khawāṣṣ*) and commoners (*ʿawāmm*), Arabs and non-Arabs, or even settled peoples and nomads, to give just a few examples. In these cases, sectarian identification would be considered (to use Haddad's terminology) "banal," meaning that while those classified as, for example, non-Arabs almost certainly possessed a sectarian affiliation after the third/ninth century, this affiliation did not operate as the primary one for the historian who chose to classify them as non-Arabs.[29] Banal sectarian identifications would not have been recorded in history books of that place and era, for the simple reason that what was considered ordinary was not considered worth recording. How, then, can the banality of sectarian identifications in these periods be "seen" by historians of later ages?

There are, of course, moments in the historical record when sectarian identifications seem to matter a great deal. Examples of sectarian violence in Muslim history are relatively easy to find. To cite just a few early medieval examples: violence in the streets of Kufa and Baghdad that was attributed to various Shiʿa groups, the Ḥanbalī riots during the *miḥna*, clashes between Ḥanbalīs and Ashʿarīs, and the ʿAbbāsid caliph al-Mutawakkil's destruction of Karbala.[30] High medieval and modern examples of sectarian strife are also relatively easy to find. Yet the visible quality of historical reports on intra-sectarian violence does not necessarily lead to the conclusion that widespread and long-term sectarian violence was the norm. Indeed, looking at the historical record as a whole it becomes intellectually irresponsible to assume that this state of affairs was usual over the *longue durée*. Put another way, I do not think that the recorded history of violence between Muslim sectarians is enough to prove that an enduring hatred exists between them, but rather it proves nothing more than that sectarian affiliation is but one strand in a complicated web of human identifications that sometimes results in polemic, friction, and violence. I suspect that neutral relations between

[29] On "banal" vs. active sectarianism, see Haddad, *Sectarianism in Iraq*, 10.

[30] For an overview and discussion of the Imāmī Shiʿi neighborhood (mini-city, in fact) of al-Karkh, see Neggaz, "Al-Karkh," 279–305.

sectarian groups is likely the default position for most, and for most of the time, but the historical record makes this position difficult to prove.

Relatedly, the banality of sectarian relations over the *longue durée* does not mean that there existed some sort of happy tolerance between them. Taking the position that Muslim confessional groups were "more than strangers" is very different from claiming that there existed some sort of amicable harmony among them, as, indeed, they were often "less than friends." For this reason, the "tolerance" thesis turns out to be just as problematic as the "ancient hatreds" thesis. It should be simultaneously remembered that the notion of tolerance is a product of the modern era and unsuited to how medieval actors operated. Likewise, "tolerance" is an unclear designator which could indicate something like an idealized social harmony or it could simply refer to putting up with people whom one does not like. Originally, it was a biological term referring to how much poison an organism could ingest before expiring. In short, the term "tolerance" has undergone a dramatic transformation in the modern period. Its premodern usages seem to fall short of the more modern idea of accepting and even celebrating differences.

The debates surrounding the nature and applicability of the idea of *convivencia* in the medieval Iberian Peninsula illustrate the difficulties in importing a modern notion of "toleration" or "coexistence" into a medieval setting. Catlos, one of the foremost historians of medieval Iberia, cautions against idealizing medieval Iberia either as a place of idyllic tolerance or one of clashing civilizations, noting that "tolerance is hardly regarded as a virtue today, let alone in the Middle Ages."[31] Different groups in the medieval Iberian Peninsula came together and worked together largely out of convenience and a perception of their own shared benefit. However, when such circumstances changed, these same groups sometimes ceased to interact harmoniously. What Catlos (and others) emphasize is how circumstances other than communal affiliation and identification play an extremely important role in determining the dynamics of group interactions in any given time and place. Generalizing civilizational clash or idyllic harmony obscures the more complicated, and more interesting, historical realities.

Another means of getting at the relations between Muslim groups is to examine marriage laws. On the one hand, if an ancient and implacable hatred existed between, for example, Sunnis and Shiʿa, then we should expect to find significant legal barriers preventing them from intermarrying. On the other hand, if the groups intermingled freely and amicably, we should expect to find few, if any, barriers between marriage. In fact, what

[31] Catlos, *Kingdoms of Faith*, 429.

we find is complicated and somewhere in between these two positions. In his *Tabṣirat al-Mutʿallimīn fī Aḥkām al-Dīn* (*The Explication of the Learned in the Ordinances of Religion*) the eighth/fourteenth-century Twelver Shiʿi scholar Abū Manṣūr Jamāl al-Dīn al-Ḥasan b. Yūsuf b. Muṭahhar al-Ḥillī stated that an Imāmī (meaning Shiʿi) woman cannot marry a Sunni man, but that an Imāmī man can marry a Sunni woman. This ruling mirrors the general Islamic legal stipulations on marriages between Muslims and non-Muslim monotheists: a Muslim man may marry a woman from the *ahl al-kitāb*, but a Muslim woman can only marry a Muslim man. One implication of al-Ḥillī's ruling, then, is that a Sunni man does not count as a full Muslim, and therefore a Shiʿi woman cannot marry him.

Aspects of al-Ḥillī's ruling, however, remained contested among Shiʿi jurists. The issue of whether or not an Imāmī woman could marry a Sunni man, despite al-Ḥillī's strong opinion on the matter, in fact garnered disagreement between Shiʿite legal scholars. Some scholars forbade it, citing the idea that "faith" (*īmān*) remains a relevant consideration for suitability (*kafāʾa*) between potential marriage partners. Other Shiʿite jurists allowed marriage between a Sunni man and Imāmī woman, considering sectarian identification separate from matters of faith and therefore not relevant to the suitability of the potential partners. So sectarian identification was only sometimes a legal issue in Shiʿi-Sunni marriages, and only in cases where a Sunni man hopes to wed a Shiʿi woman. A similar range of opinion exists among Sunni jurists on the issue, with many allowing it and some dissenting to it. What, then, does the issue of Sunni-Shiʿite marriages illuminate about the nature of sectarian relations? The issue remains unsettled, and, just as in the case of Catholic uses of birth control, legal opinions often tell only half of the story.

This sometimes-shared space of marriage is reflected in how public spaces are sometimes marked as cross-sectarian. In a study on ʿAlīd shrines in medieval Syria, Mulder notes how shrines often possessed both Sunni and Shiʿi patrons, and that the inscriptions in them often praised the *ahl al-bayt*. This was done, she argues, as a deliberately unifying act in the wake of the Crusades and found its strongest expression in the policies of the caliph al-Nāṣir li-Dīn Allāh (575–622/1180–1225).[32] So too, the medieval Ashrafiyya library in Damascus contained numerous works of Shiʿism, many specifically associated with the Twelver Shiʿite tradition. In his discussion of why such works appear to be seamlessly integrated into the library, Hirschler points to the de-confessionalization of the late medieval period, a sentiment echoed by Melvin-Koushki in his analysis of late

[32] Mulder, *Shrines of the ʿAlids*, 98–105.

medieval occult materials.[33] Such confessional ambiguity is better documented in the Muslim East, yet a modicum of such ambiguities seems to have prevailed in late medieval Syria as well.

Such instances of inter-sectarian relations and shared spaces, when Muslims of various denominational affiliations were "more than strangers" to one another or occupied a shared space together, remind us as students of sectarianism that significant ambiguity and overlap often permeate and interpenetrate how Muslims think about, or do not think about, their sectarian identities. The narrative-identity approach that I have adopted for this book posits that sectarian identity only matters when it is made to matter – when a narrative about sectarianism becomes compelling enough to warrant attention. When such narratives do not compel, sectarianism as an identification may well fade, become unimportant, or assume a secondary role.

But what of those moments when sectarian identifications are made to matter? What about those instances of sectarian friction that fall short of violence, yet still show how Muslim sectarians were "less than friends"? These examples offer another means to examine the numerous possibilities of sectarian relations, specifically the issue of polemics. Apologetic and polemic texts that previous generations of Muslims have preserved remain far more common than outright violence between sectarian groups (and likely operate as a necessary precursor to such violence). Polemical literature spans a number of genres, including heresiographical texts, legal opinions, recorded sermons, and much else, and its tenor runs the gambit from relatively light to vehement. Indeed, the scholars of the Muslim traditions argued at great length about a great many things, including communal affiliation, the benefits of their own, and the dangers of someone else's. They continue to do so up to the present moment, as do Christians, Jews, and many other deeply committed religious persons.

Ibn Taymiyya's eighth/fourteenth-century *fatwa*s on the Nuṣayrīs (ʿAlawīs) offer illustrative examples of anti-sectarian legal polemic and the issues involved in the academic study of them. Ibn Taymiyya (d. 728/1328) was a Ḥanbalī jurist from the Levant. His writings exhibit an overall polemical bent against non-Sunnis, but Shiʿites and Sufis in particular attracted his ire. As a prominent jurist of his era, Ibn Taymiyya was on a few occasions asked to render his professional legal opinion about the Nuṣayrīs. In one of his responses, he famously stated that the Nuṣayriyya "and the other kinds of Qarāmiṭa, the Bāṭiniyya, are more heretical than the Jews and the Christians, even

[33] Hirschler, *Medieval Damascus*, 125; Melvin-Koushki, "Quest for a Universal Science," 69–77.

more so than many polytheists."[34] Taken as a general statement, this opinion paints a strongly negative portrait of the Nuṣayrī Shiʿites. There exists, however, a particular context for the *fatwa*: it was likely used in conjunction with Mamluk raids into the Nuṣayrī regions of Jabala or al-Ẓanīnayn in the year 705/1305. Given this context, it is unsurprising that Ibn Taymiyya offers such bold criticism. Likewise, his other two *fatwa*s on the Nuṣayrīs appear to have been focused on another local raid and on putting down an uprising by a Nuṣayrī who claimed to be the returning Mahdī. And despite their strong language, they do not seem to have affected in any significant way how the ruling political powers ultimately dealt with the Nuṣayrīs. The Muslim traveler Ibn Baṭṭūṭa explains that the Mamluks needed them to cultivate the land, and so they were spared despite the earlier (and unsuccessful) campaign to convert them to Sunnism. Moreover, as Winter has shown, the later Ottoman state appeared fully aware of them, and of their non-Sunni communal affiliation, but left them alone, taxing them just as they taxed other religious communities within their borders. Ibn Taymiyya's wrath, it seems, was limited in its scope.

Additionally, analysis of Ibn Taymiyya's *fatwa*s has convincingly argued that he lacked firsthand knowledge of the Nuṣayrīs, and that he consistently conflated them in with other Shiʿite groups, such as the Ismāʿīlīs, or classed them alongside of other local groups such as the Druze. Nevertheless, Ibn Taymiyya's opinions have survived in the Ḥanbalī-Sunni tradition, resurfacing in the modern period as part of the polemical attacks against the Assad regime in Syria.

Ibn Taymiyya's *fatwa*s against the Nuṣayrīs thus offer a few helpful caveats when approaching polemical and apologetic literature that deals with intra-sectarian relations between Muslims. First, such literature may or may not be accurate in its depiction of sectarian groups. Ibn Taymiyya was rather uninformed about the Nuṣayrīs. Yet this is not always the case. Other polemical literature, such as al-Malaṭī's discussion of the Shiʿite Hishām b. al-Ḥakam's articulation of the Imāmī Shiʿite doctrine of the imamate in his fourth/tenth-century *al-Tanbīh wa'l-Radd ʿalā Ahl al-Ahwāʾ wa'l-Bidʿa* (*The Warning and the Refutation of the People of Whim and Innovation*), appears to match what can be found elsewhere about Ibn al-Ḥakam and Imāmī imamate theory, despite the fact that al-Malaṭī was openly hostile to Ibn al-Ḥakam in his text.[35] This range of possibilities reminds us that the many scholarly tools of textual study and comparison must be used in evaluating a medieval text. Polemical literature can range

[34] Friedman, "Ibn Taymiyya's *Fatāwā*," 351ff. [35] al-Malaṭī, *al-Tanbīh*, 25.

from uninformed to fully informed, and it is up to the researcher to pursue all of the clues that the text offers to determine its status.

Second, it should be remembered that it was the *ʿulamāʾ*, for the most part, who produced polemical and apologetic literature. Therefore, their place within the broader scope of Muslim societies, as well as the limits of their influence, must be appreciated in order to gauge the impact of their polemical writings. Again, Ibn Taymiyya's *fatwa*s on the Nuṣayrīs offer an excellent example. Although he was a towering intellectual in his time, his *fatwa*s on the Nuṣayrīs had but limited and local affect on how the Muslims of his day dealt with this group. Other Muslims – political figures, local dignitaries, military people, and many others – played an important role in how Levantine Muslims of the eighth/fourteenth century actually interacted with the Nuṣayrī community. However, these figures are mostly lost to us because few if any of their decisions and actions were recorded in the historical record. This fact offers an important reminder of how the *ʿulamāʾ* (or other producers of such literature) represent a certain segment of any given medieval society, but they do not represent all of it nor should their place and influence in such societies be grossly under- or overestimated.

Finally, the ability of Ibn Taymiyya's *fatwa*s to resurface several centuries after the death of their author in the context of modern polemics against the Syrian Assad regime should remind us that religious actors can plumb the histories of their traditions and activate aspects of their narratives that have been largely forgotten, repurposing them for contemporary concerns in a way that masks the distance between the original circumstances of the polemic and the contemporary needs of the polemicist. Such a move is made to appear seamless in how it takes literature that was once part of the broader narrative of sectarian identification, however major or minor, and makes it again part of that identification. Others have written far more elegantly about the processes of religious "tradition," but it is worth appreciating how this process works within the context of sectarian identification writ large.

Sectarian Definitions

In addition to the ambiguities and problems associated with the study of Muslim sects and schools, it is also worth remembering that the terms that we use to describe and examine our subject, and the taxonomies that we have adopted to organize this book, have a history that effects how we as scholars approach our topic. This history should be examined in some detail, if only to reveal the difficulties that arise with making the necessary linguistic and organizational choices when writing a book. One of the major hurdles of this book was how to describe the topic itself. The terms "sect" and "sectarianism" (even, to an extent, the strongly Christian notion of "salvation") are terms and categories foreign to medieval Muslims (note also how we have imported the modern idea of "religion" into the book as well). These are academic terms initially forged among German sociologists for the purpose of understanding the history of Christians. In the modern world they have taken on negative connotations of (often irrational) violence and factionalism. Nevertheless, the terms seem to approximate something(s) that had many names in medieval Muslim literature: *firaq*, *milal*, *niḥal*, *madhāhib*, and *ṭawāʾif*, to name a few. The terms "sect" or "school" might not accurately capture the range of what medieval Muslims seem to be describing when they use their own terminology. Nor does substituting another English term like "denomination" or "confessional group" solve the problem either (in fact, it seems to add to the problem by introducing confusion to an English-speaking audience over the subject of the work). This work has chosen to keep the terms "sect," "school," and "sectarianism" because they offer a kind of recognizable shorthand and because there are few acceptable alternatives appropriate to an introductory survey on the topic. At the same time, it becomes imperative to examine the terms and taxonomies themselves to find their shortcomings as definitional tools.

Knowing something about the history of the terminology and literature produced by medieval scholars can assist in appreciating its usefulness. To that end, it is helpful to remember that medieval Muslim scholars created their schemas of sects and schools to make sense of their own world and, in part, to attempt to control how it was perceived by others. They did not do so in a uniform fashion (despite what the clean organization of this book might imply), nor did they escape their own ambiguities and difficulties when attempting to define their subjects. Nevertheless, medieval *ʿulamāʾ*, by adopting and employing the genre of heresiography as the mainstay of their attempts to organize knowledge about the *firaq* of their day, engaged in an exercise of power. In other words, their taxonomies of knowledge were not neutral, but aimed at convincing others of the rightness of their own adopted affiliation at the expense of the other *firaq*, which they considered damned. It is vital to keep the polemical nature of our sources in mind when considering the usefulness of the definitions that we take from it.

It is also worth remembering that the categories of *firaq* that became the mainstays of heresiographical literature came into existence among Muslims of a specific geography, namely, Eastern (Mashriqī) Muslims. As such, it may or may not be helpful in assessing the history of the Muslim West (Maghrib). Indeed, Wansbrough cautions against attempting to solve historical issues in the Islamic West with solutions from the East, and this cautionary should lead scholars to pause when creating blanket definitions of sectarian identity.[36] It has been shown, for example, that the Almohads (al-Muwaḥḥidūn) of North Africa and Iberia understood Islam in a fashion strongly parallel to the Ismāʿīlī Shiʿite Fāṭimids. Like the Fāṭimids, the Almohads envisioned a Mahdī figure who (re)established right doctrine, giving rise to a new religious elite who aggressively propagated it, often at the expense of the local Mālikī *ʿulamāʾ*. Is it, then, more appropriate to think of their mission as the Sunnification of Fāṭimid Shiʿism and therefore as occupying a middle ground between Sunnism and Shiʿism?[37] What does this mean for how we are to conceptualize Sunnism or Shiʿism in the Islamic West? Much the same could be said for the issue of "sectarianism" in the further eastern regions of Islamdom, such as Central Asia or India. To what extent do the now dominant *firaq* schemes, created largely in the central realms of Islamdom in the medieval period, apply to other places and eras? The geographically situatedness of our definitions of sect and school might not, in the end, be appropriate for the study of Muslim groups across all times and places within Islamdom.

Similarly, the sheer range of terminology employed by Muslims to describe the divisions among them is another indicator of a variety of thinking on the subject. I have chosen to emphasize the term *firqa*/*firaq* over others, but this choice does privilege the classical, third–sixth/ninth–twelfth-century Muslim heresiographers who wrote in Arabic, lived (for the most part) in the central regions of Islamdom, and who tended to use the term *firqa* to describe the divisions among their peers. Other terminology existed, as did other divisions, some of which can seem *firqa*-like when examined closely. Moreover, these groups often seem to fulfill the criterion for the narrative-identity approach to Islamic sectarianism. Take, for example, the idea of a *madhhab*, often translated as "legal school." I have chosen, for the most part, not to examine the *madhāhib* as examples of "sectarianism," except in the chapter on Sunnis (see Chapter 6) where the medieval Ḥanbalīs of Baghdad do, in fact, behave in rather *firqa*-like ways (that is, when they possessed their own particular narrative of truth and salvation and they acted according to it, even to the point of violence in certain cases). In fact, some Shiʿite heresiographers, along with Ibāḍī heresiographers, did treat the Ḥanbalīs and other (Sunni) *madhāhib* as divisions to be described alongside of Murjiʾites,

[36] Wansbrough, "On Recomposing the Islamic History of North Africa," 170.

[37] Fierro, *The Almohad Revolution*, 164; see also Fierro, "The Almohads and the Fatimids," 161–75.

Muʿtazilites, and Khārijites.[38] There might be occasions, then, when the idea of "sect" or "school" needs to be expanded to accommodate what we think of as legal schools.

So too, the idea of "theological schools," such as the Ashʿarites (al-Ashʿariyya), might at times approximate the ways that this book has defined Muslim sects and schools. The Ashʿarites, too, often clashed with the Ḥanbalīs of the medieval period over issues of truth and salvation. In such cases, it might be prudent to consider them as a "sect"/*firqa*, or at least as sect-like. In fact, the Ibāḍī heresiographer al-Qalhātī does class the Ashʿarites among the divisions of Sunnis, though most other heresiographers do not.[39]

In a similar vein, al-Rāzī and al-Shahrastānī wrote about the medieval Muslim philosophers (*faylasūf*) in the sections of their heresiographies that were devoted to non-Muslims, likely following the lead of al-Ghazālī who excluded them from the Muslim fold.[40] And yet the Muslim philosophers declared their submission to God and their allegiance to His last Prophet. In other words, they professed *islām*, however they may have understood it. Why, then, do they not count among the divisions of Muslims? Should we, as scholars of Muslim history, simply follow al-Ghazālī, al-Rāzī, and al-Sharastānī in their taxonomies and exclude them, or is there something to be gained by reexamining our categories and including the philosophers among the other *firaq*? There might be instances when such a move is warranted.

So too, should Sufi groups be considered sect-like, especially after the fifth–sixth/eleventh–twelfth centuries when they organized themselves into *ṭarīqāt* (fraternities)? By the narrative-identity theory, there should actually be little difference between a Sufi group and a *firqa*. Yet for the most part Sufi groups did not appear in the pages of heresiographies (including later ones), suggesting that on the whole, Muslim heresiographers thought of these groups as something other than sect-like.[41] Similarly, should other esoteric and occultist groups, such as the lettrists, astrologers, and alchemists, who delved into the esoteric and soteriological symbolism of letters, stars and substances, be considered sect-like? Is it possible to speak of a Sufi or lettrist "sectarianism"?

I have left these questions unanswered in an attempt to remind the student of Muslim sects and schools that definitions and taxonomies are messy and often inaccurate. There is no way around them, as we must

[38] See Madelung and Walker, *An Ismaili Heresiography*, 43–47; al-Qalhātī, *al-Kashf wa'l-Bayān*, 2:373ff.
[39] al-Qalhātī, *al-Kashf wa'l-Bayān*, 2:372–73.
[40] al-Rāzī, *Iʿtiqādāt*, 134–50; al-Shahrastānī, *al-Milal wa'l-Niḥal*, 414ff.
[41] al-Rāzī, *Iʿtiqādāt*, 110–17.

speak in a language and organize our knowledge so as to make certain kinds of sense from it. Yet we cannot forget that language and the organization of knowledge are human endeavors, tied to the times and places where they are employed, and bounded by the agendas of those who employ them. Progress in knowledge, however, comes from a willingness to explore beyond the taxonomies that we have inherited. And it is the hope of this author that future scholars might experiment with new and more profitable ways of organizing our knowledge about Muslim sects and schools.

The questions raised in this chapter have sought to underscore one of the core concerns of this work, which is to emphasize that sectarian affiliation is something created, sustained, and continually reimagined by human beings. To study such a thing as "Muslim sects and schools" requires not only expansive methodologies that can account for the instability and scale of the topic, but also a healthy appreciation of the limits of these methodologies, married to a willingness to examine them for their shortcomings. I have here only scratched the surface of the inadequacies of this particular work, but I trust that the ranks of professors and graduate students who will follow me in my interest in this subject will prove eager to point out the remaining issues and to improve upon them.

8 Conclusions

In sketching out the history of the main sects and schools of the early to high medieval periods among Muslims, this work has attempted to avoid the common mistake of treating these divisions among Muslims as entrenched, immutable, and unchanging. This is not to argue that such differences and divisions do not exist among Muslims, but rather to ask what kind of existence these identifications might have in any given situation. It is to recognize that Muslims most often adopt sect and school affiliations (although sometimes they are thrust upon them), and as such they are as fluid and mutable as any other identification that human beings might assume. Moreover, such identifications remain connected to several other aspects of a person's identity and might be either primary, secondary, or utterly banal depending on a host of circumstances.

In order to approach the history of Muslim sects and schools in this fashion, this work has eschewed earlier scholarly attempts at defining and classing "sects" against a host of other "types" of religio-communal affiliations (e.g. "church," denomination, and cult) and proposed treating sect and school affiliations as a kind of participatory location in narrative-(s). That is, the narrative-identification approach to religious sectarianism, as I have called it, posits that human beings come to identify (or be identified) with religious sects or schools primarily by emplotting themselves (or having themselves emplotted) in the unfolding narratives of the group's existence and history. Participation within this grand narrative frame, familiarity with it such that the person orients himself or herself according to it, defines what "being" a member of any given group entails. Alternately, a person might have themselves located in that narrative without their assent, as when other groups emphasize a narrative for their own purposes, locating certain persons within that narrative even if they don't identify with that narrative on their own.

Treating sect and school affiliations as emplotments within narratives means taking the idea of narrative seriously. I'm convinced that sect and school narratives have all of the usual elements of fictional, historical, hagiographical, or other types of stories. That is, they have characters, settings, origin stories, backstories, and a plot (and many subplots). Likewise they have many who have told the story and passed it down in various guises to us (that is, they have authors/narrators). While the many elements of these grand narratives may differ, I believe that the plot is usually a stratagem qua story about how human beings achieve ultimate salvation. Thus, "being" a Shiʿite involves understanding that God chose the imams as the divinely inspired leaders of humankind, and thus devotion to the imams becomes the primary means of submitting oneself to God and enacting His religion. Similarly, "being" an Ibāḍī Muslim encompasses the historical narrative that true religion was preserved against corruption in the very early periods of Islamdom by small bands of Muslim *shurāt*, a group of whom settled in Basra and was led initially by Jābir b. Zayd, who then spread this message via a missionary apparatus to the Arabian Peninsula and North Africa, leading to the Ibāḍī communities that survive to the present and preserve God's message to humanity in its purest form. Alternately, a medieval chronicler such as al-Ṭabarī writing about the Khārijites was eager to convince his audience that these groups had deviated from the true religion, and he framed the stories that had come down to him accordingly. Despite their many guises, however, these are, at heart, stories, and they are largely stories relevant to how a person should (or should not) comport themselves if they wish to be right before God.

I have attempted in the chapters to orient them around central narratives of salvation. This is merely to give the chapters some sort of cohesion and focus. This method remains nothing more than a heuristic device and does not imply some sort of essential quality of these groups. Nevertheless, and acknowledging the problems of our source materials for the history of Muslim groups, it can be helpful to view the master narratives of the Khārijites and Ibāḍiyya as protests against the impieties of the early period. A concern for preserving piety, even dying for it, does seem to loom large in the stories that have come down about them, even if those same sources are highly problematic from the perspective of the historian. Similarly, the theme of devotion to the imams looms large in the massive literature of the Shiʿa, whether that be devotion to a rebel who promises to restore the rights of the Prophet's family or to an imam held to be a divinely guided source of knowledge. The Murjiʾites and Muʿtazilites, being largely schools of thought by the ʿAbbāsid era, are more difficult to track in terms of overarching themes. Nevertheless, they are marked by a high degree of intellectual speculation and experimentation, enabled by the mostly favorable conditions of the ʿAbbāsid period. Their grand narratives, as it were, encompassed ideas about God's nature and the structure of His creation. Still, such ideas enabled the Murjiʾites and Muʿtazilites to orient their behavior accordingly, in the hopes that their actions would prove pleasing to God. The last of the groups surveyed here, the Sunnis, remained the last to form of the classical pentad of Muslim sects and schools. In many ways, Sunnism can only be defined in the broadest of terms. It is, perhaps, an expansive consensus that looked to the example of the Prophet as a means to establish and ground the community (and one that self-consciously presented itself as unlike any of the sects and schools that preceded them). Simultaneously, an important "plot" of the grand narrative of Sunnism, as it were, was and is adhering to the broad outlines of consensus that the community of scholars built on the basis of the example of the Prophet. Many different groups, in fact, called and continue to call themselves Sunnis. This inclusive approach, combined with medieval patronage of the *madrasa* system, allowed Sunnism to become the majority communal affiliation among Muslims, which it remains to this day.

By locating themselves in these grand narratives of Muslim sects and schools, Muslims entered into sect and school traditions that, for the most part, preceded them. This work has hoped to provide accounts of some of the early episodes in Muslim history that shaped the way that the master narratives of the Muslim groups developed. Thus, it has emphasized the context of late antiquity as the stage on which the dramas of the first generations of Muslims initially played out. Late antiquity simultaneously provided much of the literary and historical frameworks in which the narratives of Muslim sects and schools were articulated, and Muslims quickly adapted the genres of the late antique world to their own uses (to say nothing of those genres that they soon established themselves). Notable among those events was the succession to the Prophet Muḥammad after his death and the early civil wars (*fitan*) that followed thereafter. Unlike the circumstances of the late antique Byzantine or Sāsānian empires, however, early Islamdom lacked a strong central government, such that religious legitimacy was often held to exist outside of the Umayyad dynasty; a situation that became entrenched in the ʿAbbāsid period with the failure of the *miḥna* and the diminishing influence of the ʿAbbāsid caliphs. Geography, of course, also played an important role in determining where certain groups could flourish outside of the influence of the dominant political powers. This fact points toward the importance of understanding how military power, the mainstay of which was the mounted archer, functioned in the medieval period, and how this situation changed with the advent of gunpowder.

Those who articulated the first narratives of Muslim sects and schools fashioned their understandings of these early historical events and conditions into the initial articulations of the grand narratives of their groups.

With time, these grand narratives acquired long histories that were not too easily altered. Yet, subsequent participation in the narratives of Muslim sects and schools was far from passive. The process of orienting oneself with a grand narrative of a Muslim sect or school necessarily entailed finding relevance to the questions that confronted a person within their time and place. And this meant that the grand narratives of sect and school evolved with the needs of those who adopted them. For the student of Muslim sects and schools, those persons who contributed to, for example, the intellectual history of a given tradition can be considered those who took the inherited narratives of their sect or school and built upon them in such a way as to make them relevant to their era. Thus, for example, the medieval Sunni scholar al-Ghazālī inherited the tradition of Sunnism and participated in it for many years. In his work *al-Munqidh min al-Ḍalāl* (*The Deliverer from Error*) he relates how at a certain point in his life he came to grapple with doubts and set about looking for certainty.[1] His solution, which the mystical traditions offered, through direct experience, a means for enlivening a tradition that stood in danger of becoming stultified, transformed Sunnism profoundly. In the language of the narrative-identity theory, al-Ghazālī was one of those luminaries who embroidered on the narrative of Sunnism, renewing it for those who followed after him. Thus, the grand narratives of communal affiliation, though they accumulate tradition over time, remain malleable. This work has attempted to present the history of Muslim groups as unfolding and dynamic, as reflective of the ways that human beings continue to find meaning as they orient themselves both within their sect or school histories and their particular situations.

Chapter 7 has attempted to reemphasize some of the ambiguity and difficulty accompanying the study of Muslim sects and schools. It examined the problems associated with reifying sectarian identifications in the earliest period of Islamdom and explored eras in later periods when sect or school affiliations seem to make less sense as a means of classifying Muslims. It looked at some of the ways that relations between sect and school groups seemed to function, noting at every turn that while communal affiliation is sometimes important as a factor in understanding how Muslims interacted, it is not always a factor, much less the main factor. So too, this chapter examined the very terms and definitions within which we as scholars operate when writing about sect and school affiliation, attempting to note the manifold problems associated with employing terms forged in a cultural context far different from the medieval Muslim context they purport to describe. Many of these issues plague

[1] McCarthy, *Al-Ghazali's Path to Sufism*, 21–24.

the very method here employed to study Muslim sects and schools, yet I have found no easy way around them.

Muslim divisions, of course, continued into the late medieval and early modern periods. In the interest of keeping this work short and readable, I have had to leave out many of the groups that emerged in these eras. I can defend this choice by pointing out that the main narratives of sect and school were developed within the early-to-medieval periods, and thus concentrating on them focused the work on the chief sect and school divisions among Muslims. That is, late medieval and early modern sects and schools identify as Sunnis, Shiʿites, or, to a lesser degree, Ibāḍīs, and this work chose to focus on the development of those earlier narratives at the expense of the later ones. However, it is not the aim of this work to imply that the high medieval and early modern periods lacked in interesting historical, intellectual, or religious development among the Muslim sects and schools. Quite the contrary, these eras offer a wealth of cases, many of which continue to exist into the modern era. For example, the Wahhābiyya (Wahhābīs), who traced themselves to Muḥammad b. ʿAbd al-Wahhāb (d. 1206/1792), could be classed as a Sunni reform movement, yet one that emphasized certain behaviors as essential to true faith in a way that other Sunni groups, who cleave to a more quasi-Murjiʾite view toward faith, would not. Another Sunni group (although many Sunnis would not consider them as such) is the Aḥmadiyya movement, whose founder, Mirza Ghulam Ahmad (d. 1326/1908), claimed that only one kind of prophecy had ended with the Prophet Muḥammad, and that he, Mirza Ghulam Ahmad, was, in fact, a prophet sent to warn (*nabī*).

Also regretfully neglected by this book are the many groups that split from various Muslim sects and schools to form something novel (even to the point of being no longer definable as Islamic). Among the Shiʿites, the Bābī movement of twelfth/eighteenth-century Iran posited that God manifested in a series of theophanies. This group, and the idea of God's manifestations, contributed to another new religious movement of twelfth/eighteenth-century Iran, the Bahāʾī faith. Among medieval Ismāʿīlīs, the teachings (and belief in the divinity) of the Fāṭimid caliph al-Ḥakam bi-ʿAmr Allāh, among others, coalesced into the Druze religion, whose inhabitants now number in the hundreds of thousands in the Levant. It is hoped that this book might have laid the foundations for further work into these post-Muslim groups, as well as the other Sunni, Shiʿite, and Ibāḍī offshoots of the high medieval and early modern period.

As a final thought, it should be noted that the title of this work – the *umma* divided – will be an uncomfortable contradiction to many Muslims. The *umma* is not supposed to be divided, and thus discussions on the history of Muslim sects and schools can be challenging ones to have. Moreover, many Muslims (among others) see themselves as non-sectarian; as Muslims full stop. It is not the aim of this work to make an awkward spectacle the history of Muslims sects and schools, or to over-balance the portrait of Muslim history in favor of its contentious and divisive moments. This book aims, simply, to appreciate how human beings sometimes come to understand who they are and what they should do in terms of narratives about group affiliation.

Yet if religious division among Muslims (and human beings in general) remains an undesirable and periodic reality, it is hoped that the instability and contingent nature of religious/sectarian identities might offer some balance to this portrait. The salience of divisions among Muslims seems to reemerge when the conditions are right for interested parties to make them paramount. These same identifications fade in importance or even disappear when such conditions change. Given the Qurʾan's insistence on human forgetfulness, as well as its overarching cautious optimism regarding humankind's ability to create a just social order on earth, perhaps the underlying qurʾanic message regarding sectarian division and difference is that they can be surmounted, just as piety can overcome human weakness and forgetfulness. Discussions of divisions among Muslims, then, might be properly counterpoised against those qurʾanic ideals that offer a means toward Islamic unity. Such universalizing notions surely emerge (in the broadest outlines) from the pages of the Qurʾan: Muslims are to cleave to the essential notion of God's oneness (*tawḥīd*). They are to recognize His propensity – stemming from His mercy – to have sent the prophets to humankind (*nubuwwa*), the last of whom Muslims believe to be the Prophet Muḥammad. And they are to remember that an essential aspect of the warning brought by the prophets cautions of the Day of Judgment (*yawm al-dīn*), when the righteous will be separated from the sinners, tyrants, and unbelievers. Surely, these broadly held notions are deceptively simple: What is the nature of God's oneness, and what, exactly, did God teach through His prophets? The answers to these questions provide the basis for sectarian and philosophical difference, and for the believer they may just mean the difference between standing with the righteous or the damned on the Day of Judgment. It would be very difficult for a student of Muslims sects and schools to walk away from their histories thinking that all Muslims cleave to the same beliefs and practices. Nevertheless, such tenets hold out the promise of Muslim unity out before the *umma*, reminding Muslims through the ages that, in the words of the Qurʾan, "you should establish religion and not be divided therein."[2]

[2] Qurʾan 42:13.

Regrettably, this study will not do justice to the many Muslims throughout the centuries who have refused to separate from their fellow Muslims on the basis of sect or scholastic differences. It will not focus on those who, either through word or action, sought to mend the fractured *umma* and realize the ideal of Islamic unity. Nevertheless, they remain as an important counterweight to the centrifugal forces analyzed in the chapters of this book. They should not be forgotten, as the history of non-sectarianism is as important to the human story as the history of difference. That, too, is the story of human beings.

Glossary

Arabic uses the prefix "al-" as the definite article. This glossary will preserve the al- prefix where appropriate, but it will ignore it when alphabetizing the terms. Those searching for a term should ignore the al- prefix when looking for a word. Names are alphabetized by the most popular and well-known element of the person's name, but I also give the full name of a person as it would appear in a bibliographic entry. Arabic uses "broken plurals" (in other words, Arabic does not usually tack on a suffix to indicate plurals as does English, but rather breaks the structure of the word), and these will be indicated, where necessary, with a slash ("/") after the singular usage of the word.

ʿAbbāsids (r. 132/749–656/1258) the second dynasty among Muslims whose caliphs traced themselves to the Prophet's uncle al-ʿAbbās. During the ʿAbbāsid period, the revolutionary concerns of the previous Umayyad era gave way, in the relative stability achieved by the ʿAbbāsids, to more theologically and philosophically minded questions.

ʿAbdullāh (var. ʿUbaydallāh) b. al-Ḥusayn al-Mahdī (d. 322/934) Ismāʿīlī imam, a descendant of Muḥammad b. Ismāʿīl, and founder of the Ismāʿīlī Fāṭimid state. In 286/899 he claimed the imamate in Salamiyya by arguing that his ancestors had always been imams, a claim that split the early Ismāʿīliyya. He then fled from the ʿAbbāsids to North Africa, where he was imprisoned at Sijilmāsa until freed by his general, Abū ʿAbdullāh al-Shīʿī, who had proselytized among the Kutāma Berbers. Proclaimed the imam and caliph, the Kutāma Berbers then conquered much of western North Africa in his name, thereby establishing the Fāṭimid state.

ʿAbdullāh b. Ibāḍ (d. early to mid-second/seventh century) eponym of the Ibāḍiyya. He is a mysterious figure about whom little is certain: the modern Ibāḍiyya regard him as a kind of colleague to the person they regard as the true founder of their school, Jābir b. Zayd.

Abū Bakr al-Ṣiddīq (d. 13/634) the first successor (caliph, *khalīfa*) to the Prophet Muḥammad, and later classed among the "rightly guided" caliphs by Sunni Muslims. Abū Bakr fought the so-called wars of apostasy (*ḥurūb al-ridda*) against tribal groups in the Arabian Peninsula who refused to pay their *zakāt* and, in so doing, consolidated the Muslim polity under his direction.

Abū Bilāl, Mirdās b. Udayya (d. 61/680–81) an early Khārijite and Ibāḍī hero. Abū Bilāl was considered a model *shārī* leader and martyr, around whose memory several disparate Khārijite groups and Ibāḍīs rallied their nascent communities.

Abū Ḥanīfa, al-Nuʿmān b. Thābit (d. 150/767) eponym of the Ḥanafī *madhhab* and legal scholar from Kufa. Abū Ḥanīfa is associated with the early Murjiʾite movement, but after some of the main tenets of Murjiʾism merged with Sunnism, Abū Ḥanīfa was reimagined as a Sunni.

Abū al-Hudhayl al-ʿAllāf (d. mid-third/ninth century) an important Muʿtazilite theologian. To him is attributed the "five principles" of Muʿtazilite theology.

ʿadl the theological concept of God's justice, which became important for Muʿtazilites and some Shiʿites. For the Muʿtazilites, God was just in a manner that human beings could comprehend, and this meant that He would not do evil, and that human beings could comprehend good and evil by their reason (and therefore they had a responsibility to do good). To the Shiʿa, God's justice implied that He would not leave human beings without access to divine guidance, a position that implied the Shiʿite doctrine of the imamate.

Aga Khan a title, meaning "reverend ruler," bestowed on the Nizārī Ismāʿīlī imams in the twelfth/eighteenth century. As of the writing of this work, there have been four imams who used the title Aga Khan. The current Aga Khan is Shah Karim Al Husseini (b. 1936), who is considered the forty-ninth Ismāʿīlī imam.

ahl al-bayt "the people of the house [of the Prophet Muḥammad]." Treating devotion and allegiance to the Prophet's family as the primary expression of one's submission to God (that is, as the fundamental means of expressing one's *islām*) distinguishes the Shiʿites from other Muslim sects and schools.

Ahl al-Ḥadīth "the people of *ḥadīth*." A group that emerged in third/ninth-century Baghdad who emphasized the importance of textual sources, namely, the written traditions (*ḥadīth*) from and about the Prophet Muḥammad, to the proper practicing of Islam. This movement was associated with Aḥmad b. Ḥanbal, and eschewed the more theologically minded discussions of their day for a more popular piety. The traditionalism of the Ahl al-Ḥadīth became an important aspect of later Sunnism.

ahl al-sunna wa'l-jamā'a "people of the *sunna* and the community." *See* **Sunni**.

ahl al-tawḥīd wa'l-'adl "people of God's oneness and justice." *See* **Mu'tazila**.

Aḥmad b. Ḥanbal (d. 241/855) eponym of the Ḥanbalī *madhhab*, legal scholar from Baghdad, and *ḥadīth* collector. Famously refused to acknowledge the createdness of the Qur'an during the *miḥna*, for which he was said to have been beaten and imprisoned. Ibn Ḥanbal lent his reputation to the growing Ahl al-Ḥadīth movement in Baghdad. His traditionalist focus in law and theology had an important influence on later Sunnism.

'Alawī Shi'ism *See* **Nuṣayrī ('Alawī) Shi'ism**.

Alevi Shi'ism a mystically oriented form of Shi'ism found in the mountainous regions of Anatolia (modern-day Turkey) that draws heavily from the teachings of the sixth/twelfth-century mystic Haji Bektāsh Veli. Not to be confused with 'Alawī (Nuṣayrī) Shi'ism.

'Alī b. Abī Ṭālib (d. 40/661) the cousin of the Prophet, fourth "rightly guided caliph," and first Shi'ite imam. An early (many consider him the first male) convert to Islam, 'Alī's closeness and familial relation to the Prophet Muḥammad, his marriage to the Prophet's daughter Fāṭima, and his intellectual and physical prowess made several of the earliest Muslims consider him the rightful successor to the Prophet. 'Alī's supporters (literally, his *shi'a*) formed the nucleus of the earliest Shi'ites.

'Alīdism reverence and support for the family of the Prophet that cuts across sectarian lines. Contrasted with Shi'ism (which elevates allegiance and devotion to the family of the Prophet as the most important aspect of submission to God), the term 'Alīdism alludes to the respect and love that Muslims have for the Prophet and his descendants.

'ālim/'ulamā' religious scholar(s). The *'ulamā'* emerged during the early period of Muslim history and constitute a vital aspect of the Islamic social fabric. Despite several attempts by the early caliphs to monopolize authority in religious matters, after the failure of the *miḥna* the *ʿulamāʾ* became the caretakers of the religious sciences (law, theology, qurʾanic commentary, etc.) and thus the primary specialists on religious questions.

amīr a title that indicates authority, especially as a military commander, leader, governor, or prince. The caliph ʿUmar b. al-Khaṭṭāb adopted the title *amīr al-muʾminīn* (Commander of the Faithful), which became caliphal titular thereafter.

ʿAmr b. ʿUbayd (144/761) early Muʿtazilite leader in Basra, and possibly one of the cofounders of the movement along with Wāṣil b. ʿAṭāʾ. A student of al-Ḥasan al-Baṣrī, he led the nascent movement into the ʿAbbāsid era, generally adopting a quietist stance toward the ruling caliphs.

ʿaql mind, but especially referring to the ability to reason. The Muʿtazilites emphasized humankind's ability to reason, considering it an aspect of God's mercy that allowed human beings to discern good from evil, and to choose between them.

al-Ashʿarī, Abū al-Ḥasan (d. between 324–33/936–45) eponymous founder of the Ashʿarī school of theology, which became an important aspect of later Sunni theology. Al-Ashʿarī began his career as a Muʿtazilite, but broke with them, criticizing many aspects of Muʿtazilite theology with their own methods of reasoning. He also penned one of the most widely consulted works of Muslim heresiography, the *Maqālāt al-Islāmiyyīn* (*The Positions of Those Who Profess Islam*).

ʿĀshūrāʾ the commemoration of the martyrdom of al-Ḥusayn. The word means the "tenth day" and it is so called because it is held on the tenth day of the lunar month of Muḥarram. Commemorations of the martyrdom of al-Ḥusayn constitute one of the oldest and most important ritual events among the Shiʿa, especially among Ithnā-ʿAsharī (Twelver) and ʿAlawī/Nuṣayrī Shiʿites.

Azraqite Khārijites (Azāriqa) a militant Khārijite group named after their first leader, Nāfiʿ b. al-Azraq. They became infamous during the second civil war (*fitna*) for their uncompromising stances regarding nonmembers, whom they considered unbelievers (*kuffār*) akin to polytheists (*mushrikūn*), who should be fought without exception. This staunch militarism resulted in their virtual annihilation at the hands of the Umayyads near the end of the second *fitna*, and in their being reviled by many of their fellow Khārijites.

bāb "gateway." ʿAlawī/Nuṣayrī Shiʿism speaks of God appearing on earth several times, always accompanied by two other figures, one of whom is the *bāb*. The *bāb* controls access to God and the secret knowledge that He dispenses to His elect. During the last incarnation of God on earth, Nuṣayrīs consider the *bāb* to have been the early Companion Salmān al-Fārisī.

al-Bāqir, Muḥammad b. ʿAlī (d. 114/733) an early Shiʿite leader, considered by quietist Shiʿites such as the Ithnā-ʿAsharīs and Ismāʿīlīs to have been the fifth imam. "Al-Bāqir" is his nickname, meaning "the discerner [of knowledge]," because he was an important religious scholar. Under al-Bāqir and his son, Jaʿfar al-Ṣādiq, the quietist Shiʿites consolidated themselves into a more discernable movement.

barāʾa "dissociation." An early Muslim doctrine, taken up by the Ibāḍiyya and elaborated extensively, that identifies and set rules concerning those outside of the group, from whom one is supposed to "dissociate" in some fashion. Among the Ibāḍiyya, such dissociation can take the form of excommunication from the group, but when practiced in relation to non-Ibāḍīs dissociation does not preclude friendship, but rather indicates an inner knowledge that the person from whom one dissociates is not among the elect. Often paired with its opposite, *walāya* (association), the principles of *walāya* and *barāʾa* establish the boundaries of group identity among the Ibāḍiyya.

Battle of Nahrawān (38/658) battle of the first Muslim civil war (*fitna*) between the armies of ʿAlī b. Abī Ṭālib and the first Khārijites (the Muḥakkima). Although the battle ended in the near total annihilation of the Khārijites, an aggrieved relative of one of the slain, ʿAbd al-Raḥmān b. Muljam, later sought revenge and murdered ʿAlī in the mosque at Kufa.

Battle of Ṣiffīn (37/657) battle during the first Muslim civil war (*fitna*) between the armies of ʿAlī b. Abī Ṭālib and Muʿāwiya b. Abī Sufyān that took place on the plain of Ṣiffīn (outside of present-day Raqqa, Syria). When it became clear ʿAlī was winning, Muʿāwiya's forces asked for arbitration according to the Qurʾan. ʿAlī accepted the offer for arbitration, which split his army. Those who left became known as the Khārijites.

bi lā kayfa "without asking how." A slogan associated with the traditionalist Ahl al-Ḥadīth movement, and later taken up by those who would play an important role in the development of Sunnism. These groups emphasized the limitations of human understanding, and thus apparent theological complications were not to be overthought, with Muslims accepting what the sources (via the interpretation of the scholars) taught without "asking how" such apparent inconsistencies (such as the question of whether God could have actual hands, as is implied in some qur'anic verses) should concern them.

Bishr al-Mārisī (218–19/833–34) an early Murji'ite theologian and Ḥanafite jurist from Baghdad. He was an advisor to the 'Abbāsid caliph al-Ma'mūn, and said to have been a "Jahmite" (a follower of Jahm b. Ṣafwān), though this appellation may not be accurate.

Bohras term (meaning "merchants/traders") referring to the adherents of the Musta'lī-Ṭayyibī branch of the Ismā'īlīs who settled in India. There are three main subsects of the Bohras: the Dāwūdī, Sulaymanī, and Alevi Bohras.

Buyruks a collection of scriptures that provide guidance to the Alevi Shi'ites of Anatolia. The Buyruks include qur'anic verses, the sayings of 'Alī b. Abī Ṭālib and the imams, as well as sayings, poems, and songs written by Yunus Emre, Pīr Sulṭān Abdal, and even the Safavid ruler Ismā'īl I.

caliph Anglicized form of *khalīfa* ("successor") and referring to the political successor to the Prophet Muḥammad. The first four caliphs were selected for their office, after which the caliphate became hereditary. The term was mostly employed by non-Shi'ites. While the caliphate was imbued with religious symbolism, the caliph fulfilled only limited religious functions (symbolically leading the *ḥajj* and expanding the realm into non-Muslim areas).

***cem* (also *jem*)** Alevi Shi'ite communal worship, usually held on Thursdays, in an edifice known as the Cemevi. A *dede* leads the service, and is assisted by twelve other persons (representing the twelve imams). A *cem* consists of music, singing, dancing, and discussion. The prototype of this service is Muḥammad's ascension into heaven (*mi'rāj*), whereby the Prophet witnessed a vision of heaven, forty saints, and their leader, 'Alī.

da'wa missionizing (literally, "calling" to Islam). Several Muslim sects and schools, such as the Ibāḍiyya and Fāṭimid (Ismā'īlī) Shi'ites, increased their numbers and spread their teachings through *da'wa*.

dede a religious leader (literally, "uncle") among the Alevi Shi'ites.

dhāt God's essence. A theological question among medieval Muslims asked whether God's essence (*dhāt*) was separate from His attributes (*ṣifāt*), or whether some (or all) of His attributes partook of His essence.

Thus, if the attribute of speech partook of God's essence, then the Qur'an, as God's speech, could be said to be uncreated in some of the same ways that God was uncreated; if God's speech was separate and distinct from His essence then the Qur'an must be considered created in time and space like other created things.

Fāṭimids (r. 297–567/909–1171) Ismā'īlī Shi'ite dynasty, founded by 'Abdullāh (var. 'Ubaydallāh) b. al-Ḥusayn, who was called al-Mahdī. The Fāṭimids first established their dynasty in North Africa, and later conquered and made Cairo their capital. At their height in the fourth/eleventh century, they rivaled the 'Abbāsid caliphs in influence and authority in Islamdom, and operated an extensive *da'wa* network that spread their form of Ismā'īlism.

fiqh Islamic law (literally "understanding"). The endeavor to understand what God's revelations imply for human beings and how they should act.

firqa/firaq sect or school of thought among Muslims (literally, "division"). Muslim heresiographers often labored to make the number of Muslim *firaq* seventy-three, in accordance with a Prophetic saying to the effect that the Muslim community would split into seventy-three *firaq*, only one of which would be the saved *firqa*.

fitna/fitan civil war or civil unrest (literally, "test"). The early period of Muslim history was wracked by several *fitan*. The first *fitna* was initiated by the assassination of the caliph 'Uthmān, and the second by the ascension of Yazīd b. Mu'āwiya to the caliphate. These *fitan* did much to solidify developing rifts in the early Muslim community into recognizable sectarian groups.

futuwwa medieval military confraternities in Islamdom. These fraternities moved from identifying as Sunni to Shi'i, and offer a good example of sectarian ambiguity among Muslim institutions.

Ghadīr Khumm A well located in present-day Saudi Arabia, and referring to an event important to the Shi'a that happened there. On the final pilgrimage before the Prophet's death, the community stopped at Ghadīr Khumm, where the Prophet was reported to have said of his cousin 'Alī b. Abī Ṭālib, "By God, of whomsoever I have been master, 'Alī is his master." Several in the community took this to mean that 'Alī was to be the Prophet's rightful successor after his death.

ghayba occultation. According to the Ithnā-'Asharī (Twelver) Shi'ites, the twelfth imam experienced two occultations: first, he remained hidden from his followers during his life. This period, 260–329/874–941, is known as the "lesser" occultation (*al-ghayba al-ṣughrā*). After 329/941, they hold that he was hidden from view until his return at the end of time, as the Mahdī. This period – still ongoing according to the Ithnā-ʿAsharīs – is known as the "greater" occultation (*al-ghayba al-kubrā*).

Ghaylān al-Dimashqī (ca. 125/743) an Umayyad bureaucrat associated with the Qadariyya (he is also identified in heresiographical sources as a Murjiʾite) who reportedly gained the confidence of the Umayyad caliph ʿUmar b. ʿAbd al-ʿAzīz for a time. Executed in Damascus, purportedly for his Qadarite beliefs.

al-Ghazālī, Abū Ḥāmid (d. 505/1111) jurist, theologian, and reformer; he has been called "the greatest Muslim after Muḥammad." Among his many achievements, al-Ghazālī ultimately made the mystical path, known as Sufism (*al-taṣawwuf*), more acceptable among Sunnis, while at the same time insisting on adherence to the legal aspects of Sunnism among the practitioners of Sufism.

ghulāt a term (and a pejorative term) for Shiʿa who, in the opinion of their enemies, went "to extremes" (that is, practiced *ghluww*) in their devotion to ʿAlī b. Abī Ṭālib and the *ahl al-bayt*. Recent research has shown that many of the so-called *ghulāt* were, in fact, integrated into the early Shiʿite community of Kufa.

ḥadīth/aḥādīth report(s), later written down and collected into books, about what the Prophet Muḥammad (or the early Companions of the Prophet) said, did, or silently confirmed. The *aḥādīth* became an important source, second to the Qurʾan, for religious guidance, especially among Sunnis. Shiʿites include reports from and about the imams in their *ḥadīth* collections.

Haji Bektāsh Veli (Arabic: Ḥājj Baktāsh Walī) (d. 669/1271) Persian mystical saint, born in Nīshāpūr, and a descendant of the seventh imam, Mūsā al-Kāẓim, who migrated to Anatolia in the wake of the Mongol invasions. His Shiʿite-infused mystical teachings became the basis for several groups that emanated out of Anatolia and the Syrian highlands, such as the Alevis and the Safavids. His teachings also influenced the (later staunchly Sunni) mystical group known as the Bektāshīs.

ḥaqq/ḥaqāʾiq literally "truth," but often referring to veiled or hidden truths, especially among certain groups of Shiʿites such as the Ismāʿīlīs or Nuṣayrī ʿAlawīs. The spiritual elites (such as the imams and those they teach) are said to be in possession of truths that are esoteric and inaccessible to regular Muslims except by initiation and instruction from the elites.

al-Ḥārith b. Surayj (d. 128/746) leader, along with Jahm b. Ṣafwān, of a "Murjiʿite" rebellion in the late Umayyad period. They united the dissatisfaction of the local Arab populace in Central Asia with those of the *mawālī*, and channeled their anger through appeals to justice, and a demand to return to the Qurʾan and *sunna*. By 119/737 the Umayyad armies had worn down the rebellion to the point where Ibn Surayj entered into an alliance with a non-Muslim Turkish prince. Jahm was captured and executed in 128/746, and although pardoned in 127/745, al-Ḥārith b. Surayj was killed and the rebellion finally scattered later in the same year.

al-Ḥasan b. ʿAlī (d. 50/670) eldest son of ʿAlī b. Abī Ṭālib and the Prophet Muḥammad's daughter Fāṭima, and considered the second imam by many Shiʿites. He chose to avoid confrontation with his father's enemy, Muʿāwiya b. Abī Sufyān, after ʿAlī's murder, conceding the caliphate to Muʿāwiya. Many believe that he was poisoned by Muʿāwiya so that the latter's son, Yazīd, could ascend to the caliphate.

al-Ḥasan al-Baṣrī (d. 110/728) Basran ascetic and popular preacher. He was said to have caught the attention of the Umayyad caliph ʿAbd al-Malik, for preaching something akin to human free will (*qadar*), and thereby suggesting that human beings were to be held accountable for their actions. A letter attributed to him, allegedly in response to the caliph's request for clarification, emphasizes that evil acts come from human beings, who have a modicum of free will. Later Muʿtazilites considered al-Ḥasan al-Baṣrī a Qadarite, though some contemporary scholars have been skeptical about the extent of his purported Qadarism, as well as the authenticity of his letter.

al-Ḥasan b. Ṣabbāḥ (Persian: Ḥasan-i-Ṣabbāḥ) (d. 518/1124) Nizārī Ismāʿīlī leader in Mesopotamia; known as the "old man in the mountain." Seizing control of a mountainous castle at Alamut (in the Alborz mountain range, in present-day Iran), Ibn Ṣabbāḥ built up the Nizārī Ismāʿīlī *daʿwa* in the region, eventually controlling a series of mountain forts stretching across modern-day Syria, Iraq, and Iran. Said to have used assassination as a tactic, but the reports of the so-called *ḥashāshīn* ("assassins") were spread by those hostile to the Nizārīs and therefore likely exaggerated.

Hāshimiyya Shiʿites Shiʿite group, later identified among the *ghulāt*, that undertook the ʿAbbāsid revolution. This group held that a descendant of Ibn al-Ḥanafiyya (Abū Hāshim ʿAbdullāh b. Muḥammad b. al-Ḥanafiyya) had transferred the imamate to the clan of ʿAbbās (their cousins) via the father (Muḥammad b. ʿAlī) of the first two ʿAbbāsid caliphs (i.e. al-Ṣaffāḥ and al-Manṣūr). Once installed in power, however, the ʿAbbāsids realized that their association with a fringe Shiʿa movement would not result in the kind of consensus that they needed to rule the empire, and so they began promoting themselves as the guardians of communal unity (*jamāʿa*).

heresiography (also heresiology) a polemical genre of writing that provides information about groups considered deviant (among Christians, "heretical") by those writing the work. The genre originated largely among late antique Christians, but it was adopted by Muslims for their own uses. Heresiography often offered a fixed number of groups for discussion or refutation: Muslim writers, for example, usually wrote about seventy-three groups after the Prophetic *ḥadīth* that predicted that the Muslim community would divide into that number of groups, only one of which would be saved.

ḥujja literally, "proof," but sometimes an epithet for the Shiʿite imams (or even their prominent disciples and spokespersons), insofar as the imams are "proof" of God's mercy and grace (*luṭf*) toward humankind. That is, the imams are the proof that God would not leave humankind without access to divine guidance, even after the death of the prophets.

al-Ḥusayn b. ʿAlī (d. 61/680) youngest son of ʿAlī b. Abī Ṭālib and the Prophet Muḥammad's daughter Fāṭima. Considered the third imam by many Shiʿites, and the "prince of martyrs" for his martyrdom at the hands of an Umayyad army on the plain of Karbala.

al-Ḥusayn al-Najjār (d. 218–21/833–36) Murjiʾite and student of Bishr al-Mārisī. Al-Najjār held what later became the Sunni stance on the issue of faith, believing that it consisted of belief and the profession of belief, but appending "acts of obedience" to these.

Ibāḍiyya (Ibāḍites) group sometimes identified with the Khārijites (the Ibāḍiyya deny this affiliation, tracing themselves to the earlier *shurāt*). They survive to the present in the Arabian Peninsula and North Africa, and can be distinguished in how they regard non-Ibāḍīs as less-than-full Muslims, and also in their unique imamate theory.

Ibn al-Ḥanafiyya, Muḥammad (d. 81/700) third son of ʿAlī b. Abī Ṭālib through a Ḥanafī concubine (thus his nickname, "the son of the Ḥanafī woman"). Several early Shiʿite groups (many later identified as *ghulāt*) considered Ibn al-Ḥanafiyya and his progeny the imams after ʿAlī.

Ibn Karrām, Abū ʿAbdullāh Muḥammad (d. 255/868) eponym of the Karrāmiyya. Ibn Karrām was a noted ascetic and preacher, born in Sijistān but establishing the Karrāmiyya in the Central Asian city of Nīshāpūr. He was jailed for a time, after which he traveled to Jerusalem, where he is buried.

Ibn Muljam, ʿAbd al-Raḥmān (d. 40/661) Khārijite, and killer of ʿAlī b. Abī Ṭālib. Ibn Muljam was reportedly seeking revenge for relatives slain at the Battle of Nahrawān.

Ibn Sabāʾ, ʿAbdullāh (d. first/seventh century) mysterious early Shiʿite figure, and supposed founder of the Sabāʾiyya Shiʿites. Often identified as the first of the *ghulāt* Shiʿites by his alleged denial of ʿAlī's death, and his waiting for his return (*rajʿa*). Historical information about Ibn Sabāʾ is extremely tenuous, and regarded with suspicion by modern scholars.

Ibn Taymiyya, Tāqī al-Dīn Aḥmad b. ʿAbd al-Ḥalīm (d. 728/1328) Ḥanbalī jurist and theologian from the Levant. Ibn Taymiyya advocated a staunch, highly scripturalist Sunnism, writing critically about several non-Sunni (especially Shiʿa) and non-scripturalist groups (such as the Sufis). Ibn Taymiyya and his writings have become important to modern-day Salafī movements (including some violent Salafī groups), but some of his legal opinions on sectarian groups (for example, the ʿAlawīs/Nuṣayrīs) have been shown to have been poorly informed.

Ibn al-Zubayr, ʿAbdullāh (d. 73/692) Umayyad-era rival to the Umayyads; sometimes called the "anti-caliph." Ibn al-Zubayr refused to pledge allegiance to Yazīd b. Muʿāwiya after the murder of the Prophet's family at Karbala, touching off what would be the second Muslim *fitna* (civil war). Seizing control of the Arabian Peninsula and parts of Iraq, Ibn al-Zubayr declared himself caliph, and ruled as such until the Umayyads reestablished their control over Islamdom. He died fighting the Umayyad army outside of Makka.

ijmāʿ the juridical concept of "consensus," meaning consensus of the religious scholars on a legal question. An example of *ijmāʿ* would be consensus on the question of whether or not Muslims should have a political leader: even though there are a variety of opinions on the person and nature of leadership, nearly all Muslims agreed that the *umma* should have a leader after the death of the Prophet.

ijtihād Islamic legal term referring to "independent reasoning" on a question.

ʿilm "knowledge," and especially referring to knowledge about religion. Among (for the most part, quietist) Shiʿa, the imams are thought to have access to an esoteric *ʿilm*; one that is available only to them as an aspect of their being the imam. This knowledge allows them to properly guide humankind.

imām term referring to different types of leader, used especially for leaders among the Shiʿa. The term can be generic for leader; but it can also refer to the person who leads the prayers. It can also be used to designate a revered scholar (for example, "Imām al-Shāfiʿī"). Among Shiʿa, *imām* became the preferred term for the persons from the *ahl al-bayt* that the various Shiʿa held to be God's divinely appointed rulers for humankind.

Imāmī Shiʿism quietist Shiʿite group organized, mainly in Kufa, around the figures of al-Bāqir and al-Ṣādiq. The Imāmī Shiʿites elucidated an apolitical theory of the imamate that allowed them to evade the scrutiny that most revolutionary Shiʿite groups experienced, while at the same time regarding the imam as the divinely appointed religious leader for humankind. The two most prevalent Shiʿite groups surviving to the present day developed out of the Imāmī Shiʿites.

īmān "faith." Questions regarding the nature of faith – such as what it is, who has it, what it entails, and whether or not it increases or decreases – remained one of the most contentious issues debated by Muslim sects and schools in the medieval periods.

al-insān al-kāmil "the perfected person." A term, taken in large part from the mystical tradition, referring to a person, such as a Sufi master, who has achieved the highest level of spiritual awareness and achievement. Several figures, such as the founder of the Safavid dynasty, Shāh Ismāʿīl, claimed to be perfected persons, and the use of such terminology points to the importance of the mystical paths to the later narratives of Muslim sects and schools.

irjāʾ the doctrine of "postponing" judgment on the sinner distinctive of the Murjiʾites (and the root of the word "Murjiʾa"). Unlike the Khārijites, who were willing to consider sinners less-than-full Muslims, Murjiʾites (and later the Sunnis) refused to pass judgment, postponing this judgment until the Day of Judgment and treating sinners as full Muslims. In the late Umayyad and early ʿAbbāsid periods, more mature articulations of the doctrine of *irjāʾ* detailed how faith was not connected to a person's actions, a position that appealed to non-Arab converts to Islam.

ism "name." ʿAlawī/Nuṣayrī Shiʿism speaks of God appearing on earth several times, always accompanied by two other figures, one of whom is the *ism*. The *ism* is the figure who speaks for God to the masses. As ʿAlawīs/Nuṣayrīs consider the last incarnation of God on earth to have been in the person of ʿAlī b. Abī Ṭālib, they hold the Prophet Muḥammad to have been His *ism*.

Ismāʿīlī Shiʿism Shiʿite group that emerged from the controversy surrounding the succession to the sixth Imāmī imam, Jaʿfar al-Ṣādiq. The Ismāʿīlīs followed a line of imams through al-Ṣādiq's son Ismāʿīl, who had been designated the imam but had predeceased his father: the Ismāʿīlīs looked therefore to Ismāʿīl's son, Muḥammad b. Ismāʿīl, as the imam. Ismāʿīlī Shiʿites went on to found one of the largest medieval empires in Islamdom, the Fāṭimids. The Nizārī subgroup, which is now the most populous of the surviving Ismāʿīlī splinter groups, claims to follow a continuous line of imams to the present day: the current imam, Shāh Karīm al-Ḥusaynī, is also known by his title, the Aga Khan.

Ithnā-ʿAsharī ("Twelver") Shiʿism Shiʿite group that emerged from the controversy surrounding the succession to the sixth Imāmī imam, Jaʿfar al-Ṣādiq. The Ithnā-ʿAsharī Shiʿites followed one of al-Ṣādiq's younger sons, Mūsā al-Kāẓim, as the imam after the death of al-Ṣādiq's eldest son, Ismāʿīl, during al-Ṣādiq's lifetime. They looked to a line of imams through al-Kāẓim's progeny, up to the twelfth imam, who they hold went into hiding during his lifetime, and then in 329/941 God hid him from view until his return at the end of time as the Mahdī. Twelver Shiʿites thus believe the twelfth imam to be alive, and await his return. After the Safavids converted the population of Iran and parts of Iraq to Ithnā-ʿAsharī Shiʿism, it became the most populous form of Shiʿism present today.

Jābir b. Zayd (d. first half of the second/eighth century) early Muslim jurist and scholar who settled in Basra, considered by the Ibāḍiyya to be their founder. Some contemporary scholars question whether something recognizable as Ibāḍism could yet have existed during Ibn Zayd's era, viewing him rather as an important early quietist Khārijite figure and predecessor to the Ibāḍīyya proper.

Jaʿfar b. Muḥammad al-Ṣādiq (d. 148/765) an early Shiʿite leader, considered by quietist Shiʿites such as the Ithnā-ʿAsharīs and Ismāʿīlīs to have been the sixth imam. "Al-Ṣādiq" is his nickname, meaning "the truthful one." Under al-Ṣādiq and his father and fifth imam, Muḥammad al-Bāqir, the quietist Shiʿites consolidated themselves into a more discernable movement: to Ja'far al-Ṣādiq and his disciples, for example, is attributed the Imāmī Shi'ite theory of the imamate.

Jahm b. Ṣafwān (d. 128/746) leader, along with al-Ḥārith b. Surayj, of a "Murji'ite" rebellion in the late Umayyad period. To him is attributed a group, known as the Jahmiyya, which is sometimes classed as Mu'tazilite and sometimes as Murji'ite. The doctrines of Jahm and the supposed Jahmiyya are often jumbled and confused in the sources, though it is likely that he was among the first Muslims to speak of the principle of reason (*'aql*) as well as the methodology of using reason to derive opinions from propositions. Jahm was captured by Umayyad forces and executed in 128/746.

jamā'a the principle of "[adhering to/keeping together the Muslim] community." A late Umayyad concept, taken up by the 'Abbāsid caliphs and eventually incorporated into Sunnism. Caliphal appeals to *jamā'a* attempted to bolster their authority by stressing that the caliphs preserved and protected the *umma*. The argument that the Sunnis were adhering to the majoritarian position (that is, the position presumed to be taken by the "community") functioned as a powerful means to legitimate Sunni positions on doctrine, ritual, and law.

kāfir/kuffār a qur'anic term referring to unbeliever(s); those guilty of *kufr* ("ungratefulness" and thus, ingrate(s)). Medieval Muslim sects and schools debated fiercely the question of who was and who was not a believer, as well as the connection of sin to unbelief. The Khārijites and Ibāḍiyya tended to treat sinners and nonmembers are somehow less-than-full Muslims, often employing the term *kāfir/kuffār* to describe them.

***kalām* (also *'ilm al-kalām*)** theology (literally "discourse"). While Muslims had from the beginning contemplated the nature of God and the consequences of God's nature for human beings, Islamic theology matured in the 'Abbāsid period with the relative stability afforded by the 'Abbāsid compromise. Likewise, Muslims sects and schools increasingly incorporated the language of theology in articulating and defending their positions.

Karbala area in present-day Iraq (100 km/62 mi. south of Baghdad) where, in 61/680 al-Ḥusayn b. 'Alī and around a hundred of his supporters and family members were surrounded by the Umayyad army. After negotiations broke down, al-Ḥusayn and his son 'Alī al-Aṣghar were killed (to the Shi'a and many others, martyred), along with seventy or seventy-two other members of his entourage. The female members of his household were taken in captivity back to the Umayyad caliph in Damascus. The events at Karbala became a distinguishing moment in Shiʿa history and identity: The tragedy and martyrdom of al-Ḥusayn became a rallying cry for several Shiʿite-inspired rebellions that followed, and the place of Karbala became a pilgrimage site. The events at Karbala are remembered annually up to the present by Ithnā-ʿAsharī and other Shiʿa.

Karrāmiyya medieval Muslim group founded by Abū ʿAbdullāh b. Karrām in the Central Asian city of Nīshāpūr. The Karrāmiyya practiced a vigorous asceticism, maintaining retreats (*khānaqā/khanāʾiq*) and eschewing money. Although they share many of the traits that would have made them candidates for the Sunni consensus, they were not, in the end, considered Sunnis, and this fact points toward the often abstruse ways that Muslim scholars later classified and organized their knowledge about the Muslim sects and schools.

***kasb* (also *iktisāb*)** the doctrine of "acquisition." Doctrine associated with Muslim theologians who stressed God's power to predestine and know all things, but who needed to make some provision for how human beings can be held responsible for their actions. Some theologians, such as al-Ashʿarī, posited that human beings "acquire" (*iktasaba*) their actions, even though it is God who creates and causes human beings to execute them.

Kaysāniyya Shiʿites early Shiʿite group, later classed among the *ghulāt*, whose leader, al-Mukhtār b. Abī ʿUbaydallāh al-Thaqafī, led a failed revolt in Kufa in the name of ʿAlī's son Muḥammad b. al-Ḥanafiyya. Some of the reported doctrines of the Kaysāniyya and its offshoots, such as the belief that Ibn al-Ḥanafiyya had not died but was in concealment (*ghayba*) in a mountain near Madina and would return (*rajʿa*) as the Mahdī, anticipate later doctrines among other Shiʿite groups (notably the Ithnā-ʿAshariyya).

Khawārij (Khārijites) the epithet (meaning "those who leave/ secessionists") given to groups of Muslim sectarians who held pious action to be the main criterion for accepting a person as a true Muslim, and who rejected the exclusive claims of the Quraysh (as well as the ʿAlīds) to the caliphate. The term enjoyed only limited use among the groups themselves as the majority of early adherents preferred the term *shurāt* (sing. *shārī*). The first Khārijites (known as the Muḥakkima) seceded from ʿAlī b. Abī Ṭālib's army in 37/657 after he agreed to subject his dispute with Muʿāwiya b. Abī Sufyān at the Battle of Ṣiffīn during the first *fitna* (civil war) to arbitration. Most groups who were considered "Khārijite" disappeared in the Umayyad and then early ʿAbbāsid eras: the only remaining subgroup to survive into the present time is the Ibāḍiyya, and they reject being associated with the Khārijites (though they embrace the Muḥakkima and early *shurāt*).

kufr unbelief (literally, "ungratefulness" or "covering up"). Qurʾanic term referring to unbelief, but connoting the idea of ungratefulness for the fullness of God's blessings; or also the idea of "covering" oneself from the truth. Those guilty of *kufr* are not considered Muslims, and can be legally fought. What constitutes *kufr* has been debated at great length among Muslims, with the various Muslim sects and schools taking a variety of positions on the issue.

lā ḥukma illā li-Llāh "no judgment but God's." The slogan associated with the Khārijites (and used also by the Ibāḍiyya). It reportedly originated after ʿAlī b. Abī Ṭālib announced the arbitration agreement (*taḥkīm*/*ḥukm al-ḥukūma*) with his enemy, Muʿāwiya b. Abī Sufyān, to which certain early Khārijites responded that there could be no human arbitration/judgment in a matter that they considered already settled by God (in favor of fighting). It was allegedly from the *lā ḥukm* slogan that the name of the first Khārijites, the Muḥakkima ("those who say the *lā ḥukm* slogan") came. The slogan also appears on coinage associated with various Khārijite groups.

luṭf the doctrine of God's "grace." Among certain (mainly quietist) Shiʿite groups, God shows His grace to humankind by providing access to divine guidance through the imams. The imams, therefore, are the manifestation of God's grace to humankind.

Maʿbad b. ʿAbdullāh al-Juhanī (d. 80/699) the alleged "founder" of the Qadariyya movement. He was a Basran *ḥadīth* scholar (*muḥaddith*) and a respected member of the Umayyad elite. He was executed, either by the caliph ʿAbd al-Malik or his deputy, al-Ḥajjāj b. Yūsuf. While many sources claim that it was his Qadarī beliefs that led to his execution, a report suggests that he participated in the failed revolt of Ibn al-Ashʿath, and may have been killed for his participation in it.

madhhab*/*madhāhib legal school(s); sectarian group. A term that refers primarily to a legal school or rite, but can secondarily refer to a sect or school insofar as Muslim sects and schools often offered their own particular interpretations of Islamic law and practice. Among Sunnis there are four recognized legal schools: the Mālikīs, Ḥanafīs, Shāfiʿīs, and Ḥanbalīs. Twelver Shiʿites claim a legal school, known as the Jaʿfarī school after Ja'far al-Ṣādiq. The Ibāḍiyya claim that they possess the oldest legal school, dating back to their purported founder, Jābir b. Zayd.

madrasa/madāris school(s), often with a religious curriculum. The *madrasa* system was established in the Muslim East by the Seljuqs in the sixth/twelfth century, and did much to make Sunnism the dominant sectarian affiliation among Muslims.

Mahdī the "guided one"; messianic figure who is said to return at the end of time to right wrongs and establish Islam. Sunnis and Shi'ites have differing interpretations of who the Mahdī is and how he functions: for Ithnā-'Asharī Shi'ites, the Mahdī is the twelfth imam, Muḥammad b. al-Ḥasan al-'Askarī, whom God caused to go into hiding during his "greater occultation" (*al-ghayba al-kubrā*) in 329/941 until he returns at the end of time. For the Fāṭimids, Mahdī became a title that the imams adopted. For Sunnis the Mahdī is a person yet unknown, but who also returns at the end of time. Many persons have claimed to be the Mahdī in Muslim history.

majlis/majālis "session(s) of learning." The Fāṭimid imams established the practice of conducting sessions of learning, whereby they instructed their closet disciples and missionaries (*dā'ī*) with the esoteric knowledge that they were believed to possess. Some of the *majālis* have been collected and preserved.

Mālik b. Anas (d. 179/795) eponym of the Mālikī legal school, *ḥadīth* collector, and legal scholar.

ma'nā "[inner] meaning." 'Alawī/Nuṣayrī Shi'ism speaks of God appearing on earth several times. He is said to appear as the inner truth of Himself made flesh, and as such He is known as the *ma'nā*. The *ma'nā* was accompanied by two others: one who spoke for Him, called His "*ism*" (literally, "name" but indicating a kind of spokesperson); as well as one who controlled a kind of access to Him (known as His "gate" – *bāb*).

al-manzila bayn al-manzilatayn the middle position (literally, "the position between the two positions"). An idea associated with the Mu'tazilites, and one of Abū al-Hudhayl's "five principles," whereby the sinner was considered neither an unbeliever (the Khārijite position) nor a full believer (the Murji'ite position), but a sinner (*fāsiq*) occupying a middle position between unbelief and belief. This doctrine allowed the Mu'tazilites to claim that they had adopted the reasonable median position between two extremes.

ma'ṣūm "protected from error." Quietist Shi'ite theology claimed that God protected the imams from serious errors (sometimes translated as "infallible," but this is misleading as the imams are thought to be protected only from major errors, not that they can commit no error whatsoever).

al-Māturīdī, Abū Manṣūr Muḥammad (d. 333/944) Muslim theologian, Ḥanafī jurist, and qur'anic interpreter from Samarkand. Al-Māturīdī's theology, slightly less predestinarian than al-Ash'arī's, also became accepted as legitimate among Sunnis, especially in the Muslim East (*mashriq*). His recognition among Sunnis illustrates well the broad inclusivism that distinguishes Sunnism from other Muslim sects and schools.

mawlā/mawālī "client(s)." A term with many meanings, but in the context of early Islamdom used to describe non-Arab converts to Islam. Especially in the Umayyad period, the *mawālī* were not always treated as equal to their Arab Muslim brethren, a fact that contributed to their dissatisfaction and willingness to join anti-Umayyad causes (as many of the Umayyad-era Muslim sects and schools tended to be).

miḥna "test" or "examination." In the context of the 'Abbāsid era, the *miḥna* (sometimes poorly translated as "inquisition") was an eighteen-year caliphal campaign beginning in 218/833 under the caliph al-Ma'mūn and ending under al-Mutawakkil aimed at forcing prominent scholars and notables to publicly recognize the doctrine of the createdness of the Qur'an or face serious punishment. It seems to have been an attempt by the 'Abbāsid caliphs to claim authority in religious matters over the *'ulamā'*. In the context of the Azraqite Khārijites, the *miḥna* was a test that they administered to prospective members.

Mongols Central Asian conglomeration of Turkic tribal groups, united under Ghengis Khan and his sons in the sixth/twelfth century, who conquered most of Asia, creating the largest continuous land empire in human history. Using mounted archers to devastating effect, the Mongol armies present a prime example of the nature of military power in the premodern period by being highly mobile and politically decentralized (by modern standards).

Mu'āwiya b. Abī Sufyān (d. 218/680) governor of Syria under the caliph 'Uthmān (his cousin), and then first Umayyad caliph. Mu'āwiya was the son of the Prophet's bitter opponent (Abū Sufyān), but became a Muslim along with his father. During the first civil war (*fitna*), he was an opponent of 'Alī, accusing 'Alī of not having punished the killers of 'Uthmān sufficiently. Their armies confronted each other at the Battle of Ṣiffīn, where Mu'āwiya escaped defeat by suing for arbitration. After

ʿAlī was murdered, Muʿāwiya assumed the caliphate, thus becoming the first of the Umayyad caliphs and the first in the dynastic rule of Islamdom.

Muḥammad b. al-Ḥasan al-ʿAskarī (lesser occultation 260/874–329/941; greater occultation 329/941–present) member of the *ahl al-bayt* and twelfth imam to the Ithnā-ʿAsharī Shiʿites, who consider him to be in occultation (*ghayba*) at the present, hidden from view as the imam until such time as God causes him to return as the Mahdī.

Muḥammad b. Ismāʿīl (d. 197/813) Jaʿfar al-Ṣādiq's grandson through Ismāʿīl b. Jaʿfar, and considered the seventh imam by the majority of Ismāʿīlīs. He was said to have gone into hiding in southwest Persia – initiating what later Fāṭimid Ismāʿīlīs would call a period of "concealment" (*satr*). This absence was said to have caused a split among his followers: some held that Muḥammad b. Ismāʿīl was the Mahdī and the Qāʾim ("one who rises") who would return at the end of time to establish justice. Others held to continuity of imamate through his progeny, but this latter group disappeared leaving the first Ismāʿīlīs to await the return of Muḥammad b. Ismāʿīl as the Mahdī.

mujāhidūn Muslim warriors. The depictions of the early Muslim warriors, especially those who fought during the conquests (*futuḥāt*), became widely idealized among Muslims, and exerted a strong influence on Muslim sects and schools. Their image was reminiscent of the way Christian monks and soldiers were portrayed in late antiquity insofar as their militancy was depicted as a form of ascetic piety, with their martyrdoms celebrated as a focal point for consolidating communities.

al-Mukhtār b. Abī ʿUbaydallāh al-Thaqafī (d. 67/687) early Shiʿite rebel and progenitor of the Kaysāniyya Shiʿites. He raised a revolt in Kufa by calling for revenge for the massacres at Karbala, claiming to have the support of ʿAlī's son, Muḥammad b. al-Ḥanafiyya (Ibn al-Ḥanafiyya neither affirmed nor denied any connection to the rebels). Al-Mukhtār attracted a large number of non-Arab Muslims (*mawālī*) and took control of the city, where they executed several Umayyads who had participated at Karbala. Despite initial successes in and around Kufa, al-Mukhtār was killed and his followers were defeated in 69/687. The group known as the Kaysāniyya likely developed after his death.

Murjiʾa (Murjiʾites) Muslim school of thought originating in the Umayyad period and associated with Abū Ḥanīfa, but surviving into the ʿAbbāsid period. Although their name alludes to the idea of *ijrāʾ*,

"postponing" judgment (initially) on ʿUthmān and ʿAlī (thus establishing an apolitical position with respect to the politics of the Umayyad period), the Murjiʾa of the later Umayyad period were willing to support revolts against the injustices of their day. Their position on faith, that a person need only declare their faith in God and the prophethood of Muḥammad without necessarily performing the attendant acts associated with these beliefs, proved popular among non-Arabs, especially in Central Asia. Maturing into a school of thought in the ʿAbbāsid period, the Murjiʾite stance on faith was eventually absorbed into Sunnism.

mushrik/mushrikūn polytheist(s); idolater(s). A qurʾanic term referring generally to those who "associate" things with God that are not God, and specifically to the polytheists/idolaters of the Prophet's era. Among the Khārijites and Ibāḍiyya, the question arose as to whether an unbeliever (*kāfir*) should be considered akin to a *mushrik* (the Qurʾan often seems to use the terms interchangeably). More militant Khārijites, such as the Azāriqa, considered nonmembers to be *kuffār* and also *mushrikūn*, meaning that they could (and should) be fought and treated as such. Quietist Khārijites, along with the Ibāḍiyya, rejected such equivalences arguing that professing monotheists could not be treated as idolaters, and that polytheism/idolatry (*shirk*) is different from other forms of *kufr*.

Muʿtazila (Muʿtazilites) Muslim rationalist school of thought that developed out of the Umayyad-era Qadariyya and matured in the ʿAbbāsid period. Muʿtazilite thought was wide-ranging and varied, but it was anchored in the idea that God provided humankind with the ability to use reason (*ʿaql*), which allowed them to discern good from evil, and to choose their actions accordingly (that is, with their free will). Muʿtazilites also held that God was just in a manner that human beings could understand, and that He committed Himself not to do evil. The Muʿtazilite school disappeared due to a variety of factors, including the disruptions caused by the Mongol invasions, as well as the criticisms of Abū al-Ḥasan al-Ashʿarī.

Nāfiʿ b. al-Azraq (d. 65–66/685) early Khārijite rebel, eponym, and founder of the Azāriqa (Azraqites). Although he was killed and the Azāriqa were routed at the Battle of Dūlāb, the group survived and followed other leaders into the mountainous regions of Fārs and Kirmān (in present-day Iran).

Najda b. ʿĀmir al-Ḥanafī (d. 73/692) [several variations of his name can be found in the sources] eponym and founder of the Najdiyya Khārijites (Najdites, also Najadāt). During the second civil war (*fitna*), he and his supporters reportedly broke with Nāfiʿ b. al-Azraq over several issues, and returned to al-Yamāma (central Arabia), where they joined their forces with a local Khārijite leader and he received the pledge of allegiance as their leader. The Najdites then scored a series of military victories that gave them control over nearly all of the Arabian Peninsula. However, friction in the group caused one of Ibn ʿĀmir's deputies to leave with several of his followers, and another deputy to kill Ibn ʿĀmir.

Najdite Khārijites (Najdiyya/Najadāt) militant Khārijite group named after their first leader, Najda b. ʿĀmir al-Ḥanafī, who for a time controlled most of the Arabian Peninsula during the second civil war (*fitna*). The Najdites eventually splintered, with some decamping to the mountainous regions of southwestern Iran where they splintered further into subsects, and others remaining in the Arabian Peninsula. Remnants of the original Najadāt in the Arabian Peninsula reportedly persisted up to the fifth/eleventh century.

naṣṣ "designation." An Imāmī, and later Ithnā-ʿAsharī and Ismāʿīlī, doctrine whereby the imam is said to designate his successor, thereby passing the authority of the imamate and attendant esoteric knowledge of religious matters to them.

nāṭiq "enunciator" or "speaker." An early Ismāʿīlī notion whereby it was held that a new prophetic era was initiated by a *nāṭiq* of a divinely revealed message, who imposed a religious law (*sharīʿa*). For early Ismāʿīlīs the first six were Adam, Noah, Abraham, Moses, Jesus, and Muḥammad. The outer teachings of religion were also accompanied by a secret, inner teaching that was reserved for a select few. The *nāṭiq* taught this secret knowledge to the figure known as the *ṣāmit* (also called the *wāṣī* or *asās*), who then passed it to his successors, the imams.

Nizārī Ismāʿīlism (Shiʿism) branch of Ismāʿīlism that traces the imamate through the eldest son (Nizār al-Muṣṭafā li-Dīn Allāh) of the eighth Fāṭimid imam, Abū Tamīm Maʿad al-Mustanṣir bi-Llāh. At present, Nizārī Ismāʿīlīs are the most populous of the surviving Ismāʿīlī groups, and their imam, who is known by his title, the Aga Khan, claims a continuous linage tracing back to ʿAlī b. Abī Ṭālib.

Nuṣayrī (ʿAlawī) Shiʿism a secretive form of gnostic Shiʿism, classed as *ghulāt* by their opponents, found in the mountainous regions of northwestern Syria/southwestern Turkey. Traced to their founder, Muḥammad b. Nuṣayr (d. after 254/868), who claimed to be the gateway (*bāb*) to the salvific knowledge of the imams, and a representative of the twelfth imam.

Ottomans (r. 697–1340/1298–1922) Muslim empire, founded in Anatolia (modern-day Turkey) with its capital eventually at Istanbul, and spreading (at its height) to much of southeastern Europe, the Middle East, and North Africa. Classed among the "gunpowder empires" because the Ottoman state adopted gunpowder weapons. As such, it is a good example of how gunpowder changed the Ottoman military and political apparatus. Several Muslim sects and schools, such as the Alevis, Nuṣayrīs, and Ithnā-ʿAsharī Shiʿites, found themselves administered by the Ottoman state.

al-qaḍāʾ God's "decree"; predestination. The notion that God decrees all things, including human actions, was the dominant assumption in the late antique and medieval world. In Islamdom, Muslim theologians who formally articulated the notion of *al-qaḍāʾ* had to grapple with the issue of human responsibility: if God decreed all actions then how could human beings be held responsible on the Day of Judgment for them? One answer to this problem, the one adopted by al-Ashʿarī and others, was that human beings "acquired" them (this is the doctrine of *kasb*).

Qadariyya (Qadarites) late Umayyad-era school of thought that emphasized *qadar* (limited free will). The movement was allegedly founded by Maʿbad b. ʿAbdullāh al-Juhanī, who was executed by the Umayyads for his supposed Qadarite views. Also associated with the movement was the popular Basran preacher and ascetic al-Ḥasan al-Baṣrī. The Qadariyya disappeared (if they ever existed as a coherent "movement"), apparently absorbed into the nascent Muʿtazila.

qāḍī/quḍāt Muslim judge(s). Often appointed by the caliph or the governors, the position was one of prestige and power in Islamdom. As such, it was sometimes shunned by the *ʿulamāʾ* (or claimed to have been shunned by those who wrote the stories of the *ʿulamāʾ* after their deaths), who held, generally speaking, that power was corrupting and should be avoided.

Qarāmiṭa (Qaramathians) Ismāʿīlī group who followed Ḥamdān Qarmaṭ in rejecting the claims of ʿAbdullāh b. al-Ḥusayn, the first Fāṭimid imam, to the imamate. The Qarāmiṭa continued to await the return of Muḥammad b. Ismāʿīl as the Mahdī. The Qarāmiṭa are remembered for sacking Makka in 319/931, stealing the black stone, and taking it back to Baḥrayn (it was ransomed to the ʿAbbāsids in 339/950). They were gradually overshadowed and missionized by the Fāṭimids, and they eventually disappeared and/or were absorbed into the Fāṭimid movement.

qiyāma "resurrection." A term usually referring to the resurrection of the dead on the Day of Judgment. Among Nizārī Ismāʿīlīs, it can also refer to an event in 559/1164, when the imam Ḥasan II, whom the Nizārīs called *ʿAlā dhikrihi al-salām* ("On whose name be peace"), declared that the *qiyāma* had arrived, and that the esoteric truths were now available, thereby abrogating the outer law (*sharīʿa*). While this event is only hazily described by the sources (all of which are hostile of the Ismāʿīlīs), it does seem as if Ḥasan II attempted to affect some changes in how the traditional religious rituals of Islam were observed. He was murdered a year and a half after the declaration. His son and successor, Nūr al-Dīn Muḥammad, modified the doctrine of *qiyāma*, claiming that his father was in fact an imam in the line of Nizār, but that the *qiyāma* was meant to emphasize commitment to the imam.

qiyās deductive "analogy" in Islamic jurisprudence. One of the "sources" (*uṣūl*) of classical Islamic jurisprudence, whereby a novel question of law can be answered through analogy with a similar issue raised in the authoritative sources (usually, in the *ḥadīth*).

***qizilbāsh* (also *kizilbāsh*)** epithet, meaning "red heads" (and referring to the red hats that they wore), given to nomadic Turkic groups that migrated into Anatolia, Iraq, and Iran in the wake of the Mongol conquests, and who became the backbone of the early Safavid movement. The *qizilbāsh* (who were often labeled as *ghulāt* by their detractors) blended Shiʿism with Sufism (especially that traced to Haji Bektāsh Veli), and looked to their leaders, such as Shāh Ismāʿīl I, the founder of the Safavid state, as perfected human beings (*al-insān al-kāmil*).

quddās Nuṣayrī/ʿAlawī "mass." Most often performed in private homes or other sequestered places, *quddās* can include the recitation of lengthy prayers praising ʿAlī's divine attributes and the trinity of ʿAlī, Muḥammad, and Salmān al-Fārisī. It also involves consecration and consumption of bread and wine (symbolizing the intoxication in and love of God, as well as the reunion of God and human beings).

al-rajʿa "return." Shiʿite doctrine of the return of the imam. First associated with so-called *ghulāt* movements, who looked to various figures from the *ahl al-bayt* as having not died, but gone into hiding and waiting to "return," usually as the Mahdī. Later adopted and modified by the Ithnā-ʿAsharī Shiʿites, the doctrine of *rajʿa* is now an integral aspect of the Ithnā-ʿAsharī conception of the twelfth imam's return as the Mahdī.

***rāshidūn* caliphs (*al-khulafāʾ al-rāshidūn*) (r. 11–40/632–61)** an ʿAbbāsid-era designation, later adopted by the Sunnis, for the era of the first four caliphs: Abū Bakr, ʿUmar, ʿUthmān, and ʿAlī. While, in fact, this early period was marked by significant turmoil and civil war (*fitna*), especially during the caliphates of ʿUthmān and ʿAlī, the idea of the first four caliphs as equally pious and worthy offered the ʿAbbāsid state, and later the Sunnis, a means to appeal broadly to Muslims by rehabilitating ʿAlī and the *ahl al-bayt* in the wake of Umayyad-era slander against them. At the same time, it placed Abū Bakr, ʿUmar, and ʿUthmān on an equal footing with ʿAlī. The ʿAbbāsids could thus appeal to the widespread and general feeling of loyalty toward the *ahl al-bayt* without subsequently ceding political authority to them.

Safavids (Arabic: Ṣafawiyya) (r. 907–1179/1501–1765) Muslim empire founded in Azerbayjān and Persia by Shāh Ismāʿīl I, with its capital at Isfahan. Classed among the "gunpowder empires" because the Safavid state adopted gunpowder weapons. The Safavids imposed Ithnā-ʿAsharī Shiʿism as the state religion, converting a population that had been predominantly Sunni and importing Shiʿite scholars to the shrine city of Qom.

samāʿ "listening." A Sufi practice, employed by some mystically inflected Muslim sects and schools such as the Alevi Shiʿites of Anatolia as part of the *cem/jem*, of listening to music and participating in or observing dance.

ṣāmit "silent one." An early Ismāʿīlī notion whereby the *nāṭiq* of each prophetic era taught the inner and hidden meaning of the divine message to a legatee (*wāṣī*), who was also called the *ṣāmit* (also the "foundation," *asās*), who propagated the secret among select elites of their age. The legatees of the first six ages were held to be Seth, Shem, Ishmael, Aaron, Simon Peter, and ʿAlī b. Abī Ṭālib. The *ṣāmit* passed this knowledge on to the imams after him.

sect subgroup of a religious or philosophical system; religious denomination; religious communal affiliation. The academic term "sect" can be problematic when deployed to describe Muslim communal affiliations, insofar as the term originates in the Christian tradition, and was initially used to describe Christians. Medieval Muslim heresiographers used several terms, such as *firqa/firaq*, to designate what the English term "sect" describes.

Seljuqs (r. 431–590/1040–1194) nomadic Turkic group from the steppes north of the Caspian, the Seljuqs seized control of the ailing ʿAbbāsid

Empire in the fifth/eleventh century and established themselves as its de facto rulers, keeping the ʿAbbāsid caliphs as figureheads. As they came to power in the wake of the so-called Shiʿite century (the fourth/tenth century, which saw the rise of the Fāṭimids in the Islamic West [Maghrib], as well as several prominent Shiʿite families who controlled large parts of the ʿAbbāsid Empire), the Seljuqs aggressively adopted Sunnism, and promoted it through their newly established *madrasa* system.

shafāʿa "intercession." Early belief, and later Sunni doctrine, whereby the Prophet Muḥammad was said to be capable of interceding on behalf of Muslims on the Day of Judgment and lessening or abrogating their time in hell. The idea of intercession was rejected by several early Muslim sects and schools, notably the Khārijites, Ibāḍiyya, and Muʿtazila, who held that God would fulfill the promises that He made in the Qurʾan to punish sinners and reward the faithful.

al-Shāfiʿī, Abū ʿAbdullāh Muḥammad b. Idrīs (d. 204/820) eponym of the Shāfiʿī *madhhab*, and legal scholar. Al-Shāfiʿī adapted the ideas of his mentor, Mālik b. Anas, arguing that the *sunna* should be primarily established using the example of the Prophet Muḥammad. He is credited with formalizing the Qurʾan, *sunna* (as found in the *ḥadīth*), *ijmāʿ*, and *qiyās* as the four main sources of jurisprudence (*uṣūl al-fiqh*). Al-Shāfiʿī's legal thought represents the culmination of the ʿAbbāsid-era project to create a universalizable law, contributing thereby to the making of Sunnism.

sharīʿa the system of Islamic law (literally, the "path"). Ideally, it is God's eternal and unchanging will for humankind, which human beings attempt to discover using the process of Islamic jurisprudence. In a more mundane sense, the term *sharīʿa* also applies to Islamic law as a whole, including the centuries-long accumulation of opinions and rulings handed down and preserved in the vast Islamic legal corpus.

Shiʿa those who looked to various lineages of the *ahl al-bayt* as the legitimate leaders of humankind after the Prophet Muḥammad (literally, "partisans"). Shiʿism emphasizes charismatic loyalty and devotion to the family of the Prophet as the primary indicator of what it means to practice Islam.

***shurāt* (sing. *shārī*)** "exchangers." Epithet adopted by the earliest Khārijites, likely after Qurʾan 9:111 which mentions those who exchange their lives in the way of God for Paradise. Early sources on the Khārijites emphasize the *shurāt*'s eagerness to perish fighting tyranny and injustice: in other words, their eagerness for martyrdom (expressed as *shirāʾ*, exchange of one's life for Paradise), as well as the attendant attitude of asceticism that was said to have permeated their group. The medieval Ibāḍiyya institutionalized the *shurāt* into a selected groups of ascetic warriors under the direction of a leader who was known as the *imām al-shārī*.

ṣifāt God's "attributes." *See* ***dhāt***.

Sufism (*al-taṣawwuf*) the mystical dimension of Islam. Sufism is often confused for a sectarian group. In fact, Sufi Muslims and Sufi confraternities (*ṭarīqāt*) can be oriented toward a sect or school. For example, they can be Sunni or Shiʿi in orientation, such as the Naqshbandī Sufi order, which is predominantly Sunni, or the Niʿmatullāhī Sufis, who are Shiʿi.

sunna authoritative example. The term *sunna* refers, on the one hand, to an authoritative example, such as that of the Prophet Muḥammad or his Companions. However, it can also refer to the body of literature – the *ḥadīth* – that Muslims hold preserves those examples. For Shiʿites, the *sunna* also includes the imams.

Sunni shortened form of *ahl al-sunna wa'l-jamāʿa* ("the people of the *sunna* and [adhering to] the community"), and one of the main communal groupings among Muslims. Since the eighth/fourteenth century, Sunni Muslims have constituted the majority of Muslims. Sunnism is marked by a broad inclusivism, whereby different legal schools and views are tolerated so long as they can be shown to be grounded in the authoritative textual sources of the Islamic tradition.

tafrīq "splintering." The fragmentation of the early Khārijite movement at the outset of the second *fitna* (that is, ca. 64/683). According to the narratives of it, the Khārijites disagreed over the status of Ibn al-Zubayr, whom they rejected for his refusal to condemn the caliph ʿUthmān b. ʿAffān. Nāfiʿ b. al-Azraq (eponym of the Azāriqa/Azraqites) took the most extreme stance when he held the sinner to be unfaithful in the same fashion as a polytheist. ʿAbdullāh b. Ibāḍ (eponym of the Ibāḍiyya) condemned Ibn al-Azraq for taking this stance, considering it too extreme, while ʿAbdullāh b. Ṣaffār (the name differs depending on the version) condemned them both – Ibn al-Azraq for going too far, Ibn Ibāḍ for not going far enough. In this way, according to the *tafrīq* narrative, the Azraqites, Ibāḍiyya, and Ṣufriyya were established. There is a strong likelihood that the *tafrīq* narrative is not historically accurate.

***taḥkīm* (also *ḥukm al-ḥukūma*)** "arbitration." ʿAlī b. Abī Ṭālib's consent to arbitrate the Battle of Ṣiffīn with his opponent, Muʿāwiya b. Abī Sufyān, led to a portion of ʿAlī's army seceding from (*kharajū*

ʿan) him, selecting their own leader, and thereby establishing the sectarian grouping known later as the Khārijites.

takfīr the act of designating a person or persons unbelievers (*kāfir/kuffār*). The practice is most often associated with the Khārijites, who were willing to employ the terminology to describe persons who professed Islam but who had fallen short in their view. In fact, a great many persons and groups other than Khārijites employed *takfīr* as a means of denigrating their opponents.

taʿlīm [doctrine of] "instruction." A Nizārī-Ismāʿīlī notion whereby each imam is held to instruct the followers of his era in the manner that befits them, but that successive imams might instruct them differently. This doctrine allowed for flexibility and responsiveness to the changing needs of the Nizārī-Ismāʿīlī community; it also provided an explanation for apparent contradictions between the teachings of the various imams over time.

taqiyya prudent dissimulation; the act of hiding aspects of one's religion to escape persecution. The practice of *taqiyya* allowed sectarian minorities to survive through these periods of political tension, and to coexist with nonsectarians in shared spaces. It was not usually practiced by Sunnis, who more often held that martyrdom was more preferable to secrecy; and certain Khārijite groups condemned it. Many Shiʿite groups, along with quietist Khārijites and the Ibāḍiyya, counseled the use of *taqiyya*, even making it obligatory under certain conditions.

tawḥīd the doctrine of God's oneness. An essential aspect of Islam, the idea of God's oneness remains deceptively simple, but in fact turns out to be quite complex. Questions regarding the nature of God's oneness, especially concerning His essence and attributes, occupied medieval Muslim sects and schools especially during the ʿAbbāsid period.

taʾwīl interpretation of religion (often qurʾanic interpretation) based on privileged knowledge. Whereas many Muslims labored at scholarly qurʾanic interpretation (called *tafsīr*), Muslim sects and schools that laid claim to a special, esoteric knowledge (such as that attributed to the Ithnā-ʿAsharī and Ismāʿīlī Shiʿite imams by their followers) claimed to have a truer/better interpretation of the Qurʾan's verses due to their possession of this knowledge. Note that Sufi groups/masters also practiced *taʾwīl*.

Tawwābūn the "Penitents." Movement in 65/684 led by Sulaymān b. Surād, who began calling on those who supported ʿAlī's family to repent for their failure to aid al-Ḥusayn b. ʿAlī, and to avenge his slaughter. His followers marched to Karbala where they pledged themselves to resist the Umayyads. After their defeat at ʿAyn al-Warda the remnants of the Tawwābūn trickled back to Kufa where they joined another militant Shiʿa uprising in the making, that of al-Mukhtār b. Abī ʿUbaydallāh al-Thaqafī, in 66/685.

taʿziya reenactments of the martyrdom of al-Ḥusayn b. ʿAlī. This practice is known especially in Iran.

ʿUmar b. al-Khaṭṭāb (d. 24/644) the second successor (caliph, *khalīfa*) to the Prophet Muḥammad, and later classed among the "rightly guided" caliphs by Sunni Muslims. Under ʿUmar the Muslim conquests (*futuḥāt*) accelerated significantly, and reflecting his concern with military matters he adopted the title *amīr al-muʾminīn* (Commander of the Faithful). Although rejected by most Shiʿa as a usurper of the rights of the *ahl al-bayt* to the leadership, Khārijites and Ibāḍīs regarded ʿUmar as a righteous caliph.

Umayyads (r. 41/661–132/750) the first Muslim dynasty after the period of the first four caliphs. The first Umayyad caliph, Muʿāwiya b. Abī Sufyān, was cousin to the third caliph, ʿUthmān, who were both members of the clan of Umayya. The Umayyads treated the caliphate as an Arab kingdom based in Syrian tribal power. For the most part, they regarded Islam as the purview of the Arabs, largely discouraging conversion among non-Arabs and treating non-Arab converts (the *mawālī*) as second-class Muslims. With notable exceptions, many of the Umayyad caliphs were unpopular, and the Umayyad period is marked by sectarian strife, particularly in the province of Iraq. The Umayyads were overthrown by a revolution that began in Central Asia with support from the *mawālī*, and led by a Shiʿite group, the Hāshimiyya, who boasted leaders from the ʿAbbāsid wing of the *ahl al-bayt*.

umma a qurʾanic term referring to the community of Muslims. This community was to be based on religious confession and piety, rather than on kinship or any other type of bond.

ʿUthmān b. ʿAffān (d. 35/656) the third successor (caliph, *khalīfa*) to the Prophet Muḥammad, and later classed among the "rightly guided" caliphs by Sunni Muslims. Among early Muslim sectarian groups ʿUthmān was a controversial figure: the Khārijites and Ibāḍiyya rejected him as a sinner who was rightfully killed; the Shiʿa regarded him along with the first two caliphs as having usurped the caliphate from ʿAlī; supporters of the Umayyads regarded him as their forbearer, and held him in esteem. A person's stance on ʿUthmān (and ʿAlī), thereby, became shorthand for their politico-religious stance in the early period.

al-waʿd wa'l-waʿīd "the promise and the threat." An idea associated with the Muʿtazilites, and one of Abū al-Hudhayl's "five principles," whereby God keeps His qurʾanic promise of Paradise for believers, and carries out His threat of hell for disbelievers. This belief precluded the idea of intercession (*shafāʿa*) that gained traction among some Murjiʾa and the nascent Sunnis.

walāya term usually referring to guardianship or governance, but taking on special meanings among Shiʿites and Ibāḍīs. Among Shiʿites the term refers to "charismatic loyalty" that is given to the *ahl al-bayt*. And as such loyalty is crucial to the soteriology of Shiʿism, *walāya* is seen as an essential component of being a Shiʿite. Among Ibāḍīs, *walāya* refers to the principle of "association" that determines who is counted as a true Muslim (meaning, an Ibāḍī Muslim). Often paired with its opposite, *barāʾa* (dissociation), the principles of *walāya* and *barāʾa* establish the boundaries of group identity among the Ibāḍiyya.

wāṣī legatee (in legal terms, the one who receives the legacy of a deceased individual). One of the titles of ʿAlī, and alluding to the idea that ʿAlī inherited the mantle of leadership and religious authority after the death of the Prophet Muḥammad. Early Ismāʿīlism posited that each prophet of his era was succeeded by his *wāṣī* (also called the "silent one" (*ṣāmit*), and the "foundation" (*asās*)), who propagated the secret among select elites of their age (the legatees of the first six ages were Seth, Shem, Ishmael, Aaron, Simon Peter, and ʿAlī b. Abī Ṭālib). These themselves had seven successors, who were the imams.

Wāṣil b. ʿAṭāʾ (d. 131/748–49) early Muʿtazilite leader in Basra, and possibly one of the cofounders of the movement along with ʿAmr b. ʿUbayd. A student of al-Ḥasan al-Baṣrī. A (historically suspect) story tells of how Ibn ʿAṭāʾ broke with his teacher over the question of the sinner, and moved (*iʿtazala*) himself to a different corner of the mosque in Basra to teach his own doctrines; his followers were allegedly called the "Muʿtaliza" after this move.

wazīr/wuzarāʾ a political position, developed especially during the ʿAbbāsid era, of the highest ranking official after the caliph, and thereby second-in-command of the caliphate (origin of the English word vizier). With the diminution of caliphal authority during and after the caliphate of al-Mutawakkil (r. 232–47/847–61), the *wuzarāʾ* assumed more and more actual power in Islamdom.

Zayd b. ʿAlī (d. 122/740) great-grandson of ʿAlī b. Abī Ṭālib, respected religious scholar, and leader of an unsuccessful revolt against the Umayyads in the late Umayyad period. Eponym of the Zaydī branch of Shiʿism.

Zaydī Shiʿism a branch of Shiʿism that takes its appellation from Zayd b. ʿAlī. Zaydī Shiʿism posits that any male descendant of ʿAlī b. Abī Ṭālib through his sons al-Ḥasan and al-Ḥusayn can become the imam by "rising with the sword" (that is, leading an uprising to claim his rights). Because Zaydī Shiʿism did not really develop a stable heartland, its doctrines have shifted somewhat over the centuries.

Bibliography

Primary Sources

ʿAbbās, Iḥsān. *Shiʿr al-Khawārij: Jamʿ wa Taqdīm Iḥsān ʿAbbās*. 3rd edition. Beirut: Dār al-Thaqāfa, 1974.

ʿAbd al-Razzāq, Abū Bakr b. Hammām b. Nāfiʿ al-Ṣanʿānī. *al-Muṣannaf*. Edited by Ayman Naṣr al-Dīn al-Azharī. Beirut: Dār al-Kutub al-ʿIlmiyya, 2000.

Abū Ḥayyān al-Tawḥīdī. *Kitāb al-Imtāʿ wa'l-Muʾānasa*. Edited by Aḥmad Amīn and Aḥmad al-Zayn. Beirut: Manshūrāt Dār Maktabat al-Ḥayāt, 1965.

Abū al-Maʿālī, Muḥammad b. ʿUbaydallāh. *Bayān al-Adyān*. Edited by Hāshim Raḍī. Tehran: Maṭbūʿātye-Farāhānī, 1964.

Adang, Camilla, Wilferd Madelung, and Sabine Schmidtke, eds. *Basran Muʿtazilite Theology: Abū ʿAlī Muḥammad b. Khallād's Kitāb al-Uṣūl and Its Reception*. Leiden: Brill, 2011.

al-Amīnī, ʿAbd al-Ḥusayn Aḥmad. *al-Ghadīr fī'l-Kitāb wa'l-Sunna wa'l-Adab*. Tehran: al-Ḥaydarī, 1974–76.

al-Ashʿarī, Abū al-Ḥasan ʿAlī b. Ismāʿīl. *Maqālāt al-Islāmiyyīn wa Ikhtilāf al-Muṣallīn*. Edited by Muḥammad Muḥyī al-Dīn al-Ḥamīd. Beirut: al-Maktaba al-ʿAṣriyya, 1999.

al-ʿAsqalānī, Ibn Ḥajar. *Fatḥ al-Bārī bi-Sharḥ Ṣaḥīḥ al-Bukhārī*. Riyadh: Bayt al-Afkār al-Dawliyya, n.d.

al-Azdī, Muḥammad b. ʿAbdullāh al-Baṣrī. *Tārīkh Futūḥ al-Shām*. Edited by ʿAbd al-Munʿim ʿAbdullāh ʿĀmir. Cairo: Muʾassasat Sijil al-ʿArab, 1970.

al-Baghdādī, Abū Qāhir b. Ṭāhir. *al-Farq bayn al-Firaq*. Beirut: Dār al-Āfāq al-Jadīda, 1987.

al-Balādhurī, Aḥmad b. Yaḥyā. *Ansāb al-Ashrāf*. Edited by Suhayl Zakkār and Riyāḍ Zarkalī. Beirut: Dār al-Fikr, 1996.

al-Barrādī, Abū al-Faḍl/al-Qāsim b. Ibrāhīm. *al-Jawhar al-Muntaqāt fī Itmām Mā Akhall bihi Kitāb al-Ṭabaqāt*. Cairo: Lithograph, 1885.

Crone, Patricia, and Fritz Zimmerman. *The Epistle of Sālim Ibn Dhakwān*. Oxford: Oxford University Press, 2001.

al-Darjīnī, Abū al-ʿAbbās Aḥmad b. Saʿīd. *Kitāb Ṭabaqāt al-Mashāyikh bi'l-Maghrib*. Edited by Ibrāhīm Tallay. Algiers: Alger-Constantine, n.d.

al-Dhahabī, Abū ʿAbdullāh Shams al-Dīn. *Kitāb Tadhkirat al-Ḥuffāẓ*. Beirut: Dār Iḥyāʾ al-Turāth al-ʿArabī, 1965.

Ibn ʿAbd Rabbih, Aḥmad b. Muḥammad. *Kitāb al-ʿIqd al-Farīd*. Edited by Barakāt Yūsuf Habdū. Beirut: Dār al-Arqam, 1999.

Ibn al-Athīr, Abū al-Ḥasan ʿAlī b. Muḥammad. *Tārīkh Ibn al-Athīr*. Riyadh: Bayt al-Afkār al-Dawliyya, n.d.

Ibn Ḥanbal, Aḥmad. *Kitāb al-Zuhd*. Beirut: Dār al-Kutub al-ʿIlmiyya, 1976.

Ibn Ḥanbal, Aḥmad. *Musnad al-Imām al-Ḥāfiẓ Abī ʿAbdullāh Aḥmad b. Ḥanbal*. Riyadh: Bayt al-Afkār al-Dawliyya, 1998.

Ibn Ḥazm, Abū Muḥammad ʿAlī b. Aḥmad. *al-Faṣl fī'l-Milal wa'l-Ahwāʾ wa'l-Niḥal*. Edited by Aḥmad Shams al-Dīn. Beirut: Dār al-Kutub al-ʿIlmiyya, 1999.

Ibn Khayyāṭ, Khalīfa. *Tārīkh Khalīfa b. Khayyāṭ*. Edited by Muṣṭafā Najīb Fawāz and Ḥikmat Kashlī Fawāz. Beirut: Dār al-Kutub al-ʿIlmiyya, 1995.

al-Isfarāʾinī, Shafūr b. Ṭāhir. *al-Tabṣīr fī'l-Dīn wa Tamyīz al-Firqa al-Nājiya ʿan al-Firaq al-Hālikīn*. Edited by Muḥammad Zāhid b. al-Ḥasan al-Kawtharī and Maḥmūd Muḥammad al-Khaḍīrī. Cairo: Maktabat al-Azhār li'l-Turāth, 1940.

Khadduri, Majid, trans. *Al-Shāfiʿī's Risāla: Treatise on the Foundations of Islamic Jurisprudence*. Cambridge: Islamic Texts Society, 1961.

al-Khaṭīb al-Baghdādī, Abū Bakr Aḥmad b. ʿAlī. *Tārīkh Baghdād*. Beirut: Dār al-Fikr, n.d.

al-Khayyāṭ, Abū al-Ḥusayn ʿAbd al-Raḥīm b. Muḥammad b. ʿUthmān. *Kitāb al-Intiṣār wa'l-Radd ʿalā Ibn al-Rawandī al-Mulḥid*. Beirut: al-Maṭbaʿa al-Kāthūlīkiyya, 1957.

al-Khwārizmī, Muḥammad b. Aḥmad. *Kitāb Mafātiḥ al-ʿUlūm*. Edited by Gerlof Van Vloten. Leiden: E. J. Brill, 1895.

Madelung, Wilferd, and Paul E. Walker, eds. and trans. *An Ismaili Heresiography: The "Bāb al-Shayṭān" from Abū Tammām's Kitāb al-Shajara*. Leiden: Brill, 1998.

al-Malaṭī, Abū al-Ḥasan Muḥammad b. Aḥmad b. ʿAbd al-Raḥmān. *al-Tanbīh wa'l-Radd ʿalā Ahl al-Ahwāʾ wa'l-Bidʿa*. Cairo: al-Maktaba al-Azhariyya li'l-Turāth, 1993.

al-Masʿūdī, Abū al-Ḥasan ʿAlī b. al-Ḥusayn b. ʿAlī. *al-Tanbīh wa'l-Ashrāf*. Beirut: Dār Maktabat al-Hilāl, 1993.

al-Māwardī, Abū al-Ḥasan ʿAlī b. Muḥammad b. Ḥabīb al-Baṣrī al-Baghdādī. *Aḥkām al-Sulṭāniyya wa'l-Wilāyat al-Dīniyya*. Beirut: Dār al-Kutub al-ʿIlmiyya, 1985.

McCarthy, R. J., trans. *Al-Ghazali's Path to Sufism: His Deliverance from Error al-Munqidh min al-Dalal*. Louisville: Fons Vitae, 2000.

al-Mubarrad, Abū al-ʿAbbās Muḥammad b. Yazīd. *al-Kāmil fī'l-Lugha wa'l-Adab*. Edited by Muḥammad Abū al-Faḍl Ibrāhīm. Beirut: al-Maktaba al-ʿAṣriyya, 2002.

al-Muqaddasī, Shams al-Dīn Abū ʿAbdullāh Muḥammad b. Aḥmad b. Abī Bakr al-Bannā al-Bashārī. *Aḥsan al-Taqāsīm fī Maʿrifat al-Taqālīm*. Edited by M. J. de Goeje. Leiden: E. J. Brill, 1906.

al-Nawbakhtī, Abū Muḥammad b. Mūsā. *Kitāb Firaq al-Shīʿa*. Edited by H. Ritter. Istanbul: Maṭbaʿat al-Dawliyya, 1931.

Poonawala, Ismail K., trans. *The History of al-Ṭabarī: Volume IX, The Last Years of the Prophet*. Albany: SUNY Press, 1990.

al-Qalhātī, Abū ʿAbdullāh Muḥammad b. Saʿīd al-Azdī. *Al-Kashf wa'l-Bayān*. Edited by Sayyida Ismāʿīl Kāshif. Muscat: Wizārat al-Turāth al-Qawmī wa'l-Thaqāfa, 1980.

al-Rāzī, Fakhr al-Dīn Muḥammad b. ʿUmar al-Khaṭīb. *Iʿtiqādāt Firaq al-Muslimīn wa'l-Mushrikīn*. Cairo: Sharikat al-Ṭibāʿa al-Fanniyya al-Muttaḥida, 1978.
Rūmī, Jalāl al-Dīn. *The Mathnawī of Jalāl ud-Dīn Rūmī*. 2 vols. Edited and translated by Reynold Alleyne Nicholson. Tehran: Nashar Booteh, 1981.
al-Sābiʿī, Nāṣir b. Sulaymān b. Saʿīd. *Al-Khawārij wa'l-Ḥaqīqa al-Ghāʾiba*. Muscat: Maktabat al-Jīl al-Waʿīd, 2003.
al-Sālimī, Nūr al-Dīn ʿAbdullāh b. Ḥumayd. *Tuḥfat al-Aʿyān bi-Sīrat Ahl ʿUmān*. Muscat: Maktabat al-Istiqāma, 1997.
Sayyid, Fuʾād, ed. *Faḍl al-Iʿtizāl wa Ṭabaqāt al-Muʿtazila*. Tunis: al-Dār al-Tūnisiyya li'l-Nashr, 1974.
al-Shahrastānī, Abū al-Fatḥ Muḥammad ʿAbd al-Karīm. *Al-Milal wa'l-Niḥal*. Edited by ʿAbd al-ʿAzīz Muḥammad al-Wakīl. Beirut: Dār al-Fikr, n.d.
al-Shammākhī, Abū al-ʿAbbās Aḥmad b. Saʿīd. *Kitāb al-Siyar*. Edited by Muḥammad Ḥasan. Beirut: Dār al-Madār al-Islāmī, 2009.
al-Ṭabarī, Muḥammad b. Jarīr. *Tārīkh al-Rusul wa'l-Mulūk*. Edited by M. J. de Goeje. Leiden: Brill, 1879.

Secondary Sources

Abdul Jabbar, Falih. *The Shiʿite Movement in Iraq*. London: Saqi, 2003.
Afsaruddin, Asma. *The First Muslims: History and Memory*. Oxford: Oneworld Publications, 2008.
Agha, Saleh Said. "A Viewpoint of the Murjiʾa in the Umayyad Period: Evolution through Application." *Journal of Islamic Studies* 8, no. 1 (1997): 1–42.
Aghaie, Kamran Scot. *The Martyrs of Karbala: Shiʿi Symbols and Rituals in Modern Iran*. Seattle: University of Washington Press, 2004.
Al-Azmeh, Aziz. *The Emergence of Islam in Late Antiquity: Allāh and His People*. Cambridge: Cambridge University Press, 2014.
Amanat, Abbas. "*Meadow of the Martyrs*: Kāshefī's Persianization of the Shiʿi Martyrdom Narrative in Late Tīmūrid Herat." In *Culture and Memory in Medieval Islam: Essays in Honour of Wilferd Madelung*. Edited by Farhad Daftary and Josef W. Meri, 250–78. London: I.B. Taurus, 2003.
Amoretti, B. S. "Religion in the Timurid and Safavid Periods." In *The Cambridge History of Iran*. Edited by Peter Jackson and Lawrence Lockhart, 610–55. Cambridge: Cambridge University Press, 1986.
Anthony, Sean. *The Caliph and the Heretic: Ibn Sabaʾ and the Origins of Shīʿism*. Leiden: Brill, 2012.
Asad, Talal. "The Idea of an Anthropology of Islam." *Qui Parle* 17, no. 2 (2009): 1–30.
Asatryan, Mushegh. "Bankers and Politics: The Network of Shiʿi Moneychangers in Eighth–Ninth Century Kufa and Their Role in the Shiʿi Community." *Journal of Persianate Studies* 7 (2014): 1–21.
Asatryan, Mushegh. *Controversies in Formative Shiʿi Islam: The Ghulat Muslims and Their Beliefs*. London: I.B. Tauris, 2017.
Ayoub, Mahmoud. *The Crisis of Muslim History: Religion and Politics in Early Islam*. Oxford: Oneworld Publications, 2003.

Baker, Christine. *Medieval Islamic Sectarianism*. Leeds: ARC Humanities Press, 2019.

Barzegar, Abbas. "'Adhering to the Community (*Luzūm al-Jamāʿa*)': Continuities between Late Umayyad Political Discourse and 'Proto-Sunni' Identity." *Review of Middle East Studies* 49, no. 2 (2015), 140–58.

Baumgarten, Albert I. *The Flourishing of Jewish Sects in the Maccabean Era: An Interpretation*. Leiden: Brill, 1997.

Becker, Howard. *Systematic Sociology on the Basis of the Beziehungslehre and Gebildelehre of Leopold von Weise*. New York: Wiley, 1932.

Becker, Howard. "Sacred and Secular Societies: Considered with Reference to Folk-State and Similar Classifications." *Social Forces* 28, no. 4 (1950): 361–76.

Bennett, David. "The Muʿtazilite Movement (II): The Early Muʿtazilites." In *The Oxford Handbook of Islamic Theology*. Edited by Sabine Schmidke, 142–58. Oxford: Oxford University Press, 2016.

Bernheimer, Teresa. "The Revolt of ʿAbdullāh b. Muʿāwiya AH 127–130: A Reconsideration through the Coinage." *Bulletin of the School of Oriental and African Studies* 69, no. 3 (2006): 381–93.

Blankinship, Khalid Yahya. *The End of the Jihâd State: The Reign of Hishām Ibn ʿAbd al-Malik and the Collapse of the Umayyads*. Albany: SUNY Press, 1994.

Blankinship, Khalid Yahya. "The Early Creed." In *Early Islamic Theology*. Edited by Tim Winter, 33–54. Cambridge: Cambridge University Press, 2008.

Bonner, Michael. *Jihad in Islamic History: Doctrines and Practices*. Princeton: Princeton University Press, 2006.

Borrut, Antoine. "Remembering Karbalāʾ: The Construction of an Early Islamic Site of Memory." *Jerusalem Studies in Arabic and Islam* 42 (2015): 249–82.

Brubaker, Rogers and Frederick Cooper. "Beyond 'Identity.'" *Theory and Society* 29 (2000): 1–47.

Bulliet, Richard W. *Conversion to Islam in the Medieval Period: An Essay in Quantitative History*. Cambridge: Harvard University Press, 1979.

Busse, Heribert. "Iran under the Būyids." In *Cambridge History of Iran, Volume 4*. Edited by R. N. Frye, 250–304. Cambridge: Cambridge University Press, 1975.

Catlos, Brian. *Kingdoms of Faith: A New History of Islamic Spain*. New York: Basic Books, 2018.

Cole, Juan. *Sacred Space and Holy War: The Politics, Culture and History of Shiʿite Islam*. New York: I.B. Tauris, 2002.

Coleman, John A. "Church-Sect Typology and Organizational Precariousness." *Sociological Analysis* 29, no. 2 (1968): 55–66.

Collins, John J. *Scriptures and Sectarianism: Essays on the Dead Sea Scrolls*. Tübingen: Mohr Siebeck, 2014.

Cook, David. "The *Aṣḥāb al-Ukhdūd*: History and *Ḥadīth* in a Martyrological Sequence." *Jerusalem Studies in Arabic and Islam* 34 (2008): 125–48.

Cook, Michael. "Weber and Islamic Sects." In *Max Weber and Islam*. Edited by Toby E. Huff and Wolfgang Schluchter, 273–80. New Brunswick: Transaction, 1999.

Crone, Patricia. "A Statement by the Najdiyya Khārijites on the Dispensability of the Imamate." *Studia Islamica* 88 (1998): 55–76.

Crone, Patricia, and Martin Hinds. *God's Caliph: Religious Authority in the First Centuries of Islam*. Cambridge: Cambridge University Press, 1986.

Dabashi, Hamid. *Authority in Islam: From the Rise of Muhammad to the Establishment of the Umayyads*. New Brunswick: Transaction, 1989.

Daftary, Farhad. *The Ismāʿīlīs: Their History and Doctrines*. Cambridge: Cambridge University Press, 1990.

Daftary, Farhad. *The Assassin Legends: Myths of the Ismaʿilis*. New York: I.B. Tauris, 1994.

Dakake, Maria Massi. *The Charismatic Community: Shiʿite Identity in Early Islam*. Albany: SUNY Press, 2007.

Dawson, Lorne L. "Creating 'Cult' Typologies: Some Strategic Considerations." *Journal of Contemporary Religion* 12, no. 3 (1997): 363–81.

Dillon, John M., and Lloyd P. Gerson, trans. and eds. *Neoplatonic Philosophy: Introductory Readings*. Indianapolis: Hackett Publishing Co., 2004.

Donner, Fred M. *Early Islamic Conquests*. Princeton: Princeton University Press, 1981.

Donner, Fred M. *Narratives of Islamic Origins*. Princeton: Darwin Press, 1998.

Dunn, Ross E. *The Adventures of Ibn Battuta: A Muslim Traveler of the 14th Century*. Berkeley: University of California Press, 1989.

Ebstein, Michael. "'Religions, Opinions and Beliefs Are Nothing but Roads and Paths ... While the Goal is One': Between Unity and Diversity in Islamic Mysticism." In *Accusations of Unbelief in Islam: A Diachronic Perspective on Takfīr*. Edited by C. Adang et al., 488–523. Leiden: Brill, 2016.

Eco, Umberto. *Six Walks in the Fictional Woods*. Cambridge, MA: Harvard University Press, 1994.

El-Omari, Racha. "The Muʿtazilite Movement (I): The Origins of the Muʿtazila." In *The Oxford Handbook of Islamic Theology*. Edited by Sabine Schmidke, 130–41. Oxford: Oxford University Press, 2016.

Ennami, Amr K. *Studies in Ibadhism (al-Ibāḍiyah)*. Muscat: Ministry of Endowments and Religious Affairs, 2008.

Fakhry, Majid. *A History of Islamic Philosophy*. New York: Columbia University Press, 2004.

Farrin, Raymond. *Abundance from the Desert: Classical Arabic Poetry*. Syracuse: Syracuse University Press, 2011.

Fierro, Maribel. "Al-Aṣfar. Again." *Jerusalem Studies in Arabic and Islam* 22 (1998): 196–213.

Fierro, Maribel. *The Almohad Revolution: Politics and Religion in the Islamic West during the Twelfth–Thirteenth Centuries*. London: Routledge, 2012.

Fierro, Maribel. "The Almohads and the Fatimids." In *Ismaili and Fatimid Studies in Honor of Paul E. Walker*. Edited by Bruce D. Craig, 161–75. Chicago: Middle East Documentation Center, 2010.

Finster, Barbara. "Arabia in Late Antiquity." In *The Qur'an in Context: Historical and Literary Investigations into the Qur'anic Milieu*. Edited by Angelika Neuwirth, Nicolai Sinai, and Michael Marx, 61–114. Leiden: Brill, 2010.

Fletcher, Richard. *Moorish Spain*. Berkeley: University of California Press, 1992.

Friedman, Yaron. "Ibn Taymiyya's *Fatāwā* against the Nuṣayrī-ʿAlawī Sect." *Der Islam* 82, no. 2 (2005): 349–63.

Gaiser, Adam. "Satan's Seven Specious Arguments: al-Shahrastānī's *Kitāb al-Milal wa'l-Niḥal* in an Ismāʿīlī Context." *Journal of Islamic Studies* 19, no. 2 (2008): 178–95.

Gaiser, Adam. *Muslims, Scholars, Soldiers: The Origin and Elaboration of the Ibāḍī Imamate Traditions*. Oxford: Oxford University Press, 2010.

Gaiser, Adam. "North African and Omani Ibāḍī Accounts of the *Munāẓara*: A Preliminary Comparison." *Revue des mondes musulmans et de la Méditerranée* 132 (2012): 63–73.

Gaiser, Adam. Shurāt *Legends, Ibāḍī Identities: Martyrdom, Asceticism, and the Making of an Early Islamic Community*. Columbia: University of South Carolina Press, 2016.

Gustafson, Paul M. "UO-US-PS-PO: A Restatement of Troeltsch's Church-Sect Typology." *Journal for the Scientific Study of Religion* 6 (1967): 64–68.

Gustafson, Paul M. "Exegesis on the Gospel according to St. Max." *Sociological Analysis* 34, no. 1 (1973): 12–25.

Gutas, Dimitri. *Greek Thought, Arabic Culture: The Graeco-Arabic Translation Movement in Baghdad and Early ʿAbbāsid Society (2nd–4th/8th–10th Centuries)*. New York: Routledge, 1998.

Haddad, Fanar. *Sectarianism in Iraq: Antagonistic Visions of Unity*. New York: Columbia University Press, 2011.

Haider, Najam. *The Origins of the Shiʿa: Identity, Ritual, and Sacred Space in Eighth-Century Kūfa*. Cambridge: Cambridge University Press, 2011.

Haider, Najam. *Shīʿī Islam: An Introduction*. New York: Cambridge University Press, 2014.

Haider, Najam. *The Rebel and the Imām in Early Islam: Explorations in Muslim Historiography*. Cambridge: Cambridge University Press, 2019.

Hallaq, Wael. "On the Authoritativeness of Sunni Consensus." *International Journal of Middle East Studies* 18, no. 4 (1986), 427–54.

Hallaq, Wael. *Authority, Continuity and Change in Islamic Law*. Cambridge: Cambridge University Press, 2001.

Hawting, Gerald R. *The Idea of Idolatry and the Emergence of Islam: From Polemic to History*. Cambridge: Cambridge University Press, 1999.

Hawting, Gerald R. *The First Dynasty of Islam: The Umayyad Caliphate AD 661–750*. New York: Routledge, 2000.

Higgins, Annie. "Faces of Exchangers, Facets of Exchange in Early *Shurāt* (Khārijī) Poetry." *Bulletin of the Royal Institute of Inter-Faith Studies* 7, no.1 (2005): 7–38.

Hirschler, Konrad. *Medieval Damascus: Plurality and Diversity in an Arabic Library*. Edinburgh: Edinburgh University Press, 2016.

Hodgson, Marshall. "How Did the Early Shiʿa Become Sectarian?" *Journal of the American Oriental Society* 75, no. 1 (1955): 1–13.

Hodgson, Marshall. *The Venture of Islam: Conscience and History in a World Civilization, Volume 1: The Classical Age of Islam*. Chicago: University of Chicago Press, 1958.

Hodgson, Marshall. *The Venture of Islam: Conscience and History in a World Civilization, Volume 2: The Expansion of Islam in the Middle Periods*. Chicago: University of Chicago Press, 1977.

Hoffman-Ladd, Valerie J. "Devotion to the Prophet and His Family in Egyptian Sufism." *International Journal of Middle East Studies* 24, no. 4 (1992): 615–37.

Hoyland, Robert. "Early Islam as a Late Antique Religion." In *The Oxford Handbook of Late Antiquity*. Edited by Scott Fitzgerald Johnson, 1053–77. Oxford: Oxford University Press, 2012.

Hughes, Aaron. "Religion without Religion: Integrating Islamic Origins into Religious Studies." *Journal of the American Academy of Religion* 85, no. 4 (2017): 867–88.

Humphreys, R. Stephen. *Mu'awiya ibn Abi Sufyan: From Arabia to Empire*. Oxford: Oneworld Publications, 2006.

Jafri, Syed Husain Mohammad. *The Origins and Early Development of Shi'a Islam*. Karachi: Oxford University Press, 2000.

Jeffery, Arthur. *The Foreign Vocabulary of the Qur'ān*. Leiden: Brill, 2007.

Johnson, Benton. "On Church and Sect." *American Sociological Review* 28 (1963): 539–49.

Jokiranta, Jutta. *Social Identity and Sectarianism in the Qumran Movement*. Leiden: Brill, 2013.

Judd, Steven C. "Ghaylan al-Dimashqi: The Isolation of a Heretic in Islamic Historiography." *International Journal of Middle East Studies* 31, no. 2 (1999): 161–84.

Judd, Steven C. "Muslim Persecution of Heretics during the Marwānid Period (64–132/684–750)." *Al-Masaq* 23, no. 1 (2011): 1–14.

Judd, Steven C. "The Early Qadariyya." In *The Oxford Handbook of Islamic Theology*. Edited by Sabine Schmidke, 44–54. Oxford: Oxford University Press, 2016.

Karamustafa, Ahmet. *God's Unruly Friends: Dervish Groups in the Islamic Middle Period 1200–1550*. Oxford: Oneworld, 2006.

Karamustafa, Ahmet. *Sufism: The Formative Period*. Berkeley: University of California Press, 2007.

Kaufman, Stuart J. *Modern Hatreds: The Symbolic Politics of Ethnic War*. New York: Cornell University Press, 2001.

Kister, Meir J. "Al-Ḥīra: Some Notes on Its Relations with Arabia." *Arabica* 15 (1968): 143–69.

Lalani, Arzina R. *Early Shi'i Thought: The Teachings of Imam Muḥammad al-Bāqir*. New York: I.B. Tauris, 2000.

Lambton, Ann K. S. "A Reconsideration of the Position of the *Marja' al-Taqlīd* and the Religious Institution." *Studia Islamica* 20 (1964): 115–35.

Layton, Bentley, ed. *Nag Hammadi Codex II, 2–7*. Leiden: E. J. Brill, 2003.

Lewinstein, Keith. "Making and Unmaking a Sect: The Heresiographers and the Ṣufriyya." *Studia Islamica* 76 (1992): 75–96.

Love, Paul M. Jr. "The Sufris of Sijilmasa: Toward a History of the Midrarids." *The Journal of North African Studies* 15 (2010): 173–88.

Madelung, Wilferd. "The Early Murji'a in Khurāsān and Transoxania and the Spread of Ḥanafism." *Der Islam* 59 (1982): 32–39.

Madelung, Wilferd. *Religious Schools and Sects in Medieval Islam*. London: Variorum Reprints, 1985.

Madelung, Wilferd. *Religious Trends in Early Islamic Iran*. Albany: Bibliotheca Persica, 1988.
Madelung, Wilferd. *The Succession to Muḥammad: A Study of the Early Caliphate*. Cambridge: Cambridge University Press, 1997.
Makdisi, Ussama. *The Culture of Sectarianism: Community, History, and Violence in Nineteenth-Century Ottoman Lebanon*. Berkeley: University of California Press, 2000.
Malamud, Margaret. "The Politics of Heresy in Medieval Khurasan: The Karramiyya in Nishapur."*Iranian Studies* 27, nos. 1–4 (1994): 37–51.
Melchert, Christopher. "The Piety of the Hadith Folk." *International Journal of Middle East Studies* 34, no. 3 (2002): 425–39.
Melchert, Christopher. "The Rightly-Guided Caliphs: The Range of Views Preserved in the *Ḥadīth*." In *Political Quietism in Islam: Sunni and Shiʿi Practice and Thought*. Edited by Saud al-Sarhan, 63–79. London: I.B. Tauris, 2020.
Melvin-Koushki, Matthew S. "The Quest for a Universal Science: The Occult Philosophy of Ṣāʿin al-Dīn Turka Iṣfahānī (1369–1432) and Intellectual Millenarianism in Early Timurid Iran." PhD diss., Yale University, 2012.
Milwright, Marcus. *An Introduction to Islamic Archaeology*. Edinburgh: Edinburgh University Press, 2010.
Modarressi, Hossein. *Crisis and Consolidation in the Formative Period of Shiʿite Islam*. Princeton: Darwin Press, 1993.
Moin, Azfar. *The Millennial Sovereign: Sacred Kingship and Sainthood in Islam*. New York: Columbia University Press, 2012.
Momen, Moojan. *An Introduction to Shiʿi Islam: The History and Doctrines of Twelver Shiʿism*. New Haven: Yale University Press, 1985.
Mottahedeh, Roy P. "Pluralism and Islamic Traditions of Sectarian Divisions." *Svensk Teologisk Kvartalskrift* 82, no. 4 (2006): 155–61.
Mulder, Stephennie. *The Shrines of the ʿAlids in Medieval Syria: Sunnis, Shiʿis and the Architecture of Coexistence*. Edinburgh: Edinburgh University Press, 2014.
Neggaz, Nassima. "Al-Karkh: The Development of an Imāmī-Shīʿī Stronghold in Early Abbasid and Būyid Baghdad (132–447/750–1055)." *Studia Islamica* 114 (2019): 265–315.
Niebuhr, Helmut Richard. *The Social Sources of Denominationalism*. New York: H. Holt and Co., 1929.
Olsson, Tord. "The Gnosis of Mountaineers and Townspeople: The Religion of the Syrian Alawites, or the Nuṣayrīs." In *Alevi Identity: Cultural, Religious and Social Perspectives*. Edited by Tord Olsson, Elisabeth Özdalga, and Catharina Raudvere, 167–83. London: Routledge, 1998.
Peters, Francis E. *Muhammad and the Origins of Islam*. Albany: SUNY Press, 1994.
Pfeiffer, Judith. "Confessional Ambiguity vs. Confessional Polarization: Politics and the Negotiation of Religious Boundaries in the Ilkhanate." In *Politics, Patronage, and the Transmission of Knowledge in 13th–15th Century Tabriz*. Edited by Judith Pfeiffer, 129–70. Leiden: Brill, 2014.
Potter, Lawrence, ed. *Sectarian Politics in the Persian Gulf*. Oxford: Oxford University Press, 2014.

al-Qāḍī, Wadād. "The Development of the Term *Ghulāt* in Muslim Literature with Special Reference to the Kaysāniyya." *Akten des VII. Kongresses für Arabistik and Islamwissenschaft* 98 (1976): 295–316.

Robertson, Roland. *The Sociological Interpretation of Religion*. New York: Schocken, 1970.

Robinson, Chase F. "Prophecy and Holy Men in Early Islam." In *The Cult of Saints in Late Antiquity and the Middle Ages: Essays on the Contribution of Peter Brown*. Edited by James Howard-Johnston and Paul Antony Hayward, 241–62. Oxford: Oxford University Press, 1999.

Robinson, Chase F. *Islamic Historiography*. Cambridge: Cambridge University Press, 2003.

Sachedina, Abdulaziz Abdulhussein. *Islamic Messianism: The Idea of the Mahdi in Twelver Shiʿism*. Albany: SUNY Press, 1981.

Scheppler, Bill. *Al-Biruni: Master Astronomer and Muslim Scholar of the Eleventh Century*. New York: Rosen Publishing Group, 2006.

Schmidtke, Sabine. "The Muʿtazilite Movement (III): The Scholastic Phase." In *The Oxford Handbook of Islamic Theology*. Edited by Sabine Schmidke, 159–80. Oxford: Oxford University Press, 2016.

Schöck, Cornelia. "Jahm b. Ṣafwān (d. 128/745–6) and the 'Jahmiyya' and Ḍirār b. ʿAmr (d. 200/815)." In *The Oxford Handbook of Islamic Theology*. Edited by Sabine Schmidke, 55–80. Oxford: Oxford University Press, 2016.

Schubel, Vernon James. *Religious Performance in Contemporary Islam: Shiʿi Devotional Rituals in South Asia*. Columbia: University of South Carolina Press, 1993.

Schubel, Vernon James. "When the Prophet Went on the *Miraç* He Saw a Lion on the Road: The *Miraç* in the Alevi-Bektaşi Tradition." In *The Prophet's Ascension: Cross-cultural Encounters with the Islamic Miʿrāj Tales*. Edited by Christiane Gruber and Frederick Colby, 330–43. Bloomington: Indiana University Press, 2010.

Sedgwick, Mark. "Sects in the Islamic World." *Nova Religio* 3, no. 2 (2000): 195–240.

Sells, Michael, ed. and trans. *Early Islamic Mysticism: Sufi, Qur'an, Miʿraj, Poetic and Theological Writings*. Mahwah: Paulist Press, 1996.

Sizgorich, Thomas. *Violence and Belief in Late Antiquity: Militant Devotion in Christianity and Islam*. Philadelphia: University of Pennsylvania Press, 2009.

Soileau, Mark. "Conforming Haji Bektash: A Saint and His Followers between Orthopraxy and Heteropraxy." *Die Welt des Islams* 54, nos. 3–4 (2014): 423–59.

Somers, Margaret R. "The Narrative Constitution of Identity: A Relational and Network Approach." *Theory and Society* 23, no. 5 (1994): 605–49.

Stark, Rodney, and William Sims Bainbridge. *The Future of Religion: Secularization, Revival and Cult Formation*. Berkeley: University of California Press, 1986.

Stark, Rodney, and William Sims Bainbridge. *A Theory of Religion*. New York: Peter Lang, 1987.

Streusand, Douglas E. *Islamic Gunpowder Empires: Ottomans, Safavids, and Mughals*. Boulder: Westview Press, 2011.

Swatos, William H. Jr. "Monopolism, Pluralism, Acceptance, and Rejection: An Integrated Model for Church-Sect Theory." *Review of Religious Research* 16, no. 3 (1975): 174–85.

Swatos, William H. Jr. "Weber or Troeltsch? Methodology, Syndrome and the Development of Church-Sect Theory." *Journal for the Scientific Study of Religion* 15, no. 2 (1976): 129–44.

Talhami, Ghada Hashem. "The Zanj Rebellion Reconsidered." *The International Journal of African Historical Studies* 10, no. 3 (1977): 443–61.

Tannous, Jack. "Between Christology and *Kalām*? The Life and Letters of George, Bishop of the Arab Tribes." In *Malphono w-Rabo d-Malphone: Studies in Honor of Sebastian P. Brock*. Edited by G. Kiraz, 671–716. Piscataway: Gorgias Press, 2008.

Tayob, Abdulkader. "An Analytical Survey of al-Ṭabarī's Exegesis of the Cultural Symbolic Construct of *Fitna*." In *Approaches to the Qur'ān*. Edited by G. R. Hawting and Abdul-Kader Shareef, 157–72. London: Routledge, 1993.

Thiele, Jan. "Between Cordoba and Nīsābūr: The Emergence and Consolidation of Ashʿarism (Fourth–Fifth/Tenth–Eleventh Century)." In *The Oxford Handbook of Islamic Theology*. Edited by Sabine Schmidke, 225–41. Oxford: Oxford University Press, 2016.

Troeltsch, Ernst. *The Social Teaching of the Christian Churches*. Translated by Olive Wyon. London: George Allen and Unwin Ltd., 1949.

Tucker, William F. *Mahdis and Millenarians: Shiʿite Extremists in Early Muslim Iraq*. Cambridge: Cambridge University Press, 2008.

Turner, John P. *Inquisition in Early Islam: The Competition for Political and Religious Authority in the Abbasid Empire*. London: I.B. Tauris, 2013.

Van Ess, Josef, ed. *Frühe muʿtazilitische Häresiographie: zwei Werke des Nāšiʾ al-Akbar (gest. 293 H.)*. Wiesbaden: Kommission bei F. Steiner, 1971.

Van Ess, Josef. *Theology and Society in the Second and Third Centuries of the Hijra, Volume 1*. Translated by John O'Kane. Leiden: Brill, 2017.

Van Ess, Josef. *Theology and Society in the Second and Third Centuries of the Hijra, Volume 2*. Translated by Gwendolin Goldbloom. Leiden: Brill, 2017.

Wallis, Roy. "Scientology: Therapeutic Cult to Religious Sect." *Sociology* 9, no. 1 (1975): 89–100.

Wansbrough, John. "On Recomposing the Islamic History of North Africa: A Review Article." In *The Journal of the Royal Asiatic Society of Great Britain and Ireland* 2 (1969): 161–70.

Watt, W. Montgomery. *Muhammad: Prophet and Stateman*. Oxford: Oxford University Press, 1961.

Watt, W. Montgomery. *Al-Ghazali: The Muslim Intellectual*. Edinburgh: Edinburgh University Press, 1963.

Watt, W. Montgomery. *The Formative Period of Islamic Thought*. Oxford: Oneworld, 1998.

Weber, Max. *From Max Weber: Essays in Sociology*. Edited and translated by Hans Heinrich Gerth and Charles Wright Mills. Oxford: Oxford University Press, 1946.

Weber, Max. *Economy and Society: An Outline of Interpretive Sociology*. Edited by Guenther Roth and Claus Wittich. New York: Bedminster Press, 1968.

Weiss, Max. *In the Shadow of Sectarianism: Law, Shi'ism, and the Making of Modern Lebanon*. Cambridge: Harvard University Press, 2010.

Wensinck, A. J. *The Muslim Creed: Its Genesis and Historical Development*. Cambridge: Cambridge University Press, 1932.

Wilkinson, John. *Ibāḍism: Origins and Early Development in Oman*. Oxford: Oxford University Press, 2010.

Wilson, Bryan. *Religious Sects: A Sociological Study*. New York: McGraw-Hill, 1970.

Winter, Stefan. *A History of the 'Alawis: From Medieval Aleppo to the Turkish Republic*. Princeton: Princeton University Press, 2016.

Yildirim, Riza. "Shī'itisation of the *Futuwwa* Tradition in the Fifteenth Century." *British Journal of Middle Eastern Studies* 40, no. 1 (2013): 53–70.

Yinger, J. Milton. *Religion, Society and the Individual*. New York: Macmillan, 1957.

Yinger, J. Milton. *Religion and the Struggle for Power: A Study in the Sociological Study of Religion (Dissertations in Sociology)*. New York: Amo Press, 1980.

Zysow, Aron. "Karrāmiyya." In *The Oxford Handbook of Islamic Theology*. Edited by Sabine Schmidke, 252–62. Oxford: Oxford University Press, 2016.

Index

For EU product safety concerns, contact us at Calle de José Abascal, 56–1°, 28003 Madrid, Spain or eugpsr@cambridge.org.

www.ingramcontent.com/pod-product-compliance
Ingram Content Group UK Ltd.
Pitfield, Milton Keynes, MK11 3LW, UK
UKHW020354140625
459647UK00020B/2463
* 9 7 8 1 0 0 9 3 1 5 2 1 0 *